RELEASED

e kept
DAYS
i for each
overtime.

an intensive course in English

ENGLISH SENTENCE PATTERNS

understanding and producing
English grammatical structures
AN ORAL APPROACH

17741

ENGLISH LANGUAGE INSTITUTE STAFF

Robert Lado and **Charles C. Fries**

ANN ARBOR | The University of Michigan Press

Foreword

These are linguistically graded lessons to teach students to speak and understand English sentences.

These lessons begin with simple but important patterns (I-X), build up cumulatively through intermediate patterns (XI-XX), and proceed into advanced patterns (XXI-XXXV).

The lessons are well adapted to intermediate students, who may proceed at the rate of one lesson per teaching hour. Beginning students, on the other hand, should proceed at no more than half a lesson per hour. Advanced students move rapidly through the first twenty lessons, omitting those exercises which do not challenge them, but working through the frames to understand better what they already know in part. Lessons XXI through XXXV challenge even the advanced students.

The lessons are most effective when used simultaneously with ENGLISH PATTERN PRACTICES, which provides additional drill for the patterns introduced here. Advanced students may not need the extra practices as much as intermediate or beginning students.

The set which together constitutes the INTENSIVE COURSE IN ENGLISH of the English Language Institute, University of Michigan, includes the following four titles: ENGLISH SENTENCE PATTERNS, ENGLISH PATTERN PRACTICES, ENGLISH PRONUNCIATION, and ENGLISH VOCABULARY.

Robert Lado

Contributors to the Revised Edition

The Third Revised Edition adds Lessons XXI through XXXV and completes the set of "grammar" lessons. GERALD DYKSTRA in close co-operation with ROBERT LADO had revised these lessons to their previous stage. THEODOSIA COPLAS helped with the exercises and prepared Lesson XXXV. The chief contributors to the revision of the lessons as they now appear are the following:

WILLIAM H. BUELL, who revised Lessons XXI through XXXV in the light of suggestions and criticisms made by the English Language Institute Staff and CHARLES C. FRIES, and made minor changes in Lessons I through XIX.

EDWARD T. ERAZMUS, who revised and expanded the exercises in these lessons, made valuable contributions to other aspects of the revision and prepared the review lessons X, XX, and XXX.

All revisions were thoroughly discussed at regular meetings of the revision staff, which included the above two and RUTH CARTER HOK, BRYCE VAN SYOC, MARY JANE MASLOOB, and myself as Director. Final copy for the printer was read and corrected by me, on whom falls ultimately the responsibility for any errors or inadequacies in the content and form of the lessons.

Robert Lado

Preface

Considerable controversy has for more than a half century centered upon the usefulness of "grammar" for the practical mastery of a foreign language. Part of the difficulty in reaching agreement in such controversies arises from the fact that "grammar" means very different materials to different persons. To some it means memorizing paradigms of declensions and conjugations; to some it means recognizing and naming the "parts of speech" and diagraming sentences; to others it means learning and applying rules of "correctness" based upon "logic" or the "laws of thought." "Knowing" grammar has most often meant the ability to use and respond to some fifty or sixty technical names and to talk about sentences in terms of these technical names. Often, one of the chief reasons offered for learning the grammar of a language is that it provides a vocabulary to facilitate explanations concerning "correct" usage.

The materials of the English Language Institute rest upon the view that learning a foreign language consists not in learning about the language but in developing a new set of habits. One may have a great deal of information about a language without being able to use the language at all. The "grammar" lessons here set forth, therefore, consist basically of exercises to develop habits, not explanations or talk about the language.

The habits to be learned consist of patterns or molds in which the "words" must be grasped. "Grammar" from the point of view of these materials is the particular system of devices which a language uses to signal one of its various layers of meaning--structural meaning (see Charles C. Fries, The Structure of English, Chapters 4 and 13). "Knowing" this grammar for practical use means being able to produce and to respond to these signals of structural meaning. To develop such habits efficiently demands practice and more practice, especially oral practice. These lessons provide the exercises for a sound sequence of such practice to cover a basic minimum of production patterns in English.

Charles C. Fries

THE SECOND EDITION

This book is part of the 1953 revision of An Intensive Course in English for Latin-American Students. Although built especially for Spanish speakers, the materials have also been used with some selection and shift of emphasis for students of other linguistic backgrounds.

Although many of the staff of the English Language Institute have contributed to the making of this revision, development of the exercises and the form of the materials presented here has been the contribution of Dr. Robert Lado, the Associate Director of the Institute, assisted by Gerald Dykstra. Mary Jane Masloob contributed suggestions throughout. Gloria Goldenberg in the typing and the proofreading, and Jack Logan also in the proofreading, rendered services of the highest quality.

Charles C. Fries

Contents

Teacher's Introduction

This introduction for teachers describes briefly the organization of the lessons and gives instructions on how the materials can be most profitably taught.

The Parts of the Lessons.

Each lesson consists of the following parts:

(1) An outline which presents the contents of the lesson. The outline consists of key examples followed by statements in brackets which describe briefly the pattern being presented. The statements are intended primarily for the guidance of the teacher, while the key examples are for student use.

(2) A frame that presents the materials to be taught to the student. The frame is preceded by a key example. Each frame presents a new pattern in three steps as follows:

(a) An-attention pointer. A sentence directing the attention of the student to the point to be emphasized. For example, "Observe the position of TO ME and ME."

(b) The structural pattern. The pattern to be taught is given in examples, often in the form of minimal contrasts that show the essential signaling elements of the pattern. A previously taught pattern will often be included for further contrast.

(c) Comments. One or more comments are provided to summarize and to verbalize the structural changes involved.

(3) Illustrative examples. Often a pattern shows minor variations in different environments. The illustrative examples show the pattern in a variety of such environments.

(4) Practice. Exercises in which the student learns to use the pattern.

(5) Notes. The notes are sometimes directed to the teacher, giving hints on teaching or on problems. Often they comment on some additional pattern which is not taught for production but which the student should learn to recognize.

(6) Review of the key examples at the end.

Presentation of the Parts of the Lessons.

Completely oral presentation has proved its value for oral mastery. Completely oral presentation, with books closed, permits also more practice per student per hour, it helps maintain the unified attention of the class, and gives the student practice in listening as well as in speaking. The usual lesson follows these steps:

(1) The teacher may begin with oral presentation of the KEY EXAMPLES of the OUTLINE of the lesson. The class repeats the key examples. The formulas are not given at this time.

(2) The class proceeds to the first section of the lesson and again repeats the KEY EXAMPLES, this time only those for this section. Several repetitions will usually be required. Books are closed.

(3) The teacher then gives the ATTENTION POINTER very clearly. Sometimes it is advisable to repeat the attention pointer later.

(4) Immediately come the EXAMPLES, given orally by the teacher, repeated by the class in chorus, several times if necessary. Often the teacher selects from the FRAME a minimally contrasting pair of examples. This is good procedure.

(5) When the class can repeat the minimal pair of examples in chorus, the teacher writes the pair of examples on the blackboard, or presents them on a poster large enough for the whole class to see comfortably.

(6) Other examples like the ones in the minimal pair are given orally from the frame. The class repeats them. The teacher often repeats the attention pointer to guide the class toward the particular point being taught.

(7) The teacher then uses leading questions or incomplete statements to draw out the inductive COMMENTS from the class. There is usually a bright pupil who discovers the contrast correctly. The teacher then tries to get other members of the class to discover the contrast also. When the teacher is convinced that most of the students in the class have got the point, the teacher then restates the point to reassure the students and help the ones who for some reason did not grasp the point but are too timid to admit it.

(8) The entire process so far should not take much more than 15 per cent of the time devoted to that pattern. The remaining 85 per cent of the time should be devoted to PRACTICE.

(9) In the PRACTICE part, instead of explaining what the exercise consists of and how it is to be worked, it is better to say,

"Let's practice. Observe the examples and continue when you understand. Examples:" Then the teacher goes ahead with three or more of the examples, rather deliberately. The class will begin to practice cautiously after about the third example and will gain confidence as the exercise progresses.

(10) When the class is doing the exercise at normal conversational speed as a group, and no gross errors are detected by the teacher, the class goes into individual practice to check for individual errors. With a class of approximately ten students it is possible and desirable for each student to recite individually at least once for each exercise.

(11) With larger classes the teacher may have to be satisfied with group practice and a spot check of individual practice. With even larger classes, it may be necessary to practice by rows, reducing individual recitation to a minimum. Even with large classes, however, when the students are trained to keep the same rhythm in group recitation, it is often possible for the teacher to detect individual errors and correct them.

(12) A number of the exercises permit more than one answer to each stimulus. Group recitation is, therefore, not possible. The entire exercise must be practiced through individual recitation in such cases.

(13) Other exercises require very long responses which would be difficult to pronounce with uniform rhythm by the entire class. Individual practice may be preferable in these cases.

(14) As a rule, when partial substitutions or changes are given, they have been carefully selected to produce responses that are both relevant to the practice and result in normal English sentences. In such cases the substitutions have to be taken in the order in which they appear, or the result might be a nonsensical construction.

(15) Normal conversational speed should always be the ultimate goal. When the teacher begins an exercise slowly, it should not remain so but should be gradually speeded up until it is rendered at somewhat normal speed. Even in slow rendition, distortions should be avoided so that the student may get a maximum of practice that will transfer to his actual use of the language in conversation.

(16) When the FRAME is followed by ILLUSTRATIVE EXAMPLES, these examples are presented orally by the teacher and repeated by the class.

(17) When all the frames and practices have been taught in a lesson, the teacher then summarizes the lesson by giving the KEY EXAMPLES at the end. These will readily be repeated by the students.

(18) When the teacher wishes to reinforce the lesson by having the students read parts of it, they maybe asked to open their books to the particular frame or exercise and to read aloud with the teacher or after the teacher. When a class knows the material well, it may be read without an immediate oral model.

(19) Homework is usually assigned as oral practice at home, using the book as the guide. Homework is checked by the teacher the following class period.

(20) Written homework consists of writing out the responses to particular exercises performed orally in class. The teacher can correct such exercises quickly and find out those who have not got the point of the pattern or are unable to apply it.

(21) Some notes found at the bottom of the page contain patterns for recognition. These are simply read aloud by the teacher, or better, presented aloud from memory by the teacher.

(22) Review lessons contain more exercises than any one class will want to do. The teacher should select those exercises that will help the particular class involved. It should be remembered that patterns are constantly being reviewed, since larger patterns often make normal use of the simpler ones taught earlier.

(23) Variety increases interest. Variety can be achieved in a thousand different ways by the resourceful teacher who lives each class with artistic vividness through the learning experience of the students.

Student's Introduction

(1) These lessons are different from most language lessons. You must expect to use them differently for best results.

(2) Remember, it isn't necessary for you to explain the grammar; it isn't necessary for you to learn the terminology. You have to UNDERSTAND the patterns and USE them. The real test is in doing the exercises rather than in discussing the frame.

(3) Learning about the problem is not your goal. You must become so familiar with the pattern that you can use it automatically. In order to attain this goal you must practice orally.

(4) Do not look at the books in class. Listen to the teacher. Listen to and repeat the examples and observe the important points. Then do the exercises with the teacher, keeping your books closed. After an exercise or lesson is finished you may want to study the book to make sure you can do the exercises orally yourself.

(5) Sometimes an exercise may be very easy for you. Use this opportunity to practice normal English intonation, speed, and rhythm.

(6) If you forget the meaning of a word in an exercise, continue the exercise and ask the teacher when it is finished.

(7) If you have questions about grammar or about the possibility of using certain words in the pattern, ask the question after the exercise has been completed. Frequently you will find that the exercise itself will have answered the question.

(8) In doing the exercises, follow the suggested sequence of substitutions as it occurs in the book. This will prevent nonsensical combinations of the material, and will permit rapid repetitions, which are so necessary to learning a second language.

(9) Get as much practice as you can in each pattern as it comes up. If the teacher asks for group practice, practice with the group. It is of little or no value simply to listen to these exercises.

(10) In individual practice, have the response ready even when it is not your turn to recite.

(11) Practice the exercises aloud after class by yourself or with a friend. Practice in the language laboratory if there is one.

(12) Use the patterns with people you meet. In short, practice as much as possible.

Lesson I

1. Statements, questions, and answers with IS, ARE, AM (forms of BE).

   la. THE LESSON IS INTERESTING. IS THE LESSON IN-
       TERESTING?
       [Word order of questions contrasted with word order of
       statements]
   lb. IT'S INTERESTING. YOU'RE BUSY. I'M BUSY.
       [Full and contracted forms of IS, ARE, AM with THE
       STUDENT, THE STUDENTS, I, YOU, HE, etc.]
   lc. IS THE LESSON INTERESTING? YES, IT IS.
       [Short answers to questions with IS, ARE, AM]
   ld. HE'S HUNGRY. HE'S IN CLASS. HE'S A DOCTOR.
       [Some uses of IS, ARE, AM]
   le. MARY IS INTERESTING. SHE'S FROM MEXICO. SHE'S
       A STUDENT.
       [HE, SHE, IT, THEY used and repeated with IS, ARE]

2. Plural contrasted with singular.

   2a. I'M A STUDENT. WE'RE STUDENTS.
       ["A" with singular, zero with plural, of Class 1 words]
   2b. THE STUDENTS ARE INTELLIGENT.
       [Invariable forms: THE and Class 3 words]

la. Key examples: The lesson IS interesting. IS the lesson interesting?

Observe the position of IS.

	STATEMENTS			QUESTIONS	
1	2	3	2	1	3
The lesson	IS	interesting.	IS	the lesson	interesting?
The lesson	IS	important.	IS	the lesson	important?
The class	IS	important.	IS	the class	important?
The student	IS	intelligent.	IS	the student	intelligent?

COMMENTS

(1) Use IS after THE LESSON, THE CLASS, THE STUDENT, etc., for
    statements.
(2) Use IS before THE LESSON, THE CLASS, THE STUDENT, etc.,
    for questions.
(3) Use a falling intonation [IN͞TERESTING] for questions. Use the
    same intonation for statements and for questions.

NOTE: LESSON, CLASS, STUDENT, etc., are Class 1 words. IS is a
      Class 2 word. INTERESTING, IMPORTANT, INTELLIGENT,
      etc., are Class 3 words.

*NOTE TO THE TEACHER. The student will often hear questions with a ris-
ing intonation in certain situations. He should use the falling intonation for questions now to learn the word order signal for questions in English. The falling
intonation [is ͡in teresting] first rises to a high pitch on "in-" (often the last
stressed syllable of the sentence) and falls to a low pitch at the end of the sentence.

PRACTICE

INSTRUCTIONS TO THE TEACHER: The examples illustrate the
exercises. The words in small letters are the teacher's part. The
words in CAPITAL LETTERS are the student's part. The teacher
says both parts in the examples. The students repeat their part after
the teacher in the examples. The teacher then continues the exercise,
saying only the teacher's part. The students continue by producing
the student's part on the pattern of the examples. The student incor-
porates in his responses the promptings supplied orally by the teacher.

EXERCISE 1a.1.* (For production of the word order of statements.)
Substitute the words INTERESTING, GOOD, BAD, etc., in the proper
position at the end in statements. For example:

The lesson is good.

bad	THE LESSON IS BAD.
necessary	THE LESSON IS NECESSARY.
interesting	THE LESSON IS INTERESTING.

(Continue the substitutions:)

1. good	4. necessary
2. bad	5. correct
3. interesting	6. important

Substitute THE ALPHABET, THE LESSON, THE ANSWER, etc., in the
proper position at the beginning. For example:

the alphabet	THE ALPHABET IS IMPORTANT.
the lesson	THE LESSON IS IMPORTANT.

(Continue the substitutions:)

7. the alphabet	10. the class
8. the lesson	11. the symbol
9. the answer	12. the spelling

Substitute GOOD, THE LESSON, IMPORTANT, THE SPELLING, etc., in
the proper positions (beginning or end). For example:

good	THE SPELLING IS GOOD.
the lesson	THE LESSON IS GOOD.
important	THE LESSON IS IMPORTANT.
the spelling	THE SPELLING IS IMPORTANT.

(Continue the substitutions:)

13. good	18. interesting	23. necessary
14. the lesson	19. the alphabet	24. the alphabet
15. important	20. the lesson	25. important
16. the spelling	21. good	26. the class
17. the answer	22. bad	

---

*The exercises are numbered to show the frame within the lesson. For ex-
ample, Exercise 1a.1. is the first exercise under Frame 1a. Exercise 1b.2
is the second exercise under Frame 1b.

The responses for exercise 1a.1. are:

1. The lesson is good.
2. The lesson is bad.
3. The lesson is interesting.
4. The lesson is necessary.
5. The lesson is correct.
6. The lesson is important.
7. The alphabet is important.
8. The lesson is important.
9. The answer is important.
10. The class is important.
11. The symbol is important.
12. The spelling is important.
13. The spelling is good.
14. The lesson is good.
15. The lesson is important.
16. The spelling is important.
17. The answer is important.
18. The answer is interesting.
19. The alphabet is interesting.
20. The lesson is interesting.
21. The lesson is good.
22. The lesson is bad.
23. The lesson is necessary
24. The alphabet is necessary.
25. The alphabet is important.
26. The class is important.

EXERCISE 1a.2. (For production of the word order of questions.) Substitute INTERESTING, GOOD, BAD, etc., in the proper position (at the end) in questions. For example:

Is the lesson interesting?

good	IS THE LESSON GOOD?
bad	IS THE LESSON BAD?
necessary	IS THE LESSON NECESSARY?

(Continue the substitutions:)

1. interesting
2. good
3. bad
4. necessary
5. correct
6. important

Substitute THE ALPHABET, THE ANSWER, etc., in the proper position (after IS). For example:

| the alphabet | IS THE ALPHABET IMPORTANT? |
| the lesson | IS THE LESSON IMPORTANT? |

(Continue:)

7. the alphabet
8. the lesson
9. the answer
10. the class
11. the symbol
12. the spelling

Substitute GOOD, THE LESSON, IMPORTANT, THE SPELLING, etc., in the proper positions (after IS or at the end). For example:

good	IS THE SPELLING GOOD?
the lesson	IS THE LESSON GOOD?
important	IS THE LESSON IMPORTANT?
the spelling	IS THE SPELLING IMPORTANT?

(Continue:)

13. good
14. the lesson
15. important
16. the spelling
17. the answer
18. interesting
19. the alphabet
20. the lesson
21. good
22. bad
23. necessary
24. the alphabet
25. important
26. the class

EXERCISE 1a.3. (To contrast statements and questions.) This is a conversation exercise. The teacher makes a statement with INTERESTING. The student asks a question with GOOD. For example:

The lesson is interesting.   IS THE LESSON GOOD?
The alphabet is interesting.   IS THE ALPHABET GOOD?
The class is interesting.   IS THE CLASS GOOD?

(Continue the conversation:)

1. The lesson is interesting.
2. The alphabet is interesting.
3. The class is interesting.
4. The spelling is interesting.
5. The answer is interesting.
6. The symbol is interesting.
7. The book is interesting.
8. The conversation is interesting.
9. The course is interesting.
10. The exercise is interesting.

1b. Key examples: IT'S interesting. YOU'RE busy. I'M busy.

Observe the correlation of IS, ARE, AM, with IT, THEY, I, etc.

Contracted Forms

THE LESSON	IS	interesting.	THE LESSON'S	interesting.
IT	IS	interesting.	IT'S	interesting.
THE TELE-PHONE	IS	busy.	THE TELE-PHONE'S	busy.
IT	IS	busy.	IT'S	busy.
JOHN	IS	busy.	JOHN'S	busy.
HE	IS	busy.	HE'S	busy.
THE SECRE-TARY	IS	busy.	MARY'S	busy.
SHE	IS	busy.	SHE'S	busy.
THE STU-DENTS	ARE	busy.	THE STUDENTS'RE	busy.
THEY	ARE	busy.	THEY'RE	busy.
THE TELE-PHONES	ARE	busy.	THE TELE-PHONES'RE	busy.
THEY	ARE	busy.	THEY'RE	busy.
YOU (one or more)	ARE	busy.	YOU'RE (one or more)	busy.
WE	ARE	busy.	WE'RE	busy.
I	AM	busy.	I'M	busy.

COMMENTS

(1) Use IS with IT, HE, SHE; THE TELEPHONE, JOHN, THE SECRETARY, etc.
(2) Use ARE with THEY, YOU, WE; THE STUDENTS, THE TELEPHONES, etc.
(3) Use AM with I.
(4) HE'S, THEY'RE, I'M, are contractions of HE IS, THEY ARE, I AM.

PRACTICE

EXERCISE 1b.1. (To correlate IS, ARE, AM, with IT, THEY, I, SHE, etc., in statements.) Substitute MARY, SHE, I, THE STUDENTS, THEY, etc., in the correct position and use the proper contracted form of BE ('S, 'RE, 'M). For example:

John's tired.

Mary	MARY'S TIRED.
She	SHE'S TIRED.
The students	THE STUDENTS'RE TIRED.
They	THEY'RE TIRED.

(Continue:)

1. Mary	7. he	13. they
2. she	8. you	14. the girls
3. I	9. we	15. they
4. the students	10. the dog	16. the students
5. they	11. it	17. they
6. John	12. the dogs	18. the teacher

EXERCISE 1b.2. (To correlate IS, ARE, AM, with HE, THEY, I, etc., in questions.) Substitute MARY, SHE, YOU, THE STUDENTS, THEY, etc., in the correct position and use the proper form of BE (IS, ARE, AM). For example:

Is John happy?

Mary	IS MARY HAPPY?
She	IS SHE HAPPY?
You	ARE YOU HAPPY?
The students	ARE THE STUDENTS HAPPY?
They	ARE THEY HAPPY?

(Continue with the substitutions in Exercise 1b.1.)

1c.   Key example: Is the lesson interesting? YES, IT IS.

Observe the short answers.

QUESTIONS			SHORT ANSWERS		
Is	John	busy?	Yes,	he	IS.
Is	Mary	busy ?	Yes,	she	IS.
Is	the lesson	important?	Yes,	it	IS.
Are	you	busy?	Yes,	we	ARE.
Am	I	right?	Yes,	you	ARE.
Are	John and Mary	busy?	Yes,	they	ARE.
Are	you	sleepy?	Yes,	I	AM.
Is	John	tired?	No,	he	ISN'T.
Is	Mary	tired?	No,	she	ISN'T.
Is	the lesson	bad?	No,	it	ISN'T.
Are	you	tired?	No,	we	AREN'T.
Am	I	wrong?	No,	you	AREN'T.
Are	John and Mary	tired?	No,	they	AREN'T.
Are	you	hungry?	No,	I'M	NOT.

COMMENTS

(1) Use the complete form of BE (IS, ARE, AM) in the short answers except in I'M NOT.

(2) IT ISN'T, YOU AREN'T, etc., are contractions of IT IS NOT, YOU ARE NOT, etc. I'M NOT is the contraction of I AM NOT.

PRACTICE

EXERCISE 1c.1. (To produce affirmative short answers.) Answer the questions with YES, HE IS; YES, SHE IS; YES, IT IS; YES, YOU ARE; YES, WE ARE; YES, THEY ARE; YES, I AM. For example:

Is John busy?	YES, HE IS.
Is the secretary busy?	YES, SHE IS.
Is the telephone busy?	YES, IT IS.
Am I right?	YES, YOU ARE.
Are you and John busy?	YES, WE ARE.
Are the students homesick?	YES, THEY ARE.
Are you busy?	YES, I AM.

(Continue:)

1. Is John busy?
2. Is the secretary busy?
3. Is the telephone busy?
4. Are you and John busy?
5. Are the students homesick?
6. Are you busy?
7. Is the alphabet important?
8. Is Mary tired?

9. Is she hungry?
10. Are you tired?
11. Is the teacher right?
12. Are the students busy?
13. Is the answer correct?
14. Am I right?
15. Is Mr. Brown a doctor?

EXERCISE 1c.2. (To produce negative short answers.) Use the questions in Exercise 1c.1. Answer the questions with NO, HE ISN'T; NO, SHE ISN'T; NO, IT ISN'T; NO, YOU AREN'T; NO, WE AREN'T; NO, THEY AREN'T; NO, I'M NOT. For example:

Is John busy?	NO, HE ISN'T.
Is the secretary busy?	NO, SHE ISN'T.
Am I right?	NO, YOU AREN'T.
Are you busy?	NO, I'M NOT.

(Continue with the questions of Exercise 1c.1.)

EXERCISE 1c.3. (To recognize statements and to answer questions with IS, ARE, AM.) Answer the questions with YES, IT IS; YES, THEY ARE; NO, IT ISN'T; NO, THEY AREN'T, etc. Make no response to the statements. For example:

Is the lesson important?	YES, IT IS.
Is the lesson bad?	NO, IT ISN'T.
Are you from Chile?	NO, I'M NOT.
The alphabet is good.	(No oral response.)
Is the alphabet necessary?	YES, IT IS.

(Continue:)

1. Is the lesson important?
2. Are you from Venezuela?
3. Are you from Spain?
4. Are you from Latin America?
5. The spelling is good.
6. Is the spelling bad?
7. The class is interesting.
8. Is the lesson interesting?
9. Is the lesson bad?
10. The lesson is scientific.
11. Is the alphabet important?
12. Are the symbols important?
13. Is the number correct?
14. Is the answer good?
15. The answer is correct.
16. The students are intelligent.
17. Are the lessons interesting?
18. Is John from Cuba?
19. Is he from Mexico?
20. Are you from Colombia?

1d. Key examples: He'S HUNGRY. He'S IN CLASS. He'S A DOC-TOR.

+---+
| Observe these uses of IS. |
| |
	John	IS	HUNGRY.	
	He	IS	COLD.	
	He	IS	RIGHT.	
	He	IS	IN CLASS.	
	He	IS	A DOCTOR.	
	He	IS	TWENTY YEARS	
			OLD.	
COMMENT
Use a form of BE (IS, ARE, AM) —not HAVE—in all
these situations.
+---+

PRACTICE

EXERCISE 1d.1. (To use a form of BE in these situations.) Substitute
the words in the proper position. For example:

John is hungry.
cold   JOHN IS COLD.
a student   JOHN IS A STUDENT.
in class   JOHN IS IN CLASS.
John and Mary   JOHN AND MARY ARE IN CLASS.

(Continue:)

1. tired	8. in class	15. homesick
2. cold	9. a student	16. you
3. hungry	10. in the United States	17. discouraged
4. from Michigan	11. I	18. nice
5. from Detroit	12. right	19. sleepy
6. John	13. busy	20. hungry
7. intelligent	14. a doctor	21. twenty years old

EXERCISE 1d.2. (To use a form of BE in these situations in questions.)
Substitute the words in the proper position. For example:

Is John hungry?

cold   IS JOHN COLD?
a student   IS JOHN A STUDENT?
in class   IS JOHN IN CLASS?
John and Mary   ARE JOHN AND MARY IN CLASS?

(Continue with the substitutions of Exercise 1d.1.)

1e.
Key examples: Mary is interesting. SHE's from Mexico. SHE's
a student.

Observe the presence of SHE, HE, IT, THEY, etc.

Mary is from New York. SHE's a student. SHE's intelligent.
John is from Chicago. HE's a student. HE's intelligent.

The lesson is interesting. IT's important.
Mary and John are students. THEY're nice. THEY're busy.

I'm from New York. I'm a teacher. I'm busy.
YOU're students. YOU're intelligent. Are YOU busy?

COMMENT

SHE, HE, IT, THEY, YOU, I are expressed—not omitted—in
English (in statements and questions).

PRACTICE

EXERCISE 1e.1. (To practice the presence of SHE, HE, IT, THEY.)
The teacher gives the name and origin or place. (JOHN IS FROM CHI-
CAGO.) Respond with the occupation or other information. (HE'S A
DOCTOR. HE'S INTELLIGENT. HE'S BUSY.) For example:

Mary is from New York.	SHE'S A NURSE. SHE'S TIRED. SHE'S HUNGRY.
Mary and John are from the United States.	THEY'RE INTERESTING. THEY'RE NICE. THEY'RE HOMESICK.
I'm from New York.	YOU'RE A TEACHER. YOU'RE INTELLIGENT. YOU'RE BUSY.

(Continue:)

1. John's from Chicago.
2. Mary's from New York.
3. John and Mary are from the U.S.
4. Mr. and Mrs. Lane are from Texas.
5. The lessons are in the book.
6. The first lesson is here.
7. I'm from the United States.
8. You're from Latin America (or Europe, or Asia).
9. The professor is from California.
10. The students are here.

2a. Key examples: I'm A student. We're studentS.

Observe the forms A STUDENT, STUDENTS, etc.	
I'm	A student.
You're	A student.
John's	A student.
He's	A student.
She's	A teacher.
It's	A class.
We're	studentS.
You're	studentS.
They're	studentS.
John and Mary are	studentS.
They're	teacherS.
They're	classES.

COMMENTS

(1) Use "A" with STUDENT, TEACHER, CLASS, etc., but not with STUDENTS, TEACHERS, CLASSES, etc.*

(2) STUDENTS, TEACHERS, CLASSES, etc.,* illustrate the formation of plurals.**

---

*For use and pronunciation of A and AN see English Pronunciation, Lesson I.
**For pronunciation of plurals see English Pronunciation, Lesson II.

EXERCISE 2a.1. (To produce singular Class 1 words with A and plural Class 1 words without A.) Substitute only the necessary parts. (A DOCTOR, A LAWYER, HE'S, JOHN AND PAUL ARE, THEY'RE, TEACHERS, MARY IS, etc.) For example:

I'm a student.

doctor	I'M A DOCTOR.
lawyer	I'M A LAWYER.
he	HE'S A LAWYER.
John and Paul.	JOHN AND PAUL ARE LAWYERS.
they	THEY'RE LAWYERS.
teachers	THEY'RE TEACHERS.
Mary	MARY'S A TEACHER.

(Continue:)

1. student
2. I
3. doctor
4. lawyer
5. he
6. John and Paul

7. they
8. teachers
9. Mary
10. she
11. Mr. and Mrs. Black
12. we
13. he

14. you
15. I
16. they
17. John
18. John and Mary
19. I

2b. Key example: THE students are INTELLIGENT.

Observe the form of THE.
Observe the form of GOOD and INTELLIGENT.

THE	lesson	is	GOOD.
THE	girl	is	INTELLIGENT.
THE	lawyer	is	INTELLIGENT.
THE	lessons	are	GOOD.
THE	girls	are	INTELLIGENT.
THE	lawyers	are	INTELLIGENT.

COMMENT

THE, GOOD, INTELLIGENT, etc., are invariable in form.

PRACTICE

EXERCISE 2b.1. (To produce THE, GOOD, etc., with singular and plural.) Substitute the words and change the statement only if necessary. For example:

The student is hungry.

| is intelligent | THE STUDENT IS INTELLIGENT. |
| are intelligent | THE STUDENTS ARE INTELLIGENT. |

is hungry	THE STUDENT IS HUNGRY.
doctor	THE DOCTOR IS HUNGRY.
professors	THE PROFESSORS ARE HUNGRY.
is intelligent	THE PROFESSOR IS INTELLIGENT.

(Continue:)

1. student	6. class	11. is good
2. is interesting	7. alphabets	12. lesson
3. are interesting	8. secretaries	13. are good
4. lessons	9. are intelligent	14. is scientific
5. lesson	10. doctor	15. teacher

SUMMARY EXERCISE FOR LESSON I. (To review Lesson I.) Give a question with the suggested word. Another student gives a short answer to the question. For example:

necessary	IS THE LESSON NECESSARY?	YES, IT IS.
practical	IS THE LESSON PRACTICAL?	YES, IT IS.
interesting	IS THE LESSON INTERESTING?	NO, IT ISN'T.
doctor	IS THE DOCTOR INTERESTING?	YES, HE IS.
doctors	ARE THE DOCTORS INTER- ESTING?	NO, THEY AREN'T.

(Continue:)

1. intelligent	7. interesting	13. bad
2. students	8. class	14. lessons
3. hungry	9. classes	15. lesson
4. you	10. students	16. necessary
5. he	11. hungry	17. alphabet
6. good	12. sick	18. good

KEY EXAMPLES OF LESSON I

1a. The lesson IS interesting.
   IS the lesson interesting?
1b. IT'S interesting.
   YOU'RE busy.
   I'M busy.
1c. Is the lesson interesting?
   YES, IT IS.
1d. He'S HUNGRY.
   He'S IN CLASS.
   He'S A DOCTOR.

1e. Mary is interesting.
   SHE's from Mexico.
   SHE's a student.

2a. I'm A student.
   We're studentS.

2b. THE students are IN- TELLIGENT.

Lesson II

1. Statements, questions, and answers with Class 2 words (BEGIN, STUDY, HAVE) other than BE.

   1a. THE STUDENTS STUDY IN THE MORNING. DO THEY STUDY AT NIGHT?
   [Word order of questions with DO contrasted with word order of statements]

   1b. JOHN STUDIES AT NIGHT.
   [-S forms with HE, SHE, IT, JOHN, etc.]

   1c. DOES HE STUDY AT NIGHT?
   [DOES with HE, SHE, IT]

   1d. DO THE STUDENTS STUDY AT NIGHT? YES, THEY DO.
   DOES JOHN STUDY IN THE AFTERNOON? YES, HE DOES.
   [Short answers to questions with DO, DOES]

2. Position of USUALLY, ALWAYS, NEVER, SOMETIMES, OFTEN.

   2a. MARY IS USUALLY BUSY. SHE ALWAYS STUDIES AT NIGHT.
   [Position of USUALLY, etc., with BE contrasted with the position of USUALLY, etc., with other Class 2 words]

   2b. IS MARY EVER HOMESICK? MARY'S NEVER HOMESICK.
   [Never in statements. Ever in questions]

1a.

Key examples: The students STUDY in the morning.
DO they STUDY at night?

Observe the order of the words. Observe DO.

Previous pattern (Lesson I):

The lessons	are	easy.

New pattern:

I	STUDY	in the morning.
We	STUDY	in the morning.
You	STUDY	in the morning.
The students	STUDY	in the morning.
The classes	BEGIN	in the morning.
The students	HAVE	coffee in the morning.

Previous pattern (Lesson I):

Are	the lessons	easy?

New pattern:

DO	you	STUDY	in the morning?
DO	Mary and John	STUDY	in the morning?
DO	they	STUDY	in the morning?
DO	the classes	BEGIN	in the morning?
DO	the students	HAVE	coffee in the morning?

12

COMMENTS

(1) Use DO in questions with Class 2 words like STUDY, BEGIN, HAVE.
(2) DO precedes YOU, THEY, THE CLASSES, THE STUDENTS, etc., in questions.
(3) Use the simple forms of Class 2 words (STUDY, BEGIN, HAVE, etc.) in expressions of repeated occurrence.
(4) Use a falling intonation for questions. Use the same intonation for the statements and the questions.

PRACTICE

EXERCISE 1a.1. (To practice questions with words like STUDY, BE-GIN, HAVE in contrast to questions with AM, IS, ARE.) Convert the statements into questions. For example:

The students arrive at eight o'clock.
DO THE STUDENTS ARRIVE AT EIGHT O'CLOCK?

They are intelligent.
ARE THEY INTELLIGENT?

The classes begin at eight o'clock.
DO THE CLASSES BEGIN AT EIGHT O'CLOCK?

They are interesting.
ARE THEY INTERESTING?

1. Mary and John study English.
2. Mary and John arrive at 8 o'clock.
3. They study in the morning.
4. The lessons are easy.
5. They're important.
6. Mary and John have coffee.
7. The students understand Spanish.
8. They practice English.
9. They are busy.
10. They have coffee at 10 o'clock.
11. The doctors are tired.
12. They study in the morning.
13. They practice pronunciation.
14. You know the answer.
15. You are tired.
16. You are busy.
17. You speak English.
18. They serve breakfast.
19. Breakfast is good.
20. Sandwiches are good.

1b.

Key example: John STUDIES at night.

Observe the form of the Class 2 words (STUDY, STUDIES).

Previous pattern:

I	study	here.
John and Mary	study	here.
They	practice	English.
The classes	begin	at 8 o'clock.
The students	have	coffee at 10 o'clock.

New pattern:

John	STUDIES	here.
He	STUDIES	in the afternoon.
Mary	STUDIES	here.
She	PRACTICES	English.
The class	BEGINS	at 8 o'clock.
John	HAS	coffee at 10 o'clock.

COMMENTS

(1) Use the -S form* of Class 2 words (STUDIES, BEGINS, etc.) with JOHN, MARY, THE CLASS, HE, SHE, IT, etc., in expressions of repeated occurrence.

(2) Use HAS (not HAVE) with JOHN, MARY, THE CLASS, HE, SHE, IT, etc.

PRACTICE

EXERCISE 1b.1. (To produce the -S form of Class 2 words in contrast to the simple form.) Substitute the words in the correct positions. For example:

I study English here.

Mary	MARY STUDIES ENGLISH HERE.
Mary and John	MARY AND JOHN STUDY ENGLISH HERE.
He	HE STUDIES ENGLISH HERE.
has coffee	HE HAS COFFEE HERE.
I	I HAVE COFFEE HERE.
study English	I STUDY ENGLISH HERE.

1. Mary	8. he	15. John
2. Mary and John	9. eats lunch	16. he
3. he	10. we	17. the student
4. has coffee	11. they	18. John and Mary
5. I	12. Mary	19. the students
6. study English	13. she	20. John
7. John	14. practices English	

---

*For pronunciation see English Pronunciation, Lesson II.

1c. Key example: DOES he study at night?

Observe the form of the Class 2 words (STUDY, STUDIES).
Observe DOES.

Previous patterns:

	I	study	in the morning.
	The students	study	in the morning.
Do	you	study	in the morning?
Do	the students	study	in the morning?
	John	studies	in the morning.
	He	studies	in the morning.

New pattern:

DOES	John	STUDY	at night?
DOES	he	STUDY	in class?
DOES	Mary	STUDY	here?
DOES	she	STUDY	in the morning?
DOES	the class	BEGIN	at 7 A.M.?
DOES	it	BEGIN	at 8 A.M.?
DOES	the teacher	HAVE	coffee at 10 A.M.?

COMMENTS

(1) Use DOES in questions with HE, SHE, IT, JOHN, MARY, THE
CLASS, etc.
(2) Always use the simple form of the Class 2 word (STUDY, BEGIN,
HAVE, etc.) in these questions.

PRACTICE

EXERCISE 1c.1. (To form questions with DOES in contrast to questions
with DO and with forms of BE.) Convert the statements into questions.
For example:

John studies at night.	DOES JOHN STUDY AT NIGHT?
Mary studies in the after-	DOES MARY STUDY IN THE AFTER-
noon	NOON?
They study in the morning.	DO THEY STUDY IN THE MORNING?
The students are busy.	ARE THE STUDENTS BUSY?
The class begins at 8 A.M.	DOES THE CLASS BEGIN AT 8 A.M.?

1. Mary arrives at 8 A.M.
2. She has coffee at 10 A.M.
3. John and Mary study at night.
4. The class begins at 8 A.M.
5. The students eat breakfast at
   7.
6. The coffee is hot.
7. The students are homesick.
8. The students study here.

9. The student studies here.
10. He has a book.
11. He understands the lessons.
12. He is here.
13. The lessons are important.
14. John lives at the English
    House.
15. He comes from Peru.
16. He is a student.

1d.

Key examples: Do the students study at night?   Yes, they DO.
Does John study in the afternoon? Yes, he DOES.

Observe the short answers.

QUESTIONS	SHORT ANSWERS

Previous pattern (Lesson I):

Is John a doctor?	Yes, he is.

New pattern:

Do you like coffee?	Yes,	I	DO.
Do the students study at night?	Yes,	they	DO.
Do I pronounce well?	Yes,	you	DO.
Do the classes begin at 7 A.M.?	No,	they	DON'T.
Do they begin at 6 A.M.?	No,	they	DON'T.
Do we have dinner at 5 P.M.?	No,	we	DON'T.
Does John like the class?	Yes,	he	DOES.
Does he like the lessons?	Yes,	he	DOES.
Does Mary like the class?	Yes,	she	DOES.
Does she eat lunch here?	No,	she	DOESN'T.
Does the class begin at 7 A.M.?	No,	it	DOESN'T.
Does it begin at 6 A.M.?	No,	it	DOESN'T.

COMMENTS

(1) DO, DOES complete the affirmative short answers to questions with DO, DOES.

(2) DON'T, DOESN'T complete the negative short answers to questions with DO, DOES.

PRACTICE

EXERCISE 1d.1. (To produce short answers with DO, DOES.) Answer the questions with YES, I DO; YES, HE DOES; YES, THEY DO; etc. For example:

Do you like coffee?   YES, I DO.
Does Mary study at night?   YES, SHE DOES.

1. Do they drink coffee?
2. Does he like the class?
3. Does the class begin at 9 A.M.?
4. Do you study in the morning?
5. Do they have class in the morning?
6. Do they have class at night?
7. Does Mary understand the lesson?
8. Do we pronounce well?
9. Does she like the class?
10. Does he eat dinner here?
11. Does it begin in the morning?
12. Do I pronounce well?

EXERCISE 1d.2. (To produce negative short answers.) Answer the questions with NO, HE DOESN'T; NO, WE DON'T; etc. For example:

Do you like coffee?   NO, I DON'T.
Does Mary study at night?   NO, SHE DOESN'T.

(Continue with the items of Exercise 1d.1.)

EXERCISE 1d.3. (To recognize statements and to answer questions.)
Give short answers to the questions. Make no response to the statements. For example:

Is the lesson interesting?   YES, IT IS.
The lesson is important.   (No oral response.)
Do you come from Cuba?   NO, I DON'T.
Does John like the class?   YES, HE DOES.

1. The lesson is important.
2. Are you from Venezuela?
3. Do you come from Venezuela?
4. Do you live here?
5. Do you like the class?
6. Does the class begin at 8
   A.M.?
7. Are the students busy?
8. Are you a student?
9. Is the class interesting?
10. The lessons are good.
11. John studies in the morning.
12. The students study in the
    morning.
13. Do they like the lessons?
14. Does John like the lessons?
15. Does Mary understand the
    lessons?
16. Does she like the classes?
17. She likes the students.
18. Do you understand English?
19. Do the students understand
    it?
20. The students are intelligent.

2a. Key examples: Mary IS USUALLY busy. She ALWAYS STUD-
IES at night.

Observe the positions of ALWAYS.					
	Mary		is	ALWAYS	busy.
	The classes		are	ALWAYS	interesting.
Is	Mary			ALWAYS	busy?
Are	the classes			ALWAYS	interesting?
	Mary	ALWAYS	studies		at night.
	We	ALWAYS	have		classes in the morning.
Does	Mary	ALWAYS	study		at night?
Do	we	ALWAYS	have		classes in the morning?

COMMENTS

(1) Use ALWAYS after forms of BE (IS, ARE, AM).
(2) Use ALWAYS before other Class 2 words (STUDY, HAVE, etc.)
(3) Use SOMETIMES, OFTEN, USUALLY, in the same positions as
    ALWAYS. See the Illustrative Examples.

ILLUSTRATIVE EXAMPLES

Mary ALWAYS drinks milk in the morning.

John USUALLY has coffee at 10 A.M.

They OFTEN eat in a restaurant.

I SOMETIMES have coffee.

Does Mary ALWAYS drink milk in the morning?

Does John USUALLY have coffee at 10 A.M.?

Do they OFTEN eat in a restaurant?

Do you SOMETIMES eat in a restaurant?

John is ALWAYS tired.

He is USUALLY sleepy.

He is OFTEN homesick.

He is SOMETIMES discouraged.

Are you ALWAYS tired?

Are the students USUALLY busy?

Is John OFTEN sleepy?

Are you SOMETIMES homesick?

PRACTICE

EXERCISE 2a.1. (To use ALWAYS, USUALLY, OFTEN, SOMETIMES, in correct positions.) Listen to the statement or question and the word before it. Repeat the statement or question with the word in the correct position. For example:

Always.   Mary drinks milk in the morning.
                  MARY ALWAYS DRINKS MILK IN THE MORNING.

Usually.   John is hungry.
                  JOHN IS USUALLY HUNGRY.

Often.   Is Mary busy?
                  IS MARY OFTEN BUSY?

1. Always.   Mary drinks milk in the morning.
2. Usually.   John is hungry.
3. Often.   Is Mary busy?
4. Usually.   I'm sleepy.
5. Sometimes.   John and Mary study at night.
6. Always.   Are the lessons easy?
7. Often.   Do they understand the lesson?
8. Sometimes.   She understands the lessons.
9. Often.   She is right.
10. Always.   The classes begin at 8 o'clock.
11. Sometimes.   The students have coffee at 10 o'clock.
12. Usually.   Do they have coffee at 10 o'clock?

EXERCISE 2a.2. (To use ALWAYS, USUALLY, OFTEN, SOMETIMES, in correct positions.) Substitute the words in the proper positions and make the necessary changes in form. For example:

John is always here.

studies	JOHN ALWAYS STUDIES HERE.
the students	THE STUDENTS ALWAYS STUDY HERE.
usually	THE STUDENTS USUALLY STUDY HERE.
are	THE STUDENTS ARE USUALLY HERE.
sometimes	THE STUDENTS ARE SOMETIMES HERE.

1. John	8. are	15. always
2. studies	9. the students	16. are
3. always	10. usually	17. I
4. Mary	11. study	18. usually
5. often	12. eat	19. eat
6. I	13. sometimes	20. always
7. we	14. we	

2b. Key examples: Is Mary EVER homesick? Mary's NEVER homesick.

Observe the use of NEVER and EVER.

QUESTIONS			STATEMENTS		
Is Mary	EVER	homesick?	Mary's	NEVER	homesick.
Are you	EVER	discouraged?	You're	NEVER	discouraged.
Do you	EVER	drink coffee?	You	NEVER	drink coffee.
Does Mary	EVER	drink coffee?	Mary	NEVER	drinks coffee.
Does John	EVER	arrive at 8?	John	NEVER	arrives at 8.

COMMENTS

(1) Use NEVER in statements.
(2) Use EVER in questions.*
(3) Use NEVER and EVER in the same position as ALWAYS, USUAL-LY, etc.

PRACTICE

EXERCISE 2b.1. (To use NEVER and EVER.) Repeat the statements and the questions. Include the word NEVER in the proper position in the statements only. Include the word EVER in the proper position in the questions only. For example:

> I have tomato juice for breakfast.
> > I NEVER HAVE TOMATO JUICE FOR BREAKFAST.
> I'm busy.
> > I'M NEVER BUSY.
> Do you have coffee for dinner?
> > DO YOU EVER HAVE COFFEE FOR DINNER?
> Are you tired?
> > ARE YOU EVER TIRED?

1. Do you have coffee for dinner?	5. Mary is homesick.
2. Are you tired?	6. Are you homesick?
3. I have tomato juice for breakfast.	7. Do you eat fish?
4. I'm busy.	8. I like breakfast.

---

*In certain special situations, you might hear EVER in statements or NEVER in questions.

9. They are hungry in the morning.
10. Does John study at night ?
11. We drink milk for breakfast.
12. Are the students late for class?

NOTE

Possible answers to questions with EVER are:

Is Mary ever homesick?	NO, NEVER.
Are you ever discouraged?	YES, SOMETIMES.
Do you ever drink coffee?	YES, OFTEN.
Do you ever have coffee for dinner?	YES, USUALLY.
Do you ever arrive at 8 A.M.?	YES, ALWAYS.

Key Examples of Lesson II

1a. The students STUDY in the morning.
Do they STUDY at night?
1b. John STUDIES at night.
1c. DOES he study at night?
1d. Do the students study at night?
Yes, they DO.
Does John study in the afternoon?
Yes, he DOES.

2a. Mary IS USUALLY busy.
She ALWAYS STUDIES at night.
2b. Is Mary EVER homesick?
Mary's NEVER homesick.

Lesson III

1. WE STUDY HERE EVERY DAY.
   [Position of expressions of "place" and expressions of "time"]

2. I WAS HERE LAST NIGHT. WERE YOU HERE LAST NIGHT?
   [Forms of BE correlated with expressions of past time]

3. I STUDIED LAST NIGHT. DID YOU STUDY LAST NIGHT?
   [Forms of other Class 2 words correlated with expressions of past time]

4. WERE YOU HERE? YES, I WAS. DID YOU STUDY? YES, I DID.
   [Short answers to questions with expressions of past time]

1.   Key example: We study HERE EVERY DAY.

Observe the position of expressions of place and expressions of time.

We study We have coffee	HERE. AT A RESTAURANT.	
We study We have coffee		EVERY DAY. AT 10 A.M.
We study We have coffee	HERE AT A RESTAURANT	EVERY DAY. AT 10 A.M.

COMMENTS

(1) Use expressions of "place" and "time" (HERE, AT A RESTAU-RANT, EVERY DAY, AT 10 A.M., etc.) at the end in this pattern.

(2) Use expressions of "place" (HERE, IN A RESTAURANT, etc.) before expressions of "time" (EVERY DAY, AT 10 A.M., etc.).

PRACTICE

EXERCISE 1.1. (To practice position of expressions of "place.")
Substitute the words in the correct position. For example:

I live in the dormitory.

here	I LIVE HERE.
eat	I EAT HERE.
we	WE EAT HERE.
in the dormitory	WE EAT IN THE DORMITORY.

1. live	5. at the restaurant	9. in that building.
2. I	6. John	10. we
3. here	7. there	11. live
4. eat	8. studies	12. in the dormitory

21

EXERCISE 1.2. (To practice position of expressions of "time.") Substitute the words in the proper position. For example:

We usually have lunch at noon.

at 1 o'clock	WE USUALLY HAVE LUNCH AT 1 O'CLOCK.
coffee	WE USUALLY HAVE COFFEE AT 1 O'CLOCK.
in the morning	WE USUALLY HAVE COFFEE IN THE MORNING.
always	WE ALWAYS HAVE COFFEE IN THE MORNING.

1. at noon
2. lunch
3. at 12 o'clock
4. usually

5. coffee
6. in the evening
7. in the afternoon
8. at night

9. dinner
10. always
11. tea
12. in the morning

EXERCISE 1.3. (To practice position of expressions of "place" and "time.") Substitute the words in the proper positions. For example:

The teacher has breakfast in the dormitory in the morning.

at 7 A.M.
   THE TEACHER HAS BREAKFAST IN THE DORMITORY AT 7 A.M.

at home
   THE TEACHER HAS BREAKFAST AT HOME AT 7 A.M.

every day
   THE TEACHER HAS BREAKFAST AT HOME EVERY DAY.

1. at a restaurant
2. coffee
3. at noon
4. here
5. in that building
6. in the afternoon

7. every day
8. we
9. at noon
10. lunch
11. there
12. at 1 o'clock

2. Key examples: I WAS here last night. WERE you here last night?

Observe WAS, WERE. Observe the time expressions.

Previous pattern (Lesson I):

I	am	right.
John	is	tired.
We	are	busy.

Am	I	right?
Is	John	tired?
Are	we	busy?

New pattern:

I	WAS	right	yester-day.
John	WAS	tired	yester-day.
He	WAS	here	last night.
Mary	WAS	busy	yester-day.
She	WAS	sleepy	last night.
It	WAS	here	yester-day.
We	WERE	busy	last night.
You	WERE	right	last night.
They	WERE	busy	yester-day.

WAS	I	right	yester-day?
WAS	John	tired	yester-day?
WAS	he	here	last night?
WAS	Mary	busy	yester-day?
WAS	she	sleepy	last night?
WAS	it	here	yester-day?
WERE	we	busy	last night?
WERE	you	right	last night?
WERE	they	busy	yester-day?

COMMENTS

(1) Use WAS, WERE for past time situations. WAS, WERE are forms of BE.
(2) Use WAS with I, HE, SHE, IT, JOHN, MARY, THE LESSON, etc.
(3) Use WERE with WE, YOU, THEY, THE LESSONS, etc.
(4) Use WAS, WERE before the Class 1 word (I, HE, JOHN, etc.) in questions.

PRACTICE

EXERCISE 2.1. (To use WAS and WERE, etc.) Substitute the words and change WAS or WERE if necessary. For example:

The boys were busy.

John	JOHN WAS BUSY.
the students	THE STUDENTS WERE BUSY.
I	I WAS BUSY.

1. the teacher	5. I	9. the class
2. the boys	6. you	10. the doctor
3. John	7. we	11. John and Mary
4. the students	8. Mary	12. they

EXERCISE 2.2. (To use WAS, WERE for past and AM, ARE, IS for the present time.) Substitute the words and change WAS, WERE, AM, ARE, IS if necessary. For example:

We were here yesterday.

John	JOHN WAS HERE YESTERDAY.
now	JOHN IS HERE NOW.
the students	THE STUDENTS ARE HERE NOW.
yesterday	THE STUDENTS WERE HERE YESTERDAY.

1. Mary	5. they	9. now
2. now	6. now	10. last night
3. last night	7. yesterday	11. the books
4. I	8. the teacher	12. now

EXERCISE 2.3. (To form questions with WAS, WERE.) Listen to the statement with present time. Make a corresponding question with an expression of past time. For example:

John is busy.	WAS HE BUSY YESTERDAY?
I'm tired.	WERE YOU TIRED YESTERDAY?
The new student is homesick.	WAS HE HOMESICK YESTERDAY?
The students are here.	WERE THEY HERE YESTERDAY?

1. Mary is busy.	6. John is tired.
2. I'm tired.	7. You are right.
3. The new student is homesick.	8. The class is interesting.
4. The new student is discouraged.	9. We are right.
5. The students are here.	10. The teacher is here.

3. Key examples: I STUDIED last night. DID you STUDY last
night?

Observe the form of the Class 2 words. Observe the time expressions.

Previous pattern (Lesson II):

	John	studies	every day.
Does	John	study	every day?

New pattern:

	John	STUDI	ED		yesterday.
	He	WANT	ED	the book	last night.
	I	PRONOUNC	ED	the words here	yesterday.
	You	CONFUS	ED	the class	yesterday.
	The students	REPEAT	ED	the exercise	last night.
	We	ARRIV	ED		yesterday.
DID	John	STUDY			yesterday?
DID	He	WANT		the book	last night?
DID	I	PRONOUNCE		the words here	yesterday?
DID	You	CONFUSE		the class	yesterday?
DID	the students	REPEAT		the exercise	last night?
DID	we	ARRIVE			yesterday?

COMMENTS

(1) Use the -ED form of the Class 2 word (STUDIED, WANTED,
PRONOUNCED, etc.) * in statements with expressions of past
time.
(2) Use DID and the simple form of the Class 2 word (STUDY, WANT,
PRONOUNCE, etc.) in questions with expressions of past time.
(3) Use the same -ED form in statements and DID in questions
[no variation] with JOHN, I, HE, SHE, YOU, WE, THEY, THE
STUDENTS.

PRACTICE

EXERCISE 3.1. (To use the -ED form with a past time expression.)
Change the time expression from "every day" to "last night" and
make the necessary change in the Class 2 word. For example:

I study every day.
I STUDIED LAST NIGHT.
John repeats the exercise every day.
JOHN REPEATED THE EXERCISE LAST NIGHT.
The doctor works every day.
THE DOCTOR WORKED LAST NIGHT.

*For pronunciation, see English Pronunciation, Lesson III.

1. I study every day.
2. John repeats the exercise every day.
3. We arrive at nine every day.
4. The students pronounce the words every day.
5. You repeat the error every day.
6. The teacher pronounces the words every day.
7. She serves orange juice every day.
8. The students repeat the intonation every day.
9. Mary wants coffee for dinner every day.
10. He studies pronunciation every day.
11. They visit John every day.
12. We walk to school every day.

EXERCISE 3.2. (To use DID and the simple form in questions with past time.) Convert the statements into questions. For example:

The students arrived yesterday.
   DID THE STUDENTS ARRIVE YESTERDAY?
They practiced the conversations.
   DID THEY PRACTICE THE CONVERSATIONS?
The teacher presented the first lesson.
   DID THE TEACHER PRESENT THE FIRST LESSON?

1. The students arrived yesterday.
2. They practiced the conversation.
3. The teacher presented the first lesson.
4. John repeated the words.
5. He entered the restaurant.
6. Mary passed the butter.
7. I repeated the intonation.
8. We studied the second lesson.
9. They wanted coffee for breakfast.
10. The class waited for the teacher.
11. The teacher pronounced the words.
12. The doctor examined the student.

EXERCISE 3.3. (To contrast the use of the -ED form in statements and the use of DID with the simple form in questions.) This is a conversation exercise. Listen to the statement with EVERY DAY. Make a corresponding statement with LAST NIGHT. Then convert the statement into a question. Use the form YOU in the question. For example:

We study every day.	WE STUDIED LAST NIGHT.
	DID YOU STUDY LAST NIGHT?
We repeat the exercises every day.	WE REPEATED THE EXERCISES LAST NIGHT.
	DID YOU REPEAT THE EXERCISES LAST NIGHT?
We study grammar every day.	WE STUDIED GRAMMAR LAST NIGHT.
	DID YOU STUDY GRAMMAR LAST NIGHT?

1. We study every day.
2. We repeat the exercises every day.
3. We study grammar every day.
4. We repeat the words every day.
5. We practice the conversation every day.
6. We arrive at seven every day.
7. We pronounce the words every day.
8. We practice the sounds every day.
9. We attend class every day.
10. We practice every day.
11. We learn new words every day.
12. We practice pronunciation every day.

4.   Key examples: Were you here? Yes, I WAS. Did you study?
              Yes, I DID.

Observe the short answers.

QUESTIONS	SHORT ANSWERS

Previous pattern (Lesson I):

Is John tired?	Yes, he is.

New pattern:

Was John tired yesterday?	Yes, he	WAS.
Were you busy last night?	Yes, I	WAS.
Was I right yesterday?	Yes, you	WERE.
Were the students here yesterday?	Yes, they	WERE.
Was John tired on Monday?	No, he	WASN'T.
Were you busy on Monday?	No, I	WASN'T.
Were we right yesterday?	No, you	WEREN'T.
Were the lessons difficult?	No, they	WEREN'T.

Previous pattern (Lesson II):

Do you study grammar every day?	Yes, I do.

New pattern:

Did you study grammar yesterday?	Yes, I	DID.
Did I answer the question?	Yes, you	DID.
Did the students arrive on Friday?	Yes, they	DID.
Did Mary want the book?	Yes, she	DID.
Did you study last night?	No, I	DIDN'T.
Did I confuse the class?	No, you	DIDN'T.
Did the students arrive on Monday?	No, they	DIDN'T.
Did the secretary want the book?	No, she	DIDN'T.

COMMENTS

(1) WAS, WERE, WASN'T, WEREN'T complete the short answers to
   questions with the forms of BE for past time (WAS, WERE).
(2) DID, DIDN'T complete the short answers to questions with DID.

PRACTICE

EXERCISE 4.1. (To use IS, WAS, WERE in affirmative and negative short answers.) Answer the questions with YES, I WAS;   NO, I WASN'T; YES, WE WERE; NO, THEY AREN'T; etc. For example:

Were the lessons important?	YES, THEY WERE.
Was John here yesterday?	YES, HE WAS.
Were you here yesterday?	YES, I WAS.
Are John and Mary homesick?	NO, THEY AREN'T.

1. Were the lessons difficult?
2. Was the teacher here yesterday?
3. Am I wrong?
4. Were you busy last night?
5. Were the students tired yesterday?
6. Was the dinner good last night?
7. Are you busy?
8. Was I right?
9. Is the teacher in the room?
10. Was the secretary here yesterday?
11. Were you in New York yesterday?
12. Were the students busy last night?
13. Was Mr. Brown here last night?

EXERCISE 4.2. (To use DO, DOES, DID in affirmative and negative short answers.) Answer the questions with YES, I DO; NO, HE DOESN'T; YES, HE DID; NO, HE DIDN'T; etc. For example:

Do you like tomato juice?	NO, I DON'T.
Did you have tomato juice for dinner?	NO, I DIDN'T.
Did the students have dinner in the	YES, THEY DID.
dormitory last night?	

1. Did you have tomato juice for dinner?
2. Did the students have dinner in the dormitory last night?
3. Does the restaurant have a different menu every day?
4. Do you like the dormitory?
5. Do you want a different room?
6. Did you arrive on Friday?
7. Does the history class interest you?
8. Did the first lesson interest you?
9. Did I answer the question?
10. Does the teacher live in the dormitory?
11. Did the new student arrive on Monday?
12. Did Mary study the second lesson last night?

EXERCISE 4.3. (To recognize statements and to practice short answers.) This is a summary exercise. Use affirmative or negative short answers in response to the questions. Make no response to the statements. For example:

Were you in New York last night?	NO, I WASN'T.
I was in Chicago yesterday.	(No oral response.)
Were the students busy last night?	YES, THEY WERE.
Are you hungry?	NO, I'M NOT.
I studied last night.	(No oral response.)
Did you visit the museum?	YES, I DID.

1. Were you in Chicago yesterday?
2. I like Chicago.
3. Do you like Chicago?
4. Did you visit the art museum?
5. Did you like it?
6. Chicago is interesting.
7. Is Caracas in Venezuela?
8. Is Paris in Italy?
9. Shakespeare was in England in 1586.
10. Did Shakespeare live in England?
11. Does John understand the question?
12. Did he study last night?
13. I studied last night.
14. Are you homesick?
15. Do you like Shakespeare?
16. Was he here yesterday?

Key Examples of Lesson III

1. We study HERE EVERY DAY.
2. I WAS here last night.
   WERE you here last night?
3. I STUDIED last night.
   DID you STUDY last night?
4. Were you here? Yes, I WAS.
   Did you study? Yes, I DID.

Lesson IV

1. WHEN DID YOU ARRIVE?
   [Word order of questions with WHAT, WHEN, WHERE, WHO(M)]

2a. I'M STUDYING GRAMMAR.
   [AM, IS, ARE + the -ING form of a Class 2 word in statements]

2b. WHAT ARE YOU STUDYING?
   [AM, IS, ARE + the -ING form of a Class 2 word in questions]

3. IT'S A GOOD CLASS. IT'S A GRAMMAR CLASS.
   [Single word modifiers before Class 1 words]

1.   Key example: WHEN DID you ARRIVE? A week ago.

Observe the word order of these questions.

QUESTIONS   ANSWERS

Previous patterns (Lessons I and II):

Does	John	study?			Yes, he does.
Is	John		a student?		Yes, he is.

New pattern:

WHAT	DOES	John	STUDY?			Grammar.
WHEN	DOES	he	STUDY?			Every day.
WHERE	DOES	he	STUDY	every day?		In class.
WHO(M) *	DOES	he	VISIT	every day?		Mary.
WHAT	DOES	he	DO	every day?		He studies.
WHAT	IS	John?				A student.
WHERE	IS	he?				In class.
WHEN	IS	he		in class?		Every day.
WHO	IS	he.?				My friend.

COMMENT

Use WHAT, WHEN, WHERE, WHO + forms of DO or BE before the
first Class 1 word (JOHN, HE, etc.) in these questions. The order
of these words is question word order (DOES HE..., IS HE..., etc.)

---

*Use WHO or WHOM before DOES, DO, DID in this pattern. WHO is informal.
WHOM is formal.

PRACTICE

EXERCISE 1.1. (To use WHAT with question word order.) This is a substitution exercise. Ask about the meaning of these words. For example:

What does "big" mean?

"intelligent"   WHAT DOES "INTELLIGENT" MEAN?
"exist"   WHAT DOES "EXIST" MEAN?
"actual"   WHAT DOES "ACTUAL" MEAN?

1. "difficult"	4. "penny"	8. "entire"
2. "duplicate"	5. "dime"	9. "funny"
3. "simple"	6. "quarter"	10. "assist"
	7. "tooth"	

EXERCISE 1.2. (To use WHEN with question word order.) This is a conversation exercise.   Listen to the information about Paul. Ask corresponding questions about John. For example:

Paul arrived in June.   WHEN DID JOHN ARRIVE?
Paul studied a year ago.   WHEN DID JOHN STUDY?
Paul telephoned yesterday.   WHEN DID JOHN TELEPHONE?

1. Paul studied a month ago.   7. Paul practiced a year ago.
2. Paul telephoned yesterday.   8. Paul telephoned at 8 o'clock.
3. Paul studied a year ago.   9. Paul returned a week ago.
4. Paul arrived yesterday.   10. Paul worked yesterday.
5. Paul called two hours ago.   11. Paul called on Wednesday.
6. Paul arrived a year ago.   12. Paul practiced in the
                                         morning.

EXERCISE 1.3. (To use WHERE with question word order.) This is a conversation exercise. Listen to the information about Paul. Ask corresponding questions about John and Mary. For example:

Paul lives in New York.   WHERE DO JOHN AND MARY LIVE?
Paul studies at the university. WHERE DO JOHN AND MARY
                                    STUDY?
Paul eats lunch in the cafe-   WHERE DO JOHN AND MARY EAT
    teria.   LUNCH?

1. Paul drinks milk in the cafe-   5. Paul studies the lessons in class.
     teria.   6. Paul teaches in New York.
2. Paul eats dinner in the res-   7. Paul speaks in Chicago.
     taurant.   8. Paul studies medicine in
3. Paul lives on Main Street.   Chicago.
4. Paul studied English in the   9. Paul eats at the English House.
     university.   10. Paul lives in New York.

EXERCISE 1.4. (To use WHO(M) with question word order.) This is a conversation exercise. Listen to the statement. Form a corresponding question using the form WHO. For example:

The teacher knows John.	WHO(M) DOES JOHN KNOW?
I visited the student.	WHO(M) DID THE STUDENT VISIT?
We talked to John.	WHO(M) DID JOHN TALK TO?

1. She telephoned Paul.
2. They see the teacher.
3. The student wants John.
4. The teacher assisted the student.
5. John called Paul.
6. He knows my friend.

7. I hear the professor.
8. Mary knows you.
9. We visited Mr. Smith.
10. They looked at the teacher.
11. Mr. Smith teaches John.
12. The teacher asked Mary.

EXERCISE 1.5. (To produce WHO(M), WHAT, WHERE, WHEN with question word order.) This is a conversation exercise. Listen to the information about Paul. Ask corresponding questions about John with the forms WHO(M), WHAT, WHERE, WHEN. For example:

Paul sees Mr. Black.	WHO(M) DOES JOHN SEE?
Paul studies every day.	WHEN DOES JOHN STUDY?
Paul is a doctor.	WHAT IS JOHN?

1. Paul was in New York.
2. Paul was in Detroit.
3. Paul is a doctor.
4. Paul was a student.
5. Paul studied English.
6. Paul studied last year.
7. Paul studied in New York.
8. Paul arrived yesterday.
9. Paul studied yesterday.
10. Paul studied grammar.

11. Paul learned grammar.
12. Paul visited the university.
13. Paul visited a friend.
14. Paul studied last week.
15. Paul studies every day.
16. Paul studies English.
17. Paul studies in New York.
18. Paul lives in New York.
19. Paul sees Mary.
20. Paul sees Mr. Black.

EXERCISE 1.6. (To establish the pattern of WHEN, WHERE, WHAT, WHO in questions with DO.) Substitute the words in the proper positions. For example:

What did John study?

eat	WHAT DID JOHN EAT?
where	WHERE DID JOHN EAT?
John and Mary	WHERE DID JOHN AND MARY EAT?
study	WHERE DID JOHN AND MARY STUDY?
when	WHEN DID JOHN AND MARY STUDY?
what	WHAT DID JOHN AND MARY STUDY?

1. eat
2. when
3. where

4. go
5. when
6. arrive

7. study
8. where
9. what

10. visit	14. learn	19. where
11. who(m)	15. he	20. study
12. see	16. she	21. what
13. what	17. you	22. John
	18. eat	

EXERCISE 1.7. (To establish the pattern of WHAT, WHERE, WHEN, WHO in questions with BE.) Substitute the words in the proper positions. For example:

What were the boys?

where	WHERE WERE THE BOYS?
are	WHERE ARE THE BOYS?
is	WHERE IS THE BOY?
who	WHO IS THE BOY?

1. where	8. are	15. the boy
2. what	9. were	16. where
3. are	10. who	17. was
4. where	11. where	18. what
5. is	12. is	19. is
6. was	13. the doctor	20. are
7. the student	14. who	21. were

2a. Key example: I'M STUDYING grammar.

Observe the Class 2 expressions.

Previous pattern (Lesson II):

I	go	to class	every day.

New pattern:

I	AM	GOING	to the door	now.
I	AM	TEACHING	grammar	now.
You	ARE	STUDYING	grammar.	
Peter	IS	WALKING	down the street.	
He	IS	COMING	to class	now.

COMMENTS

(1) Use AM, ARE, IS + the -ING form of a Class 2 word for "action" in progress at the present time (with NOW, etc.). Use I GO for repeated action (with EVERY DAY, etc.), but use I AM GOING for action in progress at the present time.

(2) Do not use the -ING form of SEE, LIKE, BE, WANT, UNDERSTAND, KNOW, in this pattern.

PRACTICE

EXERCISE 2a.1. (To use IS plus an -ING form to indicate action in progress.) Convert the statements with repeated or past action to statements with action in progress at the present time. Use the word NOW in the statement. For example:

I study every day.   I AM STUDYING NOW.
He studied his lesson yesterday.   HE IS STUDYING HIS LESSON
                                      NOW.
John works every day.   JOHN IS WORKING NOW.

1. She waits every day.
2. They visited Mary yesterday.
3. I telephoned the student yesterday.
4. We work every day.
5. They eat steak every day.
6. The students write a letter every day.
7. You studied grammar this morning.
8. John studies pronunciation every morning.
9. Peter walks to school every day.
10. He works in the cafeteria every day.
11. She studied in the library yesterday.
12. They come to class every day.

EXERCISE 2a.2. (To practice correlation of Class 2 expressions with time expressions.) Substitute the words and make necessary changes in the Class 2 expressions. For example:

Mary is watching the play.

she   SHE IS WATCHING THE PLAY.
yesterday   SHE WATCHED THE PLAY YESTERDAY.
every day   SHE WATCHES THE PLAY EVERY DAY.
now   SHE IS WATCHING THE PLAY NOW.

1. John
2. we
3. studying
4. every day
5. he
6. now
7. last week
8. they
9. now
10. watching
11. last night
12. we
13. now
14. you

2b. Key example: WHAT ARE you STUDYING? Grammar.

Observe the word order in the questions.

Previous pattern:

STATEMENT

| We | are | studying | grammar. |

New pattern:

		QUESTIONS			ANSWERS
	ARE	you	STUDYING	grammar?	Yes, I am.
	ARE	you	STUDYING	in class?	Yes, I am.
	IS	John	LEARNING	English?	Yes, he is.
	IS	he	VISITING	a friend?	Yes, he is.
	AM	I	SPEAKING	slowly?	Yes, you are.
WHAT	ARE	you	STUDYING?		Grammar.
WHERE	ARE	you	STUDYING?		In class.
WHAT	IS	John	LEARNING?		English.
WHO(M)	IS	he	VISITING?		A friend.
WHAT	IS	he	DOING	now?	Studying.

COMMENTS

(1) Use ARE, IS, AM before the first Class 1 word (YOU, JOHN, HE, etc.) in these questions with the -ING form.

(2) Use WHAT, WHEN, WHERE, WHO(M) before ARE, IS, AM.

PRACTICE

EXERCISE 2b.1. (To recognize questions and statements with -ING forms and to give short answers.) Answer the questions. Make no response to the statements. For example:

Are you studying grammar?	YES, I AM.
John's working.	(No oral response.)
Is John working?	YES, HE IS.
I'm learning English.	(No oral response.)
Are we practicing Spanish?	NO, WE AREN'T.

1. Is John learning English?
2. Is he visiting a friend?
3. He's speaking slowly.
4. Am I speaking slowly?
5. Are you writing letters?

6. Are we practicing Spanish?
7. Is he teaching grammar?
8. Is he practicing short answers?
9. I am asking questions.
10. Are you studying grammar?

EXERCISE 2b.2. (To practice the question pattern with IS, ARE, and an
-ING form.) Substitute the word in the correct position and make the
necessary changes. For example:

Are you studying grammar?

he	IS HE STUDYING GRAMMAR?
teaching	IS HE TEACHING GRAMMAR?
English	IS HE TEACHING ENGLISH?
they	ARE THEY TEACHING ENGLISH?

1. you
2. he
3. learning
4. studying

5. grammar
6. vocabulary
7. you
8. she
9. teaching

10. Spanish
11. studying
12. you
13. grammar

EXERCISE 2b.3. (To produce the question pattern with WHAT, WHERE,
WHO(M), and IS plus an -ING form.) This is a conversation exercise.
Listen to the statement about Paul. Ask corresponding questions about
his brother. For example:

Paul is studying English.	WHAT IS HIS BROTHER STUDYING?
Paul is living in New York.	WHERE IS HIS BROTHER LIVING?
Paul is eating at a restaurant.	WHERE IS HIS BROTHER EATING?
Paul is visiting a friend.	WHO IS HIS BROTHER VISITING?

1. Paul is studying English.
2. Paul is living in New York.
3. Paul is visiting a friend.
4. Paul is drinking coffee.
5. Paul is teaching in New York.
6. Paul is studying here.
7. Paul is practicing a conversation.

8. Paul is studying medicine.
9. Paul is telephoning John.
10. Paul is living in the dormitory.
11. Paul is watching the teacher.
12. Paul is eating a sandwich.

3.   Key examples: It's a GOOD class. It's a GRAMMAR class.

Observe the position and form of GOOD, etc., and of STEAK, etc.

MODIFIER → HEAD

We have a	GOOD	dinner every day.
We have	GOOD	dinners.
We have a	SMALL	class.
We have	SMALL	classes.
It's a	TALL	building.
He's a	TALL	boy.
She's a	TALL	girl.
They're	TALL	buildings.
They're	TALL	boys.
They're	TALL	girls.
We have a	STEAK	dinner every day.
We have	STEAK	dinners.
We have a	GRAMMAR	class every day.
We have	GRAMMAR	classes.
It's a	DRUG	store.
They're	DRUG	stores.
He's a	GRAMMAR	teacher.
She's a	GRAMMAR	teacher.
They're	GRAMMAR	teachers.

COMMENTS

(1) Use Class 3 words (GOOD, SMALL, TALL, etc.) and Class 1 words
(STEAK, GRAMMAR, etc.) before the word they modify (not after
it). A STEAK DINNER is a dinner (not a steak). A GOOD DIN-
NER is a dinner.
(2) Class 3 words (GOOD, etc.) are invariable in form for singular
and plural. Class 1 words (STEAK, etc.) as modifiers (before
other Class 1 words) are invariable in form for singular and
plural.
(3) The intonation of GOOD DINNER, etc., is usually different from
the intonation of STEAK DINNER, etc. (GOOD‾DIN‾NER,
STEAK‾DINNER).

PRACTICE

EXERCISE 3.1. (To use Class 3 words as describing words in the proper
position.) Substitute the words and make the necessary changes. For
example:

It's a good dinner.

lesson	IT'S A GOOD LESSON.
they	THEY'RE GOOD LESSONS.
steaks	THEY'RE GOOD STEAKS.
it	IT'S A GOOD STEAK.

1. dinner	5. they	9. interesting
2. lunch	6. big	10. they
3. breakfast	7. it	11. tall
4. sandwich	8. building	12. it

EXERCISE 3.2. (To practice recognition of the meaning in this pattern.)
Answer the questions as in these examples:

What's milk chocolate?	IT'S CHOCOLATE.
What's chocolate milk?	IT'S MILK.
What's a bus station?	IT'S A STATION.
What's a station bus?	IT'S A BUS.
What's a telephone book?	IT'S A BOOK.
What's fruit juice?	IT'S JUICE.

1. What's a milk bottle?	7. What's a car factory?
2. What's a bus station?	8. What's a factory car?
3. What's a station bus?	9. What's a telephone book?
4. What's a language problem?	10. What's a flower garden?
5. What's a pocket watch?	11. What's a garden flower?
6. What's a watch pocket?	

EXERCISE 3.3. (To use a Class 1 word before another Class 1 word.)
Listen to the word given and the statement which follows it. Identify
the word as in these examples:

A cover. It's on a magazine.
    IT'S A MAGAZINE COVER.
A watch. I carry the watch in a pocket.
    IT'S A POCKET WATCH.
A pocket. I carry my watch in the pocket.
    IT'S A WATCH POCKET.
A lesson. It teaches grammar.
    IT'S A GRAMMAR LESSON.
Lessons. They teach grammar.
    THEY'RE GRAMMAR LESSONS.
A class. It explains grammar.
    IT'S A GRAMMAR CLASS.

1. A lesson. It teaches English.
2. A store. It consists of departments.
3. A watch. I carry the watch in my pocket.
4. A cup. I use the cup for coffee.
5. Shoes. I play tennis in the shoes.
6. A watch. I wear the watch on my wrist.
7. A lamp. The lamp is on the desk.
8. Spoons. We eat soup with the spoons.
9. Dresses. I wear the dresses in the evening.
10. A class. We study pronunciation.
11. A teacher. He teaches grammar.

12. Buses. They go to the station.
13. A station. It's for buses.
14. A light. It regulates traffic.
15. A store. It sells groceries.
16. A store. It sells shoes.
17. Two stores. They sell shoes.
18. A bottle. It's for milk.
19. A tree. It has apples.
20. A ticket. It is for a trip on the railroad.
21. A ticket. It is for a baseball game.
22. A store. It sells books.
23. A room. It is for classes.
24. A class. We study English.
25. A factory. It produces automobiles.
26. A class. We study grammar.

KEY EXAMPLES OF LESSON IV

1. WHEN DID you ARRIVE?   3. It's a GOOD class.
    A week ago.   It's a GRAMMAR class.
2a. I'M STUDYING grammar.
2b. WHAT ARE you STUDYING?
    Grammar.

Lesson V

1. WE'RE GOING TO STUDY TOMORROW.
   ARE YOU GOING TO STUDY TOMORROW?
   [IS, ARE, AM + GOING TO + Class 2 in expressions of future time]

2. WE AREN'T GOING TO STUDY. WE DON'T STUDY IN THE MORNING.
   [NOT in negative statements]

3. I NEVER STUDY IN THE AFTERNOON.
   [Negative statements with NEVER, RARELY, SELDOM]

4. I DON'T NEED ANY BOOKS. I NEED SOME PENCILS.
   [Distribution of SOME and ANY]

1.

Key examples: We'RE GOING TO STUDY tomorrow.
              ARE you GOING TO STUDY tomorrow?

Observe the position and form of ARE, AM, IS with GOING TO.

Previous pattern (Lesson IV):

	They 're	studying	now.	
	Are they	studying	now?	Yes, they are.

New pattern:

		They	'RE	GOING TO STUDY		tomorrow.	
		We	'RE	GOING TO PLAY	baseball	tomorrow.	
		You	'RE	GOING TO BE	late	tomorrow.	
		I	'M	GOING TO STUDY		tomorrow.	
		John	'S	GOING TO STUDY	engineering.		
		He	'S	GOING TO BE	an engineer.		
	ARE	they		GOING TO STUDY		tomorrow?	Yes, they are.
	ARE	we		GOING TO PLAY	baseball	tomorrow?	Yes, we are.
	ARE	you		GOING TO STUDY		tomorrow?	Yes, I am.
	AM	I		GOING TO BE	late	tomorrow?	No, you aren't.
	IS	John		GOING TO STUDY	engineering?		Yes, he is.
	IS	he		GOING TO BE	a dentist?		No, he isn't.
WHAT	IS	he		GOING TO STUDY?			Engineering.
WHEN	IS	he		GOING TO GO	to New York?		Next year.

40

COMMENTS

(1) Use ARE, AM, IS + GOING TO + the simple form of a Class 2 word in expressions of future time.

(2) Use ARE, AM, IS before the first Class 1 word (THEY, I, JOHN, etc.) in questions with GOING TO. Use WHAT, WHEN, etc., before ARE, IS, AM.

(3) ARE, AM, IS, AREN'T, AM NOT, ISN'T complete the short answers to questions with GOING TO.

PRACTICE

EXERCISE 1.1. (To practice correlation of I, HE, WE, STUDENTS with the forms of BE + GOING TO.) Substitute the words and make the necessary changes. For example:

I'm going to study tomorrow.

he	HE'S GOING TO STUDY TOMORROW.
we	WE'RE GOING TO STUDY TOMORROW.
I	I'M GOING TO STUDY TOMORROW.

1. he
2. we
3. the students
4. they

5. I
6. she
7. John
8. John and Mary

9. you
10. the man
11. the doctor
12. I

EXERCISE 1.2. (To practice BE + GOING TO in questions.) Substitute the words and make the necessary changes. For example:

Are they going to study tomorrow?

he	IS HE GOING TO STUDY TOMORROW?
practice	IS HE GOING TO PRACTICE TOMORROW?
the students	ARE THE STUDENTS GOING TO PRACTICE TOMORROW?
arrive	ARE THE STUDENTS GOING TO ARRIVE TOMORROW?

1. they
2. he
3. practice

4. the students
5. next week
6. study
7. Mary

8. they
9. you
10. she

EXERCISE 1.3. (To form questions with GOING TO.) Listen to the statements. Form corresponding questions. For example:

They're going to study.   ARE THEY GOING TO STUDY?
John's going to play baseball.   IS JOHN GOING TO PLAY
                        BASEBALL?
I'm going to teach grammar.   ARE YOU GOING TO TEACH
                        GRAMMAR?

1. The boys are going to be late.
2. He's going to be an engineer.
3. I'm going to study.
4. John's going to study engineering.
5. He's going to be an engineer.
6. He's going to be here next week.
7. The students are going to eat lunch.
8. They're going to study English.
9. The girl is going to learn English.
10. She's going to visit the museum.
11. She's going to go to the university.
12. The students are going to visit the Ford factory.

EXERCISE 1.4. (To contrast the forms used with present and future time.) Substitute the words and make the necessary changes. Use ARE, AM, IS + the -ING form for present time. For example:

I'm going to study tomorrow.

now   I'M STUDYING NOW.
next week   I'M GOING TO STUDY NEXT WEEK.
we   WE'RE GOING TO STUDY NEXT WEEK.
tomorrow   WE'RE GOING TO STUDY TOMORROW.
practice   WE'RE GOING TO PRACTICE TOMORROW.
now   WE'RE PRACTICING NOW.

1. he
2. they
3. she
4. tomorrow
5. next week
6. next year
7. we
8. I
9. study
10. he
11. they
12. now (at the present moment)
13. he
14. I
15. tomorrow

EXERCISE 1.5. (To use BE + GOING TO in questions with WHAT.) This is a conversation exercise. Listen to the statements. Form corresponding questions with WHAT at the beginning and TOMORROW at the end. For example:

He's studying English today.   WHAT IS HE GOING TO STUDY
                        TOMORROW?
He's writing the assignment now. WHAT IS HE GOING TO WRITE
                        TOMORROW?
They're writing the assignments   WHAT ARE THEY GOING TO
   now.   WRITE TOMORROW?
I'm teaching Lesson V now.   WHAT ARE YOU GOING TO TEACH
                        TOMORROW?

1. I'm studying questions now.
2. I'm writing the introduction now.
3. I'm learning vocabulary now.
4. He's practicing grammar now.
5. They're studying pronunciation now.
6. She's learning the alphabet now.
7. Mary's studying Latin now.
8. She's learning the words today.
9. He's buying a book today.
10. We're writing a composition now.
11. John's reading a story now.
12. They're eating steaks today.

2.   Key examples: We AREN'T going to study.
               We DON'T study in the morning.

Observe the negative forms.

Previous pattern:

I	'm	busy.	(Lesson I)
I	'm	studying.	(Lesson IV)
I	'm	going to study.	(Lesson V)

New pattern:

I	'M NOT	busy.
I	'M NOT	studying.
I	'M NOT	going to study.
You	AREN'T	busy.
He	ISN'T	studying.
They	AREN'T	going to study.
You	WEREN'T	busy yesterday.
He	WASN'T	busy yesterday.

Previous pattern:

| You | | study. | (Lesson II) |
| You | | studied yesterday. | (Lesson III) |

New pattern:

You	DON'T	study.
He	DOESN'T	study.
You	DIDN'T	study yesterday.
He	DIDN'T	study yesterday.

COMMENTS

(1) Use I'M NOT, YOU AREN'T, HE ISN'T, YOU WEREN'T, HE WASN'T etc., in negative statements with forms of BE (I'M NOT BUSY), BE + the -ING form (I'M NOT STUDYING), and BE + GOING TO + the simple form of the Class 2 word (I'M NOT GOING TO STUDY).

(2) Use DON'T, DOESN'T, DIDN'T + the simple form of the Class 2 word in other negative statements (YOU DON'T STUDY).

(3) AREN'T, ISN'T, DOESN'T, DIDN'T, etc., are contractions of ARE NOT, IS NOT, DOES NOT, DO NOT, etc.

PRACTICE

EXERCISE 2.1. (To practice the negative with AM, IS, ARE, WAS, WERE.) Substitute the words and make the necessary changes. For example:

I'm not in Detroit now.

he	HE ISN'T IN DETROIT NOW.
last week	HE WASN'T IN DETROIT LAST WEEK.
next week	HE ISN'T GOING TO BE IN DETROIT NEXT WEEK.
here	HE ISN'T GOING TO BE HERE NEXT WEEK.
now	HE ISN'T HERE NOW.
they	THEY AREN'T HERE NOW.

1. Mary	9. tomorrow	17. yesterday
2. she	10. we	18. we
3. in Detroit	11. I	19. you
4. yesterday	12. you	20. they
5. you	13. he	21. last week
6. I	14. at home	22. I
7. they	15. Mary	23. they
8. now	16. now	24. we

EXERCISE 2.2. (To practice the negative with DO, DOES, DID.) Substitute the words and make the necessary changes. For example:

He doesn't study engineering.

they	THEY DON'T STUDY ENGINEERING.
last year	THEY DIDN'T STUDY ENGINEERING LAST YEAR.
I	I DIDN'T STUDY ENGINEERING LAST YEAR.
don't	I DON'T STUDY ENGINEERING.

1. we	8. Paul	14. I
2. John	9. we	15. he
3. he	10. I	16. they
4. they	11. Mr. and Mrs.	17. Mary
5. you	White	18. Mary and Jane
6. she	12. you	19. Paul
7. a year ago	13. don't	20. we

3.   Key example: I NEVER STUDY in the afternoon.

Observe these negative statements.

Previous pattern:

He	isn't		here in the afternoon.
He	isn't usually		here in the afternoon.
He	doesn't	study	here in the afternoon.
He	doesn't usually	study	here in the afternoon.

New pattern:

He	IS NEVER		here in the afternoon.
He	IS RARELY		here in the afternoon.
He	IS SELDOM		here in the afternoon.
He	NEVER	STUDIES	here in the afternoon.
He	RARELY	STUDIES	here in the afternoon.
He	SELDOM	STUDIES	here in the afternoon.

COMMENTS

(1) Statements with NEVER, RARELY, SELDOM are negative. Do
not use ISN'T, AREN'T, WASN'T, DOESN'T, DIDN'T, etc., with
NEVER, RARELY, SELDOM.

(2) Use NEVER, RARELY, SELDOM after forms of BE (IS, ARE,
WAS, etc.). Use NEVER, RARELY, SELDOM before other
Class 2 words (STUDY, PRACTICE, etc.).

PRACTICE

EXERCISE 3.1. (To form negative statements with USUALLY, NEVER,
etc.) Use only negative statements in this exercise. Substitute the
words and make the necessary changes. For example:

He doesn't usually smoke.

often	HE DOESN'T OFTEN SMOKE.
never	HE NEVER SMOKES.
rarely	HE RARELY SMOKES.
always	HE DOESN'T ALWAYS SMOKE.
seldom	HE SELDOM SMOKES.

1. always
2. often
3. seldom
4. rarely
5. usually

6. never
7. rarely
8. often
9. usually
10. rarely

EXERCISE 3.2. (To form negative statements with USUALLY, NEVER, etc.) This is a conversation exercise. Listen to the statement. Respond with a corresponding negative statement with AT NIGHT. For example:

He's usually here in the morning.	HE ISN'T USUALLY HERE AT NIGHT.
He's always in class in the morning.	HE ISN'T ALWAYS IN CLASS AT NIGHT.
They often study in the morning.	THEY DON'T OFTEN STUDY AT NIGHT.
He's never here in the morning.	HE'S NEVER HERE AT NIGHT.
He's seldom in class in the morning.	HE'S SELDOM IN CLASS AT NIGHT.
I rarely study in the morning.	I RARELY STUDY AT NIGHT.

1. I often study in the morning.
2. I never study in the morning.
3. I usually sing in the morning.
4. He usually sings in the morning.
5. I never run to class in the morning.
6. I always study grammar in the morning.
7. She never eats in the morning.
8. She's usually absent in the morning.
9. Mary's often hungry in the morning.
10. John's never hungry in the morning.
11. He rarely smokes in the morning.
12. He seldom runs in the morning.
13. He's seldom late in the morning.
14. He's never busy in the morning.
15. He's rarely absent in the morning.

4.

Key examples: I don't need ANY books. I need SOME pencils.

Observe SOME and ANY.

Do you need some bread? Do you need any bread?						
I need	SOME	bread.		I don't need	ANY	bread.
I need	SOME	fruit.		I don't need	ANY	fruit.
I need	SOME	stamps.		I don't need	ANY	stamps.
I need	SOME	books.		I don't need	ANY	books.

COMMENTS

1. Use SOME or ANY in questions.
2. Use SOME in affirmative statements.*
3. Use ANY after a negative.

*You will hear ANY in certain types of affirmative statements: "I would give you some money if I had any."

EXERCISE 4.1. (To contrast the use of SOME in affirmative statements with the use of ANY after a negative signal.) Substitute the words and make the necessary changes. For example:

I have some potatoes.

I don't have	I DON'T HAVE ANY POTATOES.
do you have	DO YOU HAVE ANY POTATOES?
bread	DO YOU HAVE ANY BREAD?
he doesn't have	HE DOESN'T HAVE ANY BREAD.

 1. did he have
 2. he has
 3. coffee
 4. do they have
 5. do you need
 6. I need
 7. she needed
 8. John doesn't need
 9. Mrs. White doesn't have
10. I don't need
11. we want
12. bread

13. the dog is eating
14. John didn't eat
15. Mrs. White has
16. does she have
17. she doesn't have
18. coffee
19. shoes
20. stamps
21. she needs
22. fruit
23. does she need

NOTE: SOME and ANY are also substitutes for words like "bread," "stamps," "fruit," etc.

Do you have stamps?

Yes, I do.
Yes, I have SOME.
No, I don't.
No, I don't have ANY.

Did Mary buy fruit?

Yes, she did.
Yes, she bought SOME.
No, she didn't.
No, she didn't buy ANY.

KEY EXAMPLES OF LESSON V

1. We'RE GOING TO STUDY tomorrow.
   ARE you GOING TO STUDY tomorrow?
2. We AREN'T going to study.
   We DON'T study in the morning.
3. I NEVER STUDY in the afternoon.
4. I don't need ANY books.
   I need SOME pencils.

Lesson VI

1a. I HAVE INK.
[Non-countable Class 1 words without A and without plural forms]

1b. I DIDN'T WANT MANY PENS. I DIDN'T WANT MUCH INK.
[Distribution of A FEW, MANY, A LITTLE, MUCH, A LOT OF with countable and non-countable Class 1 words]

2. DR. BROWN ALWAYS DISCUSSES PHILOSOPHY WITH STUDENTS.
THE STUDENTS LIKE THE PHILOSOPHY OF ARISTOTLE.
[Use of THE contrasted with absence of THE]

3. I WANT THIS BOOK. I WANT THESE PENCILS.
MY BOOKS ARE IN MY ROOM.
[Singular-plural contrast with THIS and THAT, but not with MY, YOUR, etc.]

4. NONE OF MY FRIENDS SPEAK ENGLISH.
[Expressions like ALL OF, NONE OF, MANY OF, NOT MANY OF, etc.]

1a. I need A PEN. I need PENS. I have INK.

Observe A PEN, PENS, INK, etc.

Previous pattern (Lesson I):

I need	A	PEN.		I need	PENS.
I have	A	PENCIL.		I have	PENCILS.
I want	AN	APPLE.		I want	APPLES.

New pattern:

I have	INK.
I like	COFFEE.
I drink	MILK.
I eat	FRUIT.
I like	BREAD.
I want	TOAST.
I need	SOAP.

COMMENTS

(1) Do not use A* with Class 1 words like INK, COFFEE, MILK, etc. ("non-countable" Class 1 words).

(2) Do not use plural forms for Class 1 words like INK, COFFEE, MILK, etc. ("non-countable" Class 1 words).

(3) Use A with singular Class 1 words like PEN, PENCIL, APPLE, etc. ("countable" Class 1 words).

---

*A is different from ONE. A is not a number. ONE is a number: ONE PEN, TWO PENS, THREE PENS, etc. "I want ONE book" implies I do not want TWO or THREE or FOUR, etc. "I want A book" implies I do not want a PEN, a PENCIL, or an APPLE, etc.

48

ILLUSTRATIVE EXAMPLES

A STUDENT uses INK every day. He uses BLACK INK and BLUE
    INK.
He drinks WATER every day.
WATER is A TRANSPARENT LIQUID. It contains OXYGEN and
    HYDROGEN.
I have INK and I have A PEN.
I have WATER. I have A GLASS. I have A GLASS of water.
I need INK. I need TWO BOTTLES of ink.
I want TOAST. I want A PIECE of toast.
I'm going to visit A GROUP of friends.

PRACTICE

EXERCISE 1a.1. (To practice the use and omission of A, AN before
Class 1 words.) Substitute the words. Use A before CAR, BOOK, etc.,
and omit it before TOAST, FRUIT, ORANGES, etc. For example:

We see a friend.

apples	WE SEE APPLES.
fruit	WE SEE FRUIT.
book	WE SEE A BOOK.
have	WE HAVE A BOOK.

1. sandwich	11. car	21. are selling
2. are eating	12. pencils	22. insurance
3. toast	13. milk	23. house
4. banana	14. are drinking	24. radios
5. apple	15. cup of milk	25. ink
6. bread	16. glass of water	26. are using
7. oranges	17. tea	27. piece of paper
8. slice of bread	18. milk shake	28. chair
9. butter	19. water	29. soap
10. are buying	20. hot coffee	30. bar of soap

1b.

    Key examples: I didn't want MANY PENS. I didn't want MUCH
        INK.

Observe A FEW, MANY, A LITTLE, MUCH, A LOT OF.

I wanted	A FEW	PENS.
I didn't want	MANY	PENS.
I wanted	A LITTLE	INK.
I didn't want	MUCH	INK.
I wanted	A LOT OF	PENS.
I wanted	A LOT OF	INK.

COMMENTS

(1) Use A FEW and MANY only with plural forms like PENS, PENCILS, etc. ("countable" Class 1 words).
(2) Use A LITTLE and MUCH only with words like INK, COFFEE, etc. ("non-countable" Class 1 words).
(3) Use A LOT OF with plural forms like PENS, PENCILS, etc., and with words like INK, COFFEE, etc.
(4) Use MANY and MUCH in negative sentences.* Use A LOT OF in negative sentences and in affirmative sentences.

ILLUSTRATIVE EXAMPLES

I want A FEW APPLES. I don't want MANY APPLES.
SOME APPLES are red. SOME are yellow.
ALL APPLES are nourishing.
I have two apples. I'm going to eat BOTH APPLES.
My friend eats SEVERAL APPLES every day.
I want A LITTLE FRUIT. I don't want MUCH FRUIT.
SOME FRUIT is rare. SOME is common.
ALL FRUIT is nourishing.

NOTE: Use BOTH and SEVERAL only with plural forms like APPLES. Use SOME and ALL with plural forms like APPLES and with words like FRUIT (non-countable Class 1 words).

PRACTICE

EXERCISE 1b.1. (To practice the distribution of A FEW, A LITTLE, MANY, MUCH, A LOT OF.) Substitute A FEW, MANY, A LITTLE, etc., in place of A SMALL QUANTITY, A LARGE NUMBER, etc. Use A FEW, A LITTLE, to indicate a small quantity or number and MANY, MUCH, A LOT OF, to indicate a large quantity or number. For example:

John drinks a large quantity of coffee.
    JOHN DRINKS A LOT OF COFFEE.
I didn't see a large number of students.
    I DIDN'T SEE MANY STUDENTS.
I need a small quantity of sugar.
    I NEED A LITTLE SUGAR.
Mary has a small number of good friends.
    MARY HAS A FEW GOOD FRIENDS.
He doesn't eat a large quantity of fruit.
    HE DOESN'T EAT MUCH FRUIT.

1. They have a small quantity of money.
2. He has a small number of dimes.
3. We don't have a large number of classes today.

---

*You will hear MANY and MUCH in affirmative sentences in some situations. But this is not natural English in many other situations.

4. We need a large quantity of bread.
5. Do you drink a large quantity of milk?
6. Does John have a large number of ties?
7. Mary drinks a small quantity of coffee.
8. We usually buy a small quantity of soap.
9. We usually buy a small number of bars of soap.
10. He doesn't usually buy a large number of pencils.
11. We don't drink a large quantity of tea in the United States.
12. Children need a large quantity of milk.
13. The students don't bring a large number of books to school.
14. The students don't drink a large quantity of fruit juice in the morning.

2. Key examples: DR. BROWN always discusses PHILOSOPHY with STUDENTS.
THE STUDENTS like THE PHILOSOPHY of Aristotle.

Observe the examples with THE and without THE.

We invited	A STUDENT.	
	STUDENTS	are usually intelligent.
	COFFEE	is a good drink.
We are drinking	COFFEE.	
We are discussing	PHILOSOPHY.	
	THE STUDENT	is from Mexico.
I often invite	THE STUDENTS	in our class.
We like	THE COFFEE	here.
	THE COFFEE	from Brazil is good.
	THE STUDENTS	in our class are intelligent.
	THE PHILOSOPHY	of Aristotle is important.
We are speaking	ENGLISH.	
	SPANISH	is an important language.
	ARGENTINA	is near Brazil.
We are going to visit	DR. BROWN.	
We are going to visit	BRAZIL.	
	MR. SMITH	is a teacher.
	MARY	is a student.
She lives on	STATE STREET.	
She goes to class at	EIGHT O'CLOCK.	

COMMENTS

(1) Use A STUDENT, STUDENTS, COFFEE, PHILOSOPHY, etc.,without THE to indicate "in general" or "not identified."
(2) Use THE STUDENT, THE STUDENTS, THE COFFEE, THE PHILOSOPHY, etc.,to indicate "specific" or "identified."
(3) Don't use THE with the names of persons, languages, most countries, streets, or the time of day.   (See Illustrative Examples for exceptions.)

ILLUSTRATIVE EXAMPLES

I like SMALL COMMUNITIES.
SMALL COMMUNITIES are interesting.
We visited LARGE and SMALL COMMUNITIES.
THE SMALL COMMUNITIES were interesting.
RIVERS are interesting too.
THE MISSISSIPPI RIVER is in THE UNITED STATES.
THE AMAZON is in BRAZIL.
BRAZIL is a large country.
THE UNITED STATES is a large country too.
THE DOMINICAN REPUBLIC is in LATIN AMERICA.
THE NETHERLANDS is not in LATIN AMERICA.
THE REPUBLIC OF ECUADOR is in SOUTH AMERICA.
ARGENTINA and CHILE are in THE SOUTHERN PART of the
    CONTINENT.
NEW YORK is in THE EASTERN PART of THE UNITED STATES.
    NOTE: We use THE with the names of a few countries.
           These names are often two words, like THE
           UNITED STATES, or have an -S ending, like
           THE NETHERLANDS.

DR. BROWN talked to MR. APPLETON about DEMOCRACY and
    ECONOMICS.
They talked about CONTEMPORARY PHILOSOPHY.
COLUMBIAN COFFEE is good.

PRACTICE

EXERCISE 2.1. (To practice the omission of THE before certain Class
1 words.) Listen to the statement. Substitute the Class 1 word which is
given. Use the form THE before the Class 1 word. Don't use THE with
the names of persons, languages, countries, streets, time of day and
when the Class 1 word has a "general" sense. For example:

Mathematics is interesting.

program	THE PROGRAM IS INTERESTING.
New York City	NEW YORK CITY IS INTERESTING.
student	THE STUDENT IS INTERESTING.
California	CALIFORNIA IS INTERESTING.
French	FRENCH IS INTERESTING.

A. Tom likes music.
  1. lady
  2. Italy
  3. professor
  4. professor Appleton
  5. South America
  6. young student

B. They arrived at three o'clock.
  1. station
  2. four fifteen
  3. airport
  4. noon
  5. apartment
  6. Taylor House

C. John and I visited Canada.
  1. Detroit
  2. English class
  3. Mexico
  4. sick student
  5. art museum
  6. University of Ohio
  7. professor Brown

D. France is beautiful.
  1. painting
  2. Nicaragua
  3. flower gardens
  4. Miss Smith
  5. Pacific Ocean
  6. Pennsylvania Avenue

3. Key examples: I want THIS BOOK. I want THESE PENCILS.
        MY BOOKS are in MY ROOM.

Observe THESE BOOKS, THIS BOOK, MY BOOKS, MY BOOK, etc.				
		THESE	BOOKS	are simple.
I	need	THESE	BOOKS.	
I	want	THOSE	BOOKS.	
		THIS	BOOK	is interesting.
I	need	THIS	BOOK.	
I	want	THAT	BOOK.	
		MY	BOOKS	are easy.
		MY	BOOK	is easy.
I	need	MY	BOOK.	
I	want	MY	BOOKS.	
I	washed	MY	FACE.	
I	washed	MY	HANDS.	
You	washed	YOUR	HANDS.	

COMMENTS

1. Use THESE [ðiz], THOSE [ðoz], with plural forms (BOOKS, LESSONS); use THIS [ðɪs], THAT [ðæt], with non-plural forms (BOOK, STUDENT, COFFEE).
2. Use MY with plural forms and non-plural forms (BOOKS, LESSONS, BOOK, STUDENT, COFFEE). MY, YOUR, HIS, HER, OUR, THEIR are invariable in form.
3. Use MY, YOUR, etc.,with parts of the body. Don't use THE.

ILLUSTRATIVE EXAMPLES

I have MY BOOK.
You know YOUR TEACHER.
John has HIS BOOK.
Mary has HER BOOK.
The class likes ITS BOOK.
We like OUR CLASS.
The students study THEIR LESSONS.
This is THEIR ROOM.
The boys visited THEIR FATHERS.
The girls visited THEIR MOTHERS.

PRACTICE

EXERCISE 3.1. (To use THESE and THOSE with plural forms and THIS
and THAT with non-plural forms.) Listen to the statements and the
words HERE and THERE. Repeat the statements and use THIS [ðɪs],
THESE [ðiz] for objects that are HERE. Use THAT [ðæt] THOSE
[ðoz] for objects that are THERE. For example:

The exercises are easy. There	THOSE EXERCISES ARE EASY.
The university is large. Here	THIS UNIVERSITY IS LARGE.
The lessons are easy. Here	THESE LESSONS ARE EASY.
The book is green. There	THAT BOOK IS GREEN.

1. The chairs are comfortable. Here
2. The ideas are new and interesting. Here
3. The student comes from Peru. There
4. The students come from Venezuela. There
5. The book has a green cover. Here
6. The girl is beautiful. There
7. I like the dictionary. There
8. I like the pencils. There
9. I like the drug store. Here
10. I need the books. Here

EXERCISE 3.2. (To produce MY, YOUR, HIS, HER, ITS, OUR, THEIR
with plural and non-plural forms including parts of the body and per-
sonal clothing.) Substitute the forms and make other necessary
changes. For example:

Mary has your watch.

John	JOHN HAS YOUR WATCH.
our	JOHN HAS OUR WATCH.
watches	JOHN HAS OUR WATCHES.
fixed	JOHN FIXED OUR WATCHES.

1. their	13. their	25. their
2. my	14. my	26. Mary and John
3. his	15. collar	27. faces
4. motor	16. ironed	28. car
5. its	17. her	29. our
6. cover	18. Mary	30. I
7. washed	19. dress	31. my
8. windows	20. washed	32. face
9. his	21. feet	33. neck
10. hands	22. hands	34. ears
11. face	23. hair	35. sweater
12. shirt	24. his	36. your

4. Key example: NONE of my friends speak English.

Observe the expressions of quantity.

	MANY	of your	books	are good.	
	MANY			are good.	
	MUCH	of this	fruit	is good.	
	MUCH			is good.	
	ALL	of this	bread	is good.	
	ALL			is good.	
NOT	MANY	of my	books	are good.	
NOT	MANY			are good.	
NOT	MUCH	of that	fruit	is good.	
NOT	MUCH			is good.	
NOT	ALL	of that	bread	is good.	
NOT	ALL			is good.	
NOT	ALL	of those	books	are good.	
NOT	ALL			are good.	
NOT	ANY	of these	books	are good.	(All are bad.)
NOT	ANY			are good.	(All are bad.)
NONE		of these	books	are good.	(All are bad.)
NONE				are good.	(All are bad.)
NONE		of that	bread	is good.	(All is bad.)
NONE				is good.	(All is bad.)

COMMENTS

(1) Use MANY, NOT MANY, NONE, etc., alone or before an expression with OF.
(2) Use NOT for the negative form with MANY, MUCH, ALL, ANY.
(3) NONE is a negative form equivalent to NOT ANY.

PRACTICE

EXERCISE 4.1. (To use the negative forms NOT and NONE to indicate quantity.) Listen to the questions which contain expressions of quantity. Answer the questions with the negative forms, NOT MANY, NOT MUCH, NOT ALL, NONE. Form two negative statements with each question. For example:

Do many of the students write letters?
        NOT MANY OF THE STUDENTS WRITE LETTERS.
        NOT MANY WRITE LETTERS.
Are any of the students sick?
        NONE OF THE STUDENTS ARE SICK.
        NONE ARE SICK.
Is any of the dessert ready?
        NOT ANY OF THE DESSERT IS READY.
        NOT ANY IS READY.

1. Are all the teachers here?
2. Was much of the coffee hot?
3. Do any of your friends want a ticket?
4. Do all of your friends speak English?
5. Is much of the building complete?
6. Is any of the milk good?
7. Are any of the exercises difficult?
8. Do many of the students live in a dormitory?
9. Was much of the program interesting?
10. Is any of the bread fresh?
11. Are any of the children lost?
12. Were many of the students at the program?

KEY EXAMPLES OF LESSON VI

1a. I need A PEN. I need PENS. I have INK.
1b. I didn't want MANY PENS. I didn't want MUCH INK.
2. DR. BROWN discusses PHILOSOPHY with STUDENTS.
    THE STUDENTS like THE PHILOSOPHY of Aristotle.
3. I want THIS BOOK. I want THESE PENCILS.
    MY BOOKS are in MY ROOM.
4. NONE of my friends speak English.

Lesson VII

1. OBSERVE THE PATTERN. LET'S REPEAT THE EXAMPLES.
   [Request sentences]

2. THE MEN ARE TIRED. THE PEOPLE ARE HUNGRY. THE NEWS IS GOOD.
   [Irregular Class 1 words]
3. THE OTHER BOOKS ARE OLD. I SEE THE OTHERS NOW.
   [OTHER as Class 1 and as modifier of Class 1]

4. I VISITED HIM YESTERDAY.
   [ME, HIM, THEM, etc.]

1.

Key examples: OBSERVE the pattern. LET'S REPEAT the examples.

Observe the request sentences.

Statement pattern:

You		speak	English in class.
You	don't	speak	Spanish in class.

Request pattern:

		SPEAK	English in.class.
		OPEN	the door.
		BE	here at 11 o'clock.
	DON'T	SPEAK	Spanish in class.
	DON'T	OPEN	the window.
PLEASE		SPEAK	English in class.
PLEASE	DON'T	BE	late.

Statement pattern:

We	speak	English in class.

Request pattern:

	LET'S		SPEAK	English in class.
	LET'S		GO	to the movies.
	LET'S	NOT	GO	to the restaurant.
PLEASE	LET'S	NOT	BE	late.

COMMENTS

(1) Do not use YOU, WE before the Class 2 word (SPEAK, OPEN, etc.) in request sentences.

(2) Begin request sentences with PLEASE as a polite form.*

(3) Request sentences with LET'S include the speaker. (Teacher: OPEN YOUR BOOKS. The students open their books. Teacher: LET'S OPEN OUR BOOKS.
The students and the teacher open their books.)

(4) Use DON'T in negative request sentences. But use NOT (without DO) in negative request sentences with LET'S.

EXERCISE 1.1. (To practice the request pattern.) Form polite request sentences with the suggested words. For example:

the door	PLEASE OPEN THE DOOR.
your book	PLEASE OPEN YOUR BOOK.
the door	PLEASE CLOSE THE DOOR.
a pen	PLEASE WRITE WITH A PEN.

1. your book
2. a pen
3. a good pen

4. a pencil
5. the paper
6. the salt
7. the door

8. the window
9. a letter
10. English

EXERCISE 1.2. (To practice the request pattern with LET'S.) Form request sentences that include the speaker. For example:

some songs	LET'S SING SOME SONGS.
to the movies	LET'S GO TO THE MOVIES.
some letters	LET'S WRITE SOME LETTERS.

1. English
2. to class
3. to the museum
4. to the new restaurant

5. to the movies
6. to Los Angeles
7. some songs
8. some letters

9. baseball
10. basketball
11. tennis
12. ping pong

---

*Other polite formulas which may precede SPEAK ENGLISH, OPEN THE DOOR, etc., are:

WOULD YOU	WOULD YOU PLEASE
WON'T YOU	WON'T YOU PLEASE
WILL YOU	WILL YOU PLEASE

Useful expressions for invitations: WOULD YOU LIKE TO GO TO THE MOVIES?
WOULD YOU LIKE TO SEE THE MUSEUM?

EXERCISE 1.3. (To practice the request pattern with a negative.) Convert the statement into a negative request with DON'T or LET'S NOT. Use the polite form. For example:

You speak rapidly.　　　　　PLEASE DON'T SPEAK RAPIDLY.
We eat dinner at the　　　　PLEASE LET'S NOT EAT DINNER
　restaurant.　　　　　　　　AT THE RESTAURANT.
You are late.　　　　　　　　PLEASE DON'T BE LATE.

1. You study in the morning.
2. We are going to eat dinner now.
3. You sleep in the afternoon.
4. You drive fast.
5. We talk Spanish to our friends.
6. We are going to the concert.
7. You are wasting time.
8. We are going to the game.
9. We are waiting for John.
10. You use red ink in your pen.
11. You miss class on Monday.
12. We hurry to school after lunch.

2.

Key examples:　The MEN ARE tired.　The PEOPLE ARE hungry.　The NEWS IS good.

Observe the plural forms:

SINGULAR			PLURAL		
Previous pattern (Lesson I):					
The	student	is here.	The	students	are here.
New pattern:					
The	MAN [mæn]	is here	The	MEN [mɛn]	are here.
The	GENTLEMAN [ǰɛntəlmən]	is here.	The	GENTLEMEN [ǰɛntəlmən]	are here.
The	WOMAN [wúmən]	is here.	The	WOMEN [wímən]	are here.
The	CHILD [čaɪld]	is here.	The	CHILDREN [číldrən]	are here.
The	WIFE [waɪf]	is here.	The	WIVES [waɪvz]	are here.
The	KNIFE [naɪf]	is here.	The	KNIVES [naɪvz]	are here.
The	FOOT [fʊt]	is here.	The	FEET [fit]	are here.
The	TOOTH [tuθ]	is here.	The	TEETH [tiθ]	are here.
The	MOUSE [maʊs]	is here.	The	MICE [maɪs]	are here.
The	SHEEP [šip]	is here.	The	SHEEP [šip]	are here.
			The	PEOPLE [pípəl]	are here.
			The	PEOPLE	come every day.
The	NEWS [nuz]	is here.			
The	NEWS	comes every day.			

COMMENTS

(1) MEN, GENTLEMEN, WOMEN, etc., are the plurals of MAN, GENTLEMAN, WOMAN, etc.
(2) Use ARE, COME, etc., with PEOPLE.
(3) Use IS, COMES, etc., with NEWS.

PRACTICE

EXERCISE 2.1. (To use the forms MEN, TEETH, NEWS, etc., in context.) Substitute the following words and make the necessary changes. For example:

The man is here.

are	THE MEN ARE HERE.
eat	THE MEN EAT HERE.
child	THE CHILD EATS HERE.
people	THE PEOPLE ARE HERE.
interesting	THE PEOPLE ARE INTERESTING.

1. news	11. happy	21. news
2. bad	12. are	22. here
3. tooth	13. woman	23. man
4. are	14. women	24. were
5. were	15. children	25. knife
6. sharp	16. is	26. children
7. knives	17. wives	27. eat
8. is	18. is	28. woman
9. good	19. people	29. eat
10. man	20. good	30. child

3.

Key examples: These books are new. The OTHER books are old.
I see the OTHERS now.

Observe the form of ANOTHER, OTHER, OTHERS.

Previous pattern:

An	old	automobile	stopped on State Street.
Three	old	automobiles	stopped on State Street.
An		automobile	stopped on State Street.
Three		automobiles	stopped on State Street.

New pattern:

AN-	-OTHER*	automobile	stopped on Huron Street.
Three	OTHER	automobiles	stopped on Main Street.
The	OTHER	automobiles	stopped on Liberty Street.
AN-		-OTHER	stopped on Huron Street.
Three		OTHERS	stopped on Main Street.
The		OTHERS	stopped on Liberty Street.

*Say and write AN + OTHER as one word: [ənə́dər], ANOTHER.

COMMENTS

(1) Use AN with OTHER in ANOTHER AUTOMOBILE, ANOTHER
    STOPPED, etc.
(2) OTHER is sometimes like OLD (a Class 3 word). OTHER is in-
    variable in form in this use.
(3) OTHER is sometimes like AUTOMOBILE (a Class 1 word).
    OTHERS is the plural form in this use.

ILLUSTRATIVE EXAMPLES

A red book is on the table. I see ANOTHER BOOK on the desk.
ANOTHER is on the chair. I see ANOTHER RED BOOK on the floor.

Three students are studying in their rooms.
THREE OTHER STUDENTS are practicing in the laboratory.
THREE OTHERS are playing baseball.

Some of the new students are from Columbia.
SOME OF THE OTHER NEW STUDENTS are from Bolivia.
SOME OF THE OTHERS are from Ecuador.

PRACTICE

EXERCISE 3.1. (To use ANOTHER and OTHER as modifiers of Class
1 words.) This is a conversation exercise. Listen to the statements.
Repeat the statements with ANOTHER or OTHER and make the necessary changes for action at the present moment. For example:

We studied the old book a week ago.
    WE ARE STUDYING ANOTHER BOOK NOW.
Mr. Brown visited Chicago a week ago.
    HE IS VISITING ANOTHER CITY NOW.
John and Mary studied the yellow book a week ago.
    THEY ARE STUDYING ANOTHER BOOK NOW.
The student learned the short conversation a week ago.
    HE IS LEARNING ANOTHER CONVERSATION NOW.

1. We studied the old book a week ago.
2. Mr. Brown visited Chicago a week ago.
3. John and Mary studied the yellow book a week ago.
4. The student learned the short conversation a week ago.
5. He studied the first lesson a week ago.
6. John played a nice game a week ago.
7. Mary practiced this conversation a week ago.
8. Mr. Brown explained this lesson a week ago.
9. Mr. White answered this question a week ago.
10. We studied the first book a week ago.

EXERCISE 3.2. (To use ANOTHER and OTHERS as substitutes.) Listen
to the statements. They are descriptions of something that occurs in the
morning. The same situation occurs at night. Describe the situation at
night by using ANOTHER or OTHERS. For example:

One automobile stops here in the morning.
　　　　ANOTHER STOPS HERE AT NIGHT.
Three hundred cars leave the factory in the morning.
　　　　THREE HUNDRED OTHERS LEAVE THE FACTORY AT NIGHT.
Four men work here in the morning.
　　　　FOUR OTHERS WORK HERE AT NIGHT.
Many people arrive in the morning.
　　　　MANY OTHERS ARRIVE AT NIGHT.

1. A few students study in the morning.
2. Two men are going to work in the morning.
3. Sixteen people work here in the morning.
4. Three students eat here in the morning.
5. Three people sleep in this room in the morning.
6. Two doctors work here in the morning.
7. A nurse helps them in the morning.
8. Many students study in the morning.
9. All of these children sleep in the morning.
10. All of the bad students write letters in the morning.
11. One man works in the morning.

4.

Key examples: I know John. I visited HIM yesterday.

Observe the forms ME, YOU, HIM, etc.

He	sees	ME.	He	studied	WITH	ME.
He	sees	YOU.	She	is standing	BESIDE	YOU.
I	followed	HIM.	She	is walking	WITH	HIM.
He	understands	HER.	John	is running	PAST	HER.
He	received	IT.	They	are	INSIDE	IT.
He	visited	US.	They	are coming	NEAR	US.
I	am teaching	YOU.	He	is standing	BETWEEN	YOU.
He	accepted	THEM.	We	are walking	UNDER	THEM.

COMMENTS

1. ME, YOU, HIM, etc., are the forms used after Class 2 words.
2. ME, YOU, HIM, etc., are used after words like WITH, BESIDE,
　　PAST.

PRACTICE

EXERCISE 4.1. (To practice the forms ME, HIM, THEM, etc.) Listen to the sentences. Substitute the words that follow the Class 2 words with ME, YOU, HIM, etc. For example:

John explains the question.	JOHN EXPLAINS IT.
They asked Mary.	THEY ASKED HER.
We followed John and Mary.	WE FOLLOWED THEM.
The boys attended the class.	THE BOYS ATTENDED IT.

1. The boys help the girls.
2. They study word order.
3. Mr. Black explains the custom.
4. Mary answers John.
5. The class learned the word.
6. I received my books yesterday.
7. I helped the new students.
8. I am going to see Mary tonight.
9. He is going to visit John.
10. I followed their car.

EXERCISE 4.2. (To contrast the forms I, HE, THEY, etc., with ME, HIM, THEM, etc.) Listen to the questions and answer them. Substitute the words that precede the Class 2 word with I, YOU, HE, etc., and substitute the words that follow the Class 2 word with ME, YOU, HIM, etc. For example:

Does John see the boy?	YES, HE SEES HIM.
Do you want the book?	YES, I WANT IT.
Do you like this class?	YES, I LIKE IT.
Are you learning English?	YES, I'M LEARNING IT.

1. Does Mary speak English?
2. Do you like Ann Arbor?
3. Does Paul know John?
4. Do you do your homework every day?
5. Do the students understand the lesson?
6. Do you see the teacher?
7. Do you hear the question?
8. Do you know Mr. and Mrs. Black?
9. Does he see Mary?
10. Do you like the movies?
11. Are you studying Lesson VII?
12. Are you going to visit the class?
13. Are they going to visit Mr. Brown?

EXERCISE 4.3. (To contrast forms like I and ME in statements and questions.) Listen to the statements and questions. Repeat the statements and questions. Substitute the forms HE, IT, THEM, SHE, etc. as the position requires. For example:

John wants the books.	HE WANTS THEM.
Children like ice cream.	THEY LIKE IT.
Does the teacher see Mary?	DOES HE SEE HER?
Are the books new?	ARE THEY NEW?

1. Mary is reading her letters.
2. Is the doctor with the students?
3. The pens are on the desk.
4. Mary and he are going with John and me.
5. Is the exercise difficult?
6. John and Mary are looking at you and me.

7. The student is writing the exercise.
8. The students are attending the classes.
9. Do the students study pronunciation?
10. John and Paul are living with Mr. Black.
11. My brother is visiting the museum.
12. Mary is reading the vocabulary lesson.
13. Did Fred see the man?

KEY EXAMPLES OF LESSON VII

1. OBSERVE the pattern.
   LET'S REPEAT the examples.
2. The MEN ARE tired.
   The PEOPLE ARE hungry.
   The NEWS IS good.
3. These books are new.
   The OTHER books are old.
   I see the OTHERS now.
4. I know John.
   I visited HIM yesterday.

Lesson VIII

1. Some forms and positions for expressions that indicate a "receiver."
   1a. HE ALWAYS SAYS "GOOD MORNING" TO ME.
       HE ASKED ME A QUESTION.
       [TO ME with Class 2 words like SAY, SPEAK, EXPLAIN, and ME with ASK]
   1b. I'M GOING TO GIVE A PENCIL TO MY BROTHER.
       [TO ME and ME with other Class 2 words like GIVE, TELL, SELL]
   1c. SHE ANSWERED THE QUESTION FOR ME.
       [FOR ME with Class 2 words like ANSWER, PRESCRIBE, CASH]

2. Class 2 words that have a vowel or consonant contrast but never have -ED.
   2a. I ATE LUNCH HERE YESTERDAY.
       [Class 2 words with a vowel contrast]
   2b. I HAD BREAKFAST AT SEVEN O'CLOCK.
       [Class 2 words with a consonant contrast]
   2c. I FELT FINE.
       [Class 2 words with a vowel and a consonant contrast]

1a. Key examples: He always says "Good morning" TO ME.
He asked ME a question.

Observe the position of TO ME and ME. Observe the Class 2 words.

He always	SAYS		"Hello"	TO ME.
He's	SPEAKING		English	TO ME.
He	EXPLAINED		the lesson	TO ME.
He	ASKED	ME	a question.	

COMMENTS

(1) Use TO ME, TO HIM, etc., after "HELLO," ENGLISH, THE LESSON, etc., with the Class 2 words SAY, SPEAK, EXPLAIN, DESCRIBE, INTRODUCE, REPEAT, ANNOUNCE, REPORT, TALK.
(2) Use ME, HIM, etc., immediately after the Class 2 word ASK.

ILLUSTRATIVE EXAMPLES

We	TALKED			TO JOHN	yesterday.
He	INTRODUCED		his father	TO US.	
His father	ASKED	US	our names.		
We	REPEATED		our names	TO HIM.	
He	ASKED	US	a lot of questions.		

65

We	DESCRIBED	our classes	TO HIM.
The teacher	ANNOUNCED	the examination	TO THE STUDENTS.
The students	REPORTED	their progress	TO THE TEACHER.

PRACTICE

EXERCISE 1a.1. (To practice TO US and US as "receiver.") Listen to the statements and repeat them. Add US or TO US in the proper position. For example:

He often speaks.	HE OFTEN SPEAKS TO US.
He explained the lesson.	HE EXPLAINED THE LESSON TO US.
He repeated it.	HE REPEATED IT TO US.
He usually says "yes."	HE USUALLY SAYS "YES" TO US.
He asked, "Where are you going?"	HE ASKED US, "WHERE ARE YOU GOING?"
They asked some questions.	THEY ASKED US SOME QUESTIONS.

1. Mary introduced it.
2. Mary usually says "Hello."
3. Mary talked.
4. She described her home.
5. She introduced John.
6. John asked the way to Detroit.
7. Mary asked our names.
8. She announced her plans.
9. The director described the English course.
10. Mr. Castro described South America.
11. She asked our telephone numbers.
12. The people explained their customs.
13. He repeated the words.
14. The teacher asked some questions.

EXERCISE 1a.2. (To practice ME, US, THE STUDENT, HIM, MR. BROWN, etc., as "receiver.") Listen to the words and the statements after them. Include the words in the statements. For example:

The student. Mary asked some questions.
    MARY ASKED THE STUDENT SOME QUESTIONS.
The student. John is explaining a problem.
    JOHN IS EXPLAINING A PROBLEM TO THE STUDENT.
Him. I'm going to speak English.
    I'M GOING TO SPEAK ENGLISH TO HIM.
Mr. Brown. I'm going to repeat the news.
    I'M GOING TO REPEAT THE NEWS TO MR. BROWN.
Them. I asked some questions.
    I ASKED THEM SOME QUESTIONS.

1. Us. He described South America.
2. Us. She talked.
3. The policeman. I asked the direction to Detroit.
4. The boys. He asked their names.
5. Me. She described her new dress.
6. The teacher. We asked a question.
7. Mary and me. They explained their customs.

8. John and Paul. He asked some questions.
9. Mary. He always says "Hello."
10. The secretary. He repeated the words.

11. Mr. and Mrs. Brown. I'm going to ask a favor.
12. My father. I'm going to introduce you.
13. Our friends. We're going to describe our house.

1b.   Key example: I'm going to give a pencil TO MY BROTHER.

Observe the position of ME and TO ME. Observe the Class 2 words.

Previous pattern:

| He always | says | | "Hello" | TO ME. |
| He's going to ask | | me | a question. | |

New pattern:

He's going to GIVE		a book	TO ME.
He's going to GIVE	ME	a book.	
He's going to TELL		the story	TO ME.
He's going to TELL	ME	the story.	
He's going to WRITE		a letter	TO ME.
He's going to WRITE	ME	a letter.	

COMMENT

Use TO ME, TO THEM, etc., after A BOOK, THE STORY, etc., or use ME, THEM, etc., immediately after the Class 2 words GIVE, TELL, WRITE, SELL, PASS, TEACH, READ, LEND, SEND, BRING, etc.

ILLUSTRATIVE EXAMPLES

Mr. Jones is going to	SELL	MARY	his car.	
He's going to	SELL		it	TO HER.
Her father is going to	LEND	HER	some money.	
He's going to	LEND		it	TO HER.
Please	PASS		the butter	TO ME.
Please	PASS	ME	the bread.	
Mr. Brown	TEACHES	US	vocabulary.	
Another teacher	TEACHES		pronunciation	TO US.
Mrs. Brown often	READS			TO THE CHILDREN.
She	READS	THEM	stories	every day.

EXERCISE 1b.1. (To use ME and/or TO ME.) Substitute the words and make the other necessary changes. For example:

He's going to ask me a favor.

question	HE'S GOING TO ASK ME THE QUESTION.
explain	HE'S GOING TO EXPLAIN THE QUESTION TO ME.
the letter	HE'S GOING TO EXPLAIN THE LETTER TO ME.
read	HE'S GOING TO READ THE LETTER TO ME.
me	HE'S GOING TO READ ME THE LETTER.

1. send	11. some books	21. the answers
2. to me	12. to me	22. explain
3. give	13. to us	23. the questions
4. me	14. they	24. ask
5. the sugar	15. send	25. repeat
6. pass	16. us	26. send
7. to me	17. some letters	27. us
8. sell	18. some news	28. the lesson
9. his car	19. tell	29. explain
10. me	20. a story	30. give

1c.

Key example: She answered a question FOR ME.

Observe FOR ME. Observe the Class 2 words.

Previous pattern:

| He always | says | | "Hello" | to me. |
| He | asked | me | a question. | |

New pattern:

The doctor	PRESCRIBED	medicine	FOR ME.
The bank	CASHED	a check	FOR ME.
The cashier	CHANGED	a $5 bill	FOR ME.
She	ANSWERED	a question	FOR ME.

COMMENTS

(1) Use FOR ME after the "direct object" with the Class 2 words PRESCRIBED, CASH, CHANGE, ANSWER, PRONOUNCE, BUY, GET, MAKE,* DO, OPEN.

(2) You are sometimes going to hear another pattern to indicate "receiver" after the Class 2 words BUY, GET, MAKE: "I'm going to buy HIM a sundae." Both patterns are correct with BUY, GET, MAKE.

---

*"He's going to read the lesson FOR ME" may also mean "He's going to read the lesson IN PLACE OF ME." In this lesson, however, we are primarily interested in FOR as any indicator of "receiver." "I don't know the lesson. He's going to teach the lesson to me. He's going to read it FOR ME. I'm going to listen."

ILLUSTRATIVE EXAMPLES

The teacher	PRONOUNCES the words		FOR THE STUDENTS.
Mr. Smith is going to	GET	a new coat	FOR MARY.
Mrs. Smith is going to	MAKE	a new dress	FOR HER.
She's going to	BUY	paper	FOR THEM.
They always	DO	their homework	FOR HER.
The man	OPENED	the door	FOR THE WOMAN.

PRACTICE

EXERCISE 1c.1. (To practice the patterns for "receiver.") This is a summary exercise. Listen to the words and the statements after them. Include the words in the statements. Use the substitute forms HER, HIM, HE, THEM, etc. For example:

The patients. The doctor prescribes medicine.
> HE PRESCRIBES MEDICINE FOR THEM.

John. The teacher explained the lesson.
> SHE EXPLAINED THE LESSON TO HIM.

Mary. The professor is going to ask some questions.
> HE'S GOING TO ASK HER SOME QUESTIONS.

The professor. Mary's going to ask some questions.
> SHE'S GOING TO ASK HIM SOME QUESTIONS.

1. John. The bank cashed a large check.
2. John. Jane's going to make a cake.
3. Me. The doctor prescribed medicine.
4. Me. Mr. Jones is going to give a book.
5. Mr. Jones. I'm going to sell a house.
6. John. I'm going to buy a sundae.
7. The director. I asked a favor.
8. The professor. I asked a question.
9. The children. I'm going to tell a story.
10. The new students. The teacher explained the lesson.
11. The patients. I always say "How are you?"
12. The engineers. I'm going to speak.
13. The engineers. Mr. Wilson described Alaska.
14. My mother. I'm going to write a letter.
15. Me. My mother is going to write a letter.

2a.   Key example: I ATE lunch here yesterday.

Observe the form of the Class 2 words with YESTERDAY.

Previous pattern (Lesson III):

We	practice	English	every day.
We	practiced	for five hours	yesterday.

New pattern:

We	eat	a good dinner	every day.
We	ATE	a steak dinner	yesterday.
We	drink	fruit juice	every day.
We	DRANK	orange juice	yesterday.
We	speak	to people	every day.
We	SPOKE	to Dr. Brown	yesterday.

COMMENT

Use ATE, DRANK, SPOKE, etc., with past time expressions. Certain Class 2 words (EAT, DRINK, SPEAK etc.) do not have an -ED ending. They have a vowel difference.

NOTE: The comment "Use the -ED form of the Class 2 word" in the frames in this book means "Use forms like PRACTICED, STUDIED, WORKED or like ATE, DRANK, SPOKE."

ILLUSTRATIVE EXAMPLES

What	did you	eat?	[it]	[et]	I	ATE	potatoes.
What	did you	give?	[gɪv]	[gev]	I	GAVE	some food.
When	did you	come?	[kəm]	[kem]	I	CAME	this morning.
What	did he	become?	[bɪkə́m]	[bɪkém]	He	BECAME	a doctor.
Who	did you	meet?	[mit]	[mɛt]	I	MET	the director.
What	did you	read?	[rid]	[rɛ̄d]	I	READ	the newspaper.
Where	did you	sit?	[sɪt]	[sæt]	I	SAT	here.
When	did you	begin?	[bɪgín]	[bɪgǽn]	I	BEGAN	two weeks ago.
What	did you	drink?	[drɪŋk]	[dræŋk]	I	DRANK	water.
What	did you	get?	[gɛt]	[gat]	I	GOT	a coat.
What	did you	forget?	[fərgɛ́t]	[fərgát]	I	FORGOT	my hat.
What	did you	see?	[si]	[sɔ]	I	SAW	your car.
What	did you	tear?	[tɛr]	[tɔr]	I	TORE	my paper.
What	did she	wear?	[wɛr]	[wɔ̄r]	She	WORE	her new dress.
When	did he	speak?	[spik]	[spok]	He	SPOKE	after dinner.
When	did it	break?	[brek]	[brōk]	It	BROKE	yesterday.
When	did you	wake up?	[wek əp]	[wōk əp]	I	WOKE UP	at 6 o'clock.
What	did he	write?	[raɪt]	[rōt]	He	WROTE	a letter.
What	did he	choose?	[čuz]	[čoz]	He	CHOSE	a brown hat.
What	did he	take?	[tek]	[tʊk]	He	TOOK	the book.
What	did he	know?	[no]	[nū]	He	KNEW	the lesson.

PRACTICE

EXERCISE 2a.1. (To recognize the forms CAME, ATE, MET, etc.)
This is a conversation exercise. Listen to the statements with YESTER-
DAY. Make corresponding statements about repeated action with
EVERY DAY. For example:

They came yesterday.	THEY COME EVERYDAY.
He ate breakfast yesterday.	HE EATS BREAKFAST EVERY DAY.
I met him yesterday.	I MEET HIM EVERY DAY.

1. He gave me a cigarette yesterday.
2. He read it yesterday.
3. It became dark at six o'clock
   yesterday.
4. I sat here yesterday.
5. I began to write yesterday.
6. I drank eight glasses of water
   yesterday.
7. I got a letter yesterday.
8. I forgot my book yesterday.
9. I saw your car yesterday.
10. I tore my paper yesterday.
11. I wore my new shoes yesterday.
12. I spoke English yesterday.
13. Mary broke some dishes
    yesterday.
14. I woke up at six yesterday.
15. We wrote letters yesterday.
16. We chose a leader yesterday.
17. He took his book yesterday.
18. He knew the lesson yesterday.

EXERCISE 2a.2. (To produce the forms CAME, ATE, MET, etc.)
Listen to the statements with DIDN'T. Make corresponding affirmative
statements about past time with THIS MORNING. For example:

He didn't come yesterday.	HE CAME THIS MORNING.
He didn't give it to me	HE GAVE IT TO ME THIS MORN-
yesterday.	ING.
I didn't eat the pie yesterday.	I ATE IT THIS MORNING.

1. I didn't choose the flowers yesterday.
2. I didn't break any dishes yesterday.
3. I didn't read it yesterday.
4. I didn't tear my shirt yesterday.
5. He didn't become president yesterday.
6. I didn't meet him yesterday.
7. I didn't give him any money yesterday.
8. I didn't sit here yesterday.
9. They didn't speak French yesterday.
10. I didn't begin my work yesterday.
11. We didn't forget our books yesterday.
12. We didn't see his wife yesterday.
13. We didn't drink the coffee yesterday.
14. I didn't get the letter yesterday.
15. I didn't wear my new shoes today.
16. I didn't wake up at six yesterday.
17. I didn't write any letters yesterday.
18. I didn't know any answers yesterday.
19. I didn't choose the correct answer yesterday.

EXERCISE 2a.3. (To produce ATE, MET, DRANK, etc.) Listen to the questions with EAT, MEET, DRINK, etc. Give answers with ATE, MET, DRANK, etc. For example:

What did you eat?	I ATE AN APPLE.
What did you give?	I GAVE SOME MONEY.
When did you come?	I CAME YESTERDAY.

(Continue with the questions in the Illustrative Examples.)

2b. Key example: I HAD breakfast at seven o'clock.

Observe the form of the Class 2 words with YESTERDAY.

We	spend	some money	every day.
We	SPENT	five dollars	yesterday.
We	have	a new lesson	every day.
We	HAD	Lesson VII	yesterday.
Our meals	cost	money	every day.
They	COST	three dollars	yesterday.

COMMENT

Use SPENT, HAD, COST, etc., with past time expressions. Certain Class 2 words without an -ED ending (SPEND, HAVE, etc.) have a difference in the final consonant. A few Class 2 words (COST, etc.) do not have a contrast.

ILLUSTRATIVE EXAMPLES

What	did you send?	[sɛnd]	[sɛnt]	I	SENT	a letter.
Where	did you spend $5?	[spɛnd]	[spɛnt]	I	SPENT	it in Detroit.
When	did you lend it?	[lɛnd]	[lɛnt]	I	LENT	it yesterday.
What	did you make?	[mek]	[med]	I	MADE	a sandwich.
What	did you have?	[hæv]	[hæd]	I	HAD	fruit juice.
What	did you cut?	[kət]	[kət]	I	CUT	the meat.
Where	did you put it?	[pʊt]	[pʊt]	I	PUT	it on the table.
How much	did it cost?	[kɔst]	[kɔst]	It	COST	$20.

PRACTICE

EXERCISE 2b.1. (To recognize SENT, SPENT, MADE, CUT, etc.) This is a conversation exercise. Listen to the statements with YESTERDAY, A MONTH AGO, and THIS MORNING. Use EVERY DAY, EVERY MONTH, EVERY MORNING in the responses. For example:

They sent a letter yesterday.	THEY SEND A LETTER EVERY DAY.
Mrs. Brown spent $500 a month ago.	SHE SPENDS $500 EVERY MONTH.
I cut the papers this morning.	I CUT THE PAPERS EVERY MORNING.

1. I made a sandwich this morning.
2. I had breakfast this morning.
3. He put the book here yesterday.
4. I lent him fifty cents yester-day.
5. Tickets cost $1 a year ago.

EXERCISE 2b.2. (To produce the forms SENT, HAD, CUT, etc.) This is a conversation exercise. Listen to the negative statements with past time expressions. Respond with affirmative statements and other past time expressions. For example:

They didn't send the letter Monday.	THEY SENT THE LETTER TUES-DAY.
She didn't spend the money today.	SHE SPENT THE MONEY YESTER-DAY.
I didn't cut the papers this week.	I CUT THE PAPERS A WEEK AGO.

1. I didn't make breakfast this morning.
2. We didn't have lunch at 1 o'clock.
3. We didn't put the papers here today.
4. I didn't lend him any money this week.
5. Tickets didn't cost $10 this year.

EXERCISE 2b.3. (To produce SENT, HAD, CUT, etc.) Listen to the questions with SEND, HAVE, CUT. Give answers with SENT, HAD, CUT, etc. For example:

What did you send?	I SENT A BOX.
Where did you spend $5?	I SPENT IT IN CHICAGO.
When did you lend it?	I LENT IT THIS MORNING.

1. What did you make?
2. What did you have?
3. What did you cut?
4. Where did you put it?
5. How much did it cost?
6. Where did you send it?
7. How much did you spend?
8. How much did you lend?
9. When did you make it?
10. When did you have it?
11. When did you cut it?
12. When did you put it there?
13. When did it cost $5?

2c. Key example: I FELT fine.

Observe the form of the Class 2 words with YESTERDAY.

We	buy	something	every day.
We	BOUGHT	some new clothes	yesterday.
We	sleep	after lunch	every day.
We	SLEPT	for an hour	yesterday.
We	tell	stories	every day.
We	TOLD	some good stories	yesterday.

COMMENT

Use BOUGHT, SLEPT, TOLD, etc., with past time expressions. Certain Class 2 words without an -ED ending (BUY, SLEEP, TELL, etc.) have both a vowel difference and a consonant difference. The final sound is [t] or [d].

ILLUSTRATIVE EXAMPLES

When	did you do this?	[du]	[dɪd]	I DID	it yesterday.
How	did you feel?	[fil]	[fɛlt]	I FELT	fine.
Where	did you sleep?	[slip]	[slɛpt]	I SLEPT	in a hotel.
What	did you mean?	[min]	[mɛnt]	I MEANT	"beautiful."
When	did you leave?	[liv]	[lɛft]	I LEFT	a year ago.
What	did you say?	[se]	[sɛd]	I SAID	"Hello."
Where	did you go?	[go]	[wɛnt]	I WENT	to New York.
What	did you hear?	[hɪr]	[hərd]	I HEARD	a car.
When	did you think that?	[Өɪŋk]	[Өɔt]	I THOUGHT	that yesterday.
What	did you bring?	[brɪŋ]	[brɔt]	I BROUGHT	an old book.
What	did you buy?	[baɪ]	[bɔt]	I BOUGHT	a new book.
What	did you teach?	[tič]	[tɔt]	I TAUGHT	mathematics.
Who	did you tell?	[tɛl]	[told]	I TOLD	my father.
What	did you sell?	[sɛl]	[sold]	I SOLD	my car.
Where	did you stand?	[stænd]	[stʊd]	I STOOD	here.
When	did you understand it?			I UNDER-STOOD	it yesterday.

PRACTICE

EXERCISE 2c.1. (To recognize the forms DID, FELT, SLEPT, etc.)
This is a conversation exercise. Listen to the statements with A WEEK
AGO, THIS MORNING, YESTERDAY. Use EVERY WEEK, EVERY
MORNING, EVERY DAY in responses. For example:

They did the exercises a week ago.
    THEY DO THEM EVERY WEEK.
I felt fine this morning.
    I FEEL FINE EVERY MORNING.
He meant that yesterday.
    HE MEANS THAT EVERY DAY.

1. They left school at noon yesterday.
2. They said "Thank you" yesterday.
3. John went to class this morning.
4. I heard the speeches yesterday.
5. I thought about it yesterday.
6. We brought some books yesterday.
7. We bought some books yesterday.
8. Mr. Brown taught mathematics yesterday.
9. He told me the answers yesterday.
10. I sold him some books a week ago.
11. I stood here this morning.
12. The students understood it this morning.
13. I slept well last night.

EXERCISE 2c.2. (To produce DID, FELT, SLEPT, etc.) This is a conversation exercise. Listen to the negative statements with TODAY. Form corresponding affirmative statements with YESTERDAY. For example:

They didn't do the exercises today. THEY DID THEM YESTERDAY.
I didn't feel well today. I FELT WELL YESTERDAY.
He didn't mean that today. HE MEANT THAT YESTERDAY.

1. They didn't leave school at noon today.
2. They didn't say "Thank you" today.
3. He didn't go to class today.
4. We didn't hear the speeches today.
5. I didn't think about it today.
6. We didn't bring our books today.
7. We didn't buy the books today.
8. Mr. Brown didn't teach mathematics today.
9. He didn't tell me the answers today.
10. I didn't sell him those books today.
11. I didn't stand there today.
12. The students didn't understand today.
13. I didn't sleep today.

EXERCISE 2c.3. (To produce DID, FELT, SLEPT, etc.) Listen to the questions with DO, FEEL, SLEEP, etc. Give answers with DID, FELT, SLEPT, etc. For example:

When did you do this? I DID IT LAST WEEK.
How did you feel? I FELT BAD.
Where did you sleep? I SLEPT AT HOME.

(Continue with the questions in the Illustrative Examples of Frame 2c.)

SUMMARY EXERCISE. (For additional practice with the Class 2 forms ATE, FELT, HAD, etc.) Substitute the words and make the necessary changes. For example:

I wanted breakfast yesterday.

ate   I ATE BREAKFAST YESTERDAY.
every day I EAT BREAKFAST EVERY DAY.
make   I MAKE BREAKFAST EVERY DAY.
coffee   I MAKE COFFEE EVERY DAY.
we   WE MAKE COFFEE EVERY DAY.

1. yesterday
2. had
3. every day
4. drink
5. yesterday
6. every morning
7. bring
8. yesterday
9. bought
10. a car
11. every year
12. I
13. sell
14. a year ago
15. he
16. every year
17. chooses
18. several days ago
19. saw
20. every 5 minutes

For more complete practice continue the exercise with these sub-stitutions: a letter, writes, 2 weeks ago, got, every week, reads, a book, yesterday, the book, forgot, every morning, I, the answer, yester-day, knew, now, a week ago, heard, the speech, every month, yesterday, understood, now, all speeches, every speech, a year ago, English, spoke, every day, teach, a year ago, wrote, a letter, began, every day, send, yesterday, some paper, lent, every day, cut, yesterday, tore, this shirt, every week, wear, a week ago, took, my friend, every day, meet, a year ago, left, New York, they, every day, see, a lot of money, give, a year ago, spent, every year, lend, cost, it, a year ago, meant, every year, a lot of food, needs, he, eats, yesterday, we, some food, I, had, a pain, felt, every day, have, a problem, study, do, yesterday, had, a typewriter, broke, every month, yesterday, saw, a desk, a doctor, told, a lawyer, every year, a year ago, became, they, were, he.

(Continue the exercise with this sentence, "We come here every day.")

1. yesterday	7. every night	14. put it
2. sat	8. there	15. a week ago
3. every morning	9. go	16. thought it
4. wake up	10. yesterday	17. every day
5. a week ago	11. stood	18. say it
6. slept	12. every day	19. a week ago
	13. I	

KEY EXAMPLES OF LESSON VIII

1a. He always says "Good morning" TO ME.
   He asked ME a question.
1b. I'm going to give a pencil TO MY BROTHER.
1c. She answered a question FOR ME.

2a. I ATE lunch here yesterday.
2b. I HAD breakfast at seven o'clock.
2c. I FELT fine.

Lesson IX

1a. JOHN SPEAKS ENGLISH RAPIDLY.
[Position for expressions of manner]

1b. JOHN PRONOUNCES ENGLISH CORRECTLY.
[Form for expressions of manner]

2. THE TALL MAN WITH BLOND HAIR IS A DOCTOR.
[Position of word-group modifiers of Class 1 words contrasted with position of single word modifiers]

3. WHO STUDIED? JOHN STUDIED.
WHEN DID HE STUDY? HE STUDIED LAST YEAR.
[Question order and statement order in questions with question words]

1a. Key example: John speaks English RAPIDLY.

Observe the position of RAPIDLY and CORRECTLY.

Previous pattern (Lesson III):

John	speaks	English		every day.

New pattern:

John	speaks	English	RAPIDLY.	
He	speaks	it	RAPIDLY	in class.
He	speaks	it in class	CORRECTLY.	
He	spoke	English to me	RAPIDLY	yesterday.
He	is speaking	it	CORRECTLY	now.

COMMENTS

(1) Use expressions of manner (RAPIDLY, CORRECTLY, etc.), after the object (ENGLISH, IT, etc.).

(2) Use expressions of manner before expressions of time (EVERY DAY, YESTERDAY, NOW, etc.).*

PRACTICE

EXERCISE 1a.1. (To use expressions of manner, RAPIDLY, CORRECTLY, etc., in the proper position.) Substitute the words in the proper positions. For example:

John spoke English rapidly last year.

correctly   JOHN SPOKE ENGLISH CORRECTLY LAST YEAR.
pronounced   JOHN PRONOUNCED ENGLISH CORRECTLY
                    LAST YEAR.

---

*Use expressions of manner before or after expressions of place: RAPIDLY IN CLASS and IN CLASS RAPIDLY are both proper.

these words	JOHN PRONOUNCED THESE WORDS CORRECTLY LAST YEAR.
yesterday	JOHN PRONOUNCED THESE WORDS CORRECTLY YESTERDAY.
he	HE PRONOUNCED THESE WORDS CORRECTLY YESTERDAY.

1. rapidly	11. I	21. explained (to me)
2. a week ago	12. you	22. the answer
3. this morning	13. the story	23. repeated
4. correctly	14. yesterday	24. told me
5. this word	15. the lesson	25. gave
6. the sentence	16. the lesson to me	26. the book
7. read [rɛd]	17. me the lesson	27. quickly
8. an hour ago	18. the words	28. this morning
9. rapidly	19. the question	29. at 8 o'clock
10. Mr. White	20. asked	30. promptly

1b.

Key examples: John pronounces English CORRECTLY.
He has a CORRECT pronunciation.

Observe the forms CORRECTLY, CAREFULLY, etc.

New pattern:

John answered	CORRECTLY.
He described the room	CAREFULLY.
Mary arrived	PROMPTLY.
She speaks	SLOWLY.
Paul arrived	PUNCTUALLY.
Mary pronounces English	WELL.
She walks	FAST.
She works	HARD.
She doesn't like sugar	VERY MUCH.
She likes milk	A LOT.

Previous patterns (Lessons I and IV):

The answer was	CORRECT.	
It was a	CORRECT	answer.
He was	CAREFUL.	
It was a	CAREFUL	description.
She's	PROMPT.	
She's a	PROMPT	girl.
She's a	SLOW	speaker.
He's a	PUNCTUAL	man.
She has a	GOOD	pronunciation.
She's a	FAST	walker.
She's a	HARD	worker.
She doesn't like	VERY MUCH	sugar.
She likes	A LOT OF	milk.

COMMENTS

(1) Add -LY to Class 3 words (CORRECT, CAREFUL, etc.) to form words of manner (CORRECTLY, CAREFULLY, etc.).

(2) Use WELL, FAST, HARD, VERY MUCH, A LOT in the position of the -LY words.

Note: The -LY words (CORRECTLY, CAREFULLY, PROMPTLY,
etc.) are Class 4 words. WELL, FAST, HARD, etc., in this
position are Class 4 words. Some expressions of time (NOW,
etc.) and some expressions of place (HERE, THERE, etc.) are
Class 4 words.

PRACTICE

EXERCISE 1b.1. (To contrast the use of CAREFULLY, SLOWLY,
QUIETLY, etc., with CAREFUL, SLOW, QUIET, etc.). Listen to the
statement with a Class 3 word (QUIET, SLOW, etc.). Form two corresponding statements, one with an -LY form and one with the Class
3 word after a form of BE. For example:

The careful student is studying.
    THE STUDENT IS STUDYING CAREFULLY. HE IS CAREFUL.
The quiet doctor worked.
    THE DOCTOR WORKED QUIETLY. HE WAS QUIET.
The sincere doctor is speaking.
    THE DOCTOR IS SPEAKING SINCERELY. HE IS SINCERE.

1. The quiet student studies.
2. The loud student is talking.
3. The careful doctor is working.
4. The prompt girl is coming.
5. The punctual student arrived.
6. The careful teacher is writing.
7. The sincere man spoke.
8. The slow teacher is talking.
9. The quiet boy is reciting.
10. The careful girl is answering questions.
11. The prompt student wrote a letter.
12. The intelligent teacher answered the questions.

EXERCISE 1b.2. (To form and use a variety of Class 4 words.) Listen
to the statements. Form additional statements with SPEAKS, WALKS,
FLIES, etc., and -LY forms. For example:

Mary's formal.   SHE SPEAKS FORMALLY.
Her English was excellent.   SHE SPOKE EXCELLENTLY.
Our friend's slow.   HE WALKS SLOWLY.
An airplane is fast.   IT FLIES FAST.

1. The new student's intelligent.
2. John's loud.
3. Mary's careful.
4. Her dress is colorful.
5. Peter's formal.
6. His answers were acceptable.
7. He's a fast swimmer.
8. Ed's a good teacher.
9. Paul's a clear speaker.
10. His answer was respectful.
11. John wore a formal suit.
12. His letters are formal.
13. John's a fast runner.
14. Paul's a good speaker.

2.

Key example: The TALL man WITH BLOND HAIR is a doctor.

Observe the position of WITH BLOND HAIR, FROM MEXICO, ON
  STATE STREET.

MODIFIER   HEAD   MODIFIER

Previous pattern (Lesson IV):

The	blond	man		is a doctor.
The	Mexican	student		speaks French.
The	State Street	shoestore		is good.

New pattern:

The		man	WITH BLOND HAIR	is a doctor.
The	TALL	man	WITH BLOND HAIR	is a doctor.
The		student	FROM MEXICO	speaks French.
The	TALL	student	FROM MEXICO	speaks French.
The		shoestore	ON STATE STREET	is good.
The	NEW	shoestore	ON STATE STREET	is good.

COMMENTS

(1) Use groups of words like WITH BLOND HAIR, ON STATE STREET,
    etc., after the Class 1 word they modify.
(2) Use words like BLOND, TALL, NEW, etc., before the Class 1
    word they modify (Lesson IV).

PRACTICE

EXERCISE 2.1. (To use single word modifiers and word-group modifiers
in proper position.) Listen to the statements. Combine them to form
one statement. Use the words TALL, SHORT, FROM SAN FRANCISCO,
FROM MEXICO, etc., as modifiers. For example:

The girl is studying. She's tall.
    THE TALL GIRL IS STUDYING.
The girl is studying here. She's from San Francisco.
    THE GIRL FROM SAN FRANCISCO IS STUDYING HERE.
The student is practicing English. He's short. He's from Mexico.
    THE SHORT STUDENT FROM MEXICO IS PRACTICING
    ENGLISH.

1. That store is very good. It's large.
2. The shoestore is very good. It's on State Street.
3. The bookstore is good. It's large. It's on State Street.
4. The man is intelligent. He's from Brazil.
5. That man is Mr. White. He's beside Mr. Black.
6. The student is my roommate. He's beside the window.
7. The student is from the English Language Institute. He's tall.
8. The doctor is learning English. He's with Mr. Black.

9. The bookstore is small. It's on the corner.
10. The bookstore is good. It's small. It's on the corner.
11. The girl is friendly. She's tall. She's from New York.
12. The boy speaks loudly. He's short. He's from Chicago.
13. The student knows the answers. He's thin. He's in my class.
14. The lawyer speaks English very well. He's at that table.
15. The man gave me a book. He's in my class.
16. That car is mine. It's red. It's on the corner.
17. The store is interesting. It's big. It's near the bank.
18. The story is interesting. It's short. It's about baseball.
19. The students speak formally. They're in my class.
20. The doctor came with his wife. He's young. He's at that table.

3. Key examples: WHO studied? JOHN studied.
WHEN DID he study? He studied LAST YEAR.

Situation: This is John.   This is Mr. King.

John   sees   Mr. King.
Mr. King doesn't see John.
John   is   in back of Mr. King.

Observe the question patterns with WHO(M) and WHERE. Observe the answers.

	QUESTIONS				ANSWERS
A	WHO(M)	DOES	John	see?	MR. KING.
	WHERE	IS	John?		IN BACK OF MR. KING.
B		WHO	sees	Mr. King?	JOHN.
		WHO	is	in back of Mr. King?	JOHN.

COMMENTS

(1) Use WHO(M), WHERE, WHAT, etc., before question word order (Pattern A) when you want to know something other than the subject (Lesson IV).

John sees MR. KING.   WHO(M) DOES John see?   MR. KING.
John is IN BACK OF   WHERE IS John?   IN BACK OF MR.
  MR. KING.   KING.

(2) Use WHO, WHAT, etc., in subject position in statement word order
    (Pattern B) when you want to know the subject.
JOHN sees Mr. King.   WHO sees Mr. King?   JOHN.
JOHN is in back of Mr. King.   WHO is in back of Mr. King?   JOHN.

(3) See the Illustrative Examples for other words in the positions of
    WHO, WHERE in these question patterns.

ILLUSTRATIVE EXAMPLES

WHO, etc., with question word order (Pattern A):

WHO(M)	DID you talk to last night?
	(We talked to) JOHN.
WHAT	DOES John do?
	(He) WORKS IN A STORE.
WHAT	DOES he sell?
	(He sells) BOOKS.
WHICH book	DO you want?
	(I want) THE HISTORY BOOK.
WHICH	DOES Paul want?
	(He wants) THE PHILOSOPHY BOOK.
HOW MUCH money	DOES the history book cost?
	(It costs) FIVE DOLLARS.
HOW MUCH	DOES the philosophy book cost?
	(It costs) TWO DOLLARS.
HOW MANY books	DO you need?
	(I need) FIVE BOOKS.
HOW MANY	DOES Paul need?
	(He needs) THREE.
WHEN	ARE you going to see John tomorrow?
	(We're going to see him) AT THREE O'CLOCK.
WHERE	DOES John live?
	(He lives) ON STATE STREET.
HOW FAR	IS his house from the store?
	(It's) FIVE BLOOKS (from the store).

WHO, etc., with statement word order (Pattern B):

	WHO	talked to John last night?
		PAUL AND I (talked to him).
	WHAT	is his business?
		BOOKS (are his business).
	WHICH book	costs five dollars?
		THE HISTORY BOOK (costs five dollars).
	WHICH	costs two dollars?
		THE PHILOSOPHY BOOK (costs two dollars).
	HOW MUCH money	is in your pocket now?
		TWO DOLLARS (is in my pocket).
	HOW MUCH	is in John's pocket?
		ONE DOLLAR (is in his pocket).

HOW MANY books   are in the store?
TWO THOUSAND BOOKS (are
   in the store).
HOW MANY   are in your room?
SEVEN (are in my room).

NOTE: Do not use WHEN, WHERE, HOW FAR with statement word
order.

PRACTICE

EXERCISE 3.1. (To use question patterns with WHO, WHAT, etc.)
Listen to the statements. They give a situation. Form questions from
the situation with WHO, WHAT, WHERE, etc. For example:

Situation: John sells cars in Texas.

    Who: WHO SELLS CARS IN TEXAS?
    What: WHAT DOES JOHN SELL?
    Where: WHERE DOES JOHN SELL CARS?

Situation: John sold a car to me.
    What: WHAT DID JOHN SELL TO YOU?
    Who: WHO SOLD A CAR TO YOU?
    Who(m): WHO(M) DID JOHN SELL A CAR TO?

Situation: John saw Mary.

    Who: WHO SAW MARY?
    Who(m): WHO(M) DID JOHN SEE?

Sit. A: John saw Mary in Detroit.
    1. who
    2. who(m)
    3. where

Sit. B: This car cost $2000 a
     year ago.
    4. what
    5. how much
    6. when

Sit. C: John visited the museum
    yesterday.
    7. who
    8. what
    9. when

Sit. D: A lot of coffee grows in
    Brazil.
    10. how much
    11. what
    12. where

Sit. E: Fifteen students visited
    the museum yesterday.
    13. how many
    14. who
    15. what
    16. when

Sit. F: Some of these doctors
    learned English here
    a year ago.
    17. how many
    18. who
    19. what
    20. where
    21. when

Sit. G: My teacher read the
    sentences to me this
    morning.
    22. who
    23. who(m)
    24. what
    25. when

EXERCISE 3.2. (To practice HOW MUCH, WHAT, WHICH, etc., with question patterns.) Listen to the statements. Notice the words with stress in the statements. Form questions and ask for similar information about THE OTHER CAR, THE OTHER WORD, THE OTHER MAN, etc. Another person answers the question. For example:

This car cost $2000.
> HOW MUCH DID THE OTHER CAR COST?
> IT COST $3000.

This word means rich.
> WHAT DOES THE OTHER WORD MEAN?
> IT MEANS POOR.

The student was in Detroit.
> WHERE WAS THE OTHER STUDENT?
> HE WAS IN NEW YORK.

This teacher writes with his left hand.
> WHICH HAND DOES THE OTHER TEACHER WRITE WITH?
> HE WRITES WITH HIS RIGHT HAND.

1. These students read 500 pages.
2. These people left 2 years ago.
3. That student studies at night.
4. One student said "poor."
5. This book cost $5.
6. These boys went to Detroit.
7. These girls went to the museum.
8. Some of this coffee comes from Brazil.
9. Twenty of the students studied last night.
10. That teacher lives in Boston.
11. These doctors arrived yesterday.
12. This student is studying English.
13. These students came from Mexico.

KEY EXAMPLES OF LESSON IX

1a. John speaks English RAPIDLY.
1b. John pronounces English CORRECTLY.
2. The TALL man WITH BLOND HAIR is a doctor.
3. WHO studied? JOHN studied.
   WHEN DID he study? He studied LAST YEAR.

Lesson X

REVIEW OF LESSONS I-IX*

1. (To review questions with BE.) Convert the following statements into questions. For example:

He is a good man.   IS HE A GOOD MAN?
It is interesting.   IS IT INTERESTING?
John was a good player.   WAS JOHN A GOOD PLAYER?

1. He was a good man.
2. These tests were hard.
3. The teacher was with the students.
4. Those books were new.
5. She is an interesting girl.
6. They are going to buy some books.
7. Mr. Smith was an important man.
8. You are late.
9. They were doing Lesson V today.
10. We are in Detroit now.
11. That man is a professor.
12. I am the winner.
13. He is going to Detroit with Paul.
14. The plane is coming this afternoon.

2. (To review questions with DO.) Convert the following statements into questions. For example:

John works every day.   DOES JOHN WORK EVERY DAY?
He worked in the factory.   DID HE WORK IN THE FACTORY?
They never walk home with John.   DO THEY EVER WALK HOME WITH JOHN?

1. Mary teaches in school.
2. They work every afternoon.
3. You frequently work at night.
4. He often studies at night.
5. He ate here regularly.
6. I study in the afternoon.
7. She never takes her book home.
8. He waited until one o'clock.
9. We recited this morning.
10. Paul talked to Mary yesterday.
11. They always want coffee.
12. My brother taught in high school.

*NOTE TO THE TEACHER: The exercises in this lesson attempt to review all of the patterns presented in Lessons I-IX. Patterns for which there is no specifically designated exercise are reviewed in exercises on other patterns. For example, there is no designated exercise on irregular Class 2 words, but these forms are practised in Exercise 11 and other exercises.

. The teacher should feel free to practice all of the exercises given here, or to practice only those which review patterns that have proved especially difficult for his class. He may wish to supplement these exercises by repeating exercises from the previous lessons.

3. (To review questions with BE and DO.) Convert the following statements into questions. For example:

He listens carefully.   DOES HE LISTEN CAREFULLY?
He is my uncle.   IS HE YOUR UNCLE?
They had eggs for breakfast.   DID THEY HAVE EGGS FOR
                               BREAKFAST?

1. They are eating at the cafeteria.
2. They ate chicken for dinner.
3. I am going to fly to Mexico.
4. He sees a movie every week.
5. She is practicing a difficult
   pattern.
6. Those students are his friends.
7. I heard the news about John.
8. The news is good.
9. They are going to visit the
   museum in Toledo.
10. The students are waiting
    for their teacher.
11. He answered the questions.
12. Mr. Black is going to sell
    his car.

4. (To review questions introduced by question words.) Convert the statements into questions. Use question words which correspond to the final items in the statements. For example:

Mary worked yesterday.   WHEN DID MARY WORK?
She saw him at the movie.   WHERE DID SHE SEE HIM?
He bought a hat.   WHAT DID HE BUY?
I met John.   WHO(M) DID YOU MEET?

1. They asked me yesterday.
2. They asked John.
3. They bought a car.
4. We drove to Cleveland.
5. We returned from Cleveland
   yesterday.
6. I saw Mary.
7. You know the story.
8. They ate steaks.
9. We found it in New York City.
10. He visited me last week.
11. The student wanted Mr. Smith.
12. He met the doctor on Main
    Street.

5. (To review questions with WHO.) Convert the statement into two questions. Use the question word WHO. In the first question ask for the subject; in the second ask for the object or receiver. For example:

Mary saw John.
       WHO SAW JOHN?   WHO(M) DID MARY SEE?
They are talking to John.
       WHO IS TALKING TO JOHN?   WHO(M) ARE THEY TALKING
                                        TO?
She told John.
       WHO TOLD JOHN?   WHO(M) DID SHE TELL?

1. Paul knows John.
2. Mr. Smith visited him.
3. They saw Mary.
4. John heard the teacher.
5. Paul met me.
6. They are visiting John today.
7. Jane waited for her.
8. My sister saw them.
9. The student asked the teacher.
10. We told Paul.
11. Mary understands him.
12. The teacher questioned Jane.

6. (To review short answers to questions.) Answer the questions with short answers. Use the forms YES, HE IS; NO HE DOESN'T; YES, HE DID; etc. For example:

Does she like her class?	YES, SHE DOES.
What does she study?	ENGLISH.
Was she in class yesterday?	YES, SHE WAS.

1. Is he busy?
2. Do you like oranges?
3. Does she sing well?
4. Did John answer the question?
5. Does John know the answer?
6. Where do you live?
7. Are you an artist?
8. Is she an engineer?
9. What are they studying?
10. When were you sick?
11. Does Mary speak French?
12. Who sent you that letter?
13. Were the students tired?
14. Is he going to see the game?
15. What are you going to do after class?

7. (To review answers with various question types.) Answer the questions with a full answer. Supply an appropriate answer to questions with WHO, WHEN, etc. For example:

Did John eat his dinner?	YES, HE ATE IT.
Was Fred at the program?	YES, HE WAS AT THE PROGRAM.
Who is with John?	MARY IS WITH HIM.
When did he arrive?	HE ARRIVED YESTERDAY.

1. Did they see the play?
2. Do the students know the way?
3. How many people are coming?
4. Does Mary like milk?
5. Who did Mary see?
6. Do you like the book?
7. Did you like the book?
8. Who saw Mary?
9. Are you a student?
10. Were they at the party?
11. Where are they living?
12. When did he come?
13. Was John with you?
14. Were we usually late?
15. Is he her friend?
16. What did he eat?
17. How much did he pay?
18. Does the bank close at three?

8. (To review the formation of past time statements.) Convert the statements with present time action into statements with past time action. For example:

I usually buy a sandwich.	I USUALLY BOUGHT A SANDWICH.
She is making a dress.	SHE MADE A DRESS.
She is homesick.	SHE WAS HOMESICK.

1. They want a book.
2. John and Paul are friends.
3. She needs a pencil.
4. The watch is on the table.
5. His book costs $5.
6. He sits in the first row.
7. He writes a letter every day.
8. We like the program.
9. They never eat steak.
10. Those ties are expensive.
11. He has a cold.
12. She always knows the answer.
13. It is on the desk.
14. She is taking a course in English.
15. He wears a hat in winter.

9. (To review the formation of future time statements.) Convert the statements with present or past time action to statements with future time action. Use BE + GOING TO + a Class 2 word. For example:

He works every day.   HE IS GOING TO WORK EVERY DAY.

He ate toast for breakfast.   HE IS GOING TO EAT TOAST FOR BREAKFAST.

He is taking philosophy.   HE IS GOING TO TAKE PHILOSOPHY.

1. Paul has a headache.
2. Professor Rok is telling a joke.
3. She made a cake for dinner.
4. They are good students.
5. The pencil broke.
6. I am writing a letter.
7. Mary told us an interesting story.
8. We went downtown in a taxi.
9. They asked him a lot of questions.
10. Fred and Bill were in the same class.
11. We eat lunch at twelve.
12. The class had a good time.
13. John woke up at 6 o'clock.
14. I drank a glass of milk for breakfast.
15. The concert began at 8.
16. They walk to school with me.

10. (To review the formation of statements with action in progress.) Convert the statements from past or future time action to statements with action in progress. Use BE + the -ING form of the Class 2 word. For example:

She walked to school with John.   SHE IS WALKING TO SCHOOL WITH JOHN.

She is going to buy a hat.   SHE IS BUYING A HAT.

I watched a good play.   I AM WATCHING A GOOD PLAY.

1. They have dinner at home.
2. He found the books.
3. They went to a concert in the auditorium.
4. We are going to wait for her.
5. The director talked to the students.
6. The store on State Street had a sale.
7. I practiced my pronunciation this morning.

8. It stood by the window.
9. We are going to bring a friend.
10. He thought of his home this morning.
11. Paul taught mathematics at the University.
12. I did the first lesson.
13. She felt fine today.
14. He is going to sell his car.

11. (To review the formation of statements with repeated or habitual action.) Convert the statements with past or future time action to statements with repeated or habitual action. Use the simple or the -S form of the Class 2 word. For example:

He did a lot of exercises every day. HE DOES A LOT OF EXERCISES
                                         EVERY DAY.

He lived in the dormitory. HE LIVES IN THE DORMITORY.
We are going to like English. WE LIKE ENGLISH.

1. She ate with her friends.
2. He took a walk every day.
3. She usually came to school early.
4. He met me in the cafeteria.
5. He got tired of the class.
6. He took an interest in baseball.
7. Paul drank a glass of milk for breakfast.
8. The student worked for his tuition.
9. The birds went south in the winter.
10. The trees lost their leaves in the fall.
11. Mary read the newspaper in the evening.
12. It cost 50 cents.
13. He spent a lot of money for clothes.

12. (To review expressions of frequency and manner.) Substitute the words in proper position. Use expressions of frequency (USUALLY, SELDOM, etc.) before the Class 2 word. Use expressions of manner (QUICKLY, CAREFULLY, etc.) at the end of the statement. For example:

He usually learns the lessons quickly.

    rapidly   HE USUALLY LEARNS THE LESSONS RAPIDLY.
    never   HE NEVER LEARNS THE LESSONS RAPIDLY.
    reads   HE NEVER READS THE LESSONS RAPIDLY.
    newspaper   HE NEVER READS THE NEWSPAPER RAPIDLY.

1. always
2. his lesson
3. carefully
4. studies
5. completely
6. seldom
7. does
8. his assignment
9. never
10. immediately
11. rarely
12. his work

13. efficiently	16. his grammar	19. usually
14. often	17. sometimes	20. badly
15. well	18. an exercise	

13.
(To review expressions of frequency, place and time.) Substitute the expressions of frequency (SOMETIMES, NEVER, etc.), of place (HERE, IN THE GARDEN, etc.), and of time (IN THE EVENING, FOR ONE HOUR, etc.) in proper positions. For example:

He usually works at home in the evening.

| always | HE ALWAYS WORKS AT HOME IN THE EVENING. |
| here | HE ALWAYS WORKS HERE IN THE EVENING. |

1. in the morning	13. in the library
2. sometimes	14. often
3. never	15. on State Street
4. at night	16. at noon
5. in the office	17. seldom
6. frequently	18. here
7. in the factory	19. at the restaurant
8. in town	20. now
9. in the evening	21. here
10. at home	22. often
11. always	23. in New York City
12. for one hour	

14.
(To review the distribution of A, AN with Class 1 words.) Substitute the words. Omit A, AN before non-countable Class 1 words and plural forms. For example:

John ate an orange.

toast	JOHN ATE TOAST.
had	JOHN HAD TOAST.
piece of toast	JOHN HAD A PIECE OF TOAST.
peaches	JOHN HAD PEACHES.

1. tea	13. two glasses of water
2. sandwich	14. used
3. coffee	15. sugar
4. party	16. teaspoon
5. milk	17. potatoes
6. chocolate milk	18. napkin
7. glass of milk	19. cream
8. fruit	20. likes
9. water	21. salt
10. drank	22. books
11. cold water	23. easy assignment
12. glass of cold water	24. red ties

15. (To review the use and omission of THE.) Substitute the words. Use the form THE before Class 1 words when possible. Do not use A in this exercise. Omit THE before names of people, countries, time of day, streets, etc. For example:

They visited the museum.

Canada	THEY VISITED CANADA.
saw	THEY SAW CANADA.
professor	THEY SAW THE PROFESSOR.

1. Professor Smith	17. grammar book
2. art gallery	18. English
3. Spain	19. instructions
4. Mississippi River	20. Shakespeare
5. New York City	21. discussed
6. old city	22. mathematics
7. football game	23. Mexico
8. Paris	24. art
9. subway	25. president
10. Paul	26. house
11. student	27. arrived at
12. book	28. two o'clock
13. read	29. Miami
14. philosophy	30. railroad station
15. books	31. noon
16. philosophy of Aristotle	

16. (To review the use of THIS, THAT, THESE, THOSE.) Listen to the statement with HERE or THERE. Use THIS, THESE to indicate objects HERE. Use THAT, THOSE to indicate objects THERE. For example:

The water here is fresh.	THIS WATER IS FRESH.
The water there is clear.	THAT WATER IS CLEAR.
The houses there are old.	THOSE HOUSES ARE OLD.
The houses here are new.	THESE HOUSES ARE NEW.

1. The trees there are pine trees.
2. The problem here is difficult.
3. The apples here are ripe.
4. The man there is my cousin.
5. The student here is from Nicaragua.
6. The lady there is a teacher.
7. The light here is bright.
8. The men there are engineers.
9. The books here belong to Mary.
10. The house there is fifty years old.
11. The boys there are my nephews.
12. The flower here is a violet.

17. (To review modifiers of Class 1 words.) Modify the Class 1 word in the first statement with a Class 3 word or a word group from the second statement. For example:

The house is on Winter street. It is old.
   THE OLD HOUSE IS ON WINTER STREET.
The house was old. It was on Winter Street.
   THE HOUSE ON WINTER STREET WAS OLD.
The red pencil is new. It is on the desk.
   THE RED PENCIL ON THE DESK IS NEW.

1. My pencil is on the desk. It is new.
2. The big house is on the hill. It is old.
3. He built a house. It is large.
4. He has a dog. The dog is small.
5. They have an apartment. It is luxurious.
6. We own a home. It is on Main Street.
7. My friend has a car. He is from Panama.
8. I study literature. It is American.
9. We know the students. They are Brazilian.
10. The cafeteria serves good meals. It's on Burns Avenue.
11. She bought a hat. It was expensive.
12. I read a book. It was about politics.
13. He took a test. It was important.
14. He wrote a check. It was bad.

18. (To review the use of Class 1 words as modifiers.) Combine the statements. Modify the Class 1 word in the first statement with a Class 1 word from the second statement. For example:

He works in a factory. It makes cars.
   HE WORKS IN A CAR FACTORY.
He is eating grapes. They come from Michigan.
   HE IS EATING MICHIGAN GRAPES.
They are students. They take engineering.
   THEY ARE ENGINEERING STUDENTS.

1. She is a student. She studies biology.
2. He went to a store. It sells shoes.
3. They went to a restaurant. They went on Main Street.
4. I know the book. It deals with physics.
5. We read the book. It discusses birds.
6. John is a student. He goes to the University.
7. They are workers. They work on the railroad.
8. We ate a dinner. We had steak.
9. The students gave a program. They gave it on Friday night.
10. We played a game. It was baseball.
11. They like fishing. They fish in the river.
12. The building is on William Street. It is a bank.

19. (To review Class 1 words as modifiers.) Convert the Class 1 words in the statements to modifiers. For example:

He works on automobiles.	HE IS AN AUTOMOBILE WORKER.
He fights fires.	HE IS A FIRE FIGHTER.
It dries dishes.	IT IS A DISH DRIER.
It cuts glass.	IT IS A GLASS CUTTER.

1. He plays baseball.
2. He plays football.
3. It dries clothes.
4. He washes windows.
5. It washes clothes.
6. It heats water.
7. It makes noise.
8. He publishes textbooks.
9. He advises students.
10. She studies French.
11. They speak Spanish.
12. He teaches English.

20. (To review Class 1 words in object position.) Substitute the words in proper position. For example:

John gave me a present.

her	JOHN GAVE HER A PRESENT.
watch	JOHN GAVE HER A WATCH.
bought	JOHN BOUGHT HER A WATCH.
his father	JOHN BOUGHT HIS FATHER A WATCH.

1. a tie
2. me
3. Paul and me
4. them
5. brought
6. book
7. his picture
8. her
9. her picture
10. me
11. him
12. the picture
13. them
14. their picture
15. you
16. me
17. your picture
18. you
19. us
20. our book
21. the book
22. a book
23. him
24. you
25. me
26. her
27. our book
28. their book
29. Mary
30. him
31. Fred

21. (To review ANY, SOME, OTHER, ANOTHER, OTHERS, ALL, MUCH, MANY, NONE, A FEW, A LITTLE, A LOT.) Substitute the following words in the request statements. Correlate ANY, MUCH, MANY with the negative form DON'T. For example:

Buy some apples.

peaches	BUY SOME PEACHES.
a few	BUY A FEW PEACHES.
get	GET A FEW PEACHES.
any	DON'T GET ANY PEACHES.
many	DON'T GET MANY PEACHES.
coffee	DON'T GET MUCH COFFEE.
some	GET SOME COFFEE.

1. a lot of	15. none	29. books
2. any	16. some	30. read
3. drink	17. a few	31. all of the
4. all of the	18. a little	32. the other
5. much	19. sugar	33. another
6. use	20. any	34. others
7. dishes	21. a lot of	35. study
8. buy	22. much	36. any
9. any	23. apples	37. many
10. car	24. some	38. all
11. another	25. a few	39. another
12. the other	26. bread	40. any
13. cars	27. coffee	41. lesson
14. the others	28. pencils	

22.

(To review the use of ME, TO ME, FOR ME, etc.) Listen to the words and the statements. Include the words in the statements. For example:

Me   She talked about music.
          SHE TALKED ABOUT MUSIC TO ME.
Them   He asked some questions.
          HE ASKED THEM SOME QUESTIONS.
John   The teacher pronounced the word.
          THE TEACHER PRONOUNCED THE WORD FOR JOHN.

1. Us. He talked about Ann Arbor.
2. Me. He visited in Miami.
3. Them. They waited.
4. Me. He told a story.
5. John. She made a cake.
6. Her. He explained the program.
7. Him. I asked for a cigarette.
8. Mary. John pronounced the sentence.
9. Him. We bought a present.
10. Me. John did the work.
11. Bill. Mary introduced us.
12. Them. He got some pencils.
13. His mother. He wrote a letter.
14. The class. He is going to speak about language.
15. Her. He always says a kind thing.

Lesson XI

1. CAN, SHOULD, MUST, WILL, MIGHT, MAY.
   1a. I CAN READ ENGLISH. CAN YOU READ IT?
   [Statements and questions]
   1b. CAN YOU PRACTICE NOW? YES, I CAN.
   [Short answers]

2. A pattern of connected statements.
   2a. JOHN CAN'T GO AND I CAN'T EITHER.
   MARY CAN GO AND BETTY CAN TOO.
   [AND . . . TOO contrasted with . . . AND . . . EITHER]
   2b. MARY CAN GO BUT JOHN CAN'T.
   [. . . BUT . . .]

1a. Key examples: I CAN READ English. Can you READ it?

Observe the position of CAN, SHOULD, etc.
Observe the form of the Class 2 words.

Previous pattern (Lesson IV):

		John	is		speaking	English.
	Is	John			speaking	English?

New pattern:

		John	CAN	SPEAK	English.
		He	SHOULD	STUDY	every day.
		You	MUST	SPEAK	English in class.
		The class	'LL	FINISH	the book next month.
		I	MIGHT	GO	to Chicago next week.
		You	MAY	SMOKE	in the dormitory.
		John	CAN'T	SPEAK	Chinese.
		He	SHOULDN'T	GO	to the movies every night.
		You	MUSTN'T	SPEAK	your native language here.
		The class	WON'T	FINISH	the book this month.
		I	MIGHT NOT	GO	to Chicago next week.
		You	MAY NOT	SMOKE	in the classroom.
	CAN	John		SPEAK	English?
	SHOULD	he		STUDY	every day?
	MUST	we		SPEAK	English in class?
	WILL	we		FINISH	the book next month?
When	WILL	we		FINISH	the book?
Where	MAY	the students		SMOKE?	

95

COMMENTS

(1) Use CAN, SHOULD, MUST, WILL ('LL), MIGHT, MAY in the positions of BE: after the subject (JOHN, HE, etc.) in statements; before the subject in questions. Don't use DO in questions with CAN, etc.

(2) Use the simple form of the Class 2 word (SPEAK, PRACTICE, etc.) with CAN, SHOULD, etc.

(3) Use CAN, SHOULD, etc., with I, YOU, WE, THEY and HE, SHE, IT. Do not add -S to words like CAN.

(4) CAN'T, SHOULDN'T, MUSTN'T, WON'T, MIGHT NOT, MAY NOT are the negative forms.

ILLUSTRATIVE EXAMPLES

Paul studied French for five years.
> He CAN speak it well.

Betty never practices her piano lessons.
> She CAN'T play well.

Paul is young and strong.
> He CAN work hard all day.

Peter is old and weak.
> He CAN'T work hard.

Mary is going to have an examination next week.
> She SHOULD study for it this week. She SHOULDN'T go to the movies.

Automobiles are dangerous.
> We SHOULD drive carefully. We SHOULDN'T drive fast.

Mrs. Smith is sick.
> She MUST stay in bed. She MUSTN'T get up.

A red light means "stop."
> Drivers MUST stop. They MUSTN'T go.

We're going to have a program next week.
> We'LL have it Friday night. All of the students WILL be there. They WON'T go to the movies that night.

> NOTE: WILL is equivalent to BE + GOING TO in most situations.

John invited me to his house tonight.
> I MIGHT go, but I MIGHT stay home. I don't know.

I sometimes see Mary in the library.
> I MIGHT see her tomorrow. I MIGHT NOT see her. I don't know.

Betty asked, "MAY I open a window?"
Her mother answered, "No. You MAY NOT open a window. I'm cold."

Betty asked her father, "MAY I go to the concert tonight?"
He gave her permission. He said, "Yes, you MAY go."

PRACTICE

EXERCISE 1a.1. (To practice MAY, CAN, etc. in proper position.)
Substitute the words. For example:

I can play the piano.
speak Spanish	I CAN SPEAK SPANISH.
they	THEY CAN SPEAK SPANISH.
may	THEY MAY SPEAK SPANISH.
ask for a visa	THEY MAY ASK FOR A VISA.

1. should	17. should
2. she	18. must
3. write home	19. practice every day
4. I	20. John and Mary
5. might	21. they
6. go to the dance	22. should
7. John	23. we
8. will	24. will
9. we	25. go to Detroit
10. study tonight	26. might
11. must	27. they
12. he	28. visit the museum
13. speak English	29. can
14. can	30. return tomorrow
15. finish the lesson	31. should
16. you	32. must

EXERCISE 1a.2. (To practice questions with CAN, MUST, MIGHT, etc.)
Convert the statements into questions. For example:

I can hear the band.	CAN YOU HEAR THE BAND?
They may miss class tomorrow.	MAY THEY MISS CLASS TOMORROW?
Professor Brown will give a speech today.	WILL PROFESSOR BROWN GIVE A SPEECH TODAY?

1. Mary should answer the letter.
2. She may use my pen.
3. The students must practice every day.
4. They should study in the evening.
5. John can play the organ.
6. He will play tonight.
7. We must report to the office now.
8. We can go to lunch later.
9. Mr. Brown will explain the lesson to you.

10. You should wait for him.
11. Paul must see a doctor immediately.
12. He might have pneumonia.
13. Mary may keep the book for seven days.
14. She should return it next Monday.

EXERCISE 1a.3. (To produce the negative forms of CAN, MAY, etc.)
Listen to the affirmative statements about John. Produce corresponding negative statements about Mary. For example:

John can go.	MARY CAN'T GO.
John may go.	MARY MAY NOT GO.
.John should go.	MARY SHOULDN'T GO.

1. John must study hard.
2. John will go tomorrow.
3. John may smoke.
4. John can play the piano.
5. John might visit us.
6. John must practice every day.
7. John will go to Chicago Saturday.
8. John must wait for his brother.
9. John can pronounce the words.
10. John should come to the program.
11. John might attend the concert.
12. John may live in an apartment.

EXERCISE 1a.4. (To practice comprehension of SHOULD, CAN, etc.,
and to produce statements with SHOULD, CAN, etc.) Answer the
questions. For example:

John's a pianist. What can he do?
    HE CAN PLAY THE PIANO.
A South American is going to study in United States. What should
    he do?
    HE SHOULD LEARN ENGLISH.
Paul and Jim permit John to play their piano. What may John do?
    HE MAY PLAY THEIR PIANO.

1. Peter goes to the movies. His mother permits it. What may he do?
2. John doesn't speak English. He needs it. What must he do?
3. John needs a lot of practice in English. What should he do?
4. Paul is going to take a train to Washington, D.C. What might he
    see there?
5. Paul is going to take a train to Washington, D.C. Who might he see
    there?
6. We had presidential elections in 1944, 1948, 1952, and 1956. What
    will we have in 1960?   ˙
7. Women may vote in the United States. The Constitution gives
    them permission. What should they do?
8. Mary is a bad student. What should she do?
9. Mary is a singer. What can she do?
10. The students drive cars on the campus. They have permission.
    What may they do?
11. Fred is sick. Who must he see?
12. Mr. Smith is a Professor of English. What can he do?

1b. Key example: Can you practice now? Yes, I CAN.

Observe the short answers.

QUESTIONS	SHORT ANSWERS

Previous pattern (Lesson IV):

Is	John	studying?		No,	he	isn't.

New pattern:

Can	John	go?		No,	he	CAN'T.
May	he	go?		No,	he	MAY NOT.
Might	he	go?		Yes,	he	MIGHT.
Must	he	go?		Yes,	he	MUST.
Should	he	go?		Yes,	he	SHOULD.
Will	he	go?		No,	he	WON'T.

COMMENTS

(1) CAN, MAY, MIGHT, MUST, SHOULD, WILL complete the affirmative short answers to questions with CAN, MAY, etc.

(2) CAN'T, MAY NOT, MIGHT NOT, MUSTN'T, SHOULDN'T, WON'T complete the negative short answers to questions with CAN, MAY, etc.

PRACTICE

EXERCISE 1b.1. (To recognize questions with CAN, SHOULD, etc., and to produce short answers.) Give short answers to the questions. Make no response to the statements. For example:

Can you play the piano?	NO, I CAN'T.
Can you play baseball?	YES, I CAN.
We should practice English.	(No oral response.)
May you speak Spanish in Class?	NO, WE MAY NOT.

1. May you speak Spanish?
2. May John take money from other people?
3. Will you be here tomorrow?
4. Might you go to the picnic?
5. John should study hard.
6. Should John study hard?
7. Can we learn a new language?
8. Can we co-operate with other countries?
9. Scientists can control diseases.
10. Must we practice constantly?
11. You can answer this question.
12. Must you answer this question?
13. Can you answer this question?
14. May you take that watch?
15. Can you read English?
16. Will the next lesson be difficult?
17. Can you go with me?
18. Should we go to the next exercise now?

2a. Key examples: John can't go AND I CAN'T EITHER.
                        Mary can go AND Betty CAN TOO.

Observe . . . AND. . . TOO; . . . AND . . . EITHER. Observe IS, CAN, DID, etc.

Previous pattern:

| John's | a student. | Mary 's | a student. |

New pattern:

John 's	a student	AND	Mary IS	TOO.
John 's	going to go	AND	Mary IS	TOO.
John can	play the piano	AND	Mary CAN	TOO.
John should	study hard	AND	Mary SHOULD	TOO.
John studied		AND	Mary DID	TOO.
John plays	every day	AND	Mary DOES	TOO.
John isn't	a teacher	AND	Mary ISN'T	EITHER.
John wasn't	there	AND	Mary WASN'T	EITHER.
John can't	go	AND	Mary CAN'T	EITHER.
John shouldn't	go	AND	Mary SHOULDN'T	EITHER.
John didn't	go	AND	Mary DIDN'T	EITHER.
John doesn't	study hard	AND	Mary DOESN'T	EITHER.

COMMENTS

(1) Use TOO when AND connects affirmative statements in this pattern.* Use EITHER when AND connects negative statements in this pattern.

(2) Use the forms that complete the short answers (MARY IS, MARY CAN, MARY DOESN'T, etc.) after AND in this pattern.

PRACTICE

EXERCISE 2a.1. (To connect statements with . . . AND . . . TOO or . . .AND. . .EITHER.) Listen to the statements and combine them. Use AND . . . TOO in affirmative statements. Use AND . . . EITHER in negative statements. For example:

John came to the meeting. Mary came to the meeting.
    JOHN CAME TO THE MEETING AND MARY DID TOO.
John played the piano. Mary played the piano.
    JOHN PLAYED THE PIANO AND MARY DID TOO.
I won't see him. My brother won't see him.
    I WON'T SEE HIM AND MY BROTHER WON'T EITHER.

---

*NOTE: They are students   AND   we ARE TOO.
            They are students   AND SO   ARE we.
            I can go   AND   John CAN TOO.
            I can go   AND SO   CAN John.
     The meanings of these pairs of sentences are the same. You will hear both patterns.

1. I can't go. My brother can't go.
2. John isn't studying. Mary isn't studying.
3. John can play the piano. Mary can play the piano.
4. We became tired. You became tired.
5. We aren't tired now. John isn't tired now.
6. They will be here tomorrow. We will be here tomorrow.
7. You can't read Chinese. I can't read Chinese.
8. You should write to the University. Mary should write to the University.
9. John may go to the movies. Mary may go to the movies.
10. John reads every day. Mary reads every day.
11. We shouldn't arrive late. The teacher shouldn't arrive late.
12. John should always be early. Mary should always be early.
13. I arrived late. My friend arrived late.
14. I can't remember all of the rules. You can't remember all of the rules.
15. John is going to visit Canada. I'm going to visit Canada.
16. My shoes were expensive. My suit was expensive.
17. They will go to the dance. I will go to the dance.
18. I'm not a doctor. He isn't a doctor.
19. I can play the piano. John can play the piano.
20. Mrs. Black isn't here. Her friends aren't here.
21. Mary won't be here. I won't be here.
22. I will begin at 8. You should begin at 8.
23. We must always be polite. They must always be polite.
24. I went to Detroit. John went to Detroit.

EXERCISE 2a.2. (To practice the correlation of EITHER with negative statements and TOO with positive statements.) Substitute the following words in the statements and make the necessary changes. For example:

John's going to study and Mary is too.

either	JOHN ISN'T GOING TO STUDY AND MARY ISN'T EITHER.
didn't sing	JOHN DIDN'T SING AND MARY DIDN'T EITHER.
too	JOHN SANG AND MARY DID TOO.
played	JOHN PLAYED AND MARY DID TOO.
either	JOHN DIDN'T PLAY AND MARY DIDN'T EITHER.

1. too
2. remembers me
3. either
4. didn't forget me
5. too
6. saw me
7. either
8. can't help me
9. too
10. either
11. shouldn't speak to me
12. too
13. must listen to me
14. must write to me
15. should write to me
16. can write to you
17. either
18. isn't writing
19. too
20. either

EXERCISE 2a.3. (To use TOO and EITHER in a conversation situation.)
Listen to the statement about one student. Make a corresponding short
statement with TOO or EITHER about another student. Omit the word
AND in this exercise. For example:

John's a student.	MARY IS TOO.
John can play the piano.	MARY CAN TOO.
John isn't going to study.	MARY ISN'T EITHER.

1. John wants that book.
2. John went to the movies last night.
3. John didn't come to class yesterday.
4. John likes engineering.
5. John read the book.
6. John needed a lot of practice.
7. John got two letters.
8. John didn't speak to the professor.
9. John doesn't eat breakfast.
10. John wasn't here Sunday.
11. John won't be here Saturday.
12. John should write a letter to the registrar.
13. John isn't a doctor.

2b. Key example: Mary can go BUT John CAN'T.

Observe the use of BUT. Observe ISN'T, CAN'T, DID, etc.

Previous pattern:

John	's	a doctor.		Mary isn't a doctor.

New pattern:

John	's	a doctor	BUT	Mary	ISN'T.
John	's	going to go	BUT	Mary	ISN'T.
John	can	play the piano	BUT	Mary	CAN'T.
John	may	play baseball	BUT	Mary	MAY NOT.
John	went		BUT	Mary	DIDN'T.
John	goes	every day	BUT	Mary	DOESN'T.
Mary	isn't	a doctor	BUT	John	IS.
Mary	wasn't	here	BUT	John	WAS.
Mary	can't	play the piano	BUT	John	CAN.
Mary	may not	play baseball	BUT	John	MAY.
Mary	didn't	go	BUT	John	DID.
Mary	doesn't	go every day	BUT	John	DOES.

COMMENTS

(1) Use BUT between a negative statement and an affirmative
statement.

(2) Use the forms that complete short answers (MARY ISN'T, MARY
CAN'T, JOHN DOES, etc.) after BUT in this pattern.

PRACTICE

EXERCISE 2b.1. (To use AND and BUT to connect statements.) Listen to the statements and combine them. Use . . . AND . . . TOO to connect affirmative statements. Use . . . AND . . . EITHER to connect negative statements. Use BUT to connect an affirmative and a negative statement. For example:

John came to the meeting. Mary didn't come to the meeting.
    JOHN CAME TO THE MEETING BUT MARY DIDN'T.
Mary can't play the piano. John can play the piano.
    MARY CAN'T PLAY THE PIANO BUT JOHN CAN.
I can go. My friends can go.
    I CAN GO AND MY FRIENDS CAN TOO.
I don't understand you. He doesn't understand you.
    I DON'T UNDERSTAND YOU AND HE DOESN'T EITHER.

1. John is studying English. Mary isn't studying English.
2. He is from Peru. She isn't from Peru.
3. I arrived early. My friends didn't arrive early.
4. John was here yesterday. Paul was here yesterday.
5. They weren't in Detroit. Mary was in Detroit.
6. Paul should go every day. Mary shouldn't go every day.
7. Mary can't go tomorrow. John can go tomorrow.
8. John went to Detroit. I didn't go to Detroit.
9. Mr. and Mrs. Black will come. Their children will come.
10. Mr. and Mrs. Brown can't come. Their friends can't come.
11. I understand you now. He doesn't understand you now.
12. I didn't understand you yesterday. She didn't understand you yesterday.
13. They don't know the answer. I know the answer.
14. John can't understand Mr. Black. I can understand him.
15. Uruguay isn't a very big country. Brazil is a very big country.
16. Not all of our coffee comes from Brazil. Most of it comes from Brazil.
17. I never go to the movies. John goes to the movies.
18. I frequently go to the movies. John frequently goes to the movies.
19. He often sees John. I rarely see John.
20. John is early. We are early.
21. They arrived yesterday. We didn't arrive yesterday.
22. He can usually do it. I can't usually do it.
23. You should see that dramatization. Your friends should see it.
24. Mr. Brown isn't here. John isn't here.

EXERCISE 2b.2. (To practice BUT in a short answer.) Listen to the question about one student. Give a corresponding short answer about another student with NO + BUT. For example:

Is John a student?	NO, BUT MARY IS.
Can John play the piano?	NO, BUT MARY CAN.
Did John go to the movies?	NO, BUT MARY DID.

1. Does John come to class every day?
2. Is John going to study?
3. Does John like literature?
4. Did John read the book?
5. Can John read Italian?
6. Did John speak to the professor?
7. Should John write a letter to the registrar?
8. Is John a doctor?
9. Was John here yesterday?
10. May John read the letter?
11. Did John talk to the director?
12. Should John practice his pronunciation?
13. Was John absent last week?

SUMMARY EXERCISE. Substitute the following words in the statements and make the necessary changes. For example:

I can help you but he can't.

too	I CAN HELP YOU AND HE CAN TOO.
either	I CAN'T HELP YOU AND HE CAN'T EITHER.
shouldn't	I SHOULDN'T HELP YOU AND HE SHOULDN'T EITHER.
won't	I WON'T HELP YOU AND HE WON'T EITHER.

1. too	6. may not	11. but
2. but	7. too	12. too
3. should	8. but	13. might
4. too	9. either	14. must
5. either	10. can't	15. either

KEY EXAMPLES OF LESSON XI

1a. I CAN READ English. CAN you READ it?
1b. Can you practice now? Yes, I CAN.
2a. John can't go AND I CAN'T EITHER.
    Mary can go AND Betty CAN TOO.
2b. Mary can go BUT John CAN'T.

Lesson XII

1. I CALLED ON HER. I CALLED HER UP.
   [Combinations like CALL ON, CALL UP]

2a. HE CAME IN ORDER TO GET THE BOOKS. HE CAME FOR
   THE BOOKS.
   [IN ORDER TO + Class 2 contrasted with FOR + Class 1]

2b. WHY DID HE COME HERE? IN ORDER TO GET THE BOOKS.
   [Answers to questions with WHY]

3a. I LEARNED ENGLISH BY STUDYING HARD.
   [BY + the -ING form of Class 2 or + Class 1]

3b. HOW DID YOU LEARN IT? BY PRACTICING CONSTANTLY.
   [Answers to questions with HOW]

1. Key examples: I CALLED ON her. I CALLED her UP.

Observe CALLED ON, CALLED UP, etc.

John	CALLED	ON	Mary.	He	CALLED	ON	her.	
John	LOOKS	LIKE	his father.	He	LOOKS	LIKE	him.	
John	GOT	OVER	his cold.	He	GOT	OVER	it.	
John	CALLED	UP	Mary. *	He	CALLED		her	UP.
John	LOOKED	UP	the word.*	He	LOOKED		it	UP.
John	PUT	ON	his coat.*	He	PUT		it	ON.

COMMENTS

(1) Use the separated pattern (CALLED her UP) with the Class 1 substitutes HIM, HER, IT, THEM, YOU, ME, US, in the combinations
CALL (her) UP, LOOK (it) UP, PUT (it) ON, TRY (it) ON, PUT
(him) UP, WAKE (him) UP, PUT (it) DOWN, TAKE (them) OFF,
TAKE (it) OUT, BREAK (him) IN, GIVE (them) OUT. You will
learn other combinations like these later.

(2) Do not use the separated pattern for CALL ON, LOOK LIKE, GET
OVER, GET ALONG WITH, LOOK OUT FOR, RUN INTO, RUN OUT
OF. You will learn other combinations like these later.

(3) Use any of these combinations (CALL ON, LOOK LIKE, GET OVER,
CALL UP, LOOK UP, PUT ON, etc.) together before MARY, HIS
FATHER, HIS COLD, THE WORK, HIS COAT, etc. (Class 1 words
and expressions).

---

*You will also hear: John CALLED Mary UP.
John LOOKED the word UP.
John PUT his coat ON.

ILLUSTRATIVE EXAMPLES OF THE SEPARATED PATTERN

John heard the alarm clock.	It	WOKE	him	UP.
	It	GOT	him	UP.
He telephoned Mary.	He	CALLED	her	UP.
He went to class. The teacher returned some examinations.	He	GAVE	them	OUT.
John had a question. He raised his hand.	He	PUT	it	UP.
He didn't know the meaning of a word.	He	LOOKED	it	UP in the dictionary.
He went to a clothing store in the afternoon. He saw a nice brown suit.	He	PUT	it	ON.
	He	TRIED	it	ON in front of the mirror.
He didn't buy it.	He	TOOK	it	OFF.
	He	PUT	it	DOWN on the counter.
He bought some new shoes.	He is	BREAKING	them	IN now.

ILLUSTRATIVE EXAMPLES OF THE NONSEPARATED PATTERN

John walked down the street. He saw Mary and her sister.	He	RAN INTO	them.
Mary resembles her sister.	She	LOOKS LIKE	her.
John likes both girls.	He	GETS ALONG WITH	them very well.
There were a lot of cars.	They	LOOKED OUT FOR	them.
They visited Paul at his apartment.	They	CALLED ON	him.
Paul served coffee, but there wasn't much cream.	They	RAN OUT OF	it.

PRACTICE

EXERCISE 1.1. (To practice the combinations CALL ON, CALL UP, etc.) Repeat the statements. Use the substitute forms HIM, HER, IT, THEM. For example:

I looked up the word.	I LOOKED IT UP.
I put on my shoes.	I PUT THEM ON.
I ran into Mr. Black.	I RAN INTO HIM.
He called up Mr. and Mrs. Black.	HE CALLED THEM UP.

1. I ran into Mary.
2. I called up Mary.
3. Your sister looks like Mary.
4. She put on her coat.
5. I looked up the answer.
6. We ran out of paper.
7. Mary called up her friends.
8. This child can put on his shoes.
9. This looks like our lesson.
10. We must look up the first lesson.
11. We are going to call up Mr. Black.
12. John ran into Mr. Black yesterday.
13. She didn't put on her new dress.
14. I'm going to call up my teacher.
15. I'm going to call on some friends.
16. He gets along with all people.
17. You must look out for children.
18. John is breaking in his new pipe.
19. Mary broke in her new shoes.
20. He's going to take out the spot.
21. I must look up his record.
22. You should put on your hat.
23. John's going to call up the man.
24. John looks like the president.
25. He ran out of sugar.

2a. Key examples:　He came IN ORDER TO GET the books.
　　　　　　　　　　　He came FOR THE BOOKS.

Observe IN ORDER TO and FOR, and the words after them.

He came	IN ORDER	TO	GET	the books.
He came	IN ORDER	TO	BUY	the coat.
He came	IN ORDER	TO	HEAR	the concert.
He came	IN ORDER	TO	LISTEN.	
He came	IN ORDER NOT	TO	MISS	the concert.
He came	IN ORDER	TO	TELL	me the news.

He came	FOR	THE BOOKS.
He came	FOR	THE COAT.
He came	FOR	THE CONCERT.

COMMENTS

(1) Use IN ORDER TO* before Class 2 words (GET, BUY, HEAR, etc.). Don't use FOR TO.
(2) Use FOR before Class 1 words (BOOKS, COAT, IT, etc.). Don't use Class 2 words after FOR.

PRACTICE

EXERCISE 2a.1. (To use IN ORDER TO with GO, HEAR, etc. and FOR with A BOOK, THE CONCERT, etc.) Substitute the following words and make the necessary changes.　For example:

---

*You will often hear TO (without IN ORDER) in the position of IN ORDER TO: HE CAME TO GET THE BOOKS. The meaning is the same.

He came in order to get the books.

for	HE CAME FOR THE BOOKS.
the concert	HE CAME FOR THE CONCERT.
hear the concert	HE CAME IN ORDER TO HEAR THE CONCERT.
study English	HE CAME IN ORDER TO STUDY ENGLISH.

1. cash the check	11. matches
2. meet me	12. lunch
3. get cigarettes	13. in order to
4. for	14. find a chair
5. his coat	15. for
6. all of his books	16. hear the radio program
7. in order to	17. for
8. tell me the news	18. a book
9. buy some matches	19. get a book
10. buy matches	20. for

2b. Key example: WHY did he come here? IN ORDER TO GET the books.

Observe the questions with WHY. Observe the answers.

QUESTIONS   ANSWERS

Previous pattern (Lesson IV):

| When | did he come here? | | Yesterday. |

New pattern:

WHY	did he come here?	FOR			THE	BOOKS.
WHY	did he come here?	FOR			THE	CONCERT.
WHY	did he come here?	IN	ORDER	TO	GET	the books.
WHY	did he come here?	IN	ORDER	TO	HEAR	the concert.
WHY	did he come here?	IN	ORDER NOT TO		MISS	the concert.

COMMENTS

(1) Use question word order in questions with WHY.*

(2) FOR THE BOOKS (FOR + Class 1) and IN ORDER TO GET THE BOOKS (IN ORDER TO + Class 2) are answers to questions with WHY.

---

*WHAT. . . FOR is equivalent to WHY:

WHY	did John come here?	In order to get his books.
WHAT	did John come here FOR?	In order to get his books.

PRACTICE

EXERCISE 2b.1. (To practice short answers with IN ORDER TO and
FOR in response to questions with WHY.) Listen to the question and the
suggested word. Use the suggested word in the short answers. For
example:

Why did you come here? learn	IN ORDER TO LEARN ENGLISH.
Why did John come here? for	FOR HIS BOOKS.
Why do people go to the bank? for	FOR MONEY.
Why do people go to the bank? cash	IN ORDER TO CASH CHECKS.
Why did Mrs. Black buy the meat? make	IN ORDER TO MAKE SANDWICHES.

1. Why did Mrs. Black buy the meat? for
2. Why are you looking for a chair? sit
3. Why do you want a cigarette? smoke
4. Why did John go to the store? buy
5. Why did John go to the store? for
6. Why did you get up at 7? study
7. Why did Mary go to the shoestore? for
8. Why did Mary go to the shoestore? buy
9. Why did you go to the movie? see
10. Why must we practice constantly? learn
11. Why did he go to Detroit? buy
12. Why did he go to Detroit? for
13. Why did you go to the barbershop? for
14. Why do other people go there? get

3a. Key example: I learned English BY STUDYING hard.

Observe BY and the words after BY.

John called	BY	TELEPHONE.	
He sent a letter	BY	AIRMAIL.	
He went	BY	TRAIN.	
He arrived early	BY	TAKING	a taxi.
He finished early	BY	TELEPHONING	his friends.
He surprised his family	BY	COMING	home early.
He pleased them	BY NOT	COMING	late.

COMMENTS

(1) Use TRAIN, TELEPHONE, etc. (Class 1 words) or TAKING,
    TELEPHONING, etc. (the -ING form of Class 2 words) after BY.
(2) Use BY (not FOR) with "communication" words like TRAIN,
    TELEPHONE, etc.

PRACTICE

EXERCISE 3a.1. (To use BY with Class 1 words and with the -ING form of Class 2 words.) Use BY and the proper form of the following words in a statement. For example:

answer . . . airmail   HE ANSWERED BY AIRMAIL.
answer . . . smile   HE ANSWERED BY SMILING.
send the letter . . . airmail   HE SENT THE LETTER BY AIRMAIL.
come . . . train   HE CAME BY TRAIN.
learn English . . . practice   HE LEARNED ENGLISH BY PRACTIC-
      ING IT.

learn English . . . go to the
  movies   HE LEARNED ENGLISH BY GOING TO
      THE MOVIES.

1. send the package . . . airmail
2. learn the words . . . repeat
3. go downtown . . . bus
4. begin the lesson . . . give examples
5. earn money . . . sell radios
6. answer . . . draw a diagram
7. go to New York . . . plane
8. learn the words . . . write them
9. come to the university . . . car
10. find your address . . . look in the telephone book
11. learn the answer . . . ask the teacher
12. learn the pronunciation . . . imitate
13. learn a lot . . . listen carefully
14. go to the station . . . taxi
15. go to Europe . . . ship
16. answer . . . smile
17. find my street . . . ask a policeman
18. learn English . . . practice constantly

3b. Key example: HOW did you learn it? BY PRACTICING
constantly.

Observe the questions with HOW. Observe the answers.

| QUESTIONS | ANSWERS |

Previous pattern (Lesson IV):

| When did he go? | | Yesterday. |

New Pattern:

HOW	did he go?	BY	TRAIN.	
HOW	did he call Mary?	BY	TELEPHONE.	
HOW	did he go?	BY	TAKING	the train.
HOW	did he anger Betty?	BY NOT	CALLING	her.
HOW	did he answer Jane?	BY	SMILING.	
HOW	did he answer her?	WITH	A SMILE.	
HOW	does he like his coffee?	WITHOUT	SUGAR.	
HOW	does he speak?	CLEARLY.		
HOW	does he sing?	SOFTLY.		

COMMENTS

(1) Use question word order in questions with HOW.
(2) In answers to questions with HOW use:
    (a) BY + Class 1 (BY TRAIN).
    (b) BY + the -ING form of Class 2 (BY SMILING).
    (c) WITH or WITHOUT + Class 1 (WITH A SMILE).
    (d) Class 4 (CLEARLY).

PRACTICE

EXERCISE 3b.1. (To use BY, WITH, and -LY words in answers to
questions with HOW.) Listen to the questions and the suggested words.
Give short answers with BY, WITH or -LY words. For example:

How did you get here?	take a taxi	BY TAKING A TAXI.
How did she answer you?	smile	BY SMILING.
		or WITH A SMILE.
How did you call her up?	telephone	BY TELEPHONE.
		or BY TELEPHONING.
How did they speak?	soft	SOFTLY.
How did he close the door?	his	
	foot	WITH HIS FOOT.

1. How did he earn money? sell radios
2. How did he send the money? telegraph
3. How did you get here? plane

4. How did you get here? take a plane
5. How did you graduate? study
6. How did John find your address? look in the telephone book
7. How did they sing? quiet
8. How did he read it? rapid
9. How did he write it? his left hand
10. How can we learn these words? repeat them
11. How did he open the box? his hands
12. How can I learn English? practice constantly
13. How can we go to Canada? bus
14. How did you go? train
15. How did he go to California? car

SUMMARY EXERCISE. Listen to the questions and give full answers. Use the suggested words and the substitutes HIM, HER, IT, THEM if possible in the answers. For example:

How can I talk to Mary? telephone
   YOU CAN TALK TO HER BY TELEPHONE.
How can I call up Mary? telephone
   YOU CAN CALL HER UP BY TELEPHONE.
Why did you call up Mary? ask her a question
   I CALLED HER UP IN ORDER TO ASK HER A QUESTION.
Why did John go to the store? for
   HE WENT TO THE STORE FOR CIGARETTES.
How did he put on his coat? quick
   HE PUT IT ON QUICKLY.
How did he answer the question? nodding his head
   HE ANSWERED IT BY NODDING HIS HEAD.

1. Why did Mary go to Detroit? see a movie
2. How did John learn the meaning of that word? looking it up in the dictionary
3. Why did he look up the word? use it
4. Why did he go to New York? visit a friend
5. How did he get here? running fast
6. How did she thank her mother? smiling
7. How did she thank her mother? a smile
8. Why did he go to Europe? see Paris
9. Why did he go to the store? for
10. Why did he put on a coat? be warm
11. How can I go to Niagara Falls? boat
12. How can we find the museum? asking a policeman
13. Why must you go to the bank? cash a check
14. How did the child put on his shoes? correctly
15. How can I get a good pronunciation? imitating native speakers

KEY EXAMPLES OF LESSON XII

1. I CALLED ON her.
    I CALLED her UP.

2a. He came IN ORDER TO GET the books.
    He came FOR THE BOOKS.

2b. WHY did he come here? IN ORDER TO GET the books.
3a. I learned English BY STUDYING hard.
3b. HOW did you learn it? BY PRACTICING constantly.

Lesson XIII

1. Class 2 + TO + Class 2
   1a. JOHN LEARNED TO SPEAK ENGLISH.
       [Class 2 + TO + Class 2 in statements]
   1b. DID MARY LEARN TO SPEAK ENGLISH? NO, SHE DIDN'T.
       [Class 2 + TO + Class 2 in questions and short answers]
   1c. MARY DIDN'T LEARN TO SPEAK ENGLISH.
       JOHN TRIES NOT TO SPEAK SPANISH IN CLASS.
       [Class 2 + TO + Class 2 with a negative]
   1d. SHE CAN'T SPEAK ENGLISH, BUT SHE'S LEARNING TO.
       [Class 2.+ TO + Class 2 in a pattern of connected statements]
2. THIS LESSON IS EASY FOR OUR CLASS TO UNDERSTAND.
   [EASY (LESSON) (FOR OUR CLASS) (TO UNDERSTAND)]
3. THESE SHOES ARE VERY BIG. THEY'RE BIG ENOUGH FOR ME.
   [Positions of VERY, TOO, ENOUGH]
4. THE TEACHER WANTS THE STUDENTS TO LEARN ENGLISH.
   [Class 2 + Class 1 + TO + Class 2]

1a. Key example: John LEARNED TO SPEAK English.

Observe the forms and positions of the Class 2 words.
Observe the position of TO.

Previous pattern (Lesson XI):

John		can		speak	English.

New pattern:

John		LEARNED	TO	SPEAK	English.
He		INTENDS	TO	SPEAK	English.
He	is	PLANNING	TO	SPEAK	English.
He	is going to	NEED	TO	SPEAK	English.
He	would	LIKE	TO	SPEAK	English.
He	must	TRY	TO	SPEAK	English.
He		HAS	TO	SPEAK	English.

COMMENTS

(1) Use TO between certain Class 2 words (LEARN, INTEND, PLAN, NEED, LIKE, TRY, HOPE, EXPECT, PROMISE, WANT, HAVE, etc.) and the simple form of another Class 2 word (SPEAK, etc.).

(2) HE HAS TO SPEAK is similar in meaning to HE MUST SPEAK. The usual pronunciations of HAS TO and HAVE TO in this pattern are [hǽstə, hǽftə].

114

PRACTICE

EXERCISE 1a.1. (To contrast LEARN TO SPEAK, LIKE TO SPEAK, etc., with CAN SPEAK, MUST SPEAK, etc.) Substitute the following words and make the necessary changes. For example:

He learned to speak English.

tried	HE TRIED TO SPEAK ENGLISH.
should	HE SHOULD SPEAK ENGLISH.
I	I SHOULD SPEAK ENGLISH.
read the lesson	I SHOULD READ THE LESSON.
have	I HAVE TO READ THE LESSON.
should try	I SHOULD TRY TO READ THE LESSON.
must	I MUST READ THE LESSON.

1. they
2. need
3. like
4. try
5. should
6. we
7. all of the students
8. study grammar
9. you
10. must
11. need
12. I
13. hope
14. expect
15. write the words

16. intend
17. promise
18. like
19. write letters
20. will
21. plan
22. might
23. want
24. can
25. we
26. should
27. tried
28. she
29. speak clearly

30. is learning
31. has
32. would like
33. must
34. must try
35. can learn
36. will
37. decided
38. is going to learn
39. needs
40. needed
41. is going to try
42. will try
43. can

1b. Key example: DID Mary LEARN TO SPEAK English? No, she DIDN'T.

Observe DOES, DID, SHOULD, IS in the questions and in the short answers.

QUESTIONS   SHORT ANSWERS

Previous patterns (Lessons II, IV, XI):

			Yes, he does.
Does	he	write?	Yes, he does.
Should	he	write?	Yes, he should.
Is	he	writing?	Yes, he is.

New pattern:

		he	TRY	TO	WRITE?	Yes, he	DOES.
	DOES	he	TRY	TO	WRITE?	Yes, he	DOES.
	DOES	he	HAVE	TO	WRITE?	No, he	DOESN'T.
	DID	he	LEARN	TO	WRITE?	Yes, he	DID.
	SHOULD	he	TRY	TO	WRITE?	Yes, he	SHOULD.
	IS	he	TRYING	TO	WRITE?	Yes, he	IS.
WHAT	DID	he	LEARN	TO	WRITE?	His name	

COMMENTS

(1) Use a form of DO, or CAN, SHOULD, etc., in questions with TRY TO, HAVE TO, etc.
(2) Use a form of BE (IS, AM, ARE) in questions with TRYING TO, GOING TO TRY TO, etc.
(3) DO, DOES, DID, SHOULD, IS, etc., complete the short answers with YES or NO.

PRACTICE

EXERCISE 1b.1. (To ask questions with CAN, WILL, etc., and with Class 2 words connected by TO; to give short answers.) Make questions with the following words and READ. Use TO if necessary. A second student answers the questions with a short answer. For example:

Does he try to read?

can	CAN HE READ?	YES, HE CAN.
like	DOES HE LIKE TO READ?	YES, HE DOES.
have	DOES HE HAVE TO READ?	YES, HE DOES.
is trying	IS HE TRYING TO READ?	YES, HE IS.
should learn	SHOULD HE LEARN TO READ?	YES, HE SHOULD.

1. plan	10. must	19. will try
2. expect	11. like	20. should try
3. will	12. prefer	21. can learn
4. can	13. refuse	22. should learn
5. may	14. might	23. will learn
6. intend	15. need	24. promise
7. need	16. want	25. expect
8. should	17. have	26. try to learn
9. try	18. is trying	27. must learn

1c. Key examples: Mary DIDN'T LEARN to speak English.
John tries NOT TO SPEAK Spanish in class.

Observe the negatives.

Previous pattern (Lesson XI):

Mary	can't	speak	English.

New patterns:

Mary	DOESN'T	PLAN	to	speak	English.
She	CAN'T	LEARN	to	speak	English.
She	ISN'T	TRYING	to	speak	English.
John		plans	NOT TO SPEAK		Spanish.
He	can	learn	NOT TO SPEAK		Spanish.
He	is	trying	NOT TO SPEAK		Spanish.

COMMENTS

(1) Use DOESN'T, CAN'T, etc., before the simple form (ISN'T, etc., before the -ING form) in order to make the first Class 2 word negative.

(2) Use NOT before TO in order to make the second Class 2 word negative.

PRACTICE

EXERCISE 1c.1. (To practice the negative expressions DOESN'T TRY TO WRITE, ISN'T TRYING TO WRITE, CAN'T WRITE, etc.) Listen to the statement about John. Make a corresponding negative statement about Mary. For example:

John tries to write.	MARY DOESN'T TRY TO WRITE.
John is trying to write.	MARY ISN'T TRYING TO WRITE.
John tried to write.	MARY DIDN'T TRY TO WRITE.
John might write.	MARY MIGHT NOT WRITE.
John should try to write.	MARY SHOULDN'T TRY TO WRITE.

1. John expects to write.
2. John must write.
3. John needs to write.
4. John plans to write.
5. John planned to write.
6. John should write.
7. John wants to write.
8. John wanted to write.
9. John expected to write.
10. John can write.
11. John can learn to write.
12. John must try to write.
13. John should continue to write.
14. John would like to go.
15. John decided to go.
16. John should go.
17. John planned to go.
18. John is planning to do it.
19. John should learn to write.
20. John is going to promise to go.
21. John likes to study.
22. John intends to go.
23. John is intending to go.
24. John must learn to write.
25. John will learn to speak clearly.
26. John is beginning to work.

EXERCISE 1c.2. (To practice the negative pattern TRY NOT TO SPEAK, MUST TRY NOT TO SPEAK, etc.) Listen to the statements about John. Make corresponding negative statements about Mary. Use the negative pattern TRY NOT TO SPEAK, MUST TRY NOT TO SPEAK, etc. For example:

John tried to speak loudly.	MARY TRIED NOT TO SPEAK LOUDLY.
John is planning to go.	MARY IS PLANNING NOT TO GO.
John expected to be here.	MARY EXPECTED NOT TO BE HERE.
John must try to work hard.	MARY MUST TRY NOT TO WORK HARD.

1. John promised to go.
2. John prefers to do it now.
3. John can learn to speak loudly.
4. John tries to pronounce correctly.
5. John must promise to do it again.
6. John will continue to answer.
7. John is planning to go.
8. John expected to go.
9. John hopes to take a vacation.
10. John should try to take a nap every afternoon.
11. John tried to be early.
12. John hopes to work hard.

1d. Key example: She can't speak English, but she's LEARNING TO.

Observe PLANS TO, HAS TO, LEARNING TO, etc.

Previous pattern (Lesson XI):

He doesn't	study	every day,	but he		should.

New pattern:

STATEMENTS

He didn't	go,		but he		PLANS TO.
He doesn't want to	go,		but he		HAS TO.
He can't	speak	English,	but he's		LEARNING TO.
He didn't have to	study	last night,	but he		WANTED TO.
He plans to	go,		but he doesn't		WANT TO.
He might	help	us,	but he doesn't		HAVE TO.
He should	study	tomorrow,	but he isn't		PLANNING TO.
He	got	a letter,	but he didn't		EXPECT TO.

QUESTIONS			ANSWERS		
Did he	go?		No, but he		PLANS TO.
Did he	get	a letter?	Yes, but he didn't		EXPECT TO.

COMMENT

PLANS TO, HAS TO, LEARNING TO, etc., complete the sentences in this pattern. Do not repeat GO, SPEAK, etc.

PRACTICE

EXERCISE 1d.1. (To contrast the WANTS TO pattern with the CAN pattern in connected statements after BUT.) Substitute the following words after BUT. Use TO when necessary. For example:

He didn't go, but he plans to.

wants	HE DIDN'T GO, BUT HE WANTS TO.
wanted	HE DIDN'T GO, BUT HE WANTED TO.
can	HE DIDN'T GO, BUT HE CAN.
is planning	HE DIDN'T GO, BUT HE'S PLANNING TO.

1. plans
2. intends
3. hopes
4. might
5. expects
6. expected
7. is expecting

8. should
9. will
10. is intending
11. hoped
12. would like
13. will try
14. needs
15. has

16. is hoping
17. must
18. might decide
19. is going to try
20. wanted
21. can
22. wants

EXERCISE 1d.2. (To practice HE PLANS TO, HE SHOULD, etc., as answers to questions.) Answer the questions with NO, BUT HE PLANS TO; NO, BUT HE SHOULD, etc. For example:

Does he have to go?	NO, BUT HE PLANS TO.
Does he want to go?	NO, BUT HE SHOULD.
Did you meet the president?	NO, BUT I WOULD LIKE TO.
Do you study every day?	NO, BUT I SHOULD.

1. Did you go to Chicago?
2. Do you like to get up at seven o'clock?
3. Did you get a letter?
4. Do you want to study tonight?
5. Must you take a four year course?
6. Do you have to take a four year course?
7. Are you going to go to a movie to night?
8. Did he pay for the ticket?
9. Does Mary play tennis?
10. Did you see the new play?
11. Did John talk to his teacher?
12. Does she understand French?

2. Key example: This lesson is easy FOR OUR CLASS TO UNDER-
STAND.

Observe FOR HIM, FOR HIM TO UNDERSTAND, TO UNDERSTAND, etc.

Previous patterns:

| This lesson is | easy. | (Lesson I) |
| This | is an easy lesson. | (Lesson IV) |

New pattern:

	HEAD	MODIFIER	
This lesson is	EASY	FOR HIM.	
This bread is	GOOD	FOR HIM.	
This	is AN EASY LESSON	FOR OUR CLASS.	
Monday	is A GOOD DAY	FOR HIM.	
This lesson is	EASY	FOR HIM	TO UNDERSTAND.
This bread is	GOOD	FOR HIM	TO EAT.
This	is AN EASY LESSON	FOR OUR CLASS	TO UNDERSTAND.
Monday	is A GOOD DAY	FOR HIM	TO GO.
This lesson is	EASY		TO UNDERSTAND.
This bread is	GOOD		TO EAT.
This	is AN EASY LESSON		TO UNDERSTAND.
Monday	is A GOOD DAY		TO GO.

COMMENT

Use FOR HIM, FOR HIM TO UNDERSTAND, TO UNDERSTAND, etc., as modifiers after words like EASY, GOOD, etc. (Class 3), and after combinations like EASY LESSON, GOOD DAY, etc.

PRACTICE

EXERCISE 2.1. (To use groups like FOR HIM, FOR HIM TO UNDER-
STAND, and TO UNDERSTAND, after EASY, etc.) Substitute the following words. For example:

This lesson is difficult for him.

for him to understand	THIS LESSON IS DIFFICULT FOR HIM TO UNDERSTAND.
to understand	THIS LESSON IS DIFFICULT TO UNDER-STAND.
easy	THIS LESSON IS EASY TO UNDERSTAND.
this exercise	THIS EXERCISE IS EASY TO UNDERSTAND.
for us	THIS EXERCISE IS EASY FOR US.
for us to write	THIS EXERCISE IS EASY FOR US TO WRITE.

1. to do
2. this lesson
3. for us to understand
4. for us
5. these words
6. difficult
7. for us to remember
8. to remember
9. to write
10. to spell
11. for our students to spell
12. for our students
13. easy
14. for them to remember
15. to remember
16. to forget
17. to write
18. for me to write
19. for you
20. for you to learn
21. these lessons
22. to learn
23. this exercise
24. to do
25. to practice

3. Key examples: These shoes are VERY big. They're big ENOUGH for me.

Observe the positions of VERY, TOO, and ENOUGH.

John	is	VERY	weak.		
He	is	TOO	weak to work.		
He	speaks	VERY	rapidly.		
He	speaks	TOO	rapidly for us to understand.		
Paul	is		strong		ENOUGH.
He	speaks		slowly		ENOUGH.

COMMENTS

(1) Use VERY and TOO before words like WEAK, STRONG (Class 3) and RAPIDLY, SLOWLY (Class 4).
(2) Use ENOUGH after these words.

ILLUSTRATIVE EXAMPLES

These shoes are size twelve.
    They are VERY big.
Your feet are size nine.
    The shoes are TOO big for you.
John's feet are size thirteen.
    The shoes are VERY big, but they are TOO small for him.
My feet are size twelve.
    The shoes are big ENOUGH for me. They aren't TOO big.
We had sixty minutes to write an examination. You didn't finish the
examination.
    You wrote TOO slowly.
John finished in thirty minutes, but he made a lot of mistakes.
    He wrote TOO fast.
    He didn't write carefully ENOUGH.
I finished in fifty-five minutes. I didn't make many mistakes.
    I wrote VERY carefully, and I wrote fast ENOUGH.

PRACTICE

EXERCISE 3.1. (To practice the positions of VERY, TOO, and ENOUGH.)
Substitute the following words. For example:

These shoes are very big.
    too   THESE SHOES ARE TOO BIG.
    enough   THESE SHOES ARE BIG ENOUGH.
    strong   THESE SHOES ARE STRONG ENOUGH.
    these boys   THESE BOYS ARE STRONG ENOUGH.
    formal   THESE BOYS ARE FORMAL ENOUGH.
    speak   THESE BOYS SPEAK FORMALLY ENOUGH.
    very   THESE BOYS SPEAK VERY FORMALLY.
    carefully   THESE BOYS SPEAK VERY CAREFULLY.
    are   THESE BOYS ARE VERY CAREFUL.

1. too	9. speaks	17. too	24. enough
2. enough	10. very	18. works	25. fast
3. old	11. enough	19. enough	26. carefully
4. John	12. Mrs. Black	20. rapidly	27. is
5. very	13. carefully	21. very	28. tall
6. Mr. Black	14. very	22. quietly	29. too
7. too	15. is	23. walks	30. short
8. slow	16. enough		

EXERCISE 3.2. (To summarize Frames 2 and 3.) Substitute the following words. For example:

This exercise is easy enough for us.
        for us to remember.   THIS EXERCISE IS EASY ENOUGH FOR
                               US TO REMEMBER.

to remember	THIS EXERCISE IS EASY ENOUGH TO REMEMBER.
to write	THIS EXERCISE IS EASY ENOUGH TO WRITE.
to write in class	THIS EXERCISE IS EASY ENOUGH TO WRITE IN CLASS.
too difficult	THIS EXERCISE IS TOO DIFFICULT TO WRITE IN CLASS.
long	THIS EXERCISE IS TOO LONG TO WRITE IN CLASS.
for me to write	THIS EXERCISE IS TOO LONG FOR ME TO WRITE.
for me	THIS EXERCISE IS TOO LONG FOR ME.
these shoes	THESE SHOES ARE TOO LONG FOR ME.

1. enough
2. good
3. too
4. old
5. for me to wear
6. for me (without "to wear")
7. for you
8. for John to wear
9. to wear (without "for John")
10. this coat
11. for you to wear
12. for you (without "to wear")
13. for Mary
14. long
15. that dress
16. enough
17. that suit
18. for John
19. big
20. too
21. that car
22. for John to drive
23. old
24. to drive (without "for John")
25. to use
26. these books
27. this coffee
28. to drink
29. hot
30. for us to drink
31. enough
32. for us (without "to drink")
33. too
34. old
35. these books
36. to read

4.

Key example: The teacher wants THE STUDENTS to learn English.

Observe the position of THE STUDENTS, THEM.

Previous pattern:

| The students wanted | | to learn | English. |

New pattern:

The teacher	wanted	THE STUDENTS	to learn	English.
He	asked	THEM	to practice	every day.
He	expected	THEM	to learn	quickly.

COMMENT

Use words like THE STUDENTS, HIM, THEM (Class 1) after WANT, ASK, EXPECT, LIKE, TELL, PERMIT, TEACH, INVITE, CHOOSE, URGE, and GET, and before TO.

PRACTICE

EXERCISE 4.1. (To practice Class 1 words before TO GO, etc.) Substitute the following words. For example:

I wanted you to go.
    asked   I ASKED YOU TO GO.
    expected   I EXPECTED YOU TO GO.
    to have breakfast here I EXPECTED YOU TO HAVE BREAKFAST HERE.
    we expected   WE EXPECTED YOU TO HAVE BREAKFAST HERE.

1. asked
2. wanted
3. they wanted
4. to become an engineer
5. your father wants
6. does he want
7. to study engineering
8. us
9. does he expect
10. did he ask
11. to be here early
12. them
13. her
14. you

KEY EXAMPLES OF LESSON XIII

1a. John LEARNED TO SPEAK English.
1b. DID Mary LEARN TO SPEAK English? No, she DIDN'T.
1c. Mary DIDN'T LEARN to speak English.
    John tries NOT TO SPEAK Spanish in class.
1d. She can't speak English, but she's LEARNING TO.
2. This lesson is easy FOR OUR CLASS TO UNDERSTAND.
3. These shoes are VERY big. They're big ENOUGH for me.
4. The teacher wants THE STUDENTS to learn English.

Lesson XIV

1a. IT'S IMPORTANT FOR US TO SPEAK ENGLISH.
   [IT in subject position]
1b. THERE'S A BOOK ON THE TABLE.
   [THERE in subject position]
2. THE WORK OF A MACHINE.
   THIS MAN'S WORK.
   [Distribution of the OF and the 'S patterns]
3a. WHOSE BOOK IS THIS? IT'S JOHN'S. YOURS IS ON THE TABLE.
   [WHOSE? MINE, YOURS, JOHN'S, etc.]
3b. I NEED A BLUE ONE AND SEVERAL WHITE ONES.
   [ONE and ONES as substitutes]

1a. Key example: IT's important for us to speak English.

Observe the use of IT.

Previous pattern (IT as a substitute):

The lesson is		short.
It	's	easy.

New pattern:

	IT	's	nine o'clock.
	IT	's	Monday.
	IT	's	May.
	IT	's	summer.
	IT	's	my birthday today.
	IT	's	getting late.
	IT	isn't	early.
	IT	's	nice weather.
	IT	seems	warm.
	IT	was	cloudy yesterday.
	IT	snows	here in the winter.
	IT	gets	hot in the summer.
	IT	will be	hot next month.
	IT	's	a long way to Alaska.
	IT	's	two blocks from here to the store.
	IT	's	Mr. Black on the telephone.
	IT	's	John (at the door).
	IT	's	easy for the teacher to speak English.
	IT	's	difficult for us.
	IT	's	important to speak clearly.
	IT	's	necessary.
Is	IT		easy to speak English? Yes, IT is.
Is	IT		late? Yes, IT is.
Does	IT	get	hot here in the summer? Yes, IT does.

125

COMMENTS

(1) Use IT in subject position in all these situations. (Time, weather, distance, identification of persons, existence of qualities, etc.) Never omit the word IT in this pattern.

(2) Use IT with IS, SEEMS, GETS, BECOMES, and words of weather like SNOWS, RAINS, etc., in this pattern.

PRACTICE

EXERCISE 1a.1. (To use IT in questions and short answers.) Use the following words in questions with IT. Another student gives the short answers, NO, IT ISN'T; YES, IT WAS; etc. For example:

early	IS IT EARLY?	YES, IT IS.
Sunday	IS IT SUNDAY?	NO, IT ISN'T.
far	IS IT FAR TO ST. LOUIS?	YES, IT IS.
rain tomorrow	IS IT GOING TO RAIN TOMORROW?	NO, IT ISN'T.
a student at the door	IS IT A STUDENT AT THE DOOR?	YES, IT IS.

1. summer	11. about two blocks
2. 1956	12. Mr. Black at the door
3. April	13. another man
4. ten o'clock now	14. a woman
5. cold yesterday	15. Mary Jones
6. warm	16. John on the telephone
7. snowing	17. the president on the radio
8. bad weather	18. Tuesday today
9. far	19. Monday yesterday
10. thirty-five miles	20. warm last year

21. easy for you to speak English
22. easy for the teacher to speak English
23. necessary to speak correctly
24. easy for you to study at night
25. difficult for John to learn English
26. necessary to write the assignment yesterday
27. easy to answer the questions tomorrow
28. important to study this lesson
29. easy for you to learn English a year ago
30. correct to say, "It's warm today"

EXERCISE 1a.2. (To use IT in statements.) Listen to the statements with -ING forms. Change the statements and use IT in subject position. These two patterns have the same meaning. Use IT + BE for production. For example:

Arriving on time is important.
　　IT'S IMPORTANT TO ARRIVE ON TIME.
Coming early will be necessary.
　　IT WILL BE NECESSARY TO COME EARLY.
Studying here is going to be easy.
　　IT'S GOING TO BE EASY TO STUDY HERE.
Writing this exercise isn't difficult.
　　IT ISN'T DIFFICULT TO WRITE THIS EXERCISE.

1. Arriving early is necessary.
2. Understanding this exercise is easy.
3. Reading this lesson is easy for you.
4. Learning a new alphabet isn't very interesting.
5. Getting up early is a good idea.
6. Speaking English is easy for us.
7. Speaking correctly is very important.
8. Studying every day is usually necessary.
9. Beginning at eight o'clock was necessary last night.
10. Beginning at eight o'clock will be necessary.
11. Beginning at nine o'clock might be necessary.
12. Beginning at eight o'clock shouldn't be necessary.
13. Beginning at eight o'clock won't be necessary.
14. Learning this lesson won't be difficult.
15. Learning a new language can be very interesting.

1b. Key example: THERE's a book on the table.

Observe the use of THERE.

Previous pattern (Lesson I):

| A book | is | | on the table. |

New pattern:

	THERE	'S	a BOOK	on the table.*
	THERE	'S	a STUDENT	in the room.
	THERE	'S	some COFFEE	in the cup.
	THERE	WAS	a PEN	on the desk yesterday.
	THERE	ARE	some BOOKS	on the table.
	THERE	WERE	several PENS	on the desk yesterday.
IS	THERE		a BOOK	on the table? Yes, THERE IS.
ARE	THERE		any BOOKS	on the table? Yes, THERE ARE.

*You will sometimes hear THERE'S SOME BOOKS ON THE TABLE in informal situations.

COMMENTS

(1) Use THERE IS, THERE WAS with BOOK, STUDENT, COFFEE, PEN, etc. (singular Class 1).

(2) Use THERE ARE, THERE WERE with BOOKS, STUDENTS, PENS, etc. (plural Class 1).

(3) THERE occupies the position of subject in this pattern.
THERE IS (WAS, etc.) indicates 'existence' in this pattern.

NOTE: THERE is also used to indicate place.

> He eats at that hotel. He eats THERE.
> The book is on the table. The book is THERE.
> Where is the book? THERE it is. THERE'S the book.

THERE, meaning place, is usually stressed at the beginning of the sentence. There are no examples of THERE meaning place in the following exercises.

PRACTICE

EXERCISE 1b.1. (To practice the use of THERE IS, THERE ARE.)
Give sentences with the following words. Use THERE IS or THERE ARE.
For example:

man	THERE'S A MAN IN THE ROOM.
chairs	THERE ARE SEVERAL CHAIRS IN THE BUILDING.
sugar	THERE'S A LOT OF SUGAR IN THE BOWL.

1. books	7. doctors	13. interesting books
2. teacher	8. intelligent student	14. old buildings
3. toast	9. difficult words	15. good restaurant
4. bread	10. tall buildings	16. money
5. meat	11. white sugar	17. good movie
6. dentist	12. very good coffee	

EXERCISE 1b.2. (To use THERE IS, THERE ARE in negative statements.) Use the following words with THERE ISN'T or THERE AREN'T.
For example:

man	THERE ISN'T A MAN FROM FRANCE IN OUR CLASS.
chairs	THERE AREN'T MANY CHAIRS IN THIS ROOM.
sugar	THERE ISN'T MUCH SUGAR IN THE BOWL.

1. papers	8. meat	14. white sugar
2. students	9. dentist	15. good coffee
3. coffee	10. doctors	16. interesting books
4. books	11. intelligent student	17. old buildings
5. teacher	12. difficult words	18. money
6. toast	13. tall buildings	19. good movies
7. bread		

EXERCISE 1b.3. (To use THERE IS, THERE ARE, etc., in questions and short answers in past, present, and future situations.) Use the following words in questions with IS THERE, IS THERE GOING TO BE, WAS THERE, etc. Another student gives a short answer. For example:

man . . . now IS THERE A MAN IN THE ROOM NOW?
YES, THERE IS.

man . . . yesterday WAS THERE A MAN IN THE ROOM YESTERDAY?
NO, THERE WASN'T.

examination . . . tomorrow IS THERE GOING TO BE AN EXAMINATION TOMORROW?
NO, THERE ISN'T.

1. students. . .a week ago
2. errors. . .yesterday
3. errors. . .today
4. improvement. . .today
5. doctor. . .now
6. dentists. . .a week ago
7. dentist. . .now
8. doctor. . .a month ago
9. books. . .yesterday
10. coffee. . .yesterday
11. good movie. . .now
12. good movie. . .a week ago

EXERCISE 1b.4. (To use THERE in questions and statements.) Form statements and questions with the following expressions containing the form THERE. For example:

was there — WAS THERE A MOVIE HERE LAST NIGHT?
there was — THERE WAS A CONCERT IN THE AUDITORIUM.
is there — IS THERE A TICKET ON MY DESK?
there's going to be — THERE IS GOING TO BE A BANQUET NEXT WEEK.
is there going to be — IS THERE GOING TO BE AN EXAMINATION?
there should be — THERE SHOULD BE MANY EXERCISES IN THE LESSONS.

1. there is
2. there were
3. there aren't
4. are there
5. is there going to be
6. there isn't
7. weren't there
8. there isn't going to be
9. was there
10. there wasn't
11. there is going to be
12. there should be
13. is there
14. there was

2.   Key examples: The work OF A MACHINE.
                        THIS MAN'S work.

Observe OF, -'S, and -S'.

	The back	OF	THIS CHAIR	is strong.
	The work	OF	A MACHINE	is precise.
THIS MAN-	-'S	work		is precise.
THE DOG-	-'S	back		is strong.
JOHN-	-'S	work		is good.
A DAY-	-'S	work		is good for us.
THIS STUDENT-	-'S	paper		is good.
THIS STUDENT-	-'S	papers		are good.
THESE STUDENT-	-S'	papers		are good.
THESE STUDENT-	-S'	paper		is good.

COMMENTS

(1) These two patterns, the OF pattern (THE WORK OF A MACHINE)
     and the -'S pattern (THIS MAN'S WORK), have the same meaning.
(2) The OF pattern is usually used with names of things. The -'S
     pattern is usually used with names that refer to people or animals.
     -'S is also used with time words (A DAY'S WORK).*
(3) In writing, -'S and -S' indicate different meanings.

> STUDENT'S PAPER refers to one student.
> STUDENTS' PAPER refers to more than one student.

There is no difference in pronunciation. The pronunciation of both
-'S and -S' is the same as for plural -S.

NOTE: The -'S word precedes other describing words:

This man'S		grammar	book.
This man'S	interesting		letter.
John'S	two	new	suits.
John'S	other	new	suit.

PRACTICE

EXERCISE 2.1. (To practice the choice between OF and -'S.) Listen to
the words and the statements. Identify the words by using them in a
statement with IT'S, THEY'RE, HE IS, etc., and the form OF or -'S.
For example:

Chair . . . Mary often sits in it.	IT'S MARY'S CHAIR.
Friend . . . She is with Mary.	SHE'S MARY'S FRIEND.
Cover . . . It's on my book.	IT'S THE COVER OF YOUR BOOK.
Vacation . . . It's for a week.	IT'S A WEEK'S VACATION.
Toys . . . The children play	
with them.	THEY'RE THE CHILDREN'S TOYS.

*You will sometimes hear expressions like THE FATHER OF THE BOY or
THE WORLD'S PROBLEMS.

1. letter...John sent it.
2. letter...John received it.
3. speech...Mr. Black gave it.
4. legs...They're on a chair.
5. legs...They're on a dog.
6. top...It's on this desk.
7. color...It's on my car.
8. friend...He is with John.
9. paper...It came today.
10. problems...John has them.
11. books...The boy has them.
12. books...The boys have them.
13. book...The boy has it.
14. wife...She married Mr. Brown.
15. books...John studied them.
16. desk...The teacher uses it.
17. two coats...Mary wears them.
18. old car...John bought it.
19. other car...John bought it.
20. other new house...John bought it.

3a. Key example: WHOSE book is this? It's JOHN'S. YOUR'S is on the table.

Observe MINE, YOURS, WHOSE, MARY'S, etc.						
This	is	my	book.	It's		MINE.
These	are	my	books.	They're		MINE.
This	is	your	book.	It's		YOURS.
These	are	your	books.	They're		YOURS.
This	is	his	book.	It's		HIS.
These	are	his	books.	They're		HIS.
This	is	her	book.	It's		HERS.
These	are	her	books.	They're		HERS.
This	is	our	book.	It's		OURS.
These	are	our	books.	They're		OURS.
WHOSE	book	is	on the table? It's			THEIRS.
WHOSE	books	are	on the table? They're			THEIRS.
WHOSE		is	on the table? It's			MARY'S.
WHOSE		are	on the table? They're			MARY'S.

COMMENTS

(1) MINE, YOURS, HIS, HERS, OURS, THEIRS complete the short statements. Never use words like BOOK, BOOKS, with these forms.
(2) Use the same form of names like MARY'S, JOHN'S with or without words like BOOK and BOOKS.
(3) Use WHOSE in questions with or without words like BOOK, BOOKS, etc.
(4) Never use THE with MINE, YOURS, MARY'S, etc.
(5) MINE, YOURS, HIS, HERS, OURS, and THEIRS are invariable in form.

PRACTICE

EXERCISE 3a.1. (To use MINE, YOURS, HIS, etc.) This is a conversation exercise. Listen to the statements with I, MY, etc. Form similar statements about JOHN, MARY, YOU, etc., and use the appropriate substitute forms HIS, HERS, YOURS, etc. For example:

I have my books. John	JOHN HAS HIS.
My books are on the desk. Mary	MARY'S ARE ON THE DESK.
I brought John's book and my book. John	JOHN BROUGHT HIS AND MINE.

1. I brought my books to class. John
2. I brought my paper to class. Mary
3. I mailed my letters this morning. Mary
4. This is my book. Fred
5. I don't like my car. Mr. and Mrs. Black
6. I visited my brothers. Mr. Smith
7. My composition isn't good, but your composition is very good. Jane
8. I bought my tickets. We
9. I read my letter before class. You
10. My books are green and John's books are too. Mary
11. I read my assignments last night. You and John
12. I showed John my books. They
13. I wrote my composition this morning. We
14. I am going to sell my car this week. Professor Brown
15. I finished my lesson, but Mary didn't finish her lesson. Fred
16. I saw John's paper and my paper. John

EXERCISE 3a.2. (To ask and answer questions with WHOSE.) Listen to the two words, WHOSE + a Class 1 word. Ask a question using these words. Then ask a similar question using WHOSE without a Class 1 word. Another student answers both questions with MINE, JOHN'S, YOURS, etc. For example:

whose books	WHOSE BOOKS ARE THOSE? THEY'RE JOHN'S. WHOSE ARE THESE? THEY'RE OURS.
whose composition	WHOSE COMPOSITION IS THIS? IT'S HERS. WHOSE IS THAT? IT'S MINE.

whose pencil	WHOSE PENCIL IS ON THE TABLE?
	   IT'S MARY'S.
	   WHOSE IS ON THE DESK? IT'S YOURS.

1. whose letter	5. whose papers	9. whose pens
2. whose dogs	6. whose pocketbook	10. whose shoes
3. whose sister	7. whose tickets	11. whose coats
4. whose brother	8. whose pen	12. whose hat

3b. Key examples: Do you need some shirts?
Yes, I need a blue ONE and several white ONES.

Observe ONE, ONES.

Previous pattern:

I want	some		shirts.

New pattern:

I want	this		ONE.
I want	that		ONE.
I want	a	small	ONE.
I want	a	good	ONE.
I want	the	red	ONE.

I want			these.
I want			some.
I want			a few.
I want			several.
I want			five.

I want	these	red	ONES.
I want	some	good	ONES.
I want	a few	nice	ONES.
I want	several	new	ONES.
I want	five	green	ONES.

COMMENTS

(1) Use ONE (plural ONES) as substitute for SHIRT, PENCIL, etc. (Class 1).
(2) Use ONE after THIS, THAT, A SMALL, THE RED, etc.
(3) Use ONES after THESE RED, SOME GOOD, FIVE NICE, etc.
(4) Don't use ONES immediately after THESE, THOSE, SOME, A FEW, SEVERAL, FIVE, etc.

PRACTICE

EXERCISE 3b.1. (To practice the use and omission of ONE and ONES.) Imagine this situation. You are going to buy some notebooks at a bookstore. Make statements with I WANT + the following words. Use ONE or ONES when necessary. For example:

this	I WANT THIS ONE.
that	I WANT THAT ONE.
five	I WANT FIVE.
a new	I WANT A NEW ONE.
some new	I WANT SOME NEW ONES.
your new	I WANT YOUR NEW ONE.
yours	I WANT YOURS.
these	I WANT THESE.

1. these new
2. those
3. those black
4. several black
5. that red
6. this old
7. ten
8. ten red
9. several
10. a few
11. a very good
12. three
13. three good
14. this green
15. five new
16. a new
17. some good
18. a few other
19. some other
20. a big
21. this big
22. this
23. these
24. those new

EXERCISE 3b.2. (To practice ONE, SOME, ONES, etc., in statements with THERE IS, THERE ARE.) Answer the following questions with THERE IS, THERE ARE. Use the expressions ONE, SOME, A LOT, GOOD ONES, etc., in the answers. For example:

Where can I find some matches?
    THERE ARE SOME IN THE OTHER ROOM.
Where can we find a pencil?
    THERE'S ONE ON MY DESK.
Where can I get a used car?
    THERE'S A GOOD ONE NEAR MY HOUSE.
Where can I get some paper?
    THERE'S A LOT ON THE TABLE.
Where can I find some apples?
    THERE ARE SOME FRESH ONES IN THE BASKET.

1. Where can I find a restaurant?
2. Where can I see a movie?
3. Where can we hear lectures?
4. Where can I go to a program on Friday?
5. Where can I get some good books?
6. Where can I find a few poems?
7. Where can I find a short story?
8. Where can I find a pen?
9. Where can I find a book about European geography?
10. Where can I buy a new suit?
11. Where can I find a telephone?
12. Where can I find a comfortable chair?
13. Where can I get some shoes?
14. Where can I get a lot of money quickly?

KEY EXAMPLES OF LESSON XIV

1a. IT's important for us to speak English.
1b. THERE's a book on the table.
2. The work OF A MACHINE.
    THIS MAN'S work.
3a. WHOSE book is this?
    It's JOHN'S. YOURS is on the table.
3b. Do you need some shirts?
    Yes, I need a blue ONE and several white ONES.

Lesson XV

1a. JOHN IS LIKE HIS FATHER.
   [Comparisons with LIKE, THE SAME AS, DIFFERENT FROM]
1b. JOHN IS THE SAME HEIGHT AS PAUL. HE IS AS TALL AS PAUL.
   HE WALKS AS SLOWLY AS PAUL.
   [Comparisons with THE SAME. . .AS, AS. . .AS]
2. JOHN IS OLDER THAN PAUL. HE IS MORE INTERESTING THAN
   PAUL.
   [Distribution of -ER THAN and MORE. . .THAN]
3. JOHN IS THE OLDEST. HE IS THE MOST INTERESTING.
   [Distribution of THE. . .-EST and THE MOST. . .]

1a. Key example: John is LIKE his father.

Observe LIKE, THE SAME AS, DIFFERENT FROM.

Situation: My coat is brown. Your coat is brown.

Pattern:

My coat	is	LIKE	yours.
John	looks	LIKE	his father.
He	works	LIKE	a horse.

Situation: Nine times three is twenty-seven. (9 x 3 = 27)
            Three times nine is twenty-seven. (3 x 9 = 27)

Pattern:

Nine times three	is	THE SAME AS	three times nine.
My pronunciation book is		THE SAME AS	yours.
This book	costs	THE SAME AS	that one.

Situation: John's coat is large. Mary's coat is small.

Pattern:

John's coat	is	DIFFERENT FROM	Mary's.
A notebook	is	DIFFERENT FROM	a book.
Mary	dresses	DIFFERENTLY FROM	Jane.

COMMENTS

(1) Use LIKE, THE SAME AS, DIFFERENT(LY) FROM to compare two
    persons or things.
(2) Use AS (not THAT) in THE SAME AS. Use FROM (not OF) in
    DIFFERENT FROM.*

---

*You will also hear: "A notebook is DIFFERENT THAN a book."

PRACTICE

EXERCISE 1a.1. (To use the expressions of comparison LIKE, THE SAME AS, DIFFERENT FROM.) Listen to the descriptive statements. Then form statements with LIKE, THE SAME AS, and DIFFERENT FROM. For example:

> My house is large and white and yours is too. There is no difference.
> > MY HOUSE IS THE SAME AS YOURS.
> John's book and Mary's book are very similar. All parts of the books are similar.
> > JOHN'S BOOK IS LIKE MARY'S.
> This book is red. It's very small. That one is black. It's big.
> > THIS BOOK IS DIFFERENT FROM THAT ONE.

1. These shoes are size ten. Those are size ten too. There is no difference.
2. My coat is warm and yours is too. Both coats are blue.
3. John is intelligent and his father is too.
4. He works hard and a horse does too.
5. Four times three is twelve and three times four is too.
6. My family consists of four sons, but yours consists of two daughters.
7. This radio is small and cheap, but that one is large and expensive.
8. Mary's address is 110 North Division Avenue. Jane lives there too.
9. John's address is 1014 East Washington Street. Paul's address is 1410 West Jefferson Street.
10. John is short. He's always happy. Paul is tall and he's seldom happy.
11. My pen is blue. His pen is green.
12. Paul looks intelligent. His father looks intelligent.
13. Your father works very hard and mine does too.
14. Paul's eyes are blue and his mother's are too.

1b. Key examples: John is THE SAME HEIGHT AS Paul. He is AS TALL AS PAUL.

Observe the words between THE SAME and AS, and between AS and AS.

My coat	is	THE SAME	COLOR	AS	yours.
It	is	THE SAME	SIZE	AS	yours.
John	isn't	THE SAME	AGE	AS	Paul.
My coat	is	AS	BROWN	AS	yours.
It	is	AS	LARGE	AS	yours.
John	isn't	AS	OLD	AS	Paul.
Mary	speaks	AS	CLEARLY	AS	John.
The professor	spoke	AS	RAPIDLY	AS	possible.
You	have	AS	MANY BOOKS	AS	John.
You	have	AS	MANY	AS	Paul.
I	work	AS	MUCH	AS	you.

COMMENTS

(1) Use THE SAME. . .AS with words like COLOR, SIZE, AGE (Class 1) not preceded by MANY, MUCH, LITTLE, FEW.

(2) Use AS. . .AS with words like BROWN, LARGE, OLD (Class 3) and like CLEARLY, RAPIDLY (Class 4), and with the quantity words MANY, MUCH, LITTLE, FEW.
Notice that AS is used after all of these. Don't use THAT in this case.

(4) Use AS RAPIDLY AS POSSIBLE. Don't say "the most rapidly possible."

NOTE: The modifiers JUST, ALMOST, EXACTLY, JUST EXACTLY, ALMOST EXACTLY, ABOUT, MORE OR LESS precede LIKE, THE SAME AS, THE SAME. . .AS, and AS. . .AS.

My coat is	JUST	LIKE	yours.
This chair is	ALMOST	THE SAME AS	that one.
My book is	EXACTLY	THE SAME SIZE AS	yours.
John is	JUST EXACTLY	AS TALL AS	Paul.

PRACTICE

EXERCISE 1b.1. (To practice the choice between THE SAME. . .AS and AS. . .AS.) Use the following words with THE SAME. . .AS or AS . . .AS. For example:

length	THIS PENCIL IS THE SAME LENGTH AS THAT ONE.
long	THIS PENCIL IS AS LONG AS THAT ONE.
thickness	THIS BOOK IS THE SAME THICKNESS AS THAT ONE.
thick	THIS BOOK IS AS THICK AS THAT ONE.

price   THIS SUIT IS THE SAME PRICE AS THAT ONE.
big   THIS CHAIR IS AS BIG AS THAT ONE.

1. expensive	9. easy	17. length	24. distance
2. cheap	10. good	18. width	25. far
3. short	11. late	19. quality	26. near
4. quiet	12. color	20. type	27. beautiful
5. quietly	13. price	21. hard	28. age
6. slow	14. size	22. hardness	29. tall
7. slowly	15. height	23. style	30. old
8. serious	16. weight		

EXERCISE 1b.2. (To use THE SAME. . .AS and AS. . .AS in situations of comparison.) Listen to the statements. Combine them to form a statement of comparison. For example:

The color of your suit is blue. The color of mine is blue too.
    YOUR SUIT IS THE SAME COLOR AS MINE.
The size of your suit is thirty-six, but the size of mine is forty.
    YOUR SUIT ISN'T THE SAME SIZE AS MINE.
(or) YOUR SUIT ISN'T AS BIG AS MINE.
Your books are interesting and mine are too.
    YOUR BOOKS ARE AS INTERESTING AS MINE.
John writes carefully and Mary does too.
    JOHN WRITES AS CAREFULLY AS MARY.

1. Mary speaks clearly and John does too.
2. John's height is five feet. Paul's height is five feet.
3. John's weight is 150 pounds. Paul's weight is 150 pounds too.
4. John's age is twenty-four. Paul's age is twenty-two.
5. John speaks rapidly. The professor speaks rapidly.
6. The color of John's hat is gray. The color of the professor's is gray too.
7. My family has two cars. Your family has two cars.
8. Mary is nineteen years old. James is nineteen years old too.
9. The price of the grammar book is three dollars. The price of the vocabulary book is three dollars too.
10. John is big. Paul is big too.
11. Mary is beautiful. Jane is beautiful too.
12. Peter ate three hamburgers. Paul ate three hamburgers too.
13. John works slowly. Paul works slowly too.
14. The quality of this shirt is excellent. The quality of that one is excellent too.

EXERCISE 1b.3. (To use some common expressions with AS. . .AS.) Use the following word groups containing AS. . .AS in statements. For example:

as quick as a wink   JOHN IS AS QUICK AS A WINK.
as hard as a rock   OUR BREAD IS USUALLY AS HARD AS A
                          ROCK.
as sharp as a razor   MY KNIFE IS AS SHARP AS A RAZOR.
as quiet as a mouse   JOHN IS AS QUIET AS A MOUSE.

1. as green as grass   7. as pretty as a picture
2. as red as fire   8. as old as the hills
3. as white as snow   9. as weak as a kitten
4. as sweet as honey   10. as light as a feather
5. as round as a ball   11. as red as a rose
6. as cold as ice   12. as free as the wind

2. Key examples: John is OLDER THAN Paul.
                     He is MORE INTERESTING THAN Paul.

Observe the comparisons with MORE. . .THAN and -ER THAN.

Previous patterns:

| A big car is | expensive. | (Lesson I) |
| You speak | carefully. | (Lesson IX) |

New pattern:

A big car is	MORE	EXPENSIVE		THAN	a small one.
You are	MORE	CAREFUL		THAN	John.
You speak	MORE	CAREFULLY		THAN	John.
You speak	MORE	CLEARLY		THAN	John.
You have	MORE	MONEY		THAN	John.
I have		MORE		THAN	you.
You are		TALL-	-ER	THAN	John.
You are		OLD-	-ER	THAN	Paul.
Paul works		HARD-	-ER	THAN	you.
He is		HAPPI-	-ER	THAN	you.
Mary is		FRIENDLI-	-ER	THAN	Betty.
Your paper is		BETTER		THAN	George's.
His is		WORSE		THAN	yours.

COMMENTS

(1) Use MORE (a) with long words like EXPENSIVE, CAREFUL (Class 3).
             (b) with words like CAREFULLY, CLEARLY (Class 4
                 ending in -LY).
             (c) with words like MONEY, FOOD, BOOKS, FRIENDS
                 (Class 1).
             (d) as substitute for MONEY, FOOD, etc. (Class 1).
(2) Use -ER (a) with words of one syllable like TALL, OLD, HARD
                 (Class 3).
             (b) with BUSY, HAPPY, HEAVY, EASY, LAZY, PRETTY,
                 EARLY, FRIENDLY (Class 3 ending in -Y or in -LY).

(3) Use BETTER as the -ER form of GOOD and of WELL.
Use WORSE as the -ER form of BAD and BADLY.
(4) Use THAN (not THAT) in all these comparisons.

NOTE 1: LESS is the contrary of MORE.

A small car is	LESS expensive than	a big one.
John is	LESS careful than	you.
John speaks	LESS carefully than	you.
John speaks	LESS clearly than	you.
John has	LESS money than	you.
You have	LESS than	I.

NOTE 2: The modifiers MUCH, EVEN, STILL, A LOT, A GREAT DEAL,
SOMEWHAT, A LITTLE, SLIGHTLY, precede MORE EXPEN-
SIVE, MORE CAREFUL, TALLER, etc.

A big car is	MUCH	MORE EXPENSIVE THAN	a small one.
You are	EVEN	MORE CAREFUL THAN	John.
You speak	STILL	MORE CAREFULLY THAN	John.
You are	A LOT	TALLER THAN	John.
You are	A GREAT DEAL	OLDER THAN	John.

NOTE 3: You will sometimes hear IS, DO, DID, CAN, etc., at the end of
the sentences found in Frames 1a, 1b, and 2.

My book is	the same as	yours	IS.
My book is	the same color as	yours	IS.
John is	as tall as	Paul	IS.
John speaks	as rapidly as	I	DO.
John spoke	as rapidly as	I	DID.
John speaks	more rapidly than	I	DO.
John spoke	more rapidly than	I	DID.
John speaks	as rapidly as	he	CAN.

PRACTICE

EXERCISE 2.1. (To practice the choice of MORE. . .THAN and -ER
THAN.) Use the following words in statements with the expressions of
comparison MORE. . .THAN and -ER THAN. For example:

slow	JOHN IS SLOWER THAN PAUL.
slowly	JOHN WALKS MORE SLOWLY THAN PAUL.
interesting	JOHN IS MORE INTERESTING THAN PAUL.

1. old	5. careful	9. important	13. rapidly
2. short	6. carefully	10. busy	14. short
3. good	7. fast	11. cold	15. tall
4. happy	8. successful	12. frequently	

EXERCISE 2.2. (To practice the choice between the expressions of comparison AS. . .AS, and MORE THAN or -ER THAN.) Listen to the statements and form equivalent statements with expressions of comparison. Use the expressions AS. . .AS, MORE. . .THAN or -ER THAN. For example:

John is six feet tall and Paul is too.
    JOHN IS AS TALL AS PAUL.
John is six feet tall. Mary is five feet tall.
    JOHN IS TALLER THAN MARY.
Jane's sister is interesting. Jane is very interesting.
    JANE IS MORE INTERESTING THAN HER SISTER.
This car is costly. The other car is very costly.
    THE OTHER CAR IS COSTLIER THAN THIS ONE.
Mary is interesting and Jane is too.
    MARY IS AS INTERESTING AS JANE.

1. Mr. Black is nice. Mr. Brown is very nice.
2. Mary is happy. Jane is very happy.
3. This lesson is easy. The other one is very easy.
4. The post office is near. The bookstore is very near.
5. Mary talks fast. John talks very fast.
6. Mary speaks rapidly. John speaks very rapidly.
7. This book is expensive. The other one is very expensive.
8. They entered quietly. We entered very quietly.
9. Mr. Brown walks slowly. Mary walks very slowly.
10. Mary is five feet tall and Jane is too.
11. Mary is twenty-two years old and Jane is too.
12. John is happy and Paul is too.
13. John is happy. Jane is very happy.
14. The second lesson was easy. The first one was very easy.
15. The other exercise is difficult. This one is very difficult.
16. The other exercise is difficult and this one is too.
17. This chair is comfortable. That one is very comfortable.
18. A small city is interesting. A large city is very interesting.
19. Mary is friendly. Jane is very friendly.
20. John's car is costly. Paul's car is very costly.

EXERCISE 2.3. (To use some common expressions with -ER THAN.) Use the following expressions with -ER THAN in statements. The meanings of these expressions are equivalent to VERY HARD, VERY SHARP, VERY QUIET, etc. For example:

harder than a rock   OUR BREAD IS HARDER THAN A ROCK.
sharper than a razor MY KNIFE IS SHARPER THAN A RAZOR.
quieter than a mouse JOHN IS QUIETER THAN A MOUSE.

1. greener than grass   3. whiter than snow
2. redder than fire   4. sweeter than honey

5. rounder than a ball
6. colder than ice
7. prettier than a picture
8. older than the hills

9. weaker than a kitten
10. lighter than a feather
11. redder than a rose
12. freer than the wind

3. Key examples: John is THE OLDEST. He is THE MOST INTER-ESTING.

Observe MOST and -EST.

Previous pattern:

| All of these cars are | very | expensive. |

New pattern:

This one is	THE	MOST	EXPENSIVE.
That one is	THE	MOST	BEAUTIFUL.
The small ones go	THE	MOST	RAPIDLY.
The big ones cost	THE	MOST	MONEY.
This one is	THE		BIGG- -EST.
That one is	THE		SMALL- -EST.
These are	THE		BEST.
Those are	THE		WORST.

COMMENTS

(1) Use THE MOST with the same words as MORE (Frame 2): [long words like EXPENSIVE (Class 3); words like CAREFULLY (Class 4) ending in -LY; words like MONEY, FOOD (Class 1); as substitute for MONEY, FOOD, etc. (Class 1).]

(2) Use THE -EST with the same words as -ER (Frame 2): [words of one syllable like TALL, OLD (Class 3); BUSY, HAPPY, etc. (Class 3 ending in -Y or -LY).]

(3) Use BEST as the "-EST form" of GOOD and WELL. Use WORST as the "-EST form" of BAD and BADLY.

(4) Use THE before MOST and before -EST forms.

NOTE: LEAST is the contrary of MOST.

This one is the cheapest.   It is the LEAST expensive.
That one is the oldest.   It is the LEAST beautiful.

PRACTICE

EXERCISE 3.1. (To practice the choice of MOST or -EST.) Produce statements with the following words. Use the forms MOST or -EST. For example:

easy   THIS IS THE EASIEST LESSON.
difficult   THIS IS THE MOST DIFFICULT LESSON.
long   THIS IS THE LONGEST LESSON.
quickly   JOHN ANSWERED THE MOST QUICKLY.

1. long	6. careful	11. easy	16. interesting
2. big	7. carefully	12. easily	17. clearly
3. tall	8. comfortable	13. quietly	18. near
4. beautiful	9. busy	14. expensive	19. fast
5. important	10. rapidly	15. intelligent	20. hard

SUMMARY EXERCISES FOR LESSON XV. 1. Imagine the following situation. You are to compare one tree with several other trees. Use the following words and the expressions of comparison AS. . .AS and SAME . . .AS. For example:

size   THIS TREE IS THE SAME SIZE AS THOSE.
type   THIS TREE IS THE SAME TYPE AS THOSE.
big   THIS TREE IS AS BIG AS THOSE.
tall   THIS TREE IS AS TALL AS THOSE.

1. beautiful	4. old	7. age	10. tall
2. color	5. height	8. big	11. good
3. short	6. shape	9. size	

2. Look at the pictures and listen to the instructions. Form statements with expressions of comparison.

MARY JOHN   PETER   PAUL

For example:

   Tell about John and Peter. Use the word HAPPY.
     JOHN IS HAPPIER THAN PETER.
   Tell about Mary and John. Use the word HAPPY.
     MARY IS AS HAPPY AS JOHN.
   Tell about Paul. Use the word HAPPY.
     PAUL IS THE HAPPIEST.
   Tell about John and Paul. Use the word SLOWLY.
     JOHN IS WALKING MORE SLOWLY THAN PAUL.

1. Tell about John and Mary.   Use the word TALL.
2. Tell about Peter and John.   Use the word TALL.
3. Tell about Mary and Peter.   Use the word SMALL.
4. Tell about John and Paul.   Use the word SHORT.
5. Tell about Paul and John.   Use the word HAPPY.
6. Tell about Paul and Mary.   Use the word RAPIDLY.
7. Tell about Mary and John.   Use the word SLOWLY.
8. Tell about Peter and John.   Use the word FAST.
9. Tell about Paul.   Use the word RAPIDLY.
10. Tell about Paul.   Use the word FAST.
11. Tell about Paul and John.   Use the word OLD.
12. Tell about Mary and Paul.   Use the word YOUNG.
13. Tell about Paul.   Use the word OLD.

3. Look at the pictures and listen to the instructions. Produce statements
with expressions of comparison. Use the patterns of this lesson.

(John bought a 1950 model car   (Mr. White bought   (Mr. Brown
yesterday and Mary did too.)   a 1940 model car.)   bought a 1960
                                                            model car.)

Tell about Mr. White's car and John's car. Use the word OLD.
    MR. WHITE'S CAR IS OLDER THAN JOHN'S.
Tell about Mary's car and Mr. White's car. Use the word RAPIDLY.
    MARY'S CAR GOES MORE RAPIDLY THAN MR. WHITE'S.
Tell about John's car and Mary's car. Use the word MODEL.
    JOHN'S CAR IS THE SAME MODEL AS MARY'S.

1. Tell about Mr. Brown's car and Mr. White's car. Use the word NEW.
2. Tell about Mr. Brown's car and Mr. White's car. Use the word OLD.
3. Tell about Mary's car and John's car.   Use the word OLD.
4. Tell about Mr. Brown's car and Mary's car.   Use the word FAST.
5. Tell about Mr. Brown's car and Mr. White's car. Use the word
                                                        BEAUTIFUL.
6. Tell about Mary's car and John's car.   Use the word
                                                        BEAUTIFUL.
7. Tell about Mr. White's car and John's car.   Use the word
                                                        EXPENSIVE.
8. Tell about John's car and Mary's car.   Use the word
                                                        STYLE.

9. Tell about Mr. White's car and Mr. Brown's car.   Use the word LONG.
10. Tell about Mr. White's car and John's car.   Use the word SHORT.
11. Tell about John's car and Mary's car.   Use the word LONG.
12. Tell about Mr. Brown's car and Mr. White's car.   Use the word NICE.

KEY EXAMPLES OF LESSON XV

1a. John is LIKE his father.
1b. John is THE SAME HEIGHT AS Paul.
He is AS TALL AS Paul.
2. John is OLDER THAN Paul.
He is MORE INTERESTING THAN Paul.
3. John is THE OLDEST.
He is THE MOST INTERESTING.

Lesson XVI

1. A MAN THAT TEACHES IS A TEACHER.
   A MAN THAT I TEACH IS A STUDENT.
   [Included sentences as modifiers of Class 1]
2a. HE CAME WHEN I CAME. HE WAITED FOR TWO HOURS.
   [Distribution of FOR, DURING, WHEN, WHILE]
2b. HE CAME AFTER I LEFT. HE CAME AFTER DINNER.
   [Distribution of BEFORE, UNTIL, AFTER]

1. Key examples: A man THAT TEACHES is a teacher.
   A man THAT I TEACH is a student.

Situation:

JOHN   MARY   MR. KING

Observe the word order of Pattern A and of Pattern B.

Previous pattern:

| John | is a | young | man. | John | sees | Mary. |
| Mr. King | is an | old | man. | Mary | sees | Mr. King. |

New patterns:

	HEAD		MODIFIER		
A	John	is the young MAN	THAT	SEES	MARY.
	John	is the young MAN	THAT IS LOOKING AT MARY.		
B	Mr. King	is the old MAN	(THAT) MARY	SEES.	
	Mr. King	is the old MAN	(THAT) MARY IS LOOKING AT.		

COMMENTS

(1) You may use included sentences (THAT SEES MARY, THAT MARY SEES) to modify words like MAN (Class 1).
(2) The difference in word order between Pattern A and Pattern B indicates an important difference in meaning.

   In Pattern A, "the man (John) sees Mary."
   In Pattern B, "Mary sees the man (Mr. King)."

(3) In Pattern A, THAT is in subject position in the included sentence (THAT SEES MARY).
   In Pattern B, MARY is in subject position in the included sentence (THAT MARY SEES).
(4) See the Illustrative Examples for other words in the positions of THAT in Patterns A and B.

147

ILLUSTRATIVE EXAMPLES OF PATTERN A

The book	THAT	CONTAINS	those exercises	is at the bookstore.
The books	THAT	CONTAIN	those exercises	are at the store.
The books	WHICH	CONTAIN	those exercises	are in the office.
The book	WHICH	CONTAINS	those exercises	is in the library.
The professor	THAT	TEACHES	your class	is from Michigan.
The professors	THAT	TEACH	your class	are very good.
The professor	WHO	TEACHES	your class	is, my friend.
The girl	WHOSE			
	FATHER TEACHES		your class	is in the office.

NOTE: Use THAT for persons and things.
       Use WHICH for things.
       Use WHO for persons.
       (Do not use WHOM in Pattern A)

ILLUSTRATIVE EXAMPLES OF PATTERN B

The student	(THAT)	YOU	VISITED		is feeling fine.
The student	(WHO[M])	YOU	VISITED		is feeling fine.
The books	(THAT)	YOU	ORDERED		came yesterday.
The books	(WHICH)	YOU	ORDERED		came yesterday.
The place	(THAT)	I	LEARNED	ENGLISH	is near here.
The place	(WHERE)	I	LEARNED	ENGLISH	is near here.
The time	(THAT)	I	PRACTICE	ENGLISH	is in the morning.
The time	(WHEN)	I	PRACTICE	ENGLISH	is in the morning.
The student	WHOSE				
	FATHER	YOU	VISITED		is in the office.

Observe these informal statements:

The man	(THAT)	I	TALKED	TO	is from Cuba.
He's the man	(THAT)	WE	TALKED	ABOUT.	
This is					
the house	(THAT)	I	LIVE	IN.	
This is					
the book	(THAT)	JOHN	WAS		
			LOOKING	AT.	

Now observe these more formal statements with the same meanings:

The man	TO WHOM I	TALKED	is from Cuba.
He's the man	ABOUT		
	WHOM	WE	TALKED.
This is the			
house	IN WHICH I	LIVE.	
This is the			
book	AT WHICH JOHN	WAS LOOKING.	

NOTE: EVER may mean "in all time" when it is used after -EST forms in this pattern.

> John is the man that I saw.
> John is the biggest man that I EVER saw.
> John is the biggest man that EVER entered this room.
> The best book that I EVER read was an old one.

PRACTICE

EXERCISE 1.1. (To contrast included sentence Patterns A and B at the end of statements.) Listen to the statements and combine them by using an included sentence. For example:

> I know the boy. The boy spoke to you.
> I KNOW THE BOY THAT SPOKE TO YOU.
> I know the boy. You spoke to the boy.
> I KNOW THE BOY THAT YOU SPOKE TO.
> I saw the man. The man helped us.
> I SAW THE MAN THAT HELPED US.
> I saw the man. We helped the man.
> I SAW THE MAN THAT WE HELPED.

1. I read the book. The book describes our federal government. A
2. I read the book. You described the book. B

3. This is the building. The building is 500 years old. A
4. This is the building. We like the building. B

5. Mr. Brown is the man. The man spoke to you. A
6. Mr. White is the man. You spoke to the man. B

7. I read the book. The book tells about the history of medicine. A
8. I read the book. You told me about the book. B

9. This is the exercise. The exercise is the most important. A
10. This is the exercise. We must write the exercise. B

11. I saw the man. The man wrote the book. A
12. I saw the man. You described the man. B

EXERCISE 1.2. (To produce included sentence Pattern B in various positions.) Listen to the statement and the question. Answer the question and include the information of the statement in the answer, or add appropriate information. For example:

> Mary sang a song. Was it beautiful?
> THE SONG THAT MARY SANG WAS BEAUTIFUL.
> You heard the program. Did you like it?
> I LIKED THE PROGRAM THAT I HEARD.
> You listened to the program. Did you like it?
> I LIKED THE PROGRAM THAT I LISTENED TO.

Paul visits a class. How many students does the class have?
   THE CLASS THAT PAUL VISITS HAS A LOT OF STUDENTS.
I visited the boy's home. Did you meet the boy?
   I MET THE BOY WHOSE HOME YOU VISITED.

1. John lives in a new house. Is this the house?
2. John lives in a new house. Where is it?
3. I bought the man's dog. Do you know the man?
4. I met the boy's father. Did you talk to the boy?
5. I am studying a famous writer's book. Do you know the writer?
6. That is the boy's book. Do you know the boy?
7. John described the beautiful park. Did you see it?
8. The teacher pronounced the words. Did you repeat them?
9. You read the book. Was it interesting?
10. I saw the letter. Was it from your mother?
11. I described the book. Did you read it?
12. I spoke to the boy. Do you know him?
13. I spoke about the man. Do you know him?
14. Professor Brown wrote the book. How much does it cost?
15. Professor Brown wrote the book. Should I buy it?

EXERCISE 1.3. (To practice included sentence Patterns A and B.)
Listen to the statement and question. Answer the question or add
appropriate information. Include the information of the statement in
your answer. For example:

   The boy spoke to me. Do you know the boy?
      NO, I DON'T KNOW THE BOY THAT SPOKE TO YOU.
   I spoke to the boy. Do you know the boy?
      YES, I KNOW THE BOY THAT YOU SPOKE TO.
   The car stopped at your house. Did you see the car?
      YES, I SAW THE CAR THAT STOPPED AT MY HOUSE.
   John bought a car. Did you see the car?
      NO, I DIDN'T SEE THE CAR THAT JOHN BOUGHT.

1. The book describes the government of my country. Did you read
   the book? A
2. Professor Black described the book. Did you read the book? B
3. The building is 500 years old. Is this the building? A
4. Professor Black likes the building. Is this the building? B
5. The man spoke to you. Is Mr. Brown the man? A
6. You spoke to the man. Is Mr. White the man? B
7. The book tells about the history of medicine. Did you read the
   book? A
8. I told you about the book. Did you read the book? B
9. The exercise is the most important. Should we omit the exercise? A
10. We practice the exercises. Do we usually forget the exercises? B
11. The man wrote the book. Did you see the man? A
12. I described the man. Did you see the man? B

13. The girl speaks French. Did you meet the girl? A
14. The boy lives in this house. Do you know the boy? A
15. The boy's father lives in this house. Do you know the boy? B
16. The girl's father is a lawyer. Do you know the girl? B
17. The professor teaches your class. Does he want to talk to me? A
18. Some problems are too difficult for you to do. Do you have some problems? A
19. The professor's daughter is in our class. Is he the professor? B
20. The doctor's work is very prominent in your country. Is he the doctor? B
21. The boy's father is living in Europe. Did you talk to the boy? B
22. The students work hard. Is it easy to teach the students? A

EXERCISE 1.4. (To practice Patterns A and B.) Answer the questions and add the information contained in the statement. For example:

> The girl spoke to me. Where is she from?
>   THE GIRL THAT SPOKE TO YOU IS FROM NEW YORK.
> The man has the papers. Who is he?
>   THE MAN THAT HAS THE PAPERS IS MR. BROWN.

1. The professors teach your class. Where are they? A
2. The books need new covers. How much do they (those books) cost? A
3. The student can speak five languages. Who met him? A
4. I need a book. How much does it cost? B
5. A room is big enough for two people. Who found it? A
6. The knife is sharp enough to cut this. Who has it? A
7. The professor teaches your class. Where is he? A
8. The books contain these exercises. Where are they? A

EXERCISE 1.5. (To produce the included sentence patterns in free composition.) Listen to the statements. Repeat them and add additional information that will identify OPERATION, ROOM, etc. For example:

> The operation was successful.
>   THE OPERATION THAT DR. GREEN DESCRIBED WAS SUCCESS-
>   FUL.
> The room is cheerful.
>   THE ROOM THAT I STUDY IN IS CHEERFUL.
> The doctor is my brother.
>   THE DOCTOR THAT GAVE THE PRESCRIPTION IS MY BROTHER.
> I know the man.
>   I KNOW THE MAN THAT BOUGHT THE HOUSE.
> This is the house.
>   THIS IS THE HOUSE THAT HE BOUGHT.
> Mr. Black is the man.
>   MR. BLACK IS THE MAN THAT SOLD THE HOUSE.

1. I want to speak to the <u>man</u>.
2. I met a <u>professor</u>.
3. I bought a <u>book</u>.
4. Let's go to a <u>store</u>.
5. I must go to a <u>university</u>.
6. I met a <u>girl</u>.
7. I don't remember the <u>day</u>.
8. The <u>books</u> were expensive.
9. The <u>day</u> was very hot.
10. The <u>lesson</u> is easy.
11. The <u>room</u> is a mile from here.
12. The <u>story</u> is very interesting.
13. The <u>question</u> is an important one.
14. The <u>program</u> was interesting.

2a. Key examples: He came WHEN I CAME. He waited FOR TWO HOURS.

Observe the expressions after FOR and DURING, WHEN and WHILE.

We studied	FOR	TWO HOURS.	
We studied	FOR	EIGHT WEEKS.	
We studied	DURING	THE EVENING.	
We studied	DURING	THE COURSE.	
We studied	WHEN	THE COURSE	BEGAN.
We studied	WHEN	WE	CAME.
We studied	WHILE	THE COURSE	WAS PROGRESSING.
We studied	WHILE	WE	WERE COMING HERE.

COMMENTS

(1) Use FOR with expressions like AN HOUR, TWO HOURS, EIGHT WEEKS, etc.
(2) Use DURING with expressions like THE EVENING, THE COURSE, THE CONCERT, etc.
(3) Use WHEN and WHILE with included sentences like THE COURSE BEGAN, THE COURSE WAS PROGRESSING, etc.

ILLUSTRATIVE EXAMPLES WITH <u>FOR</u> AND <u>DURING</u>

HOW LONG did you study?

We studied FOR	ONE	HOUR.
We studied FOR	TWENTY	MINUTES.
We studied FOR	SEVERAL	DAYS.
We studied FOR	A FEW	MINUTES.
We studied FOR	AN	HOUR.
We studied FOR	A LITTLE	WHILE.
We studied FOR	A LONG	TIME.

WHEN did you study?

We studied DURING   DINNER.
We studied DURING THE PROGRAM.
We studied DURING THE ENTIRE EVENING.
We studied DURING THE AFTERNOON.
We studied DURING THE DAY BEFORE THE EXAMINATION.

NOTE: Use FOR with expressions that indicate number or quantity.
Use FOR in answers to questions with HOW LONG.
Use DURING with expressions that do <u>not</u> indicate number or
quantity.
Use DURING in answers to questions with WHEN.
You may omit FOR. It doesn't change the meaning.
You may not omit DURING.

ILLUSTRATIVE EXAMPLES WITH <u>WHEN</u> AND <u>WHILE</u>

I was studying	WHEN	the phone rang.
I was studying	WHEN	my friends arrived.
I usually study	WHEN	my roommate sleeps.
The phone rang	WHILE	I WAS STUDYING.
My friends arrived	WHILE	I WAS STUDYING.
My roommate sleeps	WHILE	I STUDY.
The phone rang	WHEN	I WAS STUDYING.
My friends arrived	WHEN	I WAS STUDYING.
My roommate sleeps	WHEN	I STUDY.

NOTE: Use WHEN to indicate the occurrence of the action that follows.
Use WHILE to emphasize the duration of the action that follows.
You may use a form of BE + the -ING form of the Class 2 word
to emphasize the duration of the action.
You may use WHEN in all situations. You may use WHILE only
when the action that follows has duration.

PRACTICE

EXERCISE 2.1.   (To use FOR and DURING with expressions of time.)
Use the following expressions in the sentence I WORKED HARD.   For
example:

two hours	I WORKED HARD FOR TWO HOURS.
the summers	I WORKED HARD DURING THE SUMMERS.
several days	I WORKED HARD FOR SEVERAL DAYS.
the course	I WORKED HARD DURING THE COURSE.
a little while	I WORKED HARD FOR A LITTLE WHILE.

1. the night   4. the concert   7. six years   10. two days
2. three weeks   5. a few minutes 8. the day   11. several hours
3. many years   6. the war   9. my vacation 12. the school year

EXERCISE 2.2.   (To use FOR and DURING in answers to questions with
WHEN and HOW LONG.)   Answer the following questions with FOR and
DURING.   For example:

When do you usually study?
>   I USUALLY STUDY DURING THE EVENING.
How long did you study?
>   I STUDIED FOR ONE HOUR.
When did John take a nap?
>   JOHN TOOK A NAP DURING THE LECTURE.

1. When did Mary see John?
2. How long did you work?
3. When did you do it?
4. How long can you work today?
5. When was Mary here?

6. How long are you going to study tonight?
7. When did you go to New York?
8. How long did it rain last night?
9. When did you lose your pen?
10. How long did you practice?

EXERCISE 2.3. (To contrast the structures used with FOR, DURING and WHEN, WHILE.) Complete the following parts of sentences with included sentences or Class 1 words. For example:

He came during
He stayed for
He came when
He came while

HE CAME DURING LUNCH.
HE STAYED FOR THREE HOURS.
HE CAME WHEN I CALLED HIM.
HE CAME WHILE I WAS EATING.

1. He spoke for
2. He studied for
3. He studied during
4. He studied while
5. He entered while
6. He began to study when

7. He worked for
8. He waited for
9. He worked during
10. He was working while
11. I saw him when
12. I talked to him for

2b. Key examples: He came AFTER I LEFT. He came AFTER DINNER.

Observe the expressions after BEFORE, UNTIL, AFTER.			
John arrived	BEFORE	THE COURSE.	
He stayed	UNTIL	SEVEN O'CLOCK.	
He left	AFTER	DINNER.	
He arrived	BEFORE	THE COURSE	BEGAN.
He stayed	UNTIL	WE	WASHED THE DISHES.
He left	AFTER	WE	ATE DINNER.*

*Be especially careful with the word AFTER. It is different from AFTERWARDS. Compare for example,
>   John left AFTER dinner.
>   He arrived at 5 o'clock. AFTERWARDS, (not AFTER) he left.
>   He ate dinner. AFTERWARDS, (not AFTER) he left.

COMMENTS

(1) Use BEFORE, UNTIL, AFTER with THE COURSE, SEVEN O'CLOCK, DINNER, etc. (Class 1 expressions) and with included sentences (THE COURSE BEGAN, etc.).
(2) Never say "before to go," "before to eat breakfast," "after to eat," etc.**

PRACTICE

EXERCISE 2b.1. (To use BEFORE, UNTIL, AFTER with Class 1 words and included sentences.) Answer the questions and use the words BEFORE, UNTIL, AFTER. For example:

Where did you live before you came to the United States?
I LIVED IN MEXICO BEFORE I CAME TO THE UNITED STATES.
Who did you meet after you came to the United States?
I MET MY TEACHERS AFTER I CAME TO THE UNITED STATES.
What did you do after dinner yesterday?
I PLAYED BASEBALL AFTER DINNER.
How long are you going to stay here?
I'M GOING TO STAY UNTIL I GET HOMESICK.
When did you see John?
I SAW JOHN BEFORE THE PROGRAM.
How long are you staying here?
I AM STAYING HERE UNTIL MONDAY.

1. How long are you going to study English?
2. How long did you practice the question patterns?
3. When are you going to play baseball?
4. Are you going to wait until the sun shines?
5. Are you going to wait until it rains?
6. Are you going to wait until you graduate?
7. Are you going to wait until summer?
8. What did you do before you came to the United States?
9. Which languages did you study before you studied English?
10. Which languages did you learn before you studied English?
11. When did you get your first haircut?
12. What did you do after breakfast?
13. What did you do before breakfast?
14. What did you do after you got up this morning?

KEY EXAMPLES OF LESSON XVI

1. A man THAT TEACHES is a teacher.
   A man THAT I TEACH is a student.
2a. He came WHEN I CAME. He waited FOR TWO HOURS.
2b. He came AFTER I LEFT. He came AFTER DINNER.

**You will hear, and you may use, BEFORE GOING, BEFORE EATING, AFTER GOING, AFTER EATING, etc. [BEFORE (AFTER) + the -ING form of Class 2].

Lesson XVII

1. I KNOW WHO TEACHES THE CLASS. I KNOW WHEN HE TEACHES IT.
   [Included sentences with WHO, WHAT, WHEN, etc., in object position]

2. I KNOW (THAT) MR. SMITH TEACHES THE CLASS.
   [Included sentences of independent statement pattern in object position]

1.

Key examples: I know WHO TEACHES THE CLASS. I know WHEN HE TEACHES IT.

Situation:

JOHN   MARY   MR. KING

Observe the word order of Pattern A and of Pattern B.

Previous pattern:

I know	Mary.
I know	Mr. King.

New patterns:

A	I know		WHO	SEES	MARY.
	I know		WHO	IS LOOKING	AT MARY.
B	I know	WHO	MARY	SEES.	
	I know	WHO	MARY	IS LOOKING AT.	

COMMENTS

(1) You may use included sentences with WHO, WHAT, etc., (WHO SEES MARY, WHO MARY SEES, etc.) in object position after Class 2 words like KNOW, REMEMBER, UNDERSTAND, BELIEVE, EXPLAIN, ASK, etc.

(2) The difference in word order between Pattern A and Pattern B indicates an important difference in meaning:

In Pattern A, "A person sees Mary. I know the person (John)."

In Pattern B, "Mary sees a person. I know the person (Mr. King)."

(3) In Pattern A, WHO is in subject position in the included sentence (WHO SEES MARY).

In Pattern B, MARY is in subject position in the included statement (WHO MARY SEES).

(4) See the Illustrative Examples for other words in the positions of WHO in this pattern.

ILLUSTRATIVE EXAMPLES OF PATTERN A

I know	WHO	WAS	HERE.
I know	WHAT	HAPPENED	HERE.
Do you know	WHICH ANSWER	IS	CORRECT?
Please tell me	WHICH	IS	CORRECT.
Do you remember	WHOSE BOOK	WAS	ON THE DESK?
I don't remember	WHOSE	WAS	THERE.
I will ask him	HOW MANY STUDENTS	WENT	ON THE PICNIC.
He can tell me	HOW MANY	WENT.	
Please explain	HOW MUCH MONEY	IS	NECESSARY.
I don't remember	HOW MUCH	IS	NECESSARY.

ILLUSTRATIVE EXAMPLES OF PATTERN B

I remember	WHOM	I	TALKED	TO.
I remember	TO WHOM	I	TALKED.	
I believed	WHAT	HE	TOLD	ME.
Do you understand	WHICH BOOK	I	WANT?	
I won't forget	WHICH	YOU	WANT.	
Please tell me	HOW MANY BOOKS	YOU	NEED.	
Please repeat	HOW MUCH	THEY	WILL COST.	
Do you know	WHAT TIME	IT	IS?	
I can't remember	WHEN	THE TRAIN	LEAVES.	
Please explain	WHERE	BOSTON	IS.	
I can't understand	WHY	YOU	WANT TO GO	THERE.
I don't know	HOW	YOU	WILL GET	THERE.
I would like to know	HOW FAR	IT	IS.	
I learned	HOW OFTEN	JOHN	PRACTICES	ENGLISH.
I found out	HOW LONG	HE	PRACTICES	EVERY DAY.
I wonder	HOW WELL	HE	CAN SPEAK IT	NOW.
I know	HOW DIFFICULT	IT	IS.	

PRACTICE

EXERCISE 1.1. (To practice included sentence patterns after I KNOW, I ASKED, etc.) Listen to the statements and combine them. Use included sentences introduced by WHO, WHICH, HOW MANY, etc. For example:

> He sent books to you. I know how many.
> **I KNOW HOW MANY BOOKS HE SENT TO YOU.**
> He went to New York. I asked how often.
> **I ASKED HOW OFTEN HE WENT TO NEW YORK.**
> One answer is correct. I don't know which.
> **I DON'T KNOW WHICH ANSWER IS CORRECT.**
> A person was here. I didn't see who.
> **I DIDN'T SEE WHO WAS HERE.**

1. He wants a book. I don't remember which.
2. Something was on the table. I don't know what.
3. A pen was on my desk. I don't know whose.
4. Some students came here a year ago. Do you remember how many?
5. He didn't go to Chicago. I asked him why.
6. He visited a person yesterday. I asked him who.
7. His friends had money. He explained how much.
8. He wanted to go to New York. He told me why.
9. Many people become well after they have tuberculosis. I can't guess how many.
10. The doctor helped many people. I can't guess how many.
11. One car is the best. I don't know which.
12. He wanted a book. I don't remember which.

EXERCISE 1.1. (To practice the word order of included sentences after KNOW, ASK, REMEMBER, etc.) Answer the questions with NO, I DON'T KNOW, etc. + an included sentence. Then ask another student the same question. He should answer YES, I KNOW, etc. + an included sentence. For example:

> Tchr: Do you know who he is?
>
> St. A: NO, I DON'T KNOW WHO HE IS.
> DO YOU KNOW WHO HE IS?
>
> St. B: YES, I KNOW WHO HE IS.
>
> Tchr: Do you know where he comes from?
> St. B: NO, I DON'T KNOW WHERE HE COMES FROM. DO YOU KNOW WHERE HE COMES FROM?
> St. C: YES, I KNOW WHERE HE COMES FROM.
>
> Tchr: Do you remember the answer?
> St. C: NO, I DON'T REMEMBER THE ANSWER. DO YOU REMEMBER THE ANSWER?
> St. D: YES, I REMEMBER THE ANSWER.

1. Do you know who came last night?
2. Do you know who I saw last night?
3. Do you know how old he is?
4. Do you know where he is from?
5. Do you know what he said?
6. Do you know how he came?
7. Did you ask him where he went?
8. Did you ask him where his mother is?
9. Did you ask him how his family is?
10. Did you tell him why the doctor operated?
11. Do you know why the lawyer lost the argument?
12. Do you remember what is in the other grammar lesson?
13. Do you remember what Lesson XVI contains?
14. Can you find out how well the students are learning this lesson?
15. Do you remember what the professor explained?
16. Do you know where he lives?
17. Do you know where he is now?
18. Do you know what time it is?

EXERCISE 1.3. (To contrast the word order of questions with the word order of included sentences.) Answer the questions with I DON'T KNOW + an included sentence with WHERE, WHO, WHOSE, etc. For example:

Is he from Chicago or New York?
  I DON'T KNOW WHERE HE IS FROM.
Is he twenty-four or twenty-five years old?
  I DON'T KNOW HOW OLD HE IS.
Did John come or did Paul come?
  I DON'T KNOW WHO CAME.
Did John's hat fall or did Paul's hat fall?
  I DON'T KNOW WHOSE HAT FELL.
Did she meet John's father or Paul's father?
  I DON'T KNOW WHOSE FATHER SHE MET.

1. Is this answer correct or is that answer correct?
2. Was John here or was Paul here?
3. Is he a doctor or is he a lawyer?
4. Did ten people come or did fifteen people come?
5. Was the doctor here or was the lawyer here?
6. Was he here yesterday or last week?
7. Was it 3 o'clock or was it 4 o'clock?
8. Is it forty miles or is it fifty miles to Detroit?
9. Is that Paul or is that John?
10. Were there ten people or were there fifteen people at the party?
11. Does he want a course in English or a course in Geography?
12. Can I buy my books here or in a drugstore?
13. Is your friend in Detroit or is he in New York?
14. Did he come by plane or by ship?

EXERCISE 1.4. (To practice the word order of included sentences after
I DON'T KNOW, DO YOU REMEMBER, etc.) Listen to the question and
the partial response that follows. Complete the response with an included sentence. For example:

    Who is that man? I don't know—
       I DON'T KNOW WHO THAT MAN IS.
    What is the date of the party? I don't know—
       I DON'T KNOW WHAT THE DATE OF THE PARTY IS.
    Where were they? They didn't say—
       THEY DIDN'T SAY WHERE THEY WERE.
    Whose book did he find? Do you remember—
       DO YOU REMEMBER WHOSE BOOK HE FOUND?

1. When is the party? I don't know—
2. How far is Detroit from here? I don't know—
3. What did he say? I don't know—
4. Who did you meet there? Do you remember—
5. Which did he want? Do you remember—
6. What did he say? Do you remember—
7. Who is that man? Do you know—
8. What is his name? Do you know—
9. What are you going to do when you leave the United States? Do
    you know—
10. Where was the concert? Who knows—
11. How many boys were there here? Who knows—
12. What section was he in? Who knows—
13. Why wasn't he there? He didn't say—
14. Why weren't they in class? They didn't say—
15. What did she write? She didn't say—
16. Where were they going? Do you remember—
17. When did Mary arrive? Do you remember—
18. Why did they want to go? Do you remember—
19. How many did you buy? Do you remember—
20. What did he mean? I don't know—
21. What did he find? I don't know—
22. What did he do? I don't know—
23. Where is he from? Do you know—
24. Who is the girl with the blue dress? Do you know—
25. Where is the new student from? Do you know—
26. Where was the fire? Who knows—
27. Why wasn't the bank open? Who knows—
28. Where is he from? I don't remember—
29. How old is he? Do you know—
30. What is his profession? He didn't say—
31. Why was he late? I can't imagine—
32. When is he leaving? I'm not sure—
33. Where is he going? Ask him—
34. What time is it? I don't have any idea—

35. How tall is the Empire State Building? I forgot—
36. What did he lose? I don't know—
37. What did he buy? I don't know—
38. What did he choose? I don't know—
39. What is that? Do you know—
40. Whose book is that? Do you know—
41. How much time is there? Do you know—
42. What is the population of New York? Can you tell me—
43. What is he laughing at? Tell me—
44. What does he want? Ask him—
45. How much does it cost? Guess—
46. What does this word mean? Will you tell me—
47. How old is he? Do you know—
48. How far is it? Do you know—
49. Where is the bus station? Do you know—
50. What time is it? Do you know—
51. What did he sing? I don't know—
52. What did he leave? I don't know—
53. What did he tell them? I don't know—
54. What did he eat? I don't know—
55. How many students are there in the English course? Who can tell
    me—
56. What did John say? Can you remember—
57. How much did it cost? Do you know—
58. What did he say? I can't remember—
59. Where is the post office? Can you tell me—
60. Where is the Health Service? I don't know—
61. Where can I buy some towels? Can you tell me—
62. Where can I buy a good fountain pen? Can you tell me—
63. Where can I buy some flowers? Do you know—
64. What did he want? I don't know—
65. Where did he go? Do you remember—
66. Where was the lecture? Who knows—

2.   Key example: I know (THAT) MR. SMITH TEACHES THE CLASS.

Situation:

JOHN   MARY   MR. KING

Observe the included statements.

Previous patterns:

| I know | | | who | sees | | Mary. |
| I know | | who(m) | Mary | sees. |

New Pattern:

I know	(THAT)	JOHN	SEES	MARY.
I know	(THAT)	JOHN	IS LOOKING AT	MARY.
I know	(THAT)	MARY	SEES	MR. KING.
I know	(THAT)	MARY	IS LOOKING AT	MR. KING.

COMMENTS

(1) You may use an included sentence that is like an independent state-
    ment in this pattern.

(2) You may use or omit THAT in this pattern. The meaning is the
    same.

(3) Never use an included statement after WANT or LIKE. Never say
    "I want that John go" or "I like that John go." Say "I want John
    to go" and "I (would) like John to go." (See Lesson XIII)

(4) Never say "I think to go." Say "I think (that) I'll go," or, "I think
    (that) I'm going to go."

PRACTICE

EXERCISE 2.1. (To practice included sentences as objects after I
THINK.) Answer the questions with I THINK + an included statement.
For example:

Is he interesting?	I THINK HE'S INTERESTING.
Should we go?	I THINK WE SHOULD GO.
Did it rain yesterday?	I THINK IT RAINED YESTERDAY.
How did John come?	I THINK HE CAME BY BUS.

1. When did John come?
2. What did he go to the store for?
3. Why is he learning English?
4. How long did he speak?
5. How far is it to the post office?

6. Where is my hat?
7. Where is the bank?
8. How often must I take this medicine?
9. May I ask questions during the lecture?
10. Is this answer correct?
11. Are there some doctors in the Institute?
12. Is it early?
13. Are we late?
14. Can you answer his questions?

EXERCISE 2.2. (To compose sentences with included sentences in object position after I THINK, I IMAGINE, etc.) Answer the questions about the following situations. Other students may produce further responses about each situation. For example:

John came to class thirty minutes late. What do you imagine?
    I IMAGINE HE'S TIRED.
    I IMAGINE HIS CLOCK STOPPED.
    I IMAGINE HE SLEPT TOO LONG.
John came to class thirty minutes late. What do you know?
    I KNOW THE TEACHER WAS ANGRY.
    I KNOW HE FEELS BAD ABOUT IT.
John came to class thirty minutes late. What do you think?
    I THINK HE SHOULD COME EARLIER TOMORROW.
    I THINK IT'S BAD TO COME LATE.

A. John came to class with five hundred dollars in his pocket.
    1. What do you imagine?

B. Henry Smith met Helen Brown in 1925. He married her in 1935. He's usually a very quiet and good man. He came home at 5 P.M. every afternoon for more than twenty years. Last night he came home at 7 P.M. Mrs. Smith said, "Goodby, I'm going to my mother."
    2. What do you imagine?
    3. What do you think?
    4. What does Mrs. Smith probably think?
    5. What does her mother think?
    6. What does Mr. Smith think?
    7. What do you believe?

C. You agreed to meet your friend at the theater at 3 o'clock. You went to the theater at 3 o'clock but your friend wasn't there.
    8. What do you think?
    9. What do you hope?

D. Answer these questions according to your opinion.
    10. How many people do you think there are in the state of New York?
    11. How many people would you guess there are in the state of Nevada?
    12. How often do you suppose we can vote in local, state, and federal elections in a period of ten years?

13. How far do you think it is to Detroit?
14. What do you think you can buy in a drugstore?

EXERCISE 2.3. (To contrast structures after WILL, CAN, etc., HAVE, WANT, etc., and THINK, BELIEVE, etc.) Use the following words in statements that begin with the name of a student in the class. After WILL, CAN, etc., use the single form of a Class 2 word; after HAVE, WANT, etc., use TO + STUDY, WORK, etc.; after THINK, BELIEVE, etc., produce an included sentence. For example:

must	MR. DORAND MUST GO TO NEW YORK.
wants	MISS GOMEZ WANTS TO STUDY HERE.
thinks	MR. LUCAS THINKS HE WORKS VERY HARD.
knows	MR. PANZA KNOWS HE IS GOING TO STUDY HERE.
doesn't know	MR. BOLANO DOESN'T KNOW I AM HERE.
tries	MISS WORTHY TRIES TO SPEAK ENGLISH.

1. can	6. tries	11. says
2. wanted	7. needs	12. doesn't believe
3. imagines	8. plans	13. doesn't know
4. must	9. thinks	14. doesn't think
5. should	10. believes	15. said

NOTE FOR RECOGNITION: The included sentences in this lesson can also be used in subject position:

I know	WHAT HAPPENED.
It was easy to understand	WHAT HE SAID.
It was obvious	THAT JOHN WAS HAPPY.
WHAT HAPPENED	caused a big discussion.
WHAT HE SAID	was easy to understand.
THAT JOHN WAS HAPPY	was obvious.

KEY EXAMPLES OF LESSON XVII

1. I know WHO TEACHES THE CLASS. I KNOW WHEN HE TEACHES IT.
2. I know (THAT) MR. SMITH TEACHES THE CLASS.

Lesson XVIII

1. I HAVE LIVED IN THE UNITED STATES FOR SEVERAL YEARS NOW.
   [HAVE (HAS) + the -ED/-EN form of a Class 2 word]
2. I HAVE BEEN STUDYING GRAMMAR FOR THIRTY MINUTES NOW.
   [HAVE (HAS) + BEEN + the -ING form of a Class 2 word]
3. I HAD INTENDED TO GO, BUT I HAD AN ACCIDENT.
   [HAD in these patterns]
4. NO, I HAVEN'T.
   [Short answers with these patterns]
5a. WE HAVE MET A GIRL FROM MEXICO TODAY.
   [Irregular Class 2 words with a form after HAVE like the form with YESTERDAY]
5b. WE HAVE BEGUN TO PRACTICE LESSON XVIII TODAY.
   [Irregular Class 2 words with a form after HAVE different from the form with YESTERDAY]

1. Key example: I HAVE LIVED in the United States for several years now.

Observe HAVE STUDIED, HAS STUDIED, etc. Observe the time expressions.

Previous pattern:

I	studied	mathematics last year.

New pattern:

	I	HAVE	STUDIED	mathematics FOR A YEAR NOW.
	John	HAS	STUDIED	algebra FOR TWO YEARS.
	We	HAVEN'T	PRACTICED	that exercise THIS WEEK.
	John	HASN'T	PRACTICED	his speech TODAY.
HAVE	you		STUDIED	mathematics?
HAS	John		PRACTICED	his speech TODAY?

COMMENTS

(1) You can use HAVE (HAS) + the -ED form of the Class 2 word with present time expressions like NOW, TODAY, THIS WEEK, etc., and with "general" time expressions like FOR TWO YEARS. Don't use HAVE + the -ED form with past time expressions like YESTERDAY, LAST WEEK. See the Illustrative Examples for some time expressions that are frequent with this pattern.
(2) Use HAVEN'T, HASN'T as negative forms in this pattern.
(3) Use HAVE, HAS before the first Class 1 word (the subject: YOU, JOHN, etc.) in questions. Never use DO in questions in this pattern.

ILLUSTRATIVE EXAMPLES

Observe the contracted forms.

I	'VE STUDIED	mathematics.	He	'S STUDIED	history.
You	'VE STUDIED	chemistry.	She	'S STUDIED	literature.
We	'VE WORKED	very hard.	It	'S RAINED	a lot this spring.
They	'VE PRACTICED	this lesson.	John	'S OPENED	the windows.
The boys	'VE WALKED	a long way.			

Observe the time expressions.

Tomás	HAS	LIVED	in the United States	FOR THREE MONTHS.
He	'S	ATTENDED	this school	FOR ONE MONTH.
He	'S	PRACTICED	this exercise	FOR AN HOUR NOW.
He	'S	STUDIED	English	FOR A LONG TIME.
He	'S	ATTENDED	this school	SINCE LAST MONTH.
He	'S	STUDIED	hard	SINCE THE DAY HE CAME.
He	'S	LIVED	in the dormitory	SINCE THE COURSE BEGAN.
He	'S	ENJOYED	his work	EVER SINCE HE CAME HERE.
He	'S ALWAYS	LIKED	to study.	
He	'S	STUDIED		ALL NIGHT.
He	'S OFTEN	STUDIED	here.	

NOTE: You may use HAVE + the -ED form to indicate a situation that began in the past and continues in the present. Time expressions with FOR, SINCE, and ALL are frequent in indications of these situations.

We	'VE	COMPLETED	seventeen lessons	SO FAR.
We	'VE	PRACTICED	all the exercises	SO FAR.
I	'VE	PRACTICED	ten exercises	THIS MORNING.
Mary	'S	STUDIED	Lesson XVII	RECENTLY.
John	'S JUST	OPENED	the window.	
Mary	'S	OPENED	the door.	
They	'VE OFTEN	HELPED	the teacher.	

NOTE: You may use HAVE + the -ED form to indicate an action that is completed at the present time. Time expressions like SO FAR and RECENTLY are frequent in indications of these actions. HAVE + JUST + the -ED form indicates an action that was completed only a very short time ago.

PRACTICE

EXERCISE 1.1. (To contrast the use of -ED forms with past time expressions [LAST WEEK, etc.] and HAVE + -ED forms with present time expressions [NOW, etc.].) Substitute the following words in the statement, I HAVE PRACTICED FOR THREE HOURS. Use HAVE + -ED forms whenever possible. Do not use this pattern with past time expressions. For example:

I have practiced for three hours.

now	I HAVE PRACTICED FOR THREE HOURS NOW.
last night ·	I PRACTICED FOR THREE HOURS LAST NIGHT.
before I came here	I PRACTICED FOR THREE HOURS BEFORE I CAME HERE.

1. now
2. last week
3. last Monday
4. now
5. yesterday
6. before breakfast

Continue the substitutions in the statement, HE HAS COMPLETED HIS WORK. For example:

He has completed his work.

now	HE HAS COMPLETED HIS WORK NOW.
last night	HE COMPLETED HIS WORK LAST NIGHT.

7. now
8. last week
9. last Monday
10. now
11. yesterday
12. before breakfast

Produce further substitutions in the statement, THEY HAVE TRIED TO SPEAK ONLY ENGLISH. For example:

They have tried to speak only English.

since they came here	THEY HAVE TRIED TO SPEAK ONLY ENGLISH SINCE THEY CAME HERE.
last night	THEY TRIED TO SPEAK ONLY ENGLISH LAST NIGHT.

13. recently
14. so far
15. for three weeks now
16. last year
17. last month
18. since they arrived
19. for a long time now
20. yesterday

EXERCISE 1.2. (To use HAVE + the -ED form to express a situation
which began in the past and continues in the present.) Listen to the statements. They tell about situations that began in the past and continue to
the present. Give the same information using HAVE + the -ED form.
For example:

I began to live in the dormitory in January and I live there now.
  I'VE LIVED IN THE DORMITORY SINCE JANUARY.
I liked American movies in 1950 and I like them now.
  I'VE LIKED AMERICAN MOVIES SINCE 1950.
I wanted to see this movie a long time ago and I want to see it now.
  I'VE WANTED TO SEE THIS MOVIE FOR A LONG TIME.
I wasn't talking to John three hours ago and I'm not talking to him now.
  I HAVEN'T TALKED TO JOHN FOR THREE HOURS.

1. I needed a new coat four years ago and I need one now.
2. I wanted to visit Hollywood when I came to the United States and I
   want to visit it now.
3. I wasn't smoking a pipe when I entered and I'm not smoking a pipe
   now.
4. I didn't study English during the first part of this week and I'm not
   studying English now.
5. I didn't smoke last Monday and I'm not smoking now.
6. I didn't try to swim last Monday and I'm not trying to swim now.
7. I respected his opinions when I was fifteen or sixteen years old and
   I respect his opinions now.
8. I liked fish when I was a child and I like it now.
9. I didn't like to drive when I came here and I don't like to drive now.
10. I disliked mathematics in 1950 and I dislike it now.
11. I preferred history at the beginning of the course and I prefer it now.
12. I liked languages ten years ago and I like them now.

EXERCISE 1.3. (To practice HAVE + the -ED form in situations with
completed action.) Listen to the situation in present time. Produce a
statement with HAVE + the -ED form that gives information from the
past which is related. Use the Class 2 word which is given after the
statement. For example:

She is a good leader. organize
  SHE HAS ORGANIZED MANY ACTIVITIES ON THE CAMPUS.
Tom has good pronunciation. practice
  HE HAS PRACTICED MANY HOURS IN THE LAB.
Jim is a good speaker. talk
  HE HAS TALKED BEFORE MANY GROUPS.

1. Mary is a fast reader. finish
2. We want a ticket to the game. ask
3. Mr. Benitos is a famous singer. perform
4. I like to look at paintings. visit
5. Jane is an excellent student. receive
6. John is a hard worker. earn

7. My friend is a poor student.   fail
8. I like football very much.   watch
9. My sister is good at languages.   learn
10. Betty worries about her mother.   telephone
11. The students are grateful.   thank
12. Bob feels hot.   open

2.

Key example: I HAVE BEEN STUDYING grammar for thirty
minutes now.

Observe HAVE BEEN STUDYING, etc.

Previous pattern:

We	have	studied	algebra.

New Pattern:

We	HAVE	BEEN STUDYING	mathematics.
Mary	HAS	BEEN STUDYING	English.
We	HAVEN'T	BEEN STUDYING	very hard.
Mary	HASN'T	BEEN STUDYING	carefully.
HAVE	you	BEEN STUDYING	mathematics?
HAS	Mary	BEEN STUDYING	carefully?

COMMENTS

(1) Use HAVE (HAS) + BEEN + the -ING form of a Class 2 word to
emphasize the continuation of an action from some time in the
past until the present time. The previous pattern (HAVE + the
-ED form) does not emphasize this continuation.
(2) Use HAVEN'T, HASN'T as negative forms in this pattern.
(3) Use HAVE, HAS before the first Class 1 word (the subject: WE,
MARY, etc.) in questions.

ILLUSTRATIVE EXAMPLES

I	'VE BEEN STUDYING		FOR TWO HOURS NOW.
John	HAS BEEN WORKING		SINCE 8 A.M.
He	'S BEEN WRITING	his homework	SINCE 8 A.M. NOW.
You	'VE BEEN SINGING		FOR HALF AN HOUR SO FAR.
They	'VE BEEN WALKING		ALL MORNING.
It	'S BEEN RAINING		ALL DAY.
These birds	'VE BEEN RETURNING		EVERY YEAR FOR A LONG TIME.
I	'VE BEEN VISITING	my friend	REGULARLY.
We	'VE BEEN LOOKING UP	new words	ALL DAY.

NOTE: The same type of time expressions are frequent with this
pattern as with the pattern of Frame 1.

PRACTICE

EXERCISE 2.1. (To use HAVE, HAS + BEEN + the -ING form of Class 2 words.) Form a question with WHAT, WHERE, WHEN or WHY. Use HAVE or HAS + BEEN + the -ING form of the Class 2 word. Another student answers the question with a long answer. For example:

talk	WHAT HAS THE TEACHER BEEN TALKING ABOUT? HE'S BEEN TALKING ABOUT GRAMMAR.
study	WHERE HAVE YOU BEEN STUDYING? I'VE BEEN STUDYING AT THE LIBRARY.
go	WHY HAVE YOU BEEN GOING TO TOWN? I'VE BEEN GOING TO TOWN TO SEE MY UNCLE.
see	WHEN HAS BILL BEEN SEEING JIM? BILL HAS BEEN SEEING JIM IN THE AFTERNOON.

1. work	6. sing	11. visit
2. play	7. swim	12. try to learn
3. practice	8. read	13. plan to go
4. eat	9. sleep	14. intend to do
5. write	10. make	

EXERCISE 2.2. (To contrast the use of HAVE + the -ED form with the use of HAVE BEEN + the -ING form.) Listen to the statement about an action in progress at the present time. Use HAVE + the -ED form to tell about a similar action which is completed at the present time. Another student uses HAVE BEEN + the -ING form to emphasize the continuation of a similar action from some time in the past until the present. For example:

I am working on Lesson XVII.
I HAVE WORKED ON LESSON XVII NOW.
I HAVE BEEN WORKING ON LESSON XVII FOR AN HOUR.
John is talking to the teacher.
I HAVE TALKED TO THE TEACHER TODAY.
I HAVE BEEN TALKING TO THE TEACHER SINCE TWO O'CLOCK.
The teacher is explaining a difficult pattern.
THE TEACHER HAS EXPLAINED A DIFFICULT PATTERN TODAY.
HE'S BEEN EXPLAINING A DIFFICULT PATTERN ALL AFTERNOON.

1. I'm studying my lesson.
2. I'm practicing my pronunciation.
3. Bob is arguing with the teacher.
4. We are preparing a song for the program.
5. I am listening to the radio.
6. John is talking to Mary.
7. I'm visiting John in the hospital.
8. You are pronouncing that word incorrectly.
9. I'm waiting for Joe.
10. I'm answering all of the questions correctly.

11. They aren't using the library.
12. Mary is helping to wash the dishes.

3. Key example: I HAD INTENDED to go, but I had an accident.

Observe HAD LEARNED, HAD BEEN WRITING, etc.

Previous patterns:

I	have		studied	mathematics for three years now.
We	have	been	studying	English	since we arrived here.

New pattern:

I	HAD		STUDIED	French	before I began to study English.
We	HADN'T		LEARNED	English	when we came here.
John	HAD	BEEN WRITING		letters	when you entered.
Mary	HADN'T	BEEN STUDYING			until you came.
HAD you			LEARNED	French	before you began to study English?
HAD MARY		BEEN STUDYING			before you came?

COMMENTS

(1) Use HAD + the -ED form of a Class 2 word or HAD + BEEN + the -ING form of a Class 2 word to indicate occurrences in a portion of time which ended in the past. HAD BEEN + the -ING form emphasizes the continuation of the process during this portion of time. HAD + the -ED form doesn't stress this continuation or duration.
(2) I'D, YOU'D, HE'D, SHE'D, IT'D, WE'D, THEY'D are the contractions.

EXERCISE 3.1. (To use HAD + the -ED form to express an action completed in the past and which occurred previous to another situation.) Imagine that you left your country three weeks ago. Answer the questions and tell what you did before you left your country. For example:

When had you prepared your clothes?
I HAD PREPARED THEM A FEW DAYS BEFORE I LEFT.
When had you received your acceptance from this school?
I'D RECEIVED IT A WEEK BEFORE I LEFT.
Where had you learned English?
I'D LEARNED A LITTLE IN MY HIGH SCHOOL BEFORE I LEFT.
Had your teachers explained our educational system to you?
THEY HADN'T EXPLAINED IT COMPLETELY WHEN I LEFT.

1. Had your friends described this country to you?
2. Had your friends described this university to you?
3. Had you practiced English intonation?

4. In which universities had you tried to get an acceptance?
5. When had you received your acceptance?
6. Who had helped you with other things?
7. How had you learned a few words in English?
8. When had you learned them?
9. Where had you learned them?
10. How long had you practiced English intonation?
11. Where had you practiced it?
12. Where had you learned English pronunciation?
13. How long had you studied it?
14. How well had you learned English grammar?

EXERCISE 3.2. (To use HAD BEEN + the -ING form to express a situation in progress and completed before another action.) Answer the questions negatively, and complete the statement with BUT . . . HAD BEEN + the -ING form. For example:

What were you doing when John came to see you?
I WASN'T DOING ANYTHING, BUT I HAD BEEN WRITING LETTERS BEFORE.
What were you doing while it rained yesterday?
I WASN'T DOING ANYTHING, BUT I HAD BEEN WALKING IN THE PARK FOR SEVERAL HOURS BEFORE IT RAINED.
What were you doing when I entered a short time ago?
I WASN'T DOING ANYTHING, BUT I HAD BEEN STUDYING BEFORE THAT.

1. What were you doing when I saw you last night?
2. What were you doing when John came?
3. What were you doing when the war began?
4. What were you doing when the director began to speak?
5. What was Mr. X doing when the director began to speak?
6. What was he doing when you went to the factory?
7. What was he doing when you returned from the factory?
8. What were you doing when Dr. Brown arrived?
9. What was John doing when the president arrived?
10. What were they doing when the vacation ended?
11. What were you doing when the concert began?
12. What was he doing when they called him up on the telephone?

4. Key example: Have you studied in France? No, I HAVEN'T.

Observe the short answers.

QUESTIONS	ANSWERS

Previous patterns:

| Are you visiting your friend? | Yes, I am. |
| Did you visit the new hospital? | Yes, I did. |

New pattern:

Have you visited the new hospital?	Yes, I	HAVE.
Have you been visiting your friend?	Yes, I	HAVE.
Have the students been working?	No, they	HAVEN'T.
Has the class started?	No, it	HASN'T.
Had you planned to take the course (before you came)?	Yes, I	HAD.
Had you studied French (before you came here)?	No, I	HADN'T.

COMMENT

HAVE, HAS, HAD, HAVEN'T, HASN'T, HADN'T complete the short answers to questions beginning with a form of HAVE.

PRACTICE

EXERCISE 4.1. (To form questions and give short answers with HAVE, HAS, HAD.) Form questions with the following Class 2 words. Use HAVE + the -ED form to express an action completed at the present time and HAD + ED to express an action which occurred before another action. Another student answers the question with a short answer. For example:

learn	HAVE YOU LEARNED THE LESSON?
	YES, I HAVE.
learn. . .before	HAD YOU LEARNED ENGLISH BEFORE YOU LEARNED FRENCH?
	YES, I HAD.
visit	HAS YOUR FRIEND VISITED THE MUSEUM?
	NO, HE HASN'T.
visit. . .before	HAD HE VISITED YOU BEFORE HE CAME HERE?
	NO, HE HADN'T.

1. study. . .before
2. practice
3. practice. . .before
4. walk
5. walk. . .before
6. talk
7. talk. . .before
8. invite
9. invite. . .before
10. try
11. try. . .before
12. ask
13. ask. . .before
14. answer
15. answer. . .before
16. play
17. play. . .before
18. work

19. work. . .before
20. pronounce
21. pronounce. . .before
22. repeat
23. repeat. . .before
24. open
25. open. . .before

26. close
27. close. . .before
28. describe
29. describe. . .before
30. explain
31. explain. . .before

5a. Key example: We HAVE MET a girl from Mexico today.

Observe the forms of the Class 2 words after HAVE.

Previous pattern:

We		worked	very hard		yesterday.
We	have	worked	very hard		today.

New pattern:

We		met	a girl from Brazil	yesterday.
We	HAVE	MET	a girl from Mexico	today.
We		spent	ten dollars	yesterday.
We	HAVE	SPENT	twenty dollars	today.
We		bought	a lot of things	yesterday.
We	HAVE	BOUGHT	a lot of things	today.

COMMENT

Certain "irregular" Class 2 words without an -ED ending have the same form with past time expressions like YESTERDAY and after HAVE. (See Lesson VIII)

ILLUSTRATIVE EXAMPLES

meet	met	HAVE MET	[mɛt]	I saw him in 1948 but we hadn't MET before.
read	read	HAVE READ	[rɛd]	Have you READ Shakespeare's plays?
sit	sat	HAVE SAT	[sæt]	I have SAT here since 8 a.m.
bite	bit	HAVE BIT	[bɪt]	That dog has BIT two children.
find	found	HAVE FOUND	[faund]	I have FOUND three good restaurants.
fight	fought	HAVE FOUGHT	[fɔt]	The two countries had FOUGHT before.
shine	shone	HAVE SHONE	[šon]	The sun hasn't SHONE for two weeks.
hang	hung	HAVE HUNG	[həŋ]	We had HUNG our coats on the wall.
sting	stung	HAVE STUNG	[stəŋ]	It has STUNG.
dig	dug	HAVE DUG	[dəg]	We have DUG for an hour.
win	won	HAVE WON	[wən]	The allies had WON the war before 1946.
bleed	bled	HAVE BLED	[blɛd]	It has BLED for an hour.

sweep	swept	HAVE SWEPT	[swɛpt]	We haven't SWEPT the floor recently.
keep	kept	HAVE KEPT	[kɛpt]	I have KEPT my ticket in my pocket.
feed	fed	HAVE FED	[fɛd]	They have FED the birds for many years.
hold	held	HAVE HELD	[hɛld]	He has HELD his position for 5 years.
feel	felt	HAVE FELT	[fɛlt]	I have never FELT unhappy.
sleep	slept	HAVE SLEPT	[slɛpt]	You've SLEPT for more than two hours.
mean	meant	HAVE MEANT	[mɛnt]	It has MEANT a lot to me to study here.
leave	left	HAVE LEFT	[lɛft]	The students have LEFT.
say	said	HAVE SAID	[sɛd]	I have always SAID that.
hear	heard	HAVE HEARD	[hərd]	I have never HEARD a better lecture.
think	thought	HAVE THOUGHT	[Θɔt]	I haven't THOUGHT about it for a long time.
bring	brought	HAVE BROUGHT	[brɔt]	I was sure you hadn't BROUGHT any books.
buy	bought	HAVE BOUGHT	[bɔt]	I knew you had BOUGHT a new tie.
teach	taught	HAVE TAUGHT	[tɔt]	We supposed you had TAUGHT Lesson XVI.
tell	told	HAVE TOLD	[told]	John thought he had TOLD you the answer.
sell	sold	HAVE SOLD	[sold]	Mary thought you had SOLD your car.
stand	stood	HAVE STOOD	[stʊd]	I had STOOD there before.
under-stand	under-stood	HAVE UNDER-STOOD [əndərstʊd]		I have usually UNDERSTOOD your lectures.
lose	lost	HAVE LOST	[lɔst]	He has LOST his interest in good books.
send	sent	HAVE SENT	[sɛnt]	I haven't SENT a letter for a week.
spend	spent	HAVE SPENT	[spɛnt]	We've SPENT all our money.
lend	lent	HAVE LENT	[lɛnt]	John had LENT us $5 before we left.
make	made	HAVE MADE	[med]	You haven't MADE many mis-takes.
have	had	HAVE HAD	[hæd]	John has HAD his car since 1950.
bend	bent	HAVE BENT	[bɛnt]	They had BENT the aerial before.
build	built	HAVE BUILT	[bɪlt]	They have BUILT a house.
cut	cut	HAVE CUT	[kət]	I had CUT my finger before you came.

put	put	HAVE PUT	[pʊt]	They have just PUT on their coats.
cost	cost	HAVE COST	[kɔst]	It had cost a LOT before.
let	let	HAVE LET	[lɛt]	I've LET John use my book.
set	set	HAVE SET	[sɛt]	I've SET the lamp on the desk.

PRACTICE

EXERCISE 5a.1. (To use irregular Class 2 forms like MET, SPENT, BROUGHT, etc., after a form of HAVE.) Listen to the statement in past time. Add another statement pattern with BUT. . .SINCE. Use HASN'T, HAVEN'T + MET, SPENT, BROUGHT, etc., in the added statement pattern. For example:

> I met Fred last year.
> > I MET FRED LAST YEAR, BUT I HAVEN'T MET HIM SINCE.
> I read Shakespeare last semester.
> > I READ SHAKESPEARE LAST SEMESTER, BUT I HAVEN'T READ HIM SINCE.
> I sat in the first row two weeks ago.
> > I SAT IN THE FIRST ROW TWO WEEKS AGO, BUT I HAVEN'T SAT THERE SINCE.

1. I sent her a letter last week.
2. I spent ten dollars Friday.
3. John lent me five dollars last month.
4. I made a mistake in grammar yesterday.
5. He had two operations last month.
6. My brother cut his finger last week.
7. I put a nickel in the parking meter an hour ago.
8. This book cost four dollars last year.
9. I felt good yesterday.
10. The baby slept two hours last night.
11. On Thursday he meant that we should go.
12. He left a package for me Tuesday.
13. Last month he said that our work was good.
14. I heard Professor Baker lecture Friday.
15. At first I thought the course was easy.
16. Mary brought her notebook to class last week.
17. I bought myself a shirt last summer.
18. I taught English in 1955.
19. The teacher told us a story last week.
20. He sold many hats last week.
21. We understood his lecture Tuesday.
22. His dog bit me last week.
23. I found John in his room two days ago.
24. He stood by the window at two o'clock.
25. They fought for him in the election.
26. The sun shone early this morning.

27. Dan lost his wallet last week.
28. He hung his coat here Monday.
29. He dug in his garden this spring.
30. Our team won the first game.
31. The medication stung my skin at first.
32. His cut bled for an hour.
33. Fred swept his room last month.
34. We kept a record of our income in 1956.
35. They fed us steak last week.
36. They held a party two weeks ago.
37. The antenna bent in the storm last summer.
38. Mr. Rogas built two houses last summer.
39. He let me drive his car last week.
40. He set a swimming record early this year.

5b. Key example: We HAVE BEGUN to practice Lesson XVIII today.

Observe the forms of the Class 2 words after HAVE.

Previous pattern:

| We | | met | a girl from Brazil | yesterday. |
| We | HAVE | MET | a girl from Mexico | today. |

New pattern:

We		began	to study Lesson XVII	yesterday.
We	HAVE	BEGUN	to study Lesson XVIII	today.
We		drank	a lot of milk	yesterday.
We	HAVE	DRUNK	a lot of milk	today.
We		ate	lunch early	yesterday.
We	HAVE	EATEN	lunch early	today.
We		knew	our lessons	yesterday.
We	HAVE	KNOWN	our lessons	today.
We		wore	our old clothes	yesterday.
We	HAVE	WORN	our old clothes	today.
We		spoke	only English	yesterday.
We	HAVE	SPOKEN	only English	today.

COMMENTS

(1) Certain Class 2 words that do not have an -ED ending have a form after HAVE that is different from the form with past time expressions like YESTERDAY.

(2) Class 2 words like BEGIN, DRINK, etc., have a different vowel in the form after HAVE. (BEGIN, BEGAN, BEGUN; DRINK, DRANK DRUNK.)

(3) Class 2 words like EAT, KNOW, etc., have a different vowel and also an -(E)N ending after HAVE. (EAT, ATE, EATEN; KNOW, KNEW, KNOWN.)

(4) Class 2 words like WEAR, SPEAK, etc., have the same vowel in
the form with past time expressions and in the form after HAVE,
but have an -(E)N ending in the form after HAVE.

NOTE: In these lessons, the "-ED/-EN form of the Class 2 word"
means the form after HAVE, like WORKED, MET, BEGUN,
EATEN, WORN, etc.

ILLUSTRATIVE EXAMPLES

come	came	HAVE COME	[kəm]	I have COME to class regularly for 3 weeks.
become	became	HAVE BECOME	[bɪkə́m]	He has just BECOME our new representative.
begin	began	HAVE BEGUN	[bɪgə́n]	I had BEGUN to work before you came.
drink	drank	HAVE DRUNK	[drəŋk]	We have DRUNK a lot of coffee since then.
sing	sang	HAVE SUNG	[səŋ]	We have SUNG that song at every program.
ring	rang	HAVE RUNG	[rəŋ]	These bells have RUNG every Sunday.
sink	sank	HAVE SUNK	[səŋk]	Submarines have SUNK thirty of our ships now.
swim	swam	HAVE SWUM	[swəm]	He has just SWUM across the lake.
run	ran	HAVE RUN	[rən]	I knew you had RUN home.
eat	ate	HAVE EATEN	[itən]	I have just EATEN lunch.
give	gave	HAVE GIVEN	[gɪvən]	I haven't GIVEN the teacher my paper.
see	saw	HAVE SEEN	[sin]	I have SEEN him several times recently.
write	wrote	HAVE WRITTEN	[rɪtən]	I have never WRITTEN him a letter.
take	took	HAVE TAKEN	[tekən]	I have TAKEN books to class.
know	knew	HAVE KNOWN	[non]	I have KNOWN my friend since 1940.
draw	drew	HAVE DRAWN	[drɔn]	I have DRAWN diagrams for five weeks now.
fly	flew	HAVE FLOWN	[flon]	Some airplanes have FLOWN faster than sound.
throw	threw	HAVE THROWN	[Ɵron]	I had THROWN my hat away.
grow	grew	HAVE GROWN	[gron]	He has GROWN very rapidly.
blow	blew	HAVE BLOWN	[blon]	The wind has BLOWN her hair.

ride	rode	HAVE RIDDEN	[rɪdən]	I have never RIDDEN on a horse.
rise	rose	HAVE RISEN	[rɪzən]	The sun had RISEN very rapidly.
drive	drove	HAVE DRIVEN	[drɪvən]	I have DRIVEN this car since 1948.
shake	shook	HAVE SHAKEN	[sĕkən]	I have SHAKEN it well.
fall	fell	HAVE FALLEN	[fɔlən]	Have you ever FALLEN off a horse?
get	got	HAVE GOT(TEN)	[gatən]	I haven't GOTTEN a letter for a month.
forget	forgot	HAVE FORGOTTEN	[fərgatən]	She hadn't FORGOTTEN me when I returned.
tear	tore	HAVE TORN	[tɔrn]	He has TORN his clothes again.
wear	wore	HAVE WORN	[wɔrn]	I haven't WORN my blue suit recently.
swear	swore	HAVE SWORN	[swɔrn]	You have SWORN to protect your country.
steal	stole	HAVE STOLEN	[stolən]	They have STOLEN a car.
freeze	froze	HAVE FROZEN	[frozən]	The water had FROZEN.
lie	lay	HAVE LAIN	[len]	The letter has LAIN there for a week.
speak	spoke	HAVE SPOKEN	[spokən]	I have never SPOKEN at a meeting.
break	broke	HAVE BROKEN	[brokən]	Have you ever BROKEN your arm?
choose	chose	HAVE CHOSEN	[čozən]	I have never CHOSEN a better partner.
do	did	HAVE DONE	[dən]	I remembered that I hadn't DONE my work.
go	went	HAVE GONE	[gɔn]	I haven't GONE to the theater since June.
be	was	HAVE BEEN	[bɪn]	He has BEEN here for two months.

PRACTICE

EXERCISE 5b.1. (To practice the -ED/-EN form of EAT, GIVE, TEAR, etc.) Listen to the statement in past time. Repeat the statement and add another statement with a situation which occurred previously. Use AFTER and HAD + the -ED/-EN form of the Class 2 word to express the previous situation. For example:

He ate his dinner.
    HE ATE HIS DINNER AFTER WE HAD EATEN.
I gave him five dollars.
    I GAVE HIM FIVE DOLLARS AFTER HE HAD GIVEN ME THE BOOK.

I came to the university in June.
I CAME TO THE UNIVERSITY IN JUNE AFTER I HAD COME FROM COLOMBIA.

1. He became president in 1950.
2. I began English this semester.
3. He drank two cups of coffee.
4. He got a bicycle.
5. She forgot her hat.
6. We saw him.
7. He tore his shirt.
8. She wore her new coat.
9. Professor Gabor spoke to us.
10. Jim broke his hand.
11. He wrote to his friend.
12. He chose to study English.
13. He took a course in Latin.
14. He knew me.
15. He did the analysis this afternoon.
16. They went to Chicago.
17. He was a salesman in 1954.
18. We sang a farewell song.
19. They rang for John.
20. The storm sank the lifeboat.
21. He swam to shore.
22. He ran for the office of president.
23. He drew a picture of the church.
24. He swore at the car.
25. They flew to Mexico City.
26. I threw away the coat.
27. He grew tomatoes in his garden.
28. The wind blew down a tree.
29. The sick man lay on his side.
30. They rode by boat to New Orleans.
31. The sun rose over the tree.
32. She drove to New York City.
33. Mrs. Vermada shook the rug out.
34. A burglar stole my typewriter.
35. The water froze in the river.

KEY EXAMPLES OF LESSON XVIII

1. I HAVE LIVED in the United States for several years now.
2. I HAVE BEEN STUDYING grammar for thirty minutes now.
3. I HAD INTENDED to go, but I had an accident.
4. Have you studied in France? No, I HAVEN'T.
5a. We HAVE MET a girl from Mexico today.
5b. We HAVE BEGUN to practice Lesson XVIII today.

Lesson XIX

1. WE ARE ASKED TO SPEAK ONLY ENGLISH.
   [BE + the -ED/-EN form of a Class 2 word]
2. JOHN IS STILL STUDYING ENGINEERING.
   HE HASN'T FINISHED YET.
   [Use of STILL, ALREADY, ANY MORE, YET]
3. JOHN IS BORED. PAUL IS BORING.
   [-ED/-EN and -ING forms as describing words]
4. JOHN IS USED TO SMOKING.
   [BE + USED TO, etc. + -ING forms or Class 1 words]

1. Key example: We ARE ASKED to speak only English.

Observe ARE REPEATED, BEING COMPLETED, BEEN COMPLETED, etc.

Previous pattern:

We		repeat	the conversations every day.

New pattern:

The conversations		ARE	REPEATED	every day.
This building		WAS	COMPLETED	before I left last year.
Many buildings	are	BEING	COMPLETED	now.
That building	was	BEING	BUILT	when I left.
Several buildings	have	BEEN	COMPLETED	this year.
None	had	BEEN	BEGUN	before last year.
That one	is going to	BE	COMPLETED	next year.
The students	should	BE	ENCOURAGED	to speak English.
They usually	want to	BE	TOLD	about our customs.
I		WAS	BORN	in the United States.

COMMENTS

(1) Use a form of BE + the -ED/-EN form of a Class 2 word to indicate that the subject (CONVERSATIONS, BUILDING, etc.) receives the action.
(2) Use I WAS BORN. Never say "I born."

PRACTICE

EXERCISE 1.1. (To use BE + the -ED/-EN form of a Class 2 word.) Convert the statements so that the receiver of the action is in subject position. For example:

The architect completed the building in 1950.
THE BUILDING WAS COMPLETED IN 1950.
Napoleon wrote that letter many years ago.
THAT LETTER WAS WRITTEN MANY YEARS AGO.
We need action now.
ACTION IS NEEDED NOW.
You should answer their questions immediately.
THEIR QUESTIONS SHOULD BE ANSWERED IMMEDIATELY.
We are going to continue our policy in the future.
OUR POLICY IS GOING TO BE CONTINUED IN THE FUTURE.
The student is writing the letter now.
THE LETTER IS BEING WRITTEN NOW.

1. The teacher explained that lesson yesterday.
2. The federal government built this road last year.
3. A construction company finished this building recently.
4. Edison invented the electric light before I was born.
5. Bizet composed the opera "Carmen" in the nineteenth century.
6. The Romans built Rome a very long time ago.
7. Michelangelo painted that picture many years ago.
8. The doctor performed the operation last week.
9. The Egyptians constructed the pyramids many years ago.
10. Controls may reduce the cost of living soon.
11. We must stop inflation now.
12. We must build more hospitals immediately.
13. We should build more houses next year.
14. The doctor is going to perform the operation tomorrow.
15. We found a deposit of manganese last month.
16. The Ministry of Mines announced the discovery of a large deposit of manganese last year.
17. The Mining Association has announced another deposit recently.
18. The Historical Society opened an exhibition yesterday.

2. Key examples: John is STILL studying engineering.
He hasn't finished YET.

Observe STILL, ALREADY, ANY MORE, YET.

<u>Situation</u>: John and Mary came to the United States from South America last year. John hasn't learned much English. Mary speaks English very well now.

<u>Pattern</u>:

John	STILL	speaks		Spanish with his friends.
English		is	STILL	difficult for him.
He	STILL	doesn't speak		English well.
English	STILL	isn't		easy for him.

Mary	doesn't speak	Spanish	ANY MORE.*
English	isn't	difficult for her	ANY MORE.
She	speaks	English very well	ALREADY.
She	has learned	it well	ALREADY.
John	doesn't speak	English well	YET.
He	hasn't learned	much English	YET.

COMMENTS

(1) Use STILL after affirmative forms of BE, but before negative forms of BE. Use STILL before other Class 2 words.
(2) Use ANY MORE, ALREADY, YET at the end of the sentence.
(3) Use ANY MORE and YET in negative sentences. Use ALREADY in affirmative sentences. Use STILL in both negative and affirmative sentences.
(4) STILL indicates that the situation continues the same now as before. ANY MORE indicates that the situation existed before, but doesn't exist now.
(5) ALREADY indicates a time earlier or shorter than expected. YET indicates a time later or longer than expected.

ILLUSTRATIVE EXAMPLES

John is STILL here.
He can STILL speak English.
Paul STILL isn't here.
He STILL can't get up early.
"Has John gone?" "No, he is STILL here."
"Does Mary always speak English now?" "No, she STILL speaks Spanish."
"Has William gone to class?" "No, he is STILL reading the paper in the living room."
The people STILL sat in their seats after the singer finished her program.

---

*ANY LONGER is the same as ANY MORE. You will hear both. For example:
John isn't here ANY MORE.
John isn't here ANY LONGER.

"Are they using a new textbook?" "They were STILL using the old one when I left the university."
"Have you finished your lessons?" "No, I STILL have to write a composition."

Is John STILL here?
Does Mary STILL speak Spanish?
Is William STILL reading the paper?
Are they STILL using the old text book?

John isn't here ANY MORE.
Mary never speaks Spanish ANY MORE.
William isn't reading the newspaper ANY MORE.
They weren't using the old textbook at the university ANY MORE when I left.

John said that he was going to begin to study at nine o'clock; but it is only eight o'clock, and he is ALREADY studying his lessons.
Dinner begins at six-thirty. It is only six o'clock now, and two of the guests have ALREADY come.
We are late; the movie has ALREADY begun.
This has been a very pleasant evening. It is difficult for me to believe that it is ALREADY eleven o'clock.
"Are we still early enough?" "No, the program has ALREADY begun."
I was only two minutes late but Elizabeth was ALREADY impatient.

John said that he was going to begin to study at nine o'clock, but it is ten o'clock now, and he hasn't begun to study YET.
We invited the guests to come at six-thirty, but it is a quarter to seven, and they aren't here YET.
We are early; the movie hasn't begun YET.
"Are we late?" "No, the program hasn't begun YET."
"Is the taxi coming?" "Yes, but I don't see it YET."

PRACTICE

EXERCISE 2.1. (To contrast the use of STILL and ANY MORE.) Listen to the statements which describe a situation in the past and in the present. Summarize the situation by using STILL or ANY MORE. For example:

Mary often played the piano last year. She doesn't play the piano now.
MARY DOESN'T PLAY THE PIANO ANY MORE.
John didn't play the piano before. He doesn't play the piano now.
JOHN STILL DOESN'T PLAY THE PIANO.
Paul played the piano two years ago. He plays the piano now.
PAUL STILL PLAYS THE PIANO.
We needed more practice last month. We need more practice now.
WE STILL NEED MORE PRACTICE.

1. The price was five dollars. The price is five dollars.
2. John was eating breakfast. John is eating breakfast now.

3. Mr. Black was living in New York. Mr. Black isn't living in New York now.
4. Mr. Brown was living in New York. Mr. Brown is living there now.
5. Mr. Black had been living in New York. Mr. Black was living in New York when I left.
6. I wanted to study last night. I want to study now.
7. I tried to study yesterday. I am trying to study now.
8. He attended the university last semester. He doesn't attend the university now.
9. He didn't speak very well last year. He doesn't speak very well now.
10. I wanted him to study before. I want him to study now.
11. They complained about the heat last week. They are complaining now.
12. My father worked there last year. He doesn't work there now.

EXERCISE 2.2. (To contrast the use of ALREADY and YET.) Repeat the following statements and include ALREADY or YET. For example:

It's only eight o'clock and Dr. Brown is here.
   IT'S ONLY EIGHT O'CLOCK AND DR. BROWN IS HERE ALREADY.
The class should begin now, but Mr. Green isn't here.
   THE CLASS SHOULD BEGIN NOW, BUT MR. GREEN ISN'T HERE YET.
It's only 10:55, but the eleven o'clock class has begun.
   IT'S ONLY 10:55, BUT THE ELEVEN O'CLOCK CLASS HAS BEGUN ALREADY.

1. They didn't expect to come early, but they are here.
2. They expected to come yesterday, but they aren't here.
3. I expected them yesterday, but they aren't here.
4. I expected them today, but they haven't come.
5. They had a lot of work, but they have finished.
6. I expected them to go later, but they have left.
7. I expected them to go early, but they haven't left.
8. They had very little work today, but they haven't finished.
9. We have just started to work, but Mr. Appleton is tired.
10. We had just started to work when you came, but Mr. Appleton was tired.
11. I'm waiting for my friend, but he hasn't arrived.
12. These students began to study English a short time ago, but they speak very well.

3.   Key example: John is BORED. Paul is BORING.

Observe the -ED/-EN forms. Observe the -ING forms.

Previous patterns (Lessons I and IV):

John		is	young.		He's	a	young		man.

New pattern:

John	is	TIRED.		He's	a	TIRED	man.
He	's	SURPRISED.		He's	a	SURPRISED	man.
He	's	BORED.		He's	a	BORED	man.
Mary	is	INTERESTED.		She's	an	INTERESTED	girl.
This dish	is	BROKEN.		It's	a	BROKEN	dish.
That dish	is	COVERED.		It's	a	COVERED	dish.
That money	is	STOLEN.		It's		STOLEN	money.
This exercise	is	WRITTEN.		It's	a	WRITTEN	exercise.
Paul	is	TIRING.		He's	a	TIRING	man.
He	's	SURPRISING.		He's	a	SURPRISING	man.
He	's	BORING.		He's	a	BORING	man.
Betty	is	INTERESTING.		She's	an	INTERESTING	girl.

COMMENTS

(1) You may use certain -ED/-EN forms (TIRED, BROKEN, etc.) to describe Class 1 words. These forms indicate that the Class 1 word is the receiver of an action. JOHN IS A BORED MAN means that other people (or things) bore John.

(2) You may use certain -ING forms (TIRING, SURPRISING, etc.) to describe Class 1 words. These forms indicate that the Class 1 word is the performer of an action. PAUL IS A BORING MAN means that Paul bores other people.

NOTE FOR ADVANCED STUDENTS: Not all of the -ED/-EN and -ING forms used in this frame are exactly the same. You can use VERY before TIRED, SURPRISED, BORED, INTERESTED, TIRING, SURPRISING, BORING, INTERESTING.

JOHN IS VERY INTERESTING.   HE'S A VERY INTERESTING MAN.
PAUL IS VERY INTERESTED.   HE'S A VERY INTERESTED MAN.

But you cannot use very before BROKEN, COVERED, STOLEN, WRITTEN, etc.

PAUL IS BORING.   PAUL IS VERY BORING.

These sentences describe Paul. They are the pattern of this frame.

PAUL IS BORING US.   JANE IS DANCING.

These sentences indicate an action. They are not the pattern of this frame. They are the pattern of Lesson IV, Frame 2a.

JANE'S A⌐DANCING GIRL.   JANE'S A/DANCING GIRL.

Both these sentences describe Jane. The difference in intonation indicates a difference in meaning. The first sentence means Jane is a girl who is dancing now. The second sentence means Jane is a girl who dances as her profession.

THIS DISH IS BROKEN.   THIS DISH WAS BROKEN.

In some situations, these sentences describe the dish, and are the pattern of this frame. In other situations, they indicate an action, and are the pattern of Frame 1 in this lesson.

THIS DISH WAS BROKEN BY THE CHILD.

This sentence indicates an action. It is the pattern of Frame 1.

PRACTICE

EXERCISE 3.1. (To produce the -ING and -ED/-EN forms as describing words.) Listen to the situation. Produce a statement which describes a person or thing in the situation. Use the -ING or -ED/-EN form of the describing word after IS. Then give another statement with a Class 1 word following the describing word. For example:

John was tired after he played tennis. (Describe tennis.)
    TENNIS IS TIRING. IT'S A TIRING GAME.
John was tired after he played tennis. (Describe John.)
    JOHN WAS TIRED. HE WAS A TIRED MAN.
Mr. Black speaks in a monotone. He bores people. (Describe Mr. Black.)
    MR. BLACK IS BORING. HE'S A BORING MAN.
Mrs. Black broke the dish. (Describe the dish.)
    THE DISH IS BROKEN. IT'S A BROKEN DISH.

1. Mr. Black bores us with his manner of speaking. (Describe Mr. Black.)
2. Mary got a new dress. The dress pleased her. (Describe Mary.)
3. The child had some candy. The candy satisfied him. (Describe the child.)
4. My friend is watching the children. They amuse him. (Describe the children.)
5. Mr. Black is laughing. Something amuses him. (Describe Mr. Black.)
6. Mrs. Black is lovely. She charms us. (Describe Mrs. Black.)
7. John married Mary. (Describe John.)
8. It was an intelligent answer. It surprised us. (Describe the answer.)
9. Mary got a new dress. The dress pleased her. (Describe the dress.)
10. It was an intelligent answer. It surprised the people. (Describe the people.)

11. Paul sharpened his pencil. (Describe the pencil.)
12. Mr. Appleton speaks interestingly. He interests people. (Describe Mr. Appleton.)
13. All of the students respect Mr. Wilby. (Describe Mr. Wilby.)
14. John always gets sleepy in class. The class bores him. (Describe John.)
15. Somebody stole my bicycle. (Describe the bicycle.)

4.   Key example: John is USED TO SMOKING.

Observe ACCUSTOMED TO, USED TO, TIRED OF, etc. Observe the words after these combinations.

John	is	ACCUSTOMED	TO	SMOKING.	
He	is	USED	TO*	SMOKING	cigarettes.
I	'm	TIRED	OF	PRACTICING	this exercise.
Mary	is	INTERESTED	IN	LEARNING	a lot of English.
I	'm	INTERESTED	IN	MATHEMATICS.	
I	wasn't	USED	TO	cold WEATHER.	
Jane	was	BORED	WITH	her CLASSES.	

COMMENTS

(1) Learn ACCUSTOMED TO, USED TO, TIRED OF, INTERESTED IN, BORED WITH as units.
(2) Use -ING forms (SMOKING, etc.) or Class 1 words (MATHEMATICS, etc.) after these combinations.

PRACTICE

EXERCISE 4.1. (To practice USED TO, TIRED OF, etc., with words like SMOKING, LEARNING, MATHEMATICS, CLASSES, etc.) Listen to the situations. Describe the same situation by using the expressions TIRED OF, INTERESTED IN, USED TO, etc. For example:

Mary said, " I don't like this book. It bores me."
   MARY WAS BORED WITH HER BOOK.
Mary said, "I don't like to read. It makes me tired."
   MARY IS TIRED OF READING.
John said, "I smoke all the time. It has been my habit for a long time."
   JOHN IS USED TO SMOKING. (or) JOHN IS ACCUSTOMED TO SMOKING.
John said, "I like geography. I think it's very interesting."
   JOHN IS INTERESTED IN GEOGRAPHY.

1. Mary likes her classes. She says, "They are interesting."
2. She likes history. She says, "It is interesting."
3. John wants to visit us. He thinks it would be interesting.

*Don't confuse USED TO in this pattern with USED TO + the simple form of Class 2 words to indicate repeated occurrence in the past ("used to go," "used to sing" etc.).

4. Mr. Appleton doesn't work hard any more. He says, "It is tiring."
5. Mary didn't like the movie. She said, "It was boring."
6. People in this country have water with their meals. They say, "It's our custom."
7. Mrs. Brown has several dogs. She said, "They are interesting."
8. Mary said, "I would like to sing. I think it's interesting."
9. John said, 'I've been smoking for ten years. It's a habit."
10. John said, "I don't want to practice this exercise any more. I'm tired."

KEY EXAMPLES OF LESSON XIX

1. We ARE ASKED to speak only English.
2. John is STILL studying engineering.
   He hasn't finished YET.
3. John is BORED.
   Paul is BORING.
4. John is USED TO SMOKING.

Lesson XX

Review of Lessons XI-XIX*

EXERCISE 1. (To review expressions of comparison in questions.) Listen to the statement which contains an expression of comparison. Ask a question about Mary in a similar situation. For example:

John is taller than Fred.
    IS MARY TALLER THAN FRED?
He took a bigger one.
    DID MARY TAKE A BIGGER ONE?
John has the blackest hair in class.
    DOES MARY HAVE THE BLACKEST HAIR IN CLASS?

1. They know that I am shorter than Bob.
2. Rose is more beautiful than Jane.
3. They paid more money than we did.
4. She types most efficiently in the morning.
5. He was the tallest in his class.
6. His bag is heavier than mine.
7. The boy looks just like his father.
8. He seems different from the other students.
9. You are as slow as I am.
10. He works more effectively at home.
11. This course is the most practical.
12. I am going to take the earliest bus.

EXERCISE 2. (To review expressions of comparison with MORE or -ER.) Listen to the statement which describes John. Produce a statement which compares Paul. Use the form MORE or -ER, and the word THAN. For example:

John is young.   PAUL IS YOUNGER THAN JOHN.
John is patient.   PAUL IS MORE PATIENT THAN JOHN.
John has a good car.   PAUL HAS A BETTER CAR THAN JOHN.

1. John's hair is gray.
2. John has traveled often.
3. John's brother is sick.
4. John is interesting.
5. We know that John is a good student.
6. John has walked a long distance.
7. John has had experience in teaching.
8. John is going to the concert early.
9. John has a wide knowledge of physics.
10. John has a bad temper.

*TO THE TEACHER: Each teacher may plan a review lesson suited to the needs of his particular class by making a selection of exercises from the ones included in this lesson. Exercises from previous lessons may also be reviewed.

11. John talks English fluently.
12. John's nose is small.

EXERCISE 3. (To review expressions of comparison with MOST or -EST.)
Listen to the statement about one or more people. Produce a statement of
comparison about Mary. Use the expressions of comparison MOST or
-EST. For example:

> There are many good students in this class.
> 　　MARY IS THE BEST STUDENT IN THIS CLASS.
> Jane and Betty are charming.
> 　　MARY IS THE MOST CHARMING.
> Jane and Betty are pretty.
> 　　MARY IS THE PRETTIEST.

1. John and Bill work hard.
2. Those students have answered often.
3. All of the students were industrious.
4. We took a big piece of cake.
5. The girls acted silly.
6. John answered the questions promptly.
7. The students took a lot of time to write their compositions.
8. John has more ambition than Jane.
9. Their hair is long.
10. Bill and Betty traveled a long distance on their vacation.
11. John and Jane had many friends.
12. Both Mary and Jane are sick.

EXERCISE 4. (To review the expressions of comparison LIKE, THE
SAME AS, DIFFERENT FROM, THE SAME . . . AS, AS . . . AS.) Substitute the following words and make the necessary changes. Use AS . . .
AS with Class 3 and Class 4 words; use THE SAME . . . AS with Class 1
words. For example:

> John talks like his father.
> 　　same　　　JOHN TALKS THE SAME AS HIS FATHER.
> 　　differently　JOHN TALKS DIFFERENTLY FROM HIS FATHER.
> 　　clearly　　JOHN TALKS AS CLEARLY AS HIS FATHER.
> 　　loud　　　JOHN TALKS AS LOUD AS HIS FATHER.
> 　　languages　JOHN TALKS THE SAME LANGUAGES AS HIS FATHER.

1. quietly	10. brother	19. reads
2. little	11. polite	20. books
3. much	12. same	21. magazines
4. frequently	13. different	22. much
5. like	14. is	23. same
6. looks	15. like	24. practices
7. different	16. speaks	25. like
8. old	17. softly	26. acts
9. seems	18. rapidly	

EXERCISE 5. (To review the forms VERY, ENOUGH, and TOO.) Listen to the statements which describe a situation. Produce a statement with IS which summarizes the situation. Use TOO, VERY, or ENOUGH and TO + a Class 2 word in the statement. For example:

John can't wear the coat. The coat is small. John is big.
  JOHN IS TOO BIG TO WEAR THE COAT.
John wants to play ball. He is eager.
  JOHN IS VERY EAGER TO PLAY BALL.
John will do the work. He is ambitious.
  JOHN IS AMBITIOUS ENOUGH TO DO THE WORK.

1. John can afford to take a trip. He is wealthy.
2. Bill is afraid to take a trip. He is timid.
3. Mary can't study. She is sick.
4. John isn't able to see the sign. He is nearsighted.
5. Paul can swim across the lake. He is strong.
6. John can't sit up. He is weak.
7. John wants to take a trip. He is anxious.
8. John can't take a trip. He is tired.
9. Mary hates to see the team lose. She is sorry.
10. John can reach the ceiling. He is tall.
11. Bill can't reach the ceiling. He is short.
12. Fred can't play football. He is small.

EXERCISE 6. (To review the forms OF or -'S.) Listen to the following situations. Produce statements with the forms OF or -'S. Use -'S with the names of people and OF with things. For example:

This book belongs to John.
  THIS IS JOHN'S BOOK.
The table top is scratched.
  THE TOP OF THE TABLE IS SCRATCHED.
The book is interesting in the beginning.
  THE BEGINNING OF THE BOOK IS INTERESTING.
This is Webson College. Mr. Market is President.
  MR. MARKET IS PRESIDENT OF WEBSON COLLEGE.

1. He is using the book that belongs to Mary.
2. John has a new book.
3. The flower has a red color.
4. The book has the name "Flower Arrangement."
5. The typewriter keys are broken.
6. He works in Bright Hall. He works in the basement.
7. I am correcting a composition. It was written by Miss Cross.
8. I found a glove yesterday. It belongs to Mary.
9. The president lives in this house.
10. The club elected a new secretary. Bob is the secretary.
11. I bought a car. I bought it from John.
12. John has a broken hand.

EXERCISE 7. (To review HIS, HER, MINE, ONE, ONES, THESE, etc., in Class 1 position.) Listen to the statements with MY BOOK, THIS BOOK, JOHN'S BOOK, etc. Produce equivalent statements without using the word BOOK. For example:

John may use my book.	JOHN MAY USE MINE.
He bought another book.	HE BOUGHT ANOTHER ONE.
or	HE BOUGHT ANOTHER.
I have Mary's book.	I HAVE HERS.
Your book is on the desk.	YOURS IS ON THE DESK.

1. I want John's book.
2. Are these our books?
3. I lost my book.
4. I have read several books this month.
5. He lost interest in those books.
6. John borrowed a few books from the library.
7. We didn't bring our books with us.
8. John hadn't read that book.
9. They forgot their books.
10. Do you have your book with you?
11. What did you do with her books?
12. I haven't read this book yet.
13. What happened to those books?
14. Have you seen the new books for our course?
15. My friend didn't care for this book.
16. These books are too heavy to carry.

EXERCISE 8. (To review YET, STILL, ALREADY, ANY MORE.) Listen to the questions and the words which follow. Answer the questions and use the words in the answers. Use ANY MORE and YET in negative statements and ALREADY in affirmative statements. Use STILL in negative and affirmative statements. For example:

Where is John?   still
　　JOHN IS STILL EATING BREAKFAST.
Have you studied Lesson Five?   already
　　I'VE STUDIED IT ALREADY.
Have you studied Lesson Six?   yet
　　I HAVEN'T STUDIED IT YET.
Does John work here?   any more
　　JOHN DOESN'T WORK HERE ANY MORE.

1. Has John left?   yet
2. Have you seen the new auditorium?   already
3. Has Fred come here lately?   any more
4. Have you seen Mary this morning?   yet
5. Is Jane going to town this afternoon?   already
6. Do you like jazz music?   any more
7. Do you like symphony music?   still
8. Is Betty going to take the American Literature Course?   already

9. Have you been to the Union Cafeteria lately?   any more
10. Have you seen the director?   yet
11. Has Bob returned the book to you?   still
12. Where is Tom?   already

EXERCISE 9. (To review TO + a Class 2 word after LIKE, WANT, etc.)
Answer the questions with TO + a Class 2 word. Use the Class 2 word
which is given. For example:

   What does he want?   buy
      HE WANTS TO BUY A BOOK.
   What did John expect?   get
      JOHN EXPECTED TO GET A LETTER TODAY.
   What do they like?   swim
      THEY LIKE TO SWIM IN THE LAKE.

1. What is she learning?   speak
2. What does he need?   study
3. What did he promise us?   go
4. What does Paul plan?   answer
5. What did Mary decide?   drive
6. What is he beginning?   read
7. What do you hope?   see
8. What did he ask us?   come
9. What is he continuing?   use
10. What did the teacher want from you?   write
11. What is he trying?   sell
12. What did he want from us?   pay

EXERCISE 10. (To review the production of CAN, MUST, etc., in questions.) Listen to the statements. Ask parallel questions about Bob. For
example:

   I can see the top of the mountain.
      CAN BOB SEE THE TOP OF THE MOUNTAIN?
   You should report to the director immediately.
      SHOULD BOB REPORT TO THE DIRECTOR IMMEDIATELY?
   Mary must hand in her composition today.
      MUST BOB HAND IN HIS COMPOSITION TODAY?

1. John may go to the movie.
2. I should take another course in English.
3. He might forget his books.
4. Our professor will answer the letter in the morning.
5. He will answer my question tomorrow.
6. We should pay our fees now.
7. I can send the package later.
8. You could have forgotten the letter.
9. He could see the traffic light in the dark.
10. He must answer the letter today.
11. I might go to Detroit tomorrow.

12. We could go to the late show.
13. They must return the application blank next week.
14. They might find an apartment on Ann Street.
15. He would like to have a conference.
16. I can understand it.
17. We may turn the television on.
18. You can come tomorrow.
19. You can do the paper tomorrow.
20. You may use the telephone.

EXERCISE 11. (To review the use of CAN, MIGHT, WILL, MAY, MUST, SHOULD.) Listen to the situation statements. Produce statements with MIGHT, CAN, etc., which are suitable to these situations.

A. (To review MIGHT.) Listen to the statement about John and make a related statement which shows that John is undecided or that some action is possible. Use MIGHT and the Class 2 word which is given. For example:

John wants to go to the play, but he is undecided. go
    HE MIGHT GO TO THE PLAY.
John is thinking of buying a car. buy
    HE MIGHT BUY A CAR.

1. John is planning a trip to San Francisco. go
2. John is waiting for a letter. get
3. John is working for a degree. get
4. John wants to eat breakfast. go
5. John has a toothache. go
6. John drives very carelessly in his car. have
7. John is homesick. What can he do? talk
8. John is looking for an apartment. find

B. (To review CAN.) Listen to the following situations about Tom. Produce a related statement. Show what he is able to do. Use CAN plus the Class 2 word which is given. For example:

Tom is a good musician. play
    HE CAN PLAY THE PIANO.
Tom has no time to see you today. see
    HE CAN SEE YOU TOMORROW.

1. Tom has a good memory. memorize
2. Tom does not need the book today. wait
3. Tom has many hobbies. sing, dance, and paint
4. Tom has no one to go with him. go
5. Tom is looking for a copy of Moby Dick. get
6. Tom wants to talk to you. talk
7. Tom is not doing anything this afternoon. go
8. Tom understands English very well. speak

C. (To review SHOULD.) Listen to the situation about Bob. Indicate what Bob has the obligation to do in this situation. Use SHOULD and the Class 2 word which is given. For example:

Bob has low grades.　study
　HE SHOULD STUDY HARDER.
Bob is wanted by the director.　report
　HE SHOULD REPORT TO THE DIRECTOR.

1. Bob is sick.　see
2. Bob is tired from playing ball.　rest
3. Bob lost all of his money.　borrow
4. Bob is sleepy in class.　sleep
5. Bob writes home only once a month.　write
6. Bob has poor pronunciation.　practice
7. Bob comes to class late every day.　come
8. Bob has owed John five dollars for the last two years.　pay

D. (To review MUST.) Listen to the situation about Fred. Make a judgement and tell what he is required to do. Use MUST and the Class 2 word which is given. For example:

Fred is late for his class.　hurry
　HE MUST HURRY.
Fred wants to study engineering.　take
　HE MUST TAKE COURSES IN MATH.

1. Fred is using Mary's book and she needs it.　return
2. Fred refuses to take the medicine which the doctor gave him.　take
3. Fred lost his eyeglasses and he can't see.　get
4. Fred has a composition to write.　hand in
5. Fred has not studied today.　work
6. Fred has not paid his tuition yet.　pay
7. Fred found John's wallet.　return
8. Fred is going to attend summer school. Registration is tomorrow. register

E. (To review MAY.) Listen to the situation. Make a statement about Paul which indicates that he has or has not permission. Use MAY and the Class 2 word which is given. For example:

Paul has permission to be absent.　be
　HE MAY BE ABSENT.
Paul asked to use the laboratory. He was refused.　use
　HE MAY NOT USE THE LABORATORY.

1. Paul asked the director for a vacation. The director said no. have
2. Paul asked to use the television set. use
3. The landlady has given Paul permission to use her phone. use
4. Paul was forbidden to drink coffee by the doctor. drink
5. Paul has received permission to visit Canada. visit
6. The government refused to give Paul a driver's license. drive
7. Paul is allowed to take sixteen hours this semester. take
8. Paul is not allowed to take Spanish. take

F. (To review WILL.) Listen to the situations about Mary. Indicate
what Mary is or is not going to do. Use WILL and the Class 2 word
which is given. For example:

   Mary is standing in the rain. get
      SHE WILL GET WET.
   Mary missed the grammar class today. know
      SHE WON'T KNOW HER LESSON TOMORROW.

1. Mary canceled her trip to England. take
2. Mary has a book to give you tomorrow. give
3. Mary has decided to take a vacation in Mexico. take
4. Mary has promised to write when she arrives in France. write
5. Mary is writing a composition. finish
6. Mary is angry at Jane. speak
7. Mary got the letter yesterday. reply
8. Mary has chosen too many courses. find

EXERCISE 12. (To review the contrast between I WANT TO FIND, etc.,
and I CAN FIND, etc.) Substitute the following words. Do not use TO
after MUST, CAN, SHOULD, etc. For example:

   I want to see the director.
      must   I MUST SEE THE DIRECTOR.
      have   I HAVE TO SEE THE DIRECTOR.
      speak   I HAVE TO SPEAK TO THE DIRECTOR.

1. may   11. won't
2. want   12. should
3. could   13. can't
4. had   14. intend
5. should   15. may
6. will   16. wish
7. need   17. might
8. am going to   18. find
9. visit   19. must
10. must   20. intend
                              21. can

22. should
23. won't
24. have
25. report

26. can
27. should
28. am going to
29. want

30. will
31. expect
32. wish

EXERCISE 13. (To review Class 2 words + UP, ON, OFF, etc.) Listen to the statements. Repeat the statements and use substitute words like HIM, IT, THEM, etc. For example:

> I woke up John at ten this morning.
>> I WOKE HIM UP AT TEN THIS MORNING.
> I put my hat on.
>> I PUT IT ON.
> I got out of the boat.
>> I GOT OUT OF IT.

1. I picked up my books.
2. I took my hat off.
3. I paid up my debts.
4. I found out about the lesson.
5. I turned the alarm off.
6. I turned the radio on.
7. I walked over to the drugstore.
8. I called up John.
9. I jumped out of bed.
10. I jumped into bed.
11. I sat down by the man.
12. I ran into John.

EXERCISE 14. (To review short answers to questions.) Answer the questions with a short answer. You may make your answers affirmative or negative. For example:

> Can you read his writing?
>> NO, I CAN'T.
> Whose book is this?
>> MINE.
> Is there going to be a concert tonight?
>> NO, THERE ISN'T.

1. Will John go by train?
2. Have you forgotten about the play?
3. May we use your telephone?
4. Did he ask you about it?
5. Why is John here tonight?
6. How did you get to Ann Arbor?
7. Is he a member of the club?
8. Could you find his address?
9. Is it far to California?
10. Would you like to go on a picnic today?
11. Whose pencil is this?
12. Might they come for the meeting?
13. Why did Mary go to the bookstore?
14. Should he make an appointment with the doctor?
15. Has she been studying Lesson Six?
16. Do you want to study in the library?
17. Had you gotten the news before you left?
18. Can Mary play the piano?
19. Are there any mountains in this area?
20. How are you traveling to New York City?

EXERCISE 15. (To review statements with IT'S.) Answer the following
questions with IT'S or IT. For example:

Who is it at the door?   IT'S JOHN.
What do you think of the movie?   IT'S TERRIBLE.
Why are you waiting?   IT'S TOO EARLY TO GO TO
                                         THE PLAY.

Why didn't you go to the restaurant?   IT WASN'T OPEN.

1. What time is it?
2. How far is it to Detroit?
3. What is the weather like today?
4. What was the weather like yesterday?
5. What month is it?
6. What day is it?
7. What do you think of the English course?
8. Why do you practice so much?
9. What year is it?
10. Who is talking to Professor Small?
11. How is your cold?
12. When is the program?

EXERCISE 16. (To review statements with THERE IS, ARE.) Answer
the questions with THERE IS or THERE ARE. Use the words which are
given after the questions. For example:

Where is there a gasoline station?   Baker Street
    THERE'S ONE ON BAKER STREET.
Where can I find a telephone?   room
    THERE'S ONE IN THE NEXT ROOM.
Do you have any matches?   table
    THERE ARE SOME ON THE TABLE.

1. Where is there a drugstore?   Greenwood Street
2. Where can I buy some bananas?   grocery store
3. Where can I find some soap?   drugstore
4. Where can I find a mechanic?   garage
5. Do you see any pencils?   desk
6. Where can I find a room?   hotel
7. Where could I buy a candy bar?   candy counter
8. Where can I get some aspirin?   drugstore
9. Do you have a cigarette?   table
10. Where can we see a good play?   New York
11. Where are some apples?   refrigerator
12. Where can we get some good ice cream?   drugstore

EXERCISE 17. (To review included statements after KNOW, BELIEVE,
REMEMBER, etc.) Listen to the statement and the Class 2 word which
follows it. Include the Class 2 word and the statement in another statement. For example:

John is a good student.   know
  I KNOW THAT JOHN IS A GOOD STUDENT.
Mary wore a green hat to the tea.   remember
  I REMEMBER THAT MARY WORE A GREEN HAT TO THE TEA.
He has a cold.   suspect
  I SUSPECT THAT HE HAS A COLD.

1. John went to Canada by train.   wrote
2. They are going to be married.   heard
3. There is no course in statistics next semester.   found
4. Professor Giffels will not be here today.   presume
5. The New York Yankees will win the pennant.   predict
6. Nobody can survive at that altitude.   said
7. There will be no war.   believe
8. The teacher assigned a new lesson.   forgot
9. We had bought the shirt the day before.   explained
10. Jane was selected for a scholarship.   learned
11. The library is open on Sundays.   discovered
12. Tom has taken a job in Venezuela.   understand

EXERCISE 18. (To review included statements as modifiers of Class 1 words.) Listen to the statements. Combine the statements using the words WHO, WHICH, or THAT. For example:

The book is here. I want it.
  THE BOOK WHICH I WANT IS HERE.
John is a good student. He works hard.
  JOHN IS A GOOD STUDENT WHO WORKS HARD.
The math teacher is my friend. John visited him.
  THE MATH TEACHER THAT JOHN VISITED IS MY FRIEND.
The math teacher is my friend. He visited John.
  THE MATH TEACHER THAT VISITED JOHN IS MY FRIEND.

1. We saw it in the book. Jim found the book.
2. Paul met the new student. We know the student.
3. My friend teaches English. He is visiting Italy.
4. We know the man. John met him yesterday.
5. We know the man. He talked to John yesterday.
6. The professor knows my mother. He teaches Spanish.
7. Fred has the camera. We found it.
8. We returned the book. John wanted it.
9. The secretary wrote me a letter. John knows him.
10. The secretary wrote me a letter. He knows John.
11. She talked with a professor. He praised Jim.
12. She talked with a professor. Jim praised him.

EXERCISE 19. (To review included statements introduced by the words WHAT, WHERE, WHY, WHEN, HOW MUCH, WHO.) Listen to the statement about John. Indicate that you know the information. Use I KNOW plus an included statement introduced by WHAT, WHERE, etc. For example:

John studies in the morning.
    I KNOW WHEN JOHN STUDIES.
John studies algebra and physics.
    I KNOW WHAT JOHN STUDIES.
John is talking to Fred.
    I KNOW WHOM JOHN IS TALKING TO.
Professor Smith met John.
    I KNOW WHO MET JOHN.
John works for a living.
    I KNOW WHY JOHN WORKS.

1. John reads novels and plays.
2. John works in the factory.
3. Mary saw John.
4. John reads for pleasure.
5. John is acquainted with Professor Pilar.
6. John earns $100 a week.
7. John met Miss Willy.
8. Miss Brown introduced John.
9. John paid fifty dollars for his suit.
10. John is going to Florida.
11. John takes a walk in the evening.
12. Bill forgot about John.
13. John is going to buy a hat and a pair of shoes.
14. John might come this afternoon.
15. Fred went with John.
16. John is studying to become a librarian.
17. John has forgotten about Bill.
18. Mr. Brenner spoke to John.
19. John spoke to Mr. Brenner.
20. Paul is John's friend.

EXERCISE 20. (To review the receiver of the action as subject.) Listen to the statements. Make the word which receives the action the subject of a similar statement. Use a form of BE in each statement. For example:

The director wants John immediately.
    JOHN IS WANTED IMMEDIATELY.
I saw the book on the table.
    THE BOOK WAS SEEN ON THE TABLE.
They took him to the hospital.
    HE WAS TAKEN TO THE HOSPITAL.

1. I returned the books yesterday.
2. The police examined the car.
3. The doctor examined Fred thoroughly.
4. We warned Paul not to go swimming.
5. He improved his pronunciation a lot this week.
6. I found my hat under the table.

7. They are inspecting the building now.
8. We must pay the bill at once.
9. We took a picture of John and Mary.
10. John and Mary took a picture of me.
11. They promised the book to us yesterday.
12. We ate it for breakfast.

EXERCISE 21. (To review the -ING and -ED/-EN forms as modifiers.)
Listen to the statements. Produce related statements with -ING and
-ED/-EN forms after BE. One student produces an -ING form and an-
other student the -ED/-EN form. For example:

John amuses us.
    JOHN IS AMUSING.
    WE ARE AMUSED.
They entertained us.
    THEY WERE ENTERTAINING.
    WE WERE ENTERTAINED.
The newspaper convinced Mary.
    THE NEWSPAPER WAS CONVINCING.
    MARY WAS CONVINCED.

1. They deceived us.
2. The book inspired him.
3. She charmed the audience.
4. The program gratified us.
5. John displeases his teacher.
6. The long walk discouraged me.
7. The exam is going to frighten the students.
8. The movie disgusted us.
9. The examination frustrated Paul.
10. The lecture convinced us.
11. The accident depressed everybody.
12. The play interests the critic.

EXERCISE 22. (To review Class 2 constructions with HAVE, HAD and
to contrast them with other constructions.) Answer the following questions. Use the Class 2 constructions indicated in the question. For
example:
    What have you been doing lately?
        I'VE BEEN TAKING A COURSE IN MATH.
    What does he have in his hand?
        HE HAS A COIN IN HIS HAND.
    What had you been working on when I came?
        I HAD BEEN WORKING ON MY GRAMMAR LESSON.

1. Where are you going?
2. What have you been doing in your free time?
3. What have you done with your car?
4. What are you going to do next summer?

5. What did you do last summer?
6. What have you done this summer?
7. When did you sell your car?
8. What have you done with your book?
9. What have you been doing with your book?
10. What color pencil does John have?
11. What color pencil has he taken?
12. What had you bought before you came here?
13. What has John been forgetting?
14. What has John forgotten?

EXERCISE 23. (To review HAVE + the -ED/-EN form.) Listen to the statement. Add another statement with BUT . . . SINCE . . . Use HAVEN'T, HASN'T plus the -ED/-EN form of the Class 2 word that is given after the statement. For example:

John is a good student. study
   JOHN IS A GOOD STUDENT, BUT HE HASN'T STUDIED SINCE
   NOVEMBER.
They work hard. complete
   THEY WORK HARD, BUT THEY HAVEN'T COMPLETED AN
   ASSIGNMENT SINCE TUESDAY.
They earn a lot of money. buy
   THEY EARN A LOT OF MONEY, BUT THEY HAVEN'T BOUGHT
   A CAR SINCE 1950.

1. We know John. seen
2. We see John every day. talked
3. Mary wants to come. talked
4. Fred has a test. studied
5. He bought a car. driven
6. They know the rules. observed
7. My father is a dentist. worked
8. They are fishing. caught
9. I like boiled eggs. had
10. He has a camera. taken
11. He knows me. talked
12. She has a cold. taken

EXERCISE 24. (To review HAVE BEEN + the -ING form.) Listen to the statement. Add another statement with AND . . . LATELY which tells related information. Use HAVE BEEN plus the -ING form of the Class 2 word which is given. For example:

John is a good student. study
   JOHN IS A GOOD STUDENT AND HE HAS BEEN STUDYING HARD
   LATELY.
They work hard. complete
   THEY WORK HARD AND THEY HAVE BEEN COMPLETING THEIR
   WORK LATELY.
They earn a lot of money. buy
   THEY EARN A LOT OF MONEY AND THEY HAVE BEEN BUYING
   A LOT OF CLOTHES LATELY.

(Continue with the items of Exercise 23.)

EXERCISE 25. (To review HAD + the -ED/-EN form of a Class 2 word.)
Listen to the statements in past time. Repeat the statements and add
other statements which express an action which occurred previously.
Use AFTER . . . HAD + the -ED/-EN form of the Class 2 word which is
given. For example:

He recovered. get
   HE RECOVERED AFTER HE HAD GOTTEN SICK.
He waited. miss
   HE WAITED AFTER HE HAD MISSED THE BUS.
He answered. receive
   HE ANSWERED AFTER HE HAD RECEIVED THE LETTER.

1. She cried. hear
2. He protested. see
3. We left. report
4. He slept. eat
5. He went to bed. study
6. They celebrated. win
7. We rested. watch
8. We talked. hear
9. I returned home. visit
10. I dressed. sleep
11. They replied. get
12. She telephoned. arrive

EXERCISE 26. (To review HAD BEEN + the ING form of a Class 2 word.)
Listen to the two events. Give the two events in a single statement. Use
HAD BEEN + the -ING form to indicate the action in progress before the
second event took place. For example:

I was studying. John came.
   I HAD BEEN STUDYING BEFORE JOHN CAME.
I was studying. I took a walk.
   I HAD BEEN STUDYING BEFORE I TOOK A WALK.
He was reading. Mary telephoned.
   HE HAD BEEN READING BEFORE MARY TELEPHONED.

1. We were talking. They arrived.
2. Mary was working. She left town.
3. We were eating. He telephoned.
4. They were talking. The concert began.
5. He was smoking. The program began.
6. We were walking. We went to the drugstore.
7. I was eating. I telephoned John.
8. The man was singing. The police arrived.
9. I was writing a letter. John called.
10. They were eating. We knocked on the door.
11. She was reading. She called up Jane.
12. I was walking. It started to rain.

Lesson XXI

1. HE MAKES THEM PRACTICE.
   [Certain Class 2 + Class 1 + Class 2]

2. I WISH (THAT) YOU SPOKE ENGLISH.
   [WISH (THAT) + statement pattern]

3. I KNOW HOW TO SPEAK ENGLISH.
   [Class 2 + HOW, WHERE, ETC., + TO + Class 2]

1. Key example: The teacher wants the students to learn English.
HE MAKES THEM PRACTICE every day.

Observe the words after LET, HAD, MADE, etc.

Previous pattern (Lesson XIII):

I	permitted the students	to read	the newspapers.
I	wanted them	to understand	the news.
I	told them	to read	the editorial.

New pattern:

I	LET THEM	READ	the newspapers.
I	HAD THEM	READ	the news.
I	MADE THEM	BUY	the papers.
I	HEARD THEM	DISCUSS	the editorial.

COMMENT

Do not use TO after the Class 2 words HAVE, LET, MAKE, SEE, HEAR, WATCH, FEEL, OBSERVE in this pattern.*

ILLUSTRATIVE EXAMPLES WITH "TO"

Some friends	ASKED ME	TO GO	to Florida.
They	INVITED ME	TO GO	with them.
They	PERSUADED ME	TO ACCEPT	their offer.
I would	LIKE YOU	TO GIVE	me some information.
But please	PERMIT ME	TO INTERRUPT	you.
I don't	WANT YOU	TO SPEND	all your time with me.
Did you	TELL ME	TO READ	some books about Florida?
Or did you	TELL ME not	TO READ	any books?
The other students	CHOSE ME	TO REPRESENT	my class in the program.
They	URGED ME	TO MAKE	a speech about Florida.
They also	GOT ME	TO STUDY	the Spanish influence there.

---

*You will hear HELP both with and without TO: "I HELPED THEM TO UNDERSTAND the editorial" or "I HELPED THEM UNDERSTAND the editorial."

ILLUSTRATIVE EXAMPLES WITHOUT "TO"

Please	LET ME	SPEAK	about Florida.
We should	HAVE THE STUDENTS	LEARN	their speeches.
Can you	MAKE THEM	APPRECIATE	the value of good pronunciation?
Can you	FEEL YOUR TONGUE	MOVE	when you pronounce [i] and [u] rapidly?
I can't	HEAR YOU	PRONOUNCE	them.
I can't	SEE YOUR LIPS	MOVE.	
	WATCH MY LIPS	MOVE	when I pronounce [i] and [u] rapidly.

PRACTICE

EXERCISE 1.1. (To review the pattern with TO.) Substitute the following words. For example:

Did Mr. Taylor ask you to go to Florida?

persuade   DID MR. TAYLOR PERSUADE YOU TO GO TO FLORIDA?

urge   DID MR. TAYLOR URGE YOU TO GO TO FLORIDA?

1. advise   4. permit
2. tell   5. invite
3. order   6. want

Continue the exercise with this statement pattern:

He advised me to go to Florida.

told   HE TOLD ME TO GO TO FLORIDA.

7. expected   10. persuaded
8. got   11. urged
9. asked   12. wanted

Continue with this negative pattern:

You should advise John not to drive the car to Florida.

urge   YOU SHOULD URGE JOHN NOT TO DRIVE THE CAR TO FLORIDA.

13. tell   16. order
14. persuade   17. get
15. ask

EXERCISE 1.2 (To practice the pattern without TO.) Substitute the following words. For example:

Will the doctor let you take the plane?

see   WILL THE DOCTOR SEE YOU TAKE THE PLANE?

have   WILL THE DOCTOR HAVE YOU TAKE THE PLANE?

1. make   4. let
2. watch   5. see
3. observe   6. have

Continue with this statement pattern:

I'm going to have her call the airport.

let   I'M GOING TO LET HER CALL THE AIRPORT.

    7. hear   10. observe
    8. watch   11. have
    9. make   12. let

Continue with this negative pattern:

He didn't have us talk about our vacation.

make   HE DIDN'T MAKE US TALK ABOUT OUR VACATION.

    13. let   16. see
    14. hear   17. have
    15. observe   18. make

EXERCISE 1.3. (To contrast Class 2 words with TO and those without TO.) Substitute the following words. Do not use TO after LET, HAVE WATCH, MAKE, etc. For example:

The doctor persuaded me to buy a car.

made   THE DOCTOR MADE ME BUY A CAR.

wanted   THE DOCTOR WANTED ME TO BUY A CAR.

sell   THE DOCTOR WANTED ME TO SELL MY CAR.

1. told	8. saw	16. observed
2. watched	9. let	17. wreck
3. made	10. got	18. saw
4. asked	11. repair	19. forbid
5. urged	12. persuaded	20. heard
6. wash	13. saw	21. watched
7. wanted	14. heard	22. drive
	15. advised	

EXERCISE 1.4. (To force a choice in the use of the pattern with TO and without TO.) Suppose that you have planned a comprehensive program or seminar on life and people in the United States. Suppose also that you have included such topics as, for example, vacations, geography, travel and transportation, business, politics, history, co-operation, conflicts, racial discrimination, religious differences, racial harmony, spring and winter, music, folk songs. You may say, for example:

I asked one person to speak about vacations.

had   I HAD ANOTHER SPEAK ABOUT GEOGRAPHY.

invited   I INVITED ANOTHER TO SPEAK ABOUT TRAVEL.

let   I LET ANOTHER SPEAK ABOUT BUSINESS.

Continue, adding different topics:

1. asked	6. made	11. wanted	15. had
2. had	7. got	12. told	16. permitted
3. invited	8. expected	13. observed	17. let
4. let	9. heard	14. advised	18. made
5. persuaded	10. watched		

2.   Key example: I WISH you SPOKE English perfectly NOW.

Observe WENT, WANTED, DIDN'T, COULD, WAS and the time expressions. Previous pattern (Lesson XVII):

I think	that	some people	go	south	every winter.
I suppose	that	they	want	to go	every year.
I suppose		they	don't	like cold weather.	
I believe		relatively few	can	go south	every year.
I hope		I	can	go south	this year.
I think		Professor Brown	is	in Florida	now.

New pattern:

I WISH	that	all people	WENT	south	EVERY WINTER.*
I WISH	that	they	WANTED	to stay here	EVERY YEAR.
I WISH		they	DIDN'T	like warm weather.	
I WISH		all people	COULD	go south	EVERY YEAR.
I WISH		I	COULD	go south	THIS YEAR.
I WISH		I	WAS	in Florida	NOW.**

COMMENTS

(1) After WISH, use DIDN'T, COULD, and -ED forms of Class 2 words like WANTED, WENT.

(2) Use time expressions like EVERY YEAR, THIS YEAR, NOW. Don't use past-time expressions like YESTERDAY.

ILLUSTRATIVE EXAMPLES

I know that languages	are	complex. (Lesson XVII)
I wish that languages	WERE	simple. (Lesson XXI)
I think we	have	highly trained teachers now.
I wish all schools	HAD	highly trained teachers now.
I heard that many teachers	have	to accept additional jobs.
I wish that teachers never	HAD	to accept additional jobs.
I learned that some teachers	get	$6,000 a year.
I wish that all teachers	GOT	$6,000 a year.

*You will frequently hear WOULD after WISH. "I wish all people WOULD GO south every winter" is similar in meaning to "I wish all people WENT south every winter."

**You will also hear "I wish I WERE in Florida now." After WISH, the form WERE is sometimes used with words like I, HE, SHE, IT, THE TEACHER, JOHN.

I discovered almost all teachers	begin	with $3,000 or less.
I wish every teacher in the country	BEGAN	with $4,000.
I believe that many university teachers	receive	less.
I wish that all university teachers	RECEIVED	more.
I understand it	is	necessary to have $5,000 a year for an average standard of living here.
I wish it	WAS	not necessary to have so much money.
I think I	can	go from New York to Detroit by plane for $30.
I wish I	COULD	go for less.

PRACTICE

EXERCISE 2.1. (To practice the pattern after WISH.) Substitute WISH and make the entire statement affirmative. For example:

> I don't think Dr. Jones is in his office now.
> I WISH HE WAS IN HIS OFFICE NOW.
> I don't believe Paul can drive a car.
> I WISH HE COULD DRIVE A CAR.
> I know Juan doesn't speak English.
> I WISH HE SPOKE ENGLISH.

1. I don't suppose George can speak Spanish.
2. I don't think Professor Brown's lectures are interesting.
3. I don't believe this store sells shoes.
4. I discovered that these children don't go to school.
5. I heard that Mr. Smith doesn't get along with his wife.
6. I understand that John isn't coming to class today.

Continue the exercise, and make the statement after WISH negative. For example:

> I think it's going to rain today.
> I WISH IT WASN'T GOING TO RAIN TODAY.

7. I heard that Mr. Jones is sick.
8. I think he has pneumonia.
9. I just remembered that I have to go to class now.
10. I just discovered that there is going to be an examination tomorrow.
11. I understand that Mr. Peterson works at night.
12. I know it is necessary to practice every day.

Continue the exercise and use an opposite describing word. For example:

> I think this pattern is difficult.
> I WISH IT WAS EASY.

13. I heard that classes begin early.
14. I believe that Mrs. Smith is sick.
15. I understand that the streets in the city are narrow.
16. I discovered that Professor Jones speaks fast.
17. I think that John's father is old and weak.
18. I imagine that Mary feels sad.

EXERCISE 2.2. FOR ADVANCED STUDENTS. (To practice the pattern with WISH in a variety of situations.) This is a conversation exercise. Listen to the statements which present an undesirable situation. Express a more desirable situation with WISH. Use such vocabulary items as "co-operation," "beauty," "justice," "peace," "happiness," "harmony," "benefits," etc. For example:

Some people speak only about religious differences.
    I KNOW. I WISH THEY SPOKE ABOUT RELIGIOUS HARMONY TOO.
They are interested only in finding examples of racial discrimination.
    I KNOW. I WISH THEY WERE INTERESTED IN RACIAL HARMONY TOO.
A reporter I know writes only articles about crime and hate.
    I KNOW. I WISH HE WROTE ABOUT LOVE AND FRIENDSHIP TOO.

1. Newspapers emphasize disagreements.
2. Many people are interested only in conflict.
3. My friend usually speaks about the bad aspects of politics.
4. Some reporters write only about the difficulties in family life.
5. Some people are concerned only with the dangers of scientific study.
6. The book I read describes only the geography of the country.
7. Mr. Mumford emphasizes the coldness of the United Nations building.
8. The book I read emphasizes the conflict between capital and labor.
9. A recent magazine article emphasizes social injustice in this country.
10. Some tourists are concerned only with the cold statistics of a country.
11. Other tourists want to know only the unusual customs of a small group of people.
12. Some movies try to describe only war, fear, conflict, and unhappiness.

3.   Key example: I KNOW HOW TO SPEAK English.

Observe the position of WHERE TO GO, etc.

Previous patterns:

| I knew | the lesson. | (Lesson II) |
| I told them | the story. | (Lesson VII) |

New pattern:

I know	WHERE TO GO.	all of the patterns.
I know	WHAT TO DO.	
I know	HOW TO USE	
I told them	WHERE TO GO.	
I told them	WHAT TO DO.	
I told them	HOW TO FIND	the store.

COMMENT

Use WHERE TO GO, WHAT TO DO, etc., in object position (the position of Class 1 words like THE LESSON and THE STORY in this pattern).

ILLUSTRATIVE EXAMPLES

I learned	HOW TO BUY	clothes.
I knew	WHERE TO BUY	them.
I decided	WHAT TO BUY.	
I can tell you	WHERE TO BUY	clothes.
I won't advise you	WHAT TO BUY.	
Please advise me	WHEN TO GO	to Canada.
Also advise me	HOW LONG TO STAY	there.
I don't know	HOW FAR TO GO.	
I don't know	WHO(M) TO ASK	to go with me.
I can't decide	WHICH PROVINCES TO VISIT.	
Will you advise me	WHICH TO VISIT?	
Can you tell me	HOW MUCH MONEY TO TAKE?	
Also tell me	HOW OFTEN TO SEE	the immigration service.

PRACTICE

EXERCISE 3.1. (To practice constructions like WHERE TO GO.) Substitute the following words. For example:

I know where to go.
how   I KNOW HOW TO GO.
how far   I KNOW HOW FAR TO GO.

1. how often	10. where	19. what
2. to practice	11. do you know	20. who
3. when	12. which cities	21. did you tell them
4. what	13. what	22. to take
5. how much	14. to buy	23. how many students
6. I don't know	15. how much paper	24. what
7. how long	16. please tell me	25. to do
8. to visit	17. which books	26. not to do
9. who	18. to look at	27. not to read

EXERCISE 3.2. (To practice constructions like WHERE TO GO in a conversational situation.) This is a conversation exercise. Listen to the questions and give answers with I TOLD HIM + WHERE TO, HOW TO, etc., + Class 2. For example:

Do you think Bill will buy enought plates for the picnic?
    I THINK HE WILL. I TOLD HIM HOW MANY TO BUY.
Do you think your friend will come at the right time?
    I THINK HE WILL. I TOLD HIM WHEN TO COME.
Do you think he will take the right plane?
    I THINK HE WILL. I TOLD HIM WHICH PLANE TO TAKE.

1. Do you think he will meet us at the correct place?
2. Do you think he will pronounce the word correctly?
3. Do you think he will buy enough clothes?
4. Do you think he will find the restaurant?
5. Do you think he will come at the right time?
6. Do you think he will choose the correct answer?
7. Do you think he will take enough money?
8. Do you think he will speak at the right time?
9. Do you think he will give the money to the right man?
10. Do you think he will bring the right books?
11. Do you think he will send the letter to the right address?
12. Do you think he will do the work we want him to?

KEY EXAMPLES OF LESSON XXI

1. The teacher wants the students to learn English. He MAKES THEM PRACTICE every day.
2. I WISH you SPOKE English perfectly NOW.
3. I KNOW HOW TO SPEAK English.

Lesson XXII

1. SHOULD HAVE PRACTICED
   [SHOULD, COULD, MIGHT, MUST + HAVE + the -ED/-EN form of
   Class 2 words]

2. SHOULD HAVE BEEN PRACTICING
   [SHOULD, COULD, MIGHT, MUST + HAVE BEEN + the -ING form
   of Class 2 words]

3. YES, I SHOULD HAVE.
   [Short answers and connected statements with these patterns]

4. I WISH (THAT) WE HAD PRACTICED YESTERDAY.
   [WISH (THAT) + statement pattern with past-time expression]

1. Key example: We didn't practice Lesson XXI last night, but we
SHOULD HAVE PRACTICED IT.

Observe the patterns with SHOULD, COULD, etc., with time expressions
like YESTERDAY, LAST NIGHT.

Previous pattern (Lesson XI):

We	should practice	English	today.

New pattern:

We	SHOULD HAVE PRACTICED	English	YESTERDAY.
We	COULD HAVE STUDIED	for three hours	LAST NIGHT.
John	MIGHT HAVE BEEN	at the library	YESTERDAY*
The students	MUST HAVE WRITTEN	that exercise	LAST WEEK.

COMMENTS

(1) With past time expressions (YESTERDAY, LAST NIGHT, etc.), use
SHOULD, COULD, MIGHT, MUST followed by HAVE PRACTICED,
HAVE WRITTEN, HAVE BEEN, etc. Never use "had" with "should,"
etc.

(2) The usual pronunciations in conversation are [šúdəv] for SHOULD
HAVE, [kúdəv] for COULD HAVE, [máɪtəv] for MIGHT HAVE,
[mə́stəv] for MUST HAVE.

ILLUSTRATIVE EXAMPLES

The doctor didn't work in his office yesterday, but it was possible for him
to work there. He COULD HAVE WORKED there yesterday.

---

*You will also hear "John MAY HAVE BEEN at the library yesterday." The
meanings of MIGHT and MAY are similar in this pattern.

Note: The meaning indicated by COULD in this pattern is usually "possibility in a situation." COULD without HAVE is frequently used to stress "ability": "Paul could work hard when he was a young man, but he can't work hard now."

The doctor had the obligation to return from his vacation yesterday, but he didn't return. He SHOULD HAVE RETURNED YESTERDAY.
He planned to come by train, but when the train arrived he wasn't on it. I think he missed the train. He MUST HAVE MISSED the train.

Note: The meaning indicated by MUST in this pattern is "supposition" or "deduction" by the speaker. In order to express "necessity" with past-time expressions, use HAD TO as in Lesson XIII.

He probably wasn't in his office last week, but there is a chance that he was. He MIGHT HAVE BEEN there last week.
We SHOULD HAVE GONE to the library last night, but we didn't.
John COULD HAVE FINISHED his work yesterday, but he didn't.
Mary MIGHT HAVE FINISHED her work last night, but I don't think she did.
I saw the doctor's car in front of her house. She MUST HAVE BEEN sick.
SHOULD Paul HAVE GONE to Detroit yesterday?
What SHOULD he HAVE DONE?
He SHOULD HAVE CLEANED his room and WORKED in the garden.
He MIGHT NOT HAVE HAD to work this morning.
When COULD he HAVE STUDIED?
He COULDN'T HAVE STUDIED last night.

PRACTICE

EXERCISE 1.1. (To practice the form of this pattern and to contrast it with the pattern with present and future time expressions.) Substitute the following words. For example:

They could have gone to the library last night.

might   THEY MIGHT HAVE GONE TO THE LIBRARY LAST NIGHT.

tonight   THEY MIGHT GO TO THE LIBRARY TONIGHT.

should   THEY SHOULD GO TO THE LIBRARY TONIGHT.

yesterday   THEY SHOULD HAVE GONE TO THE LIBRARY YESTERDAY.

1. must	7. last week	13. now
2. could	8. might not	14. last night
3. might	9. been here	15. should they
4. seen the movie	10. must not	16. could they
5. tomorrow	11. couldn't	17. might they
6. should	12. shouldn't	18. gone to the library

EXERCISE 1.2. (To use MUST in this pattern.) Listen to the sentences which describe a situation. Use MUST HAVE + PRACTICED, LOST, etc., in order to express your impression. For example:

Your friend speaks English very well.
> HE MUST HAVE PRACTICED A LOT LAST MONTH.

He can't find his pen.
> HE MUST HAVE LOST IT IN THE PARK YESTERDAY.

He came to class a half hour late.
> HE MUST HAVE SLEPT TOO LATE THIS MORNING.

1. He missed the first class.
2. He has a cut on his face.
3. He is tired of working.
4. He is bored with the movies.
5. He knew many things even when he was a boy.
6. I never see his old car anymore. I don't know what he did with it.
7. He isn't in his room. He is interested in finding an apartment.
8. He came home with some medicine last week.
9. He was smiling after he talked to Mary.
10. I never see him with Betty any more.
11. He was very tired when he got home from the picnic.
12. He spoke English well when he came to the United States.

EXERCISE 1.3. (To use this pattern in situations.) Listen to the sentences which describe a situation. Form responses in this pattern with the suggested words. For example:

John didn't study for his chemistry test. He failed it. should
> HE SHOULD HAVE STUDIED.

Dr. Brown left Ann Arbor for Detroit in his car at 8:00 last night. It is possible to drive from Ann Arbor to Detroit in one hour. could
> HE COULD HAVE BEEN IN DETROIT AT 9:00.

Mary didn't answer the phone when I called her up last night. might
> SHE MIGHT HAVE BEEN AT THE LIBRARY.

1. Joe didn't take the medicine the doctor prescribed for him. should
2. The laboratory was open last night, but Mary didn't practice there. could
3. Mr. and Mrs. Smith weren't home when I called on them last night. might
4. George wasn't in class yesterday. I saw the doctor's car in front of his house. must
5. It is possible that John bought a new car. I don't know. might
6. Ralph had time to finish his work, but he didn't finish it. could
7. Paul didn't shave before he went to class yesterday. should
8. The teacher returned our examinations this morning. When Betty got hers, she began to cry. must
9. Mary hasn't written to her parents for a long time. She had time to write yesterday, but she didn't. should
10. I had an acceptance from Harvard University, but I didn't go there. could
11. I had an appointment with Mr. O'Conner in his office yesterday. He didn't come. might
12. Tom received a letter this morning. After he looked at it, he went to the bank. must

EXERCISE 1.4. (To use this pattern in questions.) This is a conversation exercise. Listen to the statements. Form questions with SHOULD, COULD, or MIGHT. For example:

I didn't see the doctor in his office at 9:00. might
   MIGHT HE HAVE ARRIVED LATER?
The doctor didn't come to his office last Saturday. should
   SHOULD HE HAVE COME?
I didn't write any letters yesterday. could
   COULD YOU HAVE WRITTEN SOME?

1. I waited here from 10:00 to 11:00 in order to see my friend, but he didn't arrive. might
2. I expected him last Tuesday, but he didn't come. could
3. I wasn't able to send a letter earlier. should
4. He didn't finish his work last week. could
5. He didn't go to the hospital for his operation yesterday. should
6. I didn't see him in his office this morning. might
7. He didn't rest last week. could
8. I didn't write any letters last week. could
9. His wife wasn't with him when I saw him. might
10. He didn't do any work yesterday. could
11. He didn't call up Mrs. Jones last night. should
12. I didn't ask him about his research when I saw him. could

2. Key example: We SHOULD HAVE BEEN PRACTICING Lesson XXII.

Observe the pattern with SHOULD, etc.

Previous pattern:

We	should have practiced	English last night.

New pattern:

We	SHOULD HAVE BEEN PRACTICING	English last night.
We	COULD HAVE BEEN STUDYING	grammar.
John	MIGHT HAVE BEEN RESTING	in his room.
He	MUST HAVE BEEN THINKING	about his examination.

COMMENT

After SHOULD, COULD, etc., use HAVE BEEN + the -ING form of Class 2 words to emphasize continuation of a process during a portion of time in the past.

ILLUSTRATIVE EXAMPLES

My friend was sitting in the doctor's reception room. He wasn't doing anything when I saw him. He COULD HAVE BEEN STUDYING for his examination.

Later I saw him in a restaurant. He was eating, but he hadn't seen the
doctor yet. He SHOULD HAVE BEEN WAITING in the doctor's office.
I was expecting to learn the new pattern in five minutes before I began
to practice it yesterday. I MIGHT HAVE BEEN EXPECTING too much.
I didn't hear you speak to me last night. I MUST HAVE BEEN CONCEN-
TRATING on my work.
SHOULD John HAVE BEEN LISTENING to the radio last night?
What SHOULD he HAVE BEEN DOING?
He SHOULDN'T HAVE BEEN PLAYING the radio.
He COULD HAVE BEEN DOING his algebra or PRACTICING his English.

PRACTICE

EXERCISE 2.1. (To practice SHOULD, etc., with HAVE BEEN + the -ING
form.) Listen to the situation sentences. Form responses in this pattern
with the suggested words. For example:

> He wasn't working in his office when I got there.   should
> HE SHOULD HAVE BEEN WORKING THERE.
> He was sitting in his chair when I entered this morning.   could
> HE COULD HAVE BEEN WRITING LETTERS.
> He has been studying for a long time. He has just collapsed.   might
> HE MIGHT HAVE BEEN STUDYING TOO HARD.

1. My friend was expecting a salary of $10,000 per year. No company
   has offered him that salary so far.   might
2. I saw him while he was talking to Mr. Jones a short time ago. I
   know he needs help.   must
3. He didn't answer when I knocked on his door. I thought he wasn't
   in his room.   might
4. He was sleeping while I was writing letters.   should
5. He wasn't working in the garden when I got there.   should
6. He was listening to the radio when I saw him last night.   could
7. When I came into his room, there were several open books on his
   desk.   must
8. I knew he was home, but he didn't answer the telephone.   might
9. He has an examination today, but I saw him at the movies last
   night.   should
10. He had a pen in his hand when he came to the door.   must
11. His hands were dirty when I saw him.   might
12. He was wearing his best suit when I saw him last Sunday.   must

EXERCISE 2.2. (To contrast the uses of SHOULD HAVE STUDIED, etc.,
and SHOULD HAVE BEEN STUDYING, etc.) Listen to the situation sentences. Form responses with the suggested word. You must choose
between the two patterns of this lesson. For example:

> George has an examination today, but he didn't study for it last night.
> should
> HE SHOULD HAVE STUDIED.
> Alice has an examination too, but she wasn't studying when I saw her
> last night.   should
> SHE SHOULD HAVE BEEN STUDYING.

George had enough money to buy some new shoes, but he didn't buy any.   could
  HE COULD HAVE BOUGHT SOME.
Alice could have read her new book last night, but she wasn't reading it when I went to her room.   could
  SHE COULD HAVE BEEN READING IT.

1. George received some money from his uncle, but he didn't thank him for it.   should
2. He should have written to his uncle last night, but he wasn't writing when I went to his room.   should
3. He was near the bank this morning, but he didn't cash his check. could
4. I know he has some money, but he wasn't buying anything when I saw him in the clothing store.   could
5. Alice sometimes goes to her grandmother's house on Saturday. She wasn't home when I called on her last Saturday.   might
6. She often plays tennis on Sunday. She wasn't home when I called on her last Sunday.   might
7. Alice is always tired after she plays tennis. She played tennis yesterday.   must
8. She always takes a nap when she is tired. She was tired yesterday afternoon and she didn't answer the phone.   must
9. It was raining yesterday, but George wasn't wearing a raincoat. should.
10. I know he has a raincoat, but he didn't wear it.   could
11. Alice doesn't always speak to people when she is thinking about something. She didn't answer me when I spoke to her this morning.   must
12. It is possible that she didn't see me. I don't know.   might

3.   Key example: Should you have practiced last night?   Yes, we
              SHOULD HAVE.

Observe the short answers and the connected statements.		
Should I have practiced this pattern?	Yes, you	SHOULD HAVE.
Could John have studied last night?	No, he	COULDN'T HAVE.
Might he have been reading in his room?	Yes, he	MIGHT HAVE.
Could he have been studying very hard?	No, he	COULDN'T HAVE.
We didn't study last night,	but we	COULD HAVE.
We went to the movies,	but we	SHOULDN'T HAVE.

COMMENT

Use SHOULD HAVE, COULDN'T HAVE, etc., in short answers and in this connected statement pattern.

PRACTICE

EXERCISE 3.1. (To practice short answers like YES, YOU SHOULD HAVE, and to review previous short answers.) Give short answers to the following questions. Do not respond orally to the statements. For example:

Should you have studied last night?   YES, I SHOULD HAVE.
Might your friend have been sleeping when
  you called?   YES, HE MIGHT HAVE.
Have you read Shakespeare's plays?   NO, I HAVEN'T.
He has been working in the garden.   (No oral response.)

1. Should you have practiced last night?
2. Might your friend have been practicing in the lab?
3. Did he come to class yesterday?
4. Could he have come to class?
5. Will you go to Detroit next week?
6. Have you gone to Detroit this month?
7. Should you have gone to Detroit yesterday?
8. You should have gone by train.
9. It is necessary to study grammar.
10. Could you have learned English more quickly at home?
11. You should have been working harder this week.
12. Have you been practicing pronunciation this week?
13. Did you finish your work last night?
14. Could you have finished your work?
15. Should you have been working harder this week?
16. Will you remember this pattern tomorrow?
17. Do you think this pattern is difficult?
18. Could you have answered these questions correctly a week ago?

EXERCISE 3.2. (To practice shoi. forms with COULD HAVE, etc., in connected statements.) Listen to the statements. Repeat the statement and add a connected statement with BUT and SHOULD, COULD, MIGHT, MUST + HAVE. Use the pronunciations [súdəv, súdəntəv, máɪtəv, maɪt nátəv], etc. For example:

I didn't go.
    I DIDN'T GO, BUT I COULD HAVE.
He forgot her birthday.
    HE FORGOT HER BIRTHDAY, BUT HE SHOULDN'T HAVE.
I thought that she drove the car.
    I THOUGHT THAT SHE DROVE THE CAR, BUT SHE MIGHT NOT HAVE.
He doesn't think that he fell asleep.
    HE DOESN'T THINK THAT HE FELL ASLEEP, BUT HE MUST HAVE.

1. I thought that I paid the bill.
2. I hit him on the nose.

3. He didn't play the piano tonight.
4. It looks like he didn't work hard.
5. The professor spoke rapidly.
6. It looks like he didn't finish the composition.
7. I didn't open the door for her.
8. We thought he knew English.
9. He didn't stop for the red light.
10. I don't think he paid me.
11. We stayed up all night.
12. It seems that she didn't see me.

4.   Key example: I WISH we HAD PRACTICED Lesson XXI LAST NIGHT.

Observe the Class 2 expressions after WISH.

Observe the time expressions.

Previous pattern (Lesson XXI):

I wish the doctors   were   here   now.

New pattern:

| I WISH they
I WISH my friend | HAD BEEN
HAD GONE | here   LAST WEEK.
to the doctor after the accident.* |
| I WISH he
I WISH I
I WISH I
I WISH he | HAD RESTED
HAD HAD
COULD HAVE VISITED
COULD HAVE STAYED | LAST WEEK.
enough time to visit him.
him   YESTERDAY.
home   LAST WEEK. |

COMMENTS

(1) After WISH, use HAD VISITED, COULD HAVE VISITED, etc., with past-time expressions like YESTERDAY, LAST WEEK.
(2) Do not use VISITED and COULD VISIT with past-time expressions after WISH.

PRACTICE

EXERCISE 4.1. (To practice the pattern with a past-time expressions after WISH.) Substitute WISH, and make the entire statement affirmative. For example:

I don't think Dr. Jones was in his office yesterday.
   I WISH HE HAD BEEN IN HIS OFFICE YESTERDAY.
I don't believe Paul could drive a car a year ago.
   I WISH HE COULD HAVE DRIVEN A CAR A YEAR AGO.
I know Juan didn't speak English last year.
   I WISH HE HAD SPOKEN ENGLISH LAST YEAR.

---

*You will sometimes hear WOULD HAVE after WISH. "I wish he WOULD HAVE GONE to the doctor" is similar in meaning to "I wish he HAD GONE to the doctor."

1. I don't suppose Paul spoke Spanish a year ago.
2. I don't believe Professor Brown's lecture was interesting yesterday.
3. I don't think Mr. Smith worked in the garden last week.
4. I learned that John didn't come to class yesterday.
5. I understand that Mr. Peterson didn't sell his car.
6. I heard that Mary didn't eat dinner here last night.

Continue the exercise, and make the statement after WISH negative.
For example:

I heard that Mrs. Smith was in the hospital last week.
    I WISH SHE HADN'T BEEN IN THE HOSPITAL LAST WEEK.

7. I believe that Mrs. Smith was sick last week.
8. I think she had a bad cold.
9. I just discovered that Jane broke her leg.
10. I understand that Mr. Black had to work at night last week.
11. I heard that Mary failed her examination.
12. I just discovered that Dr. White lost all of his money.

Continue the exercise, and use an opposite describing word. For example:

I think the lesson was difficult yesterday.
    I WISH IT HAD BEEN EASY.

13. I heard that the program began late.
14. I believe that Joe was sick last week.
15. I imagine that Mary felt sad last night.
16. I heard that the dinner was very bad last night.
17. I think that the teacher spoke fast yesterday.
18. I know that the lake was cold.

EXERCISE 4.2. (To practice WISH with a variety of time expressions.)
Listen to the statements. Express your desire for an opposite situation
with WISH + a statement pattern. For example:

John isn't happy now.
    I WISH HE WAS HAPPY NOW.
John wasn't happy yesterday.
    I WISH HE HAD BEEN HAPPY YESTERDAY.
He doesn't study hard.
    I WISH HE STUDIED HARD.
He didn't study hard last week.
    I WISH HE HAD STUDIED HARD LAST WEEK.

1. He didn't practice in the laboratory yesterday evening.
2. He didn't finish his work last night.
3. He isn't speaking English now.
4. He didn't remember my name when he ran into me.
5. He doesn't know how to play tennis.
6. He can't drive a car.
7. He didn't make a speech at the program last Friday.
8. He doesn't have a lot of money this month.
9. He wasn't in his room when I called on him yesterday.

10. He doesn't like to ride a bicycle in the winter.
11. He doesn't speak English perfectly.
12. He couldn't find the restaurant last night.

KEY EXAMPLES OF LESSON XXII

1. We didn't practice Lesson **XXI** last night, but we SHOULD HAVE PRACTICED it.
2. We SHOULD HAVE BEEN PRACTICING Lesson **XXII**.
3. Should you have practiced last night? YES, WE SHOULD HAVE.
4. I WISH we HAD PRACTICED Lesson **XXI** LAST NIGHT.

Lesson XXIII

1. I AM STUDYING BECAUSE I HAVE AN EXAMINATION.
[Sequences of statements connected with BECAUSE, ALTHOUGH, IF, etc.]

2. BECAUSE OF MY EXAMINATION
[BECAUSE OF, IN SPITE OF + Class 1]

1. Key example: I am studying BECAUSE I have an examination this afternoon.

Observe the connecting words between statements.

Previous connecting words (Lesson XVI):

I like to study	when	the professor is here.
I like to study	while	the professor is here.
I like to study	before	the professor arrives.
I like to study	until	the professor arrives.
I like to study	after	the professor arrives.

New connecting words:

I like to study	WHENEVER	the professor is here.
I like to study	IF	the professor is here.
I like to study	UNLESS	the professor is here.
I like to study	ALTHOUGH	the professor is here.*
I like to study	BECAUSE	the professor is here.
I like to study	WHETHER OR NOT	the professor is here.

COMMENT

WHENEVER, IF, UNLESS, ALTHOUGH, BECAUSE, WHETHER OR NOT connect statements. (See WHEN, BEFORE, etc., in Lesson XVI.)

ILLUSTRATIVE EXAMPLES

I never forget my umbrella when it rains. I take my umbrella WHEN-EVER it rains.

It was raining yesterday, but Mary didn't have her umbrella. She forgot her umbrella ALTHOUGH it was raining.

I took my umbrella BECAUSE it was raining.

It might rain this afternoon. I must take my umbrella IF it rains.

The sun was shining this morning, but Professor Taylor had his umbrella. He takes his umbrella WHETHER OR NOT it is raining.

I didn't take my umbrella BECAUSE the sun was shining. I don't take my umbrella UNLESS IT RAINS.

---

*You will often hear "I like to study THOUGH the professor is here." The meaning is the same. Other connectives with similar meanings are EVEN THOUGH, EVEN IF, and EVEN WHEN.

223

Please call Mrs. Taylor	WHEN	the professor comes.
Do you want me to call her	WHETHER OR NOT	he comes?
No, don't call her	UNLESS	he comes.
What shall I do	IF	he comes late?
Call her	WHENEVER	he arrives.

NOTE: Statements introduced by the connecting words are used in questions and requests.

I like to study WHEN the professor is here.
WHEN the professor is here, I like to study.

I might go to New York IF it doesn't cost too much.
IF it doesn't cost too much, I might go to New York.

I went to bed early last night BECAUSE I was tired.
BECAUSE I was tired, I went to bed early last night.

NOTE: The statement introduced by WHEN, IF, BECAUSE, etc., may be used before or after the other statement. The meaning is the same. The difference is a matter of style.

I like to study WHETHER OR NOT   the professor is here.
I like to study WHETHER   the professor is here OR NOT.
He takes his umbrella WHETHER OR NOT it is raining.
He takes his umbrella WHETHER   it is raining OR NOT.

NOTE: WHETHER is often separated from OR NOT. The meaning is the same as in the unseparated pattern.

PRACTICE

EXERCISE 1.1. (To practice WHETHER OR NOT.) This is a conversation exercise. Answer the questions, using WHETHER OR NOT. For example:

Do you want to go to the picnic if it rains?
    YES. I WANT TO GO WHETHER OR NOT IT RAINS.
Or YES. I WANT TO GO WHETHER IT RAINS OR NOT.
Do you usually go to the movies Friday night if you have to study?
    YES. I USUALLY GO WHETHER OR NOT I HAVE TO STUDY.
Do you like to go to the movies when your friends go with you?
    YES. I LIKE TO GO WHETHER OR NOT THEY GO WITH ME.

1. Do you often go to the movies if your homework isn't finished?
2. Can you understand the actors when they speak fast?
3. Do you like the movies if there isn't much action?
4. Do you enjoy the movies if the actresses aren't beautiful?
5. Do you want to go to the movies tonight if the teacher doesn't give us any homework?
6. Can you finish your homework before the movies if I help you?
7. Do you like to study before dinner if you are tired?
8. Can you study when your friends are talking?
9. Do you like your friends to visit you when you are studying?

10. Do you continue to study if there is a good television program?
11. Do you want to go to the movies if there is a good television program?
12. Do you want to get something to eat after the movie if it isn't too late?

EXERCISE 1.2. (To force a choice between IF and UNLESS.) Listen to the following statements. Show the relationship between the ideas with IF or UNLESS. For example:

> The weather is nice. We have a picnic every Sunday.
> WE HAVE A PICNIC EVERY SUNDAY IF THE WEATHER IS NICE.
> It's raining. We have a picnic every Sunday.
> WE HAVE A PICNIC EVERY SUNDAY UNLESS IT'S RAINING.
> John has finished his homework. He usually goes to the movies.
> HE USUALLY GOES TO THE MOVIES IF HE HAS FINISHED HIS HOMEWORK.
> John has to study. He usually goes to the movies.
> HE USUALLY GOES TO THE MOVIES UNLESS HE HAS TO STUDY.

1. I am tired. I usually go to bed early.
2. I am very tired. I seldom go to bed early.
3. The water is warm enough. I like to go swimming.
4. The water is too cold. I like to go swimming.
5. Help me. I can't work these algebra problems.
6. Help me. I can work these algebra problems.
7. Paul's too busy. He takes a nap every afternoon.
8. Paul has time. He takes a nap every afternoon.
9. The train is on time. It arrives at 11:10.
10. The train is late. It arrives at 11:10.
11. I have enough money. I might go to Florida for my vacation.
12. A student wants to learn English. He must practice every day.
13. Lend me some money. I can't buy any new shoes.
14. I finish my homework. I shouldn't go to the movies tonight.
15. People speak slowly. The new student from Peru can understand English.
16. A student knows arithmetic well. It is difficult for him to learn algebra.
17. An algebra student knows arithmetic already. He must learn it quickly.
18. An intelligent student knows arithmetic. Algebra is not difficult for him.

EXERCISE 1.3. (To force a choice between ALTHOUGH and BECAUSE.) Tomás Gómez is a friendly and polite young man. He is quite serious and wants to be co-operative. With this in mind, describe the following situations by using ALTHOUGH or BECAUSE. Use the last words in the situation sentence in the first part of your response. For example:

> It was difficult for Tomás to learn English quickly.
> HE LEARNED ENGLISH QUICKLY ALTHOUGH IT WAS DIFFICULT FOR HIM.
> It was necessary for him to attend Riverside University.
> HE ATTENDED RIVERSIDE UNIVERSITY BECAUSE IT WAS NECESSARY.

It was easy for Jack to help Tomás write the letter.
JACK HELPED TOMÁS WRITE THE LETTER BECAUSE IT WAS
EASY FOR HIM.
It was difficult for Tomás to write to the University.
HE WROTE TO THE UNIVERSITY ALTHOUGH IT WAS DIFFICULT.

1. It was difficult for Tomás to study English.
2. It was difficult for him to speak English.
3. It was difficult for him to practice constantly.
4. It was difficult for him to learn English.
5. It was necessary for him to learn English.
6. He needed English and he learned it.
7. It was necessary for him to write a letter.
8. It was necessary to apply for admission early.
9. His adviser had told him to study economics at Riverside.
10. His adviser didn't ask him to study English there.
11. He told him not to buy a lot of books.
12. The weather was very hot, but he worked hard.
13. Jack advised him to drop economics, but Tomás wanted to continue the course.
14. It was difficult, but he completed the course.
15. He had difficulty with his English, but he was one of the best students in the class.
16. English is not his native language, but he completed the course.
17. He needed the course and he completed it.
18. He wanted to attend Central University later, and he enrolled in Riverside University for the fall semester.

EXERCISE 1.4. (To use IF, BECAUSE, etc., in a particular situation.)
Listen to the situation. Repeat and complete the sentences below.
"Oscar is a playboy at the beginning of each month when he has money.
He is an amiable playboy. His friends enjoy his company. They also
appreciate his presence in town because he gets a very big check at the
beginning of every month. He lends his money freely and forgets to ask
for it again. He is always very poor, but still happy, at the end of the
month."

1. He gives money to his friends whenever—
2. They frequently ask him for money because—
3. He likes them very much although—
4. He doesn't actually spend much for himself because—
5. He goes to night clubs if—
6. He is always happy whether or not—
7. He always lends money to his friends unless—
8. He spends money and lends money whenever—
9. He couldn't take his girl friend to the dance on June 28 because—
10. He went to New York the next day although—

2.   Key example: I am studying BECAUSE OF my examination.

Observe the words after BECAUSE OF and IN SPITE OF.

Previous <u>pattern</u>:

I took my umbrella	because	it was raining.
I went to the movies	because	my friend wanted me to go.
We played tennis	although	it was raining.
We went to Detroit	although	Mr. Smith advised us not to go.

New <u>pattern</u>:

I took my umbrella	BECAUSE OF	the rain.*
I went to the movies	BECAUSE OF	my friend.
We played tennis	IN SPITE OF	the rain.**
We went to Detroit	IN SPITE OF	Mr. Smith.

COMMENT

Use Class 1 words (RAIN, FRIEND, etc.) after BECAUSE OF and IN SPITE OF.

PRACTICE

EXERCISE 2.1. (To produce Class 1 words after BECAUSE OF.) Listen to the statements with BECAUSE. Repeat with BECAUSE OF. For example:

> I came here because I wanted the English course.
> **I CAME BECAUSE OF THE ENGLISH COURSE.**
> I stayed home because it was raining.
> **I STAYED HOME BECAUSE OF THE RAIN.**
> I'm resting because my head aches.
> **I'M RESTING BECAUSE OF MY HEADACHE.**

1. The doctor wrote the book because his patients needed it.
2. He wrote it because he was interested.
3. He went to Florida because the weather was cold in the winter.
4. He went to the lake because the weather was hot in August.
5. Tomás wants one course because the professor is famous.
6. He wanted to study business administration because his father asked him to.
7. He needed help with the letter because his English was not very good.
8. The school sent him an application form because his letter requested information.
9. He didn't answer the letter immediately because he had a lot of homework to do.
10. Later the school couldn't accept him because the number of applications was too great.

---

*You will also hear "I took my umbrella ON ACCOUNT OF THE rain" and "I took my umbrella DUE to the rain." The meaning is the same.

**You will also hear "We played tennis REGARDLESS OF the rain." The meaning is the same.

The words introduced by BECAUSE OF, IN SPITE OF, etc., may be used at the beginning of the statement: "BECAUSE OF the rain, I took my umbrella."

11. He took economics because his professor advised him to.
12. He studied late at night because the assignments were very long.

EXERCISE 2.2. (To produce Class 1 words after IN SPITE OF.) Listen to the statements with ALTHOUGH. Repeat with IN SPITE OF. For example:

We went on a picnic although the weather was cool.
WE WENT ON A PICNIC IN SPITE OF THE COOL WEATHER.
Jack went with us although he had a lot of work to do.
JACK WENT WITH US IN SPITE OF HIS WORK.
Ruth went too although she had a cold.
RUTH WENT TOO IN SPITE OF HER COLD.

1. Betty went too although her mother didn't want her to.
2. George went too although he had a class.
3. We didn't wear coats although the weather was cool.
4. We went in George's car although the engine was in bad condition.
5. We decided to go to Fish Lake although the distance was great.
6. We wanted to go there although the road was not very good.
7. We got there in an hour although George's car was very old.
8. We swam in the lake although the water was cold.
9. We sat on the ground although the grass was wet.
10. We enjoyed our lunch although the coffee was cold.
11. We stayed all afternoon although it began to rain.
12. We started home at 6:00 although Betty wanted to stay longer.

SUMMARY EXERCISE. (To practice all the patterns of Lesson XXIII.) Consider the following situation. Then complete the statements by continuing the same theme.

"Oscar is friendly and carefree. He is happy to give everything to his friends who spend most of his large amounts of money."

1. Oscas has many friends because—
2. A few of his friends like him only because of—
3. Most of his friends like him because—
4. He likes all of them although—
5. He spends his money freely if—
6. He gives away his books when—
7. He acts like a poor man in spite of—
8. He is still happy at the end of the month although—
9. He is always carefree whether or not—
10. He can't take his friends to parties at the end of the month because—
11. Oscar's uncle should send him clothes in place of the check because of—
12. The size of the check is very large. His uncle doesn't send him any clothes because of—
13. Oscar can't buy any clothes in spite of—
14. He doesn't have any good shirts because—

KEY EXAMPLES OF LESSON XXIII

1. I am studying BECAUSE I have an examination this afternoon.
2. I am studying BECAUSE OF my examination.

Lesson XXIV

1. I WILL HELP YOU IF YOU NEED HELP.
   I WOULD HELP YOU IF YOU NEEDED HELP.
   [Correlations of Class 2 words and expressions in sequences of statements connected by IF, etc., in present and future time situations]*

2. I WOULD HAVE HELPED YOU LAST WEEK IF YOU HAD NEEDED HELP THEN.
   [Class 2 expressions in sequences of statements connected by IF, etc., with past-time expressions]

1. Key examples: Your adviser WILL help you IF you need help.
I WOULD help you IF you NEEDED help.

Observe the correlation of WILL, WOULD, etc., with the form of the Class 2 words after IF.

I	WILL	help you	IF	you	NEED	help.
I	CAN	help you	IF	you	NEED	help.
I	WOULD	help you	IF	you	NEEDED	help.
I	COULD	help you	IF	you	NEEDED	help.

COMMENTS

(1) Use WILL, CAN, etc., in the first statement with the simple form or the -S form of the Class 2 word (NEED, NEEDS, etc.) in the statement after IF, etc., in this pattern.

(2) Use WOULD, etc., in the first statement with the -ED form of the Class 2 word (NEEDED, etc.) in the statement after IF, etc., in this pattern.**

(3) WOULD, COULD, etc., in the first statement and the -ED form of the statement after IF, etc., indicate that the speaker thinks the situation being expressed is not probable or is contrary to fact.

(4) See illustrative examples for other words which are used in the positions of WILL, WOULD, and IF.***

---

*Both this lesson and part of Lesson XXIII are about sequences of statements connected by IF, UNLESS, etc. In Lesson XXIII, the emphasis is on the connecting words. In this lesson, the emphasis is on the form of the Class 2 words and expressions which are used in certain connected statements.

**You will sometimes hear COULD in the first statement with the simple or -S form of the Class 2 word in the statement after IF, etc. You will not hear CAN with the -ED form.

***You may hear IN CASE, PROVIDED (THAT), IN THE EVENT (THAT) in the position of IF and with the same meaning.

ILLUSTRATIVE EXAMPLES

I	WILL	study algebra next year	IF	I	HAVE	time.
I	SHOULD	study algebra next year	IF	I	HAVE	time.
I	MUST	study algebra next year	IF	I	HAVE	time.
I	MIGHT	study algebra next year	IF	I	HAVE	time.
I	AM GOING TO	study algebra next year	IF	I	HAVE	time.
I	HAVE TO	study algebra next year	IF	I	HAVE	time.
I	EXPECT TO	study algebra next year	IF	I	HAVE	time.

NOTE: SHOULD, MUST, MIGHT, AM GOING TO, HAVE TO, and the
      simple or -S forms of some Class 2 words + TO, are used in
      the position of WILL.

I	WOULD	study algebra next year	IF	I	HAD	time.
I	MIGHT	study algebra next year	IF	I	HAD	time.
I	WAS GOING TO	study algebra next year	IF	I	HAD	time.
I	EXPECTED TO	study algebra next year	IF	I	HAD	time.

NOTE: MIGHT, WAS GOING TO, and the -ED forms of some Class 2
      words + TO, are used in the position of WOULD and COULD.
      Observe that MIGHT is used with both the simple and the -ED
      forms of the Class 2 word in the statement after IF.

Juan	WOULD	enter the university next year	IF		he SPOKE English well.
He	WOULDN'T	enter the university	UNLESS		he SPOKE English well.
He	COULD	go to a smaller college	WHETHER OR NOT		he SPOKE English well.
He	WOULD	study there	UNTIL		he LEARNED English well.
He	COULD	go to the university	WHEN-EVER		he LEARNED English well.
He	WOULD	enter the university	AFTER		he LEARNED English well.

NOTE: UNLESS, WHETHER OR NOT, WHENEVER, WHEN, WHILE,
      BEFORE, AFTER, UNTIL, etc., are used in the position of IF.

SITUATION: I think Mr. Taylor is going to drive to Detroit tomorrow.
           I don't think he is going to go to New York.

PATTERN: I WILL   go with him   IF he GOES   to Detroit.
           I WILL   ride with him IF he DRIVES to Detroit.
           I WILL   go to Detroit IF he DOES.
           I WOULD go with him   IF he WENT   to New York.
           I WOULD ride with him IF he DROVE to New York.
           I WOULD go to New York IF he DID.

SITUATION: I think this geography book is in English. I can read
English. That history book is in Russian. I can't read
Russian.

PATTERN:

I CAN	read this geography book	IF		it IS	in English.
I CAN'T	read it	UNLESS		it IS	in English.
I WILL	read it	IF		it IS.	
I WILL	read it	IF		I CAN.	
I COULD	read that history book	IF		it WAS in English.	
I COULDN'T	read it	UNLESS		it WAS in English.	
I WOULD	read it	IF		it WAS.	
I WOULD	read it	IF		I COULD.	

SITUATION: There is going to be a football game next Saturday. It
might be nice weather then, or it might be raining. I don't
think it is going to snow.

PATTERN:

I WILL	go	IF	it	IS	nice weather.
I WON'T	go	UNLESS	it	IS	nice weather.
I WILL	go	IF	it	ISN'T	raining.
I WON'T	go	UNLESS	it	ISN'T	raining.
I WOULDN'T	go	IF	it	WAS	snowing.
Some of my friends WOULD	go	WHETHER OR NOT	it	WAS	snowing.

PRACTICE

EXERCISE 1.1. (To practice the correlation of WILL, WOULD, etc., with
the forms of the Class 2 word after IF, etc.) Imagine you are talking to
a person who hopes to go to Europe next summer. You want to go to
Europe, but you don't have enough money. Respond to his statements as
in the examples.

I will go by plane if I go to Europe.
   I WOULD GO BY PLANE IF I WENT TO EUROPE.
I will arrive in London in a few hours after I leave New York.
   I WOULD ARRIVE IN LONDON IN A FEW HOURS AFTER I LEFT
   NEW YORK.

1. I will fly on to Paris after I see London.
2. I can see the cathedral of Notre Dame while I am in Paris.
3. I will visit Sweden after I leave Paris.
4. I can see Stockholm while I am in Sweden.
5. I will go to Germany after I visit Sweden.
6. I can stop in Berlin if I want to.
7. I will go through Switzerland after I leave Germany.
8. I will cross the Alps when I go through Switzerland.
9. I will arrive in Italy after I cross the Alps.
10. I can ride in a gondola if I go to Venice.
11. I expect to see many famous museums if I stop in Florence.

EXERCISE 1.2. (To practice WOULD, etc., and the -ED forms in situations.) Give complete answers to the following questions. For example:

What would you do if you were sick?
  I WOULD GO TO A DOCTOR IF I WAS SICK.
What would you do if you were rich?
  I WOULD TRAVEL AROUND THE WORLD IF I WAS RICH.
What would you do if someone stole your car?
  I WOULD TELL THE POLICE IF SOMEONE STOLE MY CAR.

1. What would you do if you were a millionaire?
2. What would you do if you had a car?
3. What would you do if you were president?
4. What would you do if you were a child again?
5. What would you do if you had all the money you wanted?
6. What would you do if you discovered a gold mine?
7. What would you do if you found $50 on the street?
8. What could you do if you needed money?
9. What could you do if you were sick?
10. What could you do if you tore your coat?
11. What might you do if you had a vacation next week?
12. What might you do if you were a king?
13. What might you do if you became blind?

EXERCISE 1.3. FOR ADVANCED STUDENTS. (To practice WILL with the simple forms in a series of statements.) Imagine the following situations. Make a series of statements, as in the examples.

SITUATION: We might go to New York during the vacation. It depends on our receiving money.

Student A: IF WE RECEIVE OUR MONEY, WE WILL GO TO NEW YORK DURING THE VACATION.
       B: IF WE GO TO NEW YORK, WE WILL GO BY PLANE.
       C: IF WE GO BY PLANE, WE WILL ARRIVE AT LA GUARDIA AIRPORT.
       D: IF WE ARRIVE AT LA GUARDIA AIRPORT, OUR FRIENDS WILL MEET US.
       E: IF OUR FRIENDS MEET US, WE WILL STAY WITH THEM.
       F: IF WE STAY WITH THEM WE WILL VISIT SOME MUSEUMS, THEATERS, AND PLACES OF INTEREST.
       G: IF WE VISIT SOME MUSEUMS, THEATERS, AND PLACES OF INTEREST, WE WILL SPEND ALL OUR MONEY.
       H: IF WE SPEND ALL OUR MONEY, WE WILL COME BACK "BROKE."
       I: IF WE COME BACK "BROKE," WE WILL HAVE TO STAY HOME FOR A MONTH.

SITUATION 1: Perhaps you will have some extra time this month. What will you do?

       A: IF WE HAVE SOME EXTRA TIME THIS MONTH, WE WILL GO TO CHICAGO.

B: IF WE GO TO CHICAGO, WE WILL GO BY BUS.

SITUATION 2:   It is possible for Mr. Gonzales to learn English. What
will he do then?

A: IF MR. GONZALES LEARNS ENGLISH, HE WILL WORK IN
THE CONSULATE.
B: IF HE WORKS IN THE CONSULATE, HE WILL HAVE A
GOOD POSITION.

SITUATION 3:   Oscar might receive a check this month. What will he do?

A: IF OSCAR RECEIVES A CHECK THIS MONTH, HE WILL
BUY A CAR.
B: IF HE BUYS A CAR, HE WILL DRIVE TO ST. LOUIS.

EXERCISE 1.4.   FOR ADVANCED STUDENTS. (To practice WOULD
with the -ED forms in a series of statements.) Imagine the following
situations. Make a series of statements, as in the examples.

SITUATION: I can't go to New York during the vacation. I won't receive
my money in time. BUT

Student A: IF I RECEIVED MY MONEY IN TIME, I WOULD GO TO NEW
YORK DURING THE VACATION.
B: IF I WENT TO NEW YORK, I WOULD GO BY PLANE.
C: IF I WENT BY PLANE, I WOULD ARRIVE AT LA GUARDIA
AIRPORT.
D: IF I ARRIVED AT LA GUARDIA AIRPORT, MY FRIEND
WOULD MEET ME.
E: IF MY FRIEND MET ME, I WOULD STAY WITH HIM.
F: IF I STAYED WITH HIM, WE WOULD VISIT SOME MUSEUMS,
THEATERS, AND PLACES OF INTEREST.
G: IF WE VISITED SOME MUSEUMS, THEATERS, AND PLACES
OF INTEREST, I WOULD SPEND ALL MY MONEY.
H: IF I SPENT ALL MY MONEY, I WOULD COME BACK
"BROKE."
I: IF I CAME BACK "BROKE," I WOULD HAVE TO STAY
HOME FOR A MONTH.

SITUATION 1:   You don't have any extra time this week, but let's
imagine that you do.

A: IF I HAD SOME EXTRA TIME THIS WEEK, I WOULD TAKE
A TRIP TO CANADA.
B: IF I TOOK A TRIP TO CANADA, I WOULD GO WITH MY
FRIEND.

SITUATION 2:   Oscar will not receive a check this week, but let's pre-
tend that he will.

A: IF OSCAR RECEIVED A CHECK THIS WEEK, HE WOULD
BUY A CAR.
B: IF HE BOUGHT A CAR, HE WOULD DRIVE TO ST. LOUIS.

SITUATION 3: You don't live in California, but let's imagine that you do.

A: IF I LIVED IN CALIFORNIA, I WOULD LIVE ON A RANCH.
B: IF I LIVED ON A RANCH, I WOULD OWN A HORSE.

2. Key example: Your adviser WOULD HAVE HELPED you LAST WEEK IF you HAD NEEDED help THEN.

Observe the Class 2 expressions. Observe the time expressions.

Previous pattern:

| I | would help | you tomorrow | if you | needed | help then. |
| I | would help | you now | if you | needed | help today. |

New pattern:

I	WOULD HAVE HELPED	you YESTERDAY	IF you	HAD NEEDED	help THEN.
I	MIGHT HAVE SEEN	you	IF you	HAD BEEN	here LAST WEEK.
I	COULD HAVE MET	you LAST WEEK	IF you	HAD COME	by train.

COMMENT

With past-time expressions (YESTERDAY, LAST WEEK, etc.) in this pattern, use WOULD, COULD, MIGHT + HAVE + the -ED/-EN forms (HELPED, SEEN, etc.) in the first statement and HAD + the -ED/-EN forms in the statement after IF, etc.

ILLUSTRATIVE EXAMPLES

I COULD HAVE ATTENDED a school board meeting LAST NIGHT IF I HAD WANTED to.
I WOULDN'T HAVE STAYED home UNLESS I HAD HAD a lot of work to do.
I'm sure that I WOULD HAVE ENJOYED it IF I HAD GONE.
My friends tell me that I WOULD HAVE LEARNED a lot IF I HAD BEEN there.
I MIGHT HAVE GONE IF I HAD HAD a little more time.

PRACTICE

EXERCISE 2.1. (To practice this pattern with past-time expressions.) Substitute a past-time expression. Change the Class 2 expressions as necessary. For example:

I would go to Chicago next week if I had a car.
    I WOULD HAVE GONE TO CHICAGO LAST WEEK IF I HAD HAD A CAR.

I might see the art museum if I went to Chicago next week.
> I MIGHT HAVE SEEN THE ART MUSEUM IF I HAD GONE TO CHICAGO LAST WEEK.

I couldn't take a vacation next month unless my father sent me some money.
> I COULDN'T HAVE TAKEN A VACATION LAST MONTH UNLESS MY FATHER HAD SENT ME SOME MONEY.

1. I would go to the football game next Saturday if the weather was nice.
2. I would wear my raincoat today if it was cloudy.
3. I would study tonight if I had to.
4. I could see you tonight if you weren't too busy.
5. I would finish my homework this evening if you helped me.
6. I might listen to the radio tonight if I didn't have too much homework.
7. I might pass my examinations next week if I studied harder.
8. George wouldn't bring his friends tomorrow unless you asked him to.
9. Mary wouldn't be happy unless George was here.
10. Paul couldn't go to the picnic today unless his cold was better.
11. Betty might not come to the party this Friday if you didn't send her a special invitation.
12. I might buy a new car this year if you lent me the money.

EXERCISE 2.2. (To convert meanings presented through a pattern of Lesson XII into the new pattern.) Listen to these statements with BY and change the words to the forms necessary in the pattern with IF. For example:

Mr. Gonzales didn't learn much about the system of education. He could have learned more by visiting school board meetings.
> HE COULD HAVE LEARNED MORE IF HE HAD VISITED SCHOOL BOARD MEETINGS.

He didn't learn much English. He would have learned more by practicing.
> HE WOULD HAVE LEARNED MORE IF HE HAD PRACTICED.

He didn't see many plays. He could have seen a lot by watching television.
> HE COULD HAVE SEEN A LOT IF HE HAD WATCHED TELEVISION.

1. He didn't learn any songs. He could have learned several by going to activity hours.
2. He didn't learn much about education. He might have learned a lot by borrowing my book.
3. I didn't help him very much. I could have helped him by giving him my book.
4. I didn't discuss the subject very intelligently. I would have discussed it better by reading my book first.
5. He never understood people. He would have understood them better by talking to them.
6. He didn't notice the customs. He could have learned them by observing people.

7. He didn't finish the assignment. He could have finished it by working harder.
8. He didn't do well on the examination. He could have done better by studying more.
9. He didn't arrive on time. He would have arrived earlier by taking a plane.
10. I didn't find his house. I might have found it by looking harder.

EXERCISE 2.3. (To practice this pattern in various situations.) Give complete answers to the following questions. For example:

What would you have done if you had been sick yesterday?
   I WOULD HAVE CALLED A DOCTOR IF I HAD BEEN SICK YESTERDAY.
What might you have done if you hadn't studied last night?
   I MIGHT HAVE GONE TO THE MOVIES IF I HADN'T STUDIED LAST NIGHT.
What would you have done if someone had stolen your car?
   I WOULD HAVE TOLD THE POLICE IF SOMEONE HAD STOLEN MY CAR.

1. What would you have done if you had stayed in your country?
2. What would you have done if you had gone to France last year?
3. What would you have done if you had found a $50 bill on the street yesterday?
4. What would you have done if you had been Napoleon?
5. What would you have done if you had been born in 1400?
6. What could you have done if you had needed money last week?
7. What could you have done if you had torn your coat yesterday?
8. What could you have done if you had lost all your money last week?
9. What might you have done if you had had a vacation last week?
10. What might you have done if you had been Adam?
11. What might you have done if you had lived 100 years ago?
12. What would you have done if you had been Columbus?

EXERCISE 2.4. FOR ADVANCED STUDENTS. (To practice this pattern in a series of statements.) Imagine the following situations. Make a series of statements, as in the examples.

SITUATION: I didn't go to New York during the last vacation. I didn't receive my money in time. BUT

Student A: IF I HAD RECEIVED MY MONEY ON TIME, I WOULD HAVE GONE TO NEW YORK DURING THE VACATION.
   B: IF I HAD GONE TO NEW YORK, I WOULD HAVE GONE BY PLANE.
   C: IF I HAD GONE BY PLANE, I WOULD HAVE ARRIVED AT LA GUARDIA AIRPORT.
   D: IF I HAD ARRIVED AT LA GUARDIA AIRPORT, MY FRIEND WOULD HAVE MET ME.
   E: IF MY FRIEND HAD MET ME, I WOULD HAVE STAYED WITH HIM.

F: IF I HAD STAYED WITH HIM, WE WOULD HAVE VISITED SOME MUSEUMS, THEATERS, AND PLACES OF INTEREST.

G: IF WE HAD VISITED SOME MUSEUMS, THEATERS, AND PLACES OF INTEREST, I WOULD HAVE SPENT ALL MY MONEY.

H: IF I HAD SPENT ALL MY MONEY, I WOULD HAVE COME BACK "BROKE."

I: IF I HAD COME BACK "BROKE," I WOULD HAVE HAD TO STAY HOME FOR A MONTH.

SITUATION 1: You didn't have any extra time last week, but let's imagine that you did.

A: IF I HAD HAD SOME EXTRA TIME LAST WEEK, I WOULD HAVE TAKEN A TRIP TO CANADA.

B: IF I HAD TAKEN A TRIP TO CANADA, I WOULD HAVE GONE WITH MY FRIEND.

SITUATION 2: You weren't hungry at 10 o'clock yesterday, but let's imagine that you were.

A: IF I HAD BEEN HUNGRY AT 10 O'CLOCK YESTERDAY, I WOULD HAVE GONE TO THE SNACK BAR.

B: IF I HAD GONE TO THE SNACK BAR, I WOULD HAVE TAKEN MY FRIEND.

KEY EXAMPLES OF LESSON XXIV

1. Your adviser WILL help you IF you NEED help.
   I WOULD help you IF you NEEDED help.
2. Your adviser WOULD HAVE HELPED you LAST WEEK IF you HAD NEEDED help THEN.

Lesson XXV

1. SO BUSY THAT, SUCH A BUSY MAN THAT
   [SO. . .THAT, SUCH. . .THAT + statement pattern]

2. Isn't the professor busy? YES, HE IS.
   [Responses to negative questions]

3. THE PROFESSOR IS BUSY, ISN'T HE? YES, HE IS.
   [Attached questions]

1. Key examples: The professor is SO BUSY THAT he can't leave his office. He is SUCH A BUSY MAN THAT he can't leave his office.

Observe the words after SO and SUCH, and the pattern after THAT.

Previous patterns (Lesson XIII):

The professor is	very busy.	
He is	too busy	to leave his office.
His secretary spoke	too rapidly	for me to understand.
The professor is	a very busy man.	

New Pattern:

The professor is	SO	BUSY	THAT	he can't leave his office.*
His secretary spoke	SO	RAPIDLY	THAT	I couldn't understand her.
The professor had	SO	MUCH WORK	THAT	I had to wait for him.
The professor is	SUCH A BUSY MAN		THAT	he can't leave his office.
His secretary was	SUCH A NICE PERSON		THAT	I enjoyed the visit.
The professor had	SUCH A LOT OF WORK		THAT	I had to wait for him.

COMMENTS

(1) Use SO with words like BUSY, RAPIDLY, etc., (Class 3 and Class 4) and with the quantity words MUCH, MANY, LITTLE, FEW.
(2) Use SUCH with Class 1 words (MAN, PERSON, etc.) that are not preceded by MANY, MUCH, LITTLE, FEW.
(3) Use a statement pattern after SO. . .THAT, SUCH. . .THAT to indicate a result or consequence of the first statement.

ILLUSTRATIVE EXAMPLES

What did you say is	SO	NICE	THAT Mary wants to buy it?
I said this dress is	SO	NICE	THAT Mary wants to buy it.
Why is it	SO	NICE	THAT she wants to buy it?

*You will also hear this pattern without THAT: THE PROFESSOR IS SO BUSY HE CAN'T LEAVE HIS OFFICE.

It is made	SO	NICELY	THAT she wants to buy it.
Is it	SUCH	A NICE DRESS	THAT she wants it very much?
Yes, but it is	SO	EXPENSIVE	THAT she can't buy it.
Does it cost	SO	MUCH MONEY	THAT her father can't buy it for her?
Yes, he has	SO	LITTLE MONEY	THAT he can't buy it either.
But he wishes he had	SUCH	A LOT OF MONEY	THAT he could buy it for her.

PRACTICE

EXERCISE 1.1. (To connect statements and indicate consequence with SO. . .THAT.) Connect these statements with SO. . .THAT. For example:

The system of education is interesting. I wanted to learn all about it.
THE SYSTEM OF EDUCATION IS SO INTERESTING THAT I WANTED TO LEARN ALL ABOUT IT.
I went to hear many speeches. I learned all about it.
I WENT TO HEAR SO MANY SPEECHES THAT I LEARNED ALL ABOUT IT.
One speech was long. I got sleepy.
ONE SPEECH WAS SO LONG THAT I GOT SLEEPY.

1. The class on education was interesting. I never missed an assignment.
2. The teacher gave many assignments. I was always busy.
3. The class textbook was good. I had to finish it before I could sleep.
4. The book was long. I didn't finish it until 2:00 a. m.
5. It was written simply. I could read it rapidly.
6. It was interesting. I didn't get sleepy.
7. The system of education here is complex. It is difficult to understand.
8. There are many books in the education library. I can never read them all.
9. Some of the books are important. I must read them.
10. I can buy few books. I have to take a lot from the library.
11. The library has many books. It is difficult to find the ones I want.
12. There are many librarians. I can always find one to help me.

EXERCISE 1.2. (To connect statements and indicate consequence with SUCH. . .THAT.) Connect these statements with SUCH. . .THAT. For example:

A lot of people came. We had to move the class to a bigger room.
SUCH A LOT OF PEOPLE CAME THAT WE HAD TO MOVE THE CLASS TO A BIGGER ROOM.
We had a difficult problem. We couldn't solve it.
WE HAD SUCH A DIFFICULT PROBLEM THAT WE COULDN'T SOLVE IT.
The instructor gives long assignments. We are always busy.
THE INSTRUCTOR GIVES SUCH LONG ASSIGNMENTS THAT WE ARE ALWAYS BUSY.

1. He's an interesting speaker. I don't want to miss him.
2. He talks about important problems. They deserve our complete attention.
3. I have a lot of difficulty with the work. I have to ask many questions.
4. This is an easy exercise. I can do it in two minutes.
5. The instructor gave me a long assignment. I will have to work late tonight.
6. Professor Taylor is an interesting teacher. We like to go to his classes.
7. He gives clear explanations. We learn a lot from him.
8. Paul is an intelligent young man. He learns more than his classmates.
9. He is a good student. I want to be like him.
10. English is an easy language. We can learn it quickly.
11. We have to do a lot of homework. We can't go to many parties.
12. We have a good time here. We don't want to go home.

EXERCISE 1.3. (To contrast SO. . .THAT, SUCH. . .THAT and the expression TOO. . .TO from Lesson XIII.) Listen to the statements with TOO SHORT TO, etc.,+ a Class 2 word. Produce a similar statement with SO SHORT THAT, etc., + a statement pattern. Another student produces a similar statement with SUCH A SHORT BOY THAT, etc. For example:

Paul is too short to reach the apple on the tree.
STUD. A: PAUL IS SO SHORT THAT HE CAN'T REACH THE APPLE ON THE TREE.
STUD. B: PAUL IS SUCH A SHORT BOY THAT HE CAN'T REACH THE APPLE ON THE TREE.
Peter is too old to become a soldier.
STUD. A: PETER IS SO OLD THAT HE CAN'T BECOME A SOLDIER.
STUD. B: PETER IS SUCH AN OLD MAN THAT HE CAN'T BECOME A SOLDIER.
This shoe is too small for me to wear.
STUD. A: THIS SHOE IS SO SMALL THAT I CAN'T WEAR IT.
STUD. B: THIS IS SUCH A SMALL SHOE THAT I CAN'T WEAR IT.

1. This coffee is too hot for anybody to drink.
2. This book is too difficult for the new students to read.
3. The professor is too busy to leave his office.
4. He is too sick to stand up.
5. This car is too expensive for us to buy.
6. She is too young to go to school.
7. This town is too small to have a fire department.
8. This coat is too long for me to wear.
9. My suitcase is too heavy to carry.
10. This hill is too steep for us to climb.
11. It is too stormy for planes to fly.
12. This lake is too wide for Fred to swim across.

2.   Key example: Isn't the professor busy today? YES, HE IS.

Observe the answers to the negative questions.*

Previous <u>patterns</u>:

Is	the professor busy today?	Yes, he is.	(Lesson I)
Does	he have a lot of work?	Yes, he does.	(Lesson II)
Can	he leave his office?	No, he can't.	(Lesson XI)
Have	you talked to his secretary?	Yes, I have.	(Lesson XVIII)

New <u>pattern</u>:

Isn't	the professor busy today?	YES, HE IS.
Doesn't	he have a lot of work?	YES, HE DOES.
Can't	he leave his office?	NO, HE CAN'T.
Haven't	you talked to his secretary?	YES, I HAVE.

COMMENTS

(1)   Negative forms (ISN'T, DOESN'T, etc.) are sometimes used to begin questions. When the question is spoken with a falling intonation, the speaker usually expects an answer of YES.**

(2)   The answer to a negative question is the same as the answer to an affirmative question in a similar situation.

(3)   Negative questions with a falling intonation are used (a) as a stylistic variation of the statement; (b) to ask for confirmation or agreement; (c) to promote conversation.

ILLUSTRATIVE EXAMPLES

SPEAKER A: Good morning. Haven't I seen you before?
SPEAKER B: YES, YOU HAVE. I have a class here every morning.
       A: Aren't you from South America?
       B: YES. I'm from Argentina.
       A: Oh. Don't they grow a lot of coffee in Argentina?
       B: NO, THEY DON'T. Aren't you thinking of Brazil?
       A: YES. I guess I was. I have to go to class now. Can't you talk to me again sometime and tell me something about Argentina?
       B: YES, I CAN. Won't you have a cup of coffee with me after class?
       A: YES. I'll meet you here then.

---

*It is not important for elementary or intermediate students to practice negative <u>questions</u> because attached questions may be used in the same situations. It is, however, important for them to practice the <u>answers</u> to negative questions.

**Negative questions with a rising intonation are used in certain situations. When the rising intonation is used, the speaker does not necessarily expect an answer of "YES."

PRACTICE

EXERCISE 2.1. (To practice answers to negative questions.) Give
short answers to the following questions. For example:

Isn't Brazil in South America?   YES, IT IS.
Didn't Columbus discover China?   NO, HE DIDN'T.
Shouldn't we always speak English?   YES, WE SHOULD.

1. Isn't Spain in Europe?
2. Isn't France in South America?
3. Isn't English an easy language?
4. Don't most of the people in the United States speak English?
5. Don't most of the people in Brazil speak Portuguese?
6. Don't most of the students in this class speak English well?
7. Can't a plane go faster than a train can?
8. Can't more people ride in a plane than in a train?
9. Can't a man work harder than a woman can?
10. Didn't Edison invent the electric light?
11. Didn't Edison invent the automobile?
12. Haven't you learned to speak English perfectly yet?
13. Shouldn't you practice ten hours every day?
14. Don't you expect to speak English perfectly next year?
15. Don't you think the answers to negative questions are easy?

3.   Key example: The professor is very busy, ISN'T HE? YES,
HE IS.

Observe the attached questions and their answers.		
The professor is very busy,	ISN'T HE?	YES, HE IS.
He has a lot of work,	DOESN'T HE?	YES, HE DOES.
You can wait for him,	CAN'T YOU?	YES, I CAN.
You have talked to his secretary,	HAVEN'T YOU?	YES, I HAVE.
The secretary isn't very careful,	IS SHE?	NO, SHE ISN'T.
She doesn't speak slowly,	DOES SHE?	NO, SHE DOESN'T.
The professor can't leave his office,	CAN HE?	NO, HE CAN'T.
You haven't talked to him yet,	HAVE YOU?	NO, I HAVEN'T.

COMMENTS

(1) Use ISN'T HE, DOESN'T HE, IS SHE, DOES SHE, etc., to form
attached questions. Do not use "Yes?" or "No?"

(2) Use a negative form in the attached question if the preceding
statement is affirmative. Use an affirmative form in the attached
question if the statement is negative.

(3) An attached question with a falling intonation indicates that the speaker thinks his statement is true. He expects the answer to agree with his statement.*

(4) Attached questions with falling intonation are used (a) as a stylistic variation of the statement; (b) to ask for confirmation or agreement; (c) to promote conversation.

ILLUSTRATIVE EXAMPLES

It's a nice day today, ISN'T IT?	YES, IT IS.
It wasn't very nice yesterday, WAS IT?	NO, IT WASN'T.
There's going to be a football game tomorrow, ISN'T THERE?	YES, THERE IS.
There isn't going to be a dance, IS THERE?	NO, THERE ISN'T.
It hasn't been very cold this winter, HAS IT?	NO, IT HASN'T.
It had snowed at this time last winter, HADN'T IT?	YES, IT HAD.
We should study tonight, SHOULDN'T WE?	YES, WE SHOULD.
We shouldn't have gone to the party last night, SHOULD WE?	NO, WE SHOULDN'T.
You're going to be home tonight, AREN'T YOU?	YES, I AM.
We must try to practice more, MUSTN'T WE?	YES, WE MUST.
Argentina is the largest country in South America, ISN'T IT?	NO, IT ISN'T.

NOTE: In the last example above, the first speaker expects an answer of YES to agree with his statement. But the second speaker thinks the statement is wrong and gives an answer of NO.

EXERCISE 3.1. (To form attached questions.) Repeat the following statements and add attached questions with a falling intonation. For example:

There's a party tonight.
THERE'S A PARTY TONIGHT, ISN'T THERE?
You were at one last night.
YOU WERE AT ONE LAST NIGHT, WEREN'T YOU?
There weren't many people there.
THERE WEREN'T MANY PEOPLE THERE, WERE THERE?

1. I didn't like it.
2. I asked you to come.
3. You came early.
4. You can't come tonight.
5. You like parties.
6. Your friend couldn't have come last night.
7. He hasn't received his degree yet.
8. He was probably busy.
9. He has been invited for tonight.
10. He won't forget to come.
11. There are going to be a lot of people.
12. We aren't going to stay very late.

---

*Attached questions with a rising intonation are used in certain situations. When the rising intonation is used, the speaker does not necessarily expect the answer to agree with his statement.

EXERCISE 3.2. (To practice attached questions and their answers.)
Observe the people, the room, the furniture and the weather around you.
Form obvious statements and attached questions. Another student
should answer the questions. For example:

STUDENT A: IT'S NICE WEATHER TODAY, ISN'T IT?
STUDENT B: YES, IT IS. IT ISN'T AS COLD AS YESTERDAY, IS IT?
STUDENT C: NO, IT ISN'T. MR. X HAS A NEW SUIT, DOESN'T HE?
STUDENT D: YES, HE DOES.

Continue the exercise.

KEY EXAMPLES OF LESSON XXV

1. The professor is SO BUSY THAT he can't leave his office.
   He is SUCH A BUSY MAN THAT he can't leave his office.
2. Isn't the professor busy today? YES, HE IS.
3. The professor is very busy, ISN'T HE? YES, HE IS.

Lesson XXVI

1. I SEE MYSELF IN THE MIRROR.
   I SEE THE MIRROR/MYSELF.*
   [-SELF forms as receiver and as emphasizer]

2. THE TEACHER ENJOYS WORKING WITH STUDENTS.
   [Certain Class 2 + the -ING form of Class 2]

1.

Key examples: I see MYSELF in the mirror.
                I see the mirror/MYSELF.

Observe the position of the -SELF forms.

Previous pattern (Lesson VI):

I	see	you	in the mirror.
You	see	me	in the mirror.

New pattern:

I	see	MYSELF	in the mirror.	
You	see	YOURSELF	in the mirror.	
I	see	the mirror/		MYSELF.
You	see	the mirror/		YOURSELF.
You	see	the mirror/		ITSELF.

COMMENTS

(1) Use -SELF forms in the same position as ME, HIM, etc., to indicate that the receiver and the performer are the same person or thing.

(2) Use -SELF forms at the end to indicate emphasis. Use a pause before these -SELF forms. (MYSELF emphasizes I; YOURSELF emphasizes YOU; ITSELF emphasizes MIRROR.)**

ILLUSTRATIVE EXAMPLES

I	hurt MYSELF.	We	hurt OURSELVES.
You	hurt YOURSELF.	You	hurt YOURSELVES.
The man	hurt HIMSELF.	The men	hurt THEMSELVES.
The woman	hurt HERSELF.		
The bird	hurt ITSELF.		

NOTE: - SELVES is the plural of -SELF.
       Use MY-, YOUR-, HIM-, HER-, IT-, OUR-, YOUR-, THEM-
       before SELF (or SELVES).

---

*The slant bar represents a tentative pause.
**You will also hear -SELF forms indicating emphasis immediately after the word they emphasize. I/MYSELF/SEE THE MIRROR is the same in meaning as I SEE THE MIRROR/MYSELF.

246

I must weigh MYSELF.
Don't cut YOURSELF with that knife.
Mary bought HERSELF some ice cream.
Jack asked HIMSELF a question.
Paul talks to HIMSELF.
He always thinks of HIMSELF.

NOTE: You may use -SELF forms in various positions of HIM, ME, etc.

John didn't ask his friends to help him with his work. He did it/HIMSELF.
You don't have to read the paper to me. I can read it/MYSELF.
Mary didn't buy that dress. She made it/HERSELF.

Observe the special meaning of BY + -SELF:

If he can't help me, I will do it BY MYSELF.
No one accompanied her. She went there BY HERSELF.
They like to be BY THEMSELVES.
John always sits BY HIMSELF.

NOTE: BY + -SELF has the same meaning and use as ALONE.*

PRACTICE

EXERCISE 1.1. (To practice -SELF forms as receiver.) Repeat the
statements, adding a -SELF form as a receiver. For example:

He bought a book.	HE BOUGHT HIMSELF A BOOK.
He told a story.	HE TOLD HIMSELF THE STORY.
She is sewing a dress.	SHE IS SEWING HERSELF A DRESS.

1. She's going to write a letter.
2. He asked a question.
3. I'm going to buy a coat.
4. He brought the book.
5. She taught the lesson.
6. I sent a package.
7. John made a sandwich.
8. Mrs. Whitney told a lie.
9. The students understood.
10. You answered correctly.
11. She's going to bake a cake.
12. Tom's going to find a job.
13. Bill cut a slice of bread.
14. John and Mary are going to build a house.

EXERCISE 1.2. (To practice -SELF forms as emphasizer.) Repeat the
above exercise, adding a -SELF form as emphasizer. For example:

He bought a book.	HE BOUGHT A BOOK/ HIMSELF.
He told the story.	HE TOLD THE STORY/ HIMSELF.
She is sewing a dress.	SHE IS SEWING A DRESS/ HERSELF.

(Continue with the items of exercise 1.3.)

---

*Some other combinations with -SELF forms have special meanings. For
example, "They ENJOYED THEMSELVES" means "They had an enjoyable time."
"BEHAVE YOURSELF" means "Behave properly."

EXERCISE 1.3. (To practice BY + -SELF.) Substitute BY + -SELF for ALONE. For example:

I'm going alone.　　　　　　　I'M GOING BY MYSELF.
Do you live alone?　　　　　　DO YOU LIVE BY YOURSELF?
John likes to be alone.　　　　JOHN LIKES TO BE BY HIMSELF.

1. You can't play tennis alone.
2. The children are singing alone.
3. I don't like to go to the movies alone.
4. A baby shouldn't be left in the house alone.
5. Professor Taylor prefers to work alone.
6. There was too much work for us to do alone.
7. Mary is going to go downtown alone.
8. Do you like to study alone?
9. John and Mary were alone.
10. There was so much work that I couldn't do it alone.

2.　Key example: The teacher ENJOYS WORKING with students.

Observe the -ING forms and the Class 2 words before them.

Previous pattern (Lesson XIII):

I	wanted	to sing.

New pattern:

I	ENJOYED	SINGING.
I	KEPT (ON)	SINGING.
I	FINISHED	SINGING.

COMMENT

Use the -ING form of Class 2 words after ENJOY, KEEP (ON), AVOID, FINISH, CONSIDER, GET THROUGH, INSIST ON. Do not use "to sing," etc., after these words.

ILLUSTRATIVE EXAMPLES

Observe the following examples with Class 2 words that are followed by the -ING form but not by TO + the simple form.

I	ENJOY	DANCING	very much.
I can	KEEP (ON)	DANCING	all night.
Paul	AVOIDS	GOING	to dances whenever he can.
He	INSISTS ON	STAYING	home tonight.
I must	FINISH	DOING	my homework before the dance.
I hope I	GET THROUGH	WORKING	early tonight.
Will you	CONSIDER	HELPING	me with my work?

Observe the following examples with Class 2 words that are followed by either the -ING form or TO + the simple form with approximately the same meaning.

Those students	BEGAN	STUDYING	here last year.
Those students	BEGAN	TO STUDY	here last year.
They	STARTED	LEARNING	English immediately.
They	STARTED	TO LEARN	English immediately.
They always	TRY	PRONOUNCING	correctly.
They always	TRY	TO PRONOUNCE	correctly.
They are going to	CONTINUE	PRACTICING	every day.
They are going to	CONTINUE	TO PRACTICE	every day.
I don't think they will	NEGLECT	WORKING	in the lab.
I don't think they will	NEGLECT	TO WORK	in the lab.
They usually	PREFER	STUDYING	together.
They usually	PREFER	TO STUDY	together.
They	LIKE	LEARNING	new patterns.
They	LIKE	TO LEARN	new patterns.

Observe the following examples with Class 2 words that are followed by either the -ING form or by TO + the simple form but with different meanings.

John	STOPPED	EATING.
John	STOPPED	TO EAT.

NOTE: STOPPED EATING means stopped the activity of eating. STOPPED TO EAT means stopped some other activity in order to eat.

Mary	REMEMBERS WRITING	to her family.
Mary	REMEMBERS TO WRITE	to her family.

NOTE: REMEMBERS WRITING means that she wrote some time in the past and that now she remembers that she wrote. REMEMBERS TO WRITE means that she does not forget to write.

George	CAN'T HELP ASKING	questions.
George	CAN'T HELP (ME) (TO) ASK	questions.

NOTE: CAN'T HELP ASKING means that he can't stop asking questions. CAN'T HELP TO ASK means that he can't help someone else ask questions.

Observe the following examples with a few of the Class 2 words that are followed by TO + the simple form but not by the -ING form. This is the pattern of Lesson XVIII.

Betty	EXPECTS	TO FINISH	high school this year.
She	HOPES	TO GO	to the university next year.
She has	DECIDED	TO STUDY	education.
She	WANTS	TO BE A	teacher.
She will	NEED	TO STUDY	many different subjects.

PRACTICE

EXERCISE 2.1. (To practice the use of a Class 2 word followed by an -ING form.) Substitute the following words. For example:

Betty considered dancing.
enjoys   BETTY ENJOYS DANCING.
kept on   BETTY KEPT ON DANCING.
working   BETTY KEPT ON WORKING.

1. insisted on
2. stopped
3. the boys
4. avoided
5. studying
6. finished
7. eating
8. enjoy
9. I
10. kept on
11. laughing
12. started
13. the baby
14. crying
15. can't help
16. Betty
17. continued
18. dancing
19. got through
20. considered

EXERCISE 2.2. (To force a choice between the -ING form and TO + the simple form.) Combine the words and phrases you hear into a sentence. Use the -ING form or TO + the simple form of the second Class 2 word. For example:
Mary enjoys. Very. Swim
    MARY ENJOYS SWIMMING VERY MUCH.
She likes. In the lake. Swim
    SHE LIKES SWIMMING IN THE LAKE.
or SHE LIKES TO SWIM IN THE LAKE.
She wanted. There last Saturday. Go
    SHE WANTED TO GO THERE LAST SATURDAY.

1. She decided. Bill and John to go with her. Ask
2. They wanted. Very much. Go
3. They considered. The bus. Take
4. John insisted on. His car. Take
5. They needed. A tire first. Change
6. They got through. At 10:00. Change it
7. They started. Immediately. Drive

8. They enjoyed.   Through the country.   Drive
9. They kept.   All the way.   Laugh and sing
10. They learned.   Some new songs.   Sing
11. They stopped.   When they got to the lake.   Sing
12. They had expected.   Before lunch.   Swim
13. But Bill insisted on.   Immediately.   Eat
14. Mary had remembered.   A lunch.   Bring
15. They finished.   At 1:00.   Eat
16. They began.   At 1:30.   Swim
17. They avoided.   Into deep water.   Go
18. They continued.   All afternoon.   Swim
19. John couldn't help.   About his homework.   Think
20. He had planned.   That afternoon.   Do it

KEY EXAMPLES OF LESSON XXVI

1. I see MYSELF in the mirror.
   I see the mirror/MYSELF.
2. The teacher ENJOYS WORKING with students.

Lesson XXVII

1. WE ELECTED TOM SECRETARY.
   [Certain Class 2 words followed by two Class 1 words with the same referent]
2. WE WANT OUR HOUSE PAINTED WHITE.
   [Class 2 words followed by an object and one or two describing words]
3. WE PASSED A GIRL STANDING ON THE CORNER.
   [Class 2 words followed by an object and a describing word or word group in the -ING form]

1. Key example: We elected Tom SECRETARY.

Observe the words which follow the Class 2 word.

Previous pattern (Lesson II):

We	elected	Tom.

New pattern:

We	elected	TOM	SECRETARY.
The president	appointed	ME	CHAIRMAN OF THE COMMITTEE.
The Italians	made	ROME	THEIR CAPITAL.

COMMENTS

(1) The words in the position of SECRETARY represent a name or designation given to the words in the position of TOM.
(2) Class 2 words which may be used in this pattern are ELECT, NOMINATE, APPOINT, CALL, NAME, CHOOSE, SELECT, MAKE, CONSIDER.

ILLUSTRATIVE EXAMPLES

What did	they	elect	Paul?	
	They	elected	him	PRESIDENT.

Who(m) did	they	elect		PRESIDENT?
	They	elected	Paul	PRESIDENT.

What did	the school board	make	Mr. Martin?	
	They	made	him	SUPERINTENDENT.

Who(m) did	they	make		SUPERINTENDENT?
	They	made	Mr. Martin	SUPERINTENDENT.

252

What are	the Clarks	going to name	the new baby?	
	They	are going to name	her	BETTY.
Who(m) are	they	going to name		BETTY?
	They	are going to name	the new baby	BETTY.
Do	they	call	William Brown	WILL?
	No, they	call	him	BILL.

PRACTICE

EXERCISE 1.1. (To practice the use of two Class 1 words with the same referent after certain Class 2 words.) Substitute the following words. For example:

The president named John treasurer.

secretary	THE PRESIDENT NAMED JOHN SECRETARY.
appointed	THE PRESIDENT APPOINTED JOHN SECRETARY.
him	THE PRESIDENT APPOINTED HIM SECRETARY.
Jim	THE PRESIDENT APPOINTED JIM SECRETARY.

1. chairman of the committee
2. selected
3. considers
4. appoints
5. the younger man
6. selected
7. treasurer
8. Mary
9. secretary
10. the student
11. Tom
12. manager of the team
13. nominated
14. Jack

EXERCISE 1.2. (To practice using this pattern in response to questions.) Answer the following questions. For example:

Bill is from Texas. What do they call him?
    THEY CALL HIM A TEXAN.
Who(m) did the people elect president in 1860?
    THEY ELECTED LINCOLN PRESIDENT.
What did the boys call Robert?
    THEY CALLED HIM BOB.

1. What did you name your dog?
2. Who(m) did the President appoint Secretary of State?
3. Who(m) did your country make its delegate to the U. N.?
4. What did the French name their capital city?
5. Who(m) did the people elect president at the last election?
6. Who appointed Smith chairman?
7. What did they name the organization of the nations of the world?
8. Who(m) did the team select captain?
9. What do you call your father?
10. What did your friends call you when you were a boy?
11. What do you call the country that is north of the United States?
12. Who(m) did you elect president of your club?

2.   Key example: We want our house PAINTED WHITE.

Observe the position of the describing words.

Previous patterns:

| We want | the white | house. | (Lesson IV) |
| We want | the painted | house. | (Lesson XIX) |

New pattern:

We want	the house		WHITE.
We should keep	our clothes		CLEAN.
We want	the house	PAINTED.	
We should keep	our clothes	WASHED.	
We want	the house	PAINTED	WHITE.
We should keep	our clothes	WASHED	CLEAN.

COMMENT

Use words like WHITE, PAINTED, etc., after the object (HOUSE, etc.) to indicate its condition or quality as a receiver of the action.

ILLUSTRATIVE EXAMPLES

We painted	the yellow house	WHITE.
The Smiths had	their house	PAINTED BROWN.
Betty had	her hair	CUT.
She wanted	it	CUT SHORT.
Norma wears	her hair	LONG.
The general believed	the enemy	DEFEATED.
He considered	them	BADLY DEFEATED IN THE BATTLE.
We found	the lecture	INTERESTING.
How do you drink	your coffee?	
I drink	it	BLACK.
How do you want	your bread?	
I want	it	TOASTED.
How do you prefer	it	TOASTED?
I prefer	it	TOASTED BROWN.

PRACTICE

EXERCISE 2.1. (To practice using a describing word after the receiver.) Listen to the sentences. Change them to fit the pattern with a describing word after the receiver. For example:

   I want fried potatoes.
      I WANT MY POTATOES FRIED.
   The boys washed their shirts until they were clean.
      THE BOYS WASHED THEIR SHIRTS CLEAN.
   John made a mistake. It was corrected.
      JOHN HAD HIS MISTAKE CORRECTED.

1. I like hot coffee.
2. He cut my hair. It was short when he had finished.
3. Mr. Smith painted the house. He used green paint.
4. Bill had the laundry wash his clothes.
5. We need to heat the water.
6. I am going to have a photographer take my picture.
7. God created men. Men are equal.
8. He had someone send the books.
9. I'll take fresh fruit.
10. He believed that we were lost.
11. Peter bought a red tie and he wants to exchange it.
12. I had the dentist clean my teeth.

EXERCISE 2.2. (To practice using this pattern in various situations.)
Listen to the situation sentences. Complete the sentences that follow
them, using an object followed by a describing word. Use HIM, HER, IT,
THEM as the object. For example:

> John doesn't like to lose at chess. It makes. . .
> IT MAKES HIM ANGRY.
> We were inspired by the violinist. We found. . .
> WE FOUND HIM INSPIRING.
> John took his car to the mechanic for repairs. He wanted. . .
> HE WANTED IT FIXED.

1. Mary did not understand the lesson very well. She found. . .
2. The coffee was too strong for John. It made. . .
3. Mr. Smith used red paint on his car. He painted. . .
4. John took Mary to the movies. It made her. . .
5. Jim doesn't like weak tea. He likes. . .
6. George was interested in the lecture. He found. . .
7. She doesn't care for cream in her coffee. She likes. . .
8. Dick dislikes cooked tomatoes. He prefers. . .
9. The professor is pleased with the students. He considers. . .
10. The child was frightened by the animals. He found. . .
11. She was bored by the professor. She found. . .
12. Fred won't drink cold coffee. He wants. . .
13. The teacher will not accept incomplete assignments. He wants. . .

EXERCISE 2.3. (To practice using this pattern in answers to questions.)
Answer the following questions. For example:

> What is Mary going to do with her dirty coat?
> SHE IS GOING TO HAVE IT CLEANED.
> How do you like your coffee?
> I LIKE IT BLACK.
> What effect does work usually have on a person?
> IT MAKES HIM TIRED.
> What color did he have his car painted?
> HE HAD HIS CAR PAINTED RED.

1. How did Sue have her hair cut?
2. What color did Dorothy paint her fingernails?
3. How did they serve the steak?
4. What effect does the smell of dinner have on you?
5. What does Mrs. Hastings want done to the floor?
6. What color did Mr. Alcott paint the yellow house?
7. How did Jim have his steak this evening?
8. How do we say that the cook serves vegetables if she doesn't cook them?
9. How does Mrs. Clark like her coffee?
10. How do you like to wear your hair?
11. How does the cook usually serve potatoes?
12. What did he do with the fish he caught?
13. How do you want your potatoes today?
14. What did Mary do with her dress that was too long?

3.   Key example: We passed a girl STANDING ON THE CORNER.

Observe the -ING expressions.

Previous pattern (Lesson XXI):

| We watched | the boys | PLAY. |

New pattern:

We watched	the boys	PLAYING.
We met	Professor Brown	GOING TO THE LIBRARY.
We avoided	the car	COMING TOWARD US.

COMMENTS

(1) The -ING form and the words after it describe the words in the position of BOYS.
(2) Do not use a pause after the words in the position of BOYS.*

EXERCISE 3.1. (To practice the use of -ING expressions to describe an object.) Combine the statements below to make a shorter utterance. For example:

I saw him. He was going to the movies.
   I SAW HIM GOING TO THE MOVIES.
You heard us. We were singing.
   YOU HEARD US SINGING.
We found the boys. They were playing baseball.
   WE FOUND THE BOYS PLAYING BASEBALL.

1. We passed an old man. He was sitting beside the road.
2. Jim watched the soldiers. They were marching down the street.
3. I jumped to avoid the car. It was coming toward me.

_____
*"We met Professor Brown/going to the library," with a pause after "Professor Brown," could mean that "we" were going to the library. "We met Professor Brown going to the library," without a pause, usually means that Professor Brown was going to the library.

4. Mr. Clark looked at the girl. She was speaking.
5. Larry talked to the boy. He was putting stamps in an album.
6. She bumped into people. They were hurrying in the rain.
7. The room was full of people. They were dancing in the dark.
8. They spoke to the man. He was selling shoes.
9. I heard the leaves. They were moving in the trees.
10. I could feel my heart. It was beating rapidly.
11. The light was on the girl. She was singing a song.
12. I saw him. He was standing on the stairs.
13. He left his coat. It was hanging on a hook.
14. Jack remembered the book. It was lying open on his desk.
15. They thought of me. I was studying in my room.
16. They stared at Don. He was shouting at the crowd.
17. They recognized us. We were going into the restaurant.
18. Miss Jackson looked at Sam. He was jumping into the water.
19. We saw them. They were falling.
20. He noticed the dog. It was barking.

KEY EXAMPLES OF LESSON XXVII

1. We elected Tom SECRETARY.
2. We want our house PAINTED WHITE.
3. We passed a girl STANDING ON THE CORNER.

Lesson XXVIII

1. WORKING ALL DAY MADE HIM TIRED.
   [-ING expressions in the position of subject]

2. WORKING ALL DAY/JOHN GOT TIRED.
   [-ING expressions at the beginning of sentences and referring to to the subject]

1.

Key example: WORKING ALL DAY made him tired.

Observe the position and function of the -ING expressions.

Previous pattern:

| Life | can be difficult. |
| Daily practice | improves our English. |

New Pattern:

LIVING	can be difficult.
PRACTICING EVERY DAY	improves our English.
BEING HERE ON TIME	is important.
WORKING ALL DAY	made him tired.

COMMENT

-ING expressions can be used in subject position.*

PRACTICE

EXERCISE 1.1. (To practice -ING expressions in subject position.)
Listen to the two statements. Combine them to form a generalization with an -ING expression in subject position. For example:

Bill teaches English. It is hard work.
   TEACHING ENGLISH IS HARD WORK.
Betty likes fishing. She finds it relaxing.
   FISHING IS RELAXING.
Ted writes short stories. It requires great talent.
   WRITING SHORT STORIES REQUIRES GREAT TALENT.

---

*NOTE: Expressions with TO+ the simple form of a Class 2 word can also be used in subject position.
   TO LIVE can be difficult.
   TO PRACTICE EVERY DAY improves our English.
   TO BE HERE ON TIME is important.
   TO WORK ALL DAY made him tired.
You should recognize this pattern, but you do not need to practice it.

258

1. Carlos writes home often. It takes a lot of time.
2. Tom takes pictures. It is a good hobby.
3. Our family plays chess. It provides many hours of entertainment.
4. John sells cars. It is a profitable business.
5. We must take an examination. That means extra hours of study.
6. Mary visited Niagara Falls. It was wonderful.
7. I read the newspaper every day. It helps in learning English.
8. Jerry completed the forms. It fulfilled the requirements.
9. Fred sent a telegram. It was faster than writing a letter.
10. Bob drinks a quart of milk every day. It is healthful.
11. Ted plays baseball. It provides relaxation.
12. Betty learned to speak Chinese. It was difficult.

EXERCISE 1.2. (To convert a pattern of Lesson XIV into this new pattern.) Listen to the statements. Change them to statements with an -ING expression in subject position. For example:

It delights the boy to eat ice cream.
    EATING ICE CREAM DELIGHTS THE BOY.
It is fun to ride in a convertible.
    RIDING IN A CONVERTIBLE IS FUN.
It is necessary to practice every day.
    PRACTICING EVERY DAY IS NECESSARY.

1. It is possible to see them.
2. It makes Jim tired to run.
3. It bores David to study.
4. It is hard to read Chinese.
5. It frightens Barbara to be alone.
6. It annoys Mrs. Hastings to hear them argue.
7. It makes me happy to win a contest.
8. It pleases the cat to get fish for dinner.
9. It requires time and effort to learn a language.
10. It thrills Jane to get a letter.
11. It is pleasant to go to the lake on a hot day.
12. It makes Sue happy to see her brother.

2. Key examples: WORKING ALL DAY/ John got tired.
                    HAVING WORKED ALL DAY/ he was tired.

Observe the -ING expressions.	
GOING TO THE LIBRARY/	WE met Professor Brown.
EATING A GOOD DINNER/	GEORGE began to feel better.
HAVING GONE TO THE LIBRARY/	WE went to the museum.
HAVING EATEN A GOOD DINNER/	GEORGE felt better.

COMMENTS

(1) This pattern does not usually begin a conversation.
(2) This pattern is more frequent in writing than in speaking.
(3) The -ING expression before the subject refers to the subject.*
     (GOING TO THE LIBRARY refers to WE, etc.)
(4) Expressions like GOING TO THE LIBRARY indicate an action that
     takes place at the same time as the action or situation that follows.
(5) Expressions with HAVING + the -ED/-EN form (HAVING GONE TO
     THE LIBRARY, etc.) refer to an action that has taken place before
     the action or situation that follows.
(6) Use a pause between the -ING expression and the subject.

PRACTICE

EXERCISE 2.1. (To practice -ING expressions at the beginning of sentences and referring to the subject.) Combine the two sentences to form one sentence with an -ING expression at the beginning. For example:

John walked to town. He saw an interesting sight.
> WALKING TO TOWN/JOHN SAW AN INTERESTING SIGHT.
John washed his hands. He noticed a cut on his finger.
> WASHING HIS HANDS/JOHN NOTICED A CUT ON HIS FINGER.
Mary is intelligent. She learned geometry quickly.
> BEING INTELLIGENT/MARY LEARNED GEOMETRY QUICKLY.

1. The car turned the corner. It hit a tree.
2. The program lasted two hours. It was a success.
3. Jim was feeling sick. He called a doctor.
4. The photographer was waving to the child. He took the picture.
5. Mary fell down stairs. She broke her arm.
6. John felt tired. He stopped at a hotel to rest.
7. The barber cut John's hair. He talked about fishing.
8. Fred had no assignments. He went to a movie.
9. Tom expected a call. He waited in the dormitory.
10. Dorothy was sick. She couldn't go to school.
11. The director saw the new student. He tried to help him.
12. Thomas flew to the United States. He made the trip in one day.

EXERCISE 2.2. (To practice expressions with HAVING + the -ED/-EN form in this position.) Combine the two sentences to form one sentence with HAVING + the -ED/-EN form at the beginning. For example:

---

*You will also hear WE MET PROFESSOR BROWN/GOING TO THE LIBRARY, usually with a pause before the -ING expression, used to refer to the same situation. WE MET PROFESSOR BROWN GOING TO THE LIBRARY, without a pause, usually means that Professor Brown was going to the library. See Lesson XXVII.

He saw the police. He became worried.
> HAVING SEEN THE POLICE/HE BECAME WORRIED.

Paul forgot his notebook. He is unhappy now.
> HAVING FORGOTTEN HIS NOTEBOOK/PAUL IS UNHAPPY.

He is looking at her picture. He will feel sad later.
> HAVING LOOKED AT HER PICTURE/HE WILL FEEL SAD.

He was nominated. He began a campaign then.
> HAVING BEEN NOMINATED/HE BEGAN A CAMPAIGN.

1. He read a newspaper. He went to a movie later.
2. The firemen put the fire out. They investigated the cause afterwards.
3. He worked very hard. He became tired.
4. He is working very hard. He will be tired.
5. He will examine the report. He is going to write a letter afterwards.
6. Tom arrived at the airport. He took a taxi to the dormitory.
7. We are visiting the art gallery. We will go through the library next.
8. He stayed up all night. He looked weary in his classes the next day.
9. She purchased a stamp. She mailed a letter to her family later.
10. The boys are playing baseball. They will eat a big lunch.
11. He was worried. He then went to the doctor.
12. Dave worked all summer. He was able to go to college in the fall.

EXERCISE 2.3. (To produce the pattern with an -ING expression at the beginning of the sentence more freely.) Listen to the two key words. Then form a sentence around them with an -ING expression at the beginning. For example:

going. . .saw   GOING TO THE MOVIES/I SAW JIM.
hearing. . .looked   HEARING A NOISE/MARY LOOKED OUT OF THE
                       WINDOW.
walking. . .met   WALKING IN THE PARK/WE MET SOME FRIENDS.

1. working. . .finished
2. passing. . .looked
3. feeling. . .rested
4. driving. . .hit
5. finding. . .went
6. liking. . .hoped
7. shouting. . .called
8. seeing. . .spoke
9. walking. . .heard
10. swimming. . .enjoyed
11. singing. . .remembered
12. listening to. . .forgot
13. looking for. . .found
14. pointing. . .talked

EXERCISE 2.4. (To produce expressions with HAVING + the -ED/-EN form at the beginning of the sentence more freely.) Change the -ING expressions of Exercise 2.3. into expressions with HAVING + the -ED/-EN form. For example:

going. . .saw   HAVING GONE TO THE MOVIES/I SAW JIM.
hearing. . .looked   HAVING HEARD A NOISE/MARY LOOKED OUT OF
                       THE WINDOW.
walking. . .met   HAVING WALKED IN THE PARK/WE MET SOME
                       FRIENDS.

(Continue with the items of Exercise 2.3.)

EXERCISE 2.5. (To review the patterns with -ING expressions of Lessons **XXVII** and **XXVIII**.) Combine the statements to form one statement with an -ING expression. For example:

I saw him. He was going to lunch.
   I SAW HIM GOING TO LUNCH.
I saw him. I was going to lunch.
   GOING TO LUNCH/I SAW HIM.
I saw him. I went to lunch then.
   HAVING SEEN HIM/I WENT TO LUNCH.

1. She smiled at him. He was standing there.
2. She smiled at him. She was standing there.
3. I looked at the leaves. They were blowing in the breeze.
4. Jim wrote a letter. He mailed it on the way to the program.
5. He had a good time. He was sailing to Europe.
6. Norman met an old friend. Norman was hurrying home.
7. Norman met an old friend. The friend was hurrying home.
8. Tom ate breakfast. He walked to school with Jim after breakfast.
9. The ship creaked noisily. It was tossing in the storm.
10. We parked our car. We began to do our shopping then.
11. Jane heard me. I was laughing loudly.
12. The kitten imitated its mother. Its mother was washing its face.
13. The kitten imitated its mother. The kitten washed its face.
14. Bob worried about Sue. She was typing too much.
15. He finished his lesson. He went to the program later.
16. They ran through the streets. They were shouting his name.
17. Dorothy and Helen walked all afternoon. They felt hungry afterward.
18. He hit the tree. He was driving too fast.
19. John finished school. He took a vacation in Cuba.

KEY EXAMPLES OF LESSON XXVIII.

1. WORKING ALL DAY made him tired.
2. WORKING ALL DAY/John got tired.
   HAVING WORKED ALL DAY/he was tired.

Lesson XXIX

1. I HAVEN'T TALKED TO MY ADVISER YET. THEREFORE/MY PLANS ARE STILL INDEFINITE.
   [Sequences of sentences related by THEREFORE, ALSO, HOWEVER]

2. I WILL FINISH THIS COURSE FIRST. THEN I'M GOING TO STUDY BUSINESS ADMINISTRATION.
   [Sequences of sentences related by initial expressions of time or place]

3. BUSINESS ADMINISTRATION REQUIRES ECONOMICS. IT REQUIRES MATHEMATICS. IN OTHER WORDS/IT IS A COMPLEX SUBJECT.
   [Sentences of restatement introduced by IN OTHER WORDS]

1. Key example: I haven't talked to my advisor yet. THEREFORE/ my plans are still indefinite.

Observe the use of THEREFORE, ALSO, HOWEVER.

Situation: You have asked me to talk to my brother for you.

Pattern:

He isn't here.	THEREFORE/	I can't talk to him.
He isn't here.	ALSO/	I don't like to disturb him.
He was here yesterday.	HOWEVER/	I didn't talk to him.

COMMENTS

(1) Use THEREFORE, ALSO, HOWEVER at the beginning of sentences that come after other sentences in conversation.

(2) Use a pause after THEREFORE, ALSO, HOWEVER.

(3) Use these words to relate sentences. Use THEREFORE to indicate that the second sentence is a consequence of the first. Use ALSO to indicate that the second sentence gives information you consider similar in some way to that in the first. Use HOWEVER to indicate that the second sentence gives information you consider contrary in some way to that in the first.

ILLUSTRATIVE EXAMPLES

The water in the lake was very cold yesterday.
　THEREFORE/ we didn't go swimming.
George studied until 3:00 last night.
　THEREFORE/ he feels very tired today.
Spanish and Italian are similar languages.
　THEREFORE/ it is easy for a Spanish speaker to learn Italian.
The water in the lake was very cold yesterday.
　ALSO/ there were clouds in the sky.

263

George studied until 3:00 last night.
    ALSO/ he has a bad cold.
Spanish and Italian are similar languages.
    ALSO/ they are both derived from Latin.
The water in the lake was very cold yesterday.
    HOWEVER/ it should be warmer next week.
George studied until 3:00 last night.
    HOWEVER/ he is going to go to bed early tonight.
Spanish and Italian are similar languages.
    HOWEVER/ Italian has more vowel sounds than Spanish.

Observe the position of THEREFORE, ALSO, HOWEVER, in the following sentences.

It is necessary to practice with native speakers.
    You should/ THEREFORE/ try to talk to them frequently.
    It is/ ALSO/ helpful to read newspapers.
    Newspapers/ HOWEVER/ are not always easy to read.

NOTE: You will often hear THEREFORE, ALSO, HOWEVER, in the middle of the second sentence. This is a matter of style.

Many more words and expressions are used to relate sentences. You should learn to recognize these other words, but elementary and intermediate students do not need to practice using all of them.* Observe the following examples.

Francisco Gómez practiced many hours every day while he was taking the English course.

THEREFORE/   he can speak English very well now.
SO/ **
CONSEQUENTLY/
THUS/
AS A RESULT/

NOTE: SO, CONSEQUENTLY, THUS, AS A RESULT, are used to indicate consequence relationship.

He found that it was helpful to practice conversation with native speakers.

ALSO/   he learned a lot about the customs of the
BESIDES/   country by talking with them.
MOREOVER/
FURTHERMORE/
INDEED/

---

    *Advanced students who wish to practice these words should remember that, although they indicate the three general types of relations described above, each word has slightly different characteristics of style and meaning.
    **SO is not used in the middle of the second sentence.

AND/*
LIKEWISE/
SIMILARLY/
IN ADDITION/
IN FACT/
AS A MATTER OF FACT/

NOTE: BESIDES, MOREOVER, FURTHERMORE, etc., are used to introduce information that is considered similar.

His friends told him that he spoke English almost as well as a native
speaker.

HOWEVER/   his teachers told him that he still
YET/*   needed to keep studying and
NEVERTHELESS/   practicing every day.
STILL/
BUT/*
ON THE CONTRARY/
ON THE OTHER HAND/
IN CONTRAST/
IN SPITE OF THAT/
CONVERSELY/

NOTE: YET, NEVERTHELESS, STILL, etc., are used to introduce information that is considered contrary.

PRACTICE

EXERCISE 1.1. (To use THEREFORE to relate sentences.) Listen to
the two statements in sequence which are related by THEREFORE.
Substitute the following statements in the proper position in the sequence.
For example:

Jim likes English. Therefore, he finds English easy.
He studies hard.
  HE STUDIES HARD. THEREFORE, HE FINDS ENGLISH EASY.
Therefore, he makes progress.
  HE STUDIES HARD. THEREFORE, HE MAKES PROGRESS.

1. He talks with native speakers.   7. Therefore, he understands English.
2. He speaks only English.   8. He reads the newspaper.
3. He uses the lab.   9. He practices his sentence patterns.
4. Therefore, he has a good   10. He writes his exercises.
   pronunciation.   11. He practices all of the time.
5. He imitates his teacher.   12. Therefore, people understand him.
6. He listens to the radio.

EXERCISE 1.2. (To use ALSO to relate sentences.) Listen to the two
statements in sequence which are related by ALSO. Substitute the following statements in the proper position in the sequence. For example:

---

*AND, YET, BUT are not used in this way in the middle of the second sentence.

Tomás speaks Spanish. Also, he knows English.
He has learned French.
HE HAS LEARNED FRENCH. ALSO, HE KNOWS ENGLISH.
Also, he can speak English.
HE HAS LEARNED FRENCH. ALSO, HE CAN SPEAK ENGLISH.

1. He reads English.
2. He understands English.
3. Also, he writes English.
4. He is able to write French.
5. He has read several English books.
6. He speaks English fluently.
7. Also, he has a good pronunciation.
8. He has a large vocabulary.
9. The structure of his sentences is correct.
10. Also, he can discuss many things.
11. He is interested in the culture of the United States.
12. Also, he asks many questions about it.

EXERCISE 1.3. (To use HOWEVER to relate sentences.) Listen to the
two statements in sequence which are related by HOWEVER. Substitute
the following statements in the proper position in the sequence. For
example:

Learning a language is interesting. However, it takes a lot of work.
We are able to learn English rapidly.
WE ARE ABLE TO LEARN ENGLISH RAPIDLY. HOWEVER, IT
TAKES A LOT OF WORK.
However, it requires constant practice.
WE ARE ABLE TO LEARN ENGLISH RAPIDLY. HOWEVER, IT
REQUIRES CONSTANT PRACTICE.

1. The students learn a good pronunciation.
2. They use only English.
3. However, they make mistakes at first.
4. They speak in sentence patterns.
5. They use English intonation.
6. They learn a new vocabulary.
7. However, the vocabulary is small.
8. They use many sentence patterns.
9. They learn the English sound system.
10. However, they do not learn rules.
11. They study English structure.
12. They speak English correctly.

EXERCISE 1.4. (To relate sentences with THEREFORE, ALSO, HOW-
EVER.) Listen to the sentences. Use either THEREFORE, ALSO, or
HOWEVER, to relate them more closely. For example:

It seems impossible to learn a language in a short time. We must try.
IT SEEMS IMPOSSIBLE TO LEARN A LANGUAGE IN A SHORT
TIME. HOWEVER, WE MUST TRY.

1. Other people have done it. We know that it is possible.
2. It has been done. It is still done frequently.
3. We may hope for perfection. We must be prepared to accept something less than perfection.
4. Learning a new language is difficult. The student must work hard.
5. Learning a new language means learning new habits. Constant practice is necessary.
6. Translation takes too much time. It slows up the establishment of language habits.
7. The use of the student's native language is discouraged. Some students continue to use it.
8. The language laboratory helps in listening. It gives an opportunity to practice speaking.
9. Constant practice is necessary. Every opportunity should be taken to use the language.
10. Pronunciation of a new language is difficult at first. It becomes easier in time.
11. Talking with native speakers helps our understanding. Listening to lectures is helpful.
12. Reading a newspaper is good practice. The best practice is talking with native speakers.

2.　Key example: I will finish this course first. THEN/I'm going to study business administration.

Observe the position of expressions of time and place. Observe the pattern with THERE.

Previous pattern (Lesson III):

We have breakfast at 8:00.	We have class at 9:00.
Farms are usually small in the East.	You will find much larger ones farther west.

New pattern:

We have breakfast at 8:00.	AT 9:00/	we have class.
We have classes all morning.	IN THE AFTERNOON/	THERE IS the laboratory period.
Farms are usually small in the East.	FARTHER WEST/	you will find much larger ones.
There are cotton fields in the South.	IN THE NORTH/	THERE ARE many cornfields.

COMMENTS

(1) Use expressions of time or place at the beginning of sentences to relate sequences of sentences more closely and to indicate time or space organization.
(2) Use a pause after expressions of time or place at the beginning of a sentence.
(3) After an expression of time or place, use THERE before the forms of BE (Lesson XIV) to indicate existence. Do not say "In the afternoon/ the laboratory period is."*

---

*You will also hear sentences without THERE: IN THE AFTERNOON/ IS THE LABORATORY PERIOD.

ILLUSTRATIVE EXAMPLES

We begin our practice of English sentence patterns with short sentences.
 THEN/ we practice long and complex sentences.
 LATER/
 NEXT/
 AFTERWARDS/
We are practicing long and complex sentences now.
 EARLIER/ we practiced short sentences.
We began practicing intonation the first day of class.
 BEFORE/ we had never heard of it.
 SINCE/ we have realized how important it is.
It never snows in my home country.
 HERE/ it snows a lot.
The winter is very cold here.
 THERE/ it is warm.
I don't like the winter here.
 ELSEWHERE/ I have enjoyed it.

Observe the use of THERE in the following sentences.

New Mexico and Arizona were the first states we visited.
 NEXT/ THERE WAS California.
Los Angeles was the first city we visited there.
 NEXT/ THERE CAME San Francisco.
Driving to San Francisco, we had the ocean on our left.
 ON OUR RIGHT/ THERE ROSE high mountains.
San Francisco is on the west side of a large bay.
 ON THE EAST SIDE/ THERE LIES the city of Berkeley.
We hadn't seen many forests in Southern California.
 NORTH OF SAN FRANCISCO/ THERE GROW large forests of tall
 trees.

NOTE: The pattern with THERE is used with certain Class 2 words
 other than BE after expressions of time or place.*

Observe the time and space organization of the following sequences of
sentences.

I came here eight weeks ago. SEVEN WEEKS AGO, I enrolled in this
 course. THREE WEEKS AGO, I took an examination. LAST WEEK,
 I applied for admission to the School of Business Administration.
 TODAY, I attended my first class there.
The state of Washington is in the northwest corner of the United
 States. SOUTH OF WASHINGTON, there is Oregon. EAST OF
 OREGON AND WASHINGTON, we find Idaho. SOUTH OF OREGON,
 ALONG THE PACIFIC COAST, the long state of California extends
 to the Mexican border. EASTWARD FROM CALIFORNIA, there
 lie Nevada and Arizona.

---

*THERE is sometimes omitted with all of these Class 2 words: NEXT/
CAME SAN FRANCISCO, etc.

PRACTICE

EXERCISE 2.1. (To relate sentences more closely with time and place expressions.) Listen to the two sentences. Arrange the time or place expressions so that they relate the second statement more closely to the first. For example:

He gets up at 8:00. He eats breakfast at 8:30.
   HE GETS UP AT 8:00. AT 8:30/ HE EATS BREAKFAST.
They grow cherries in Michigan. They grow peaches in Georgia.
   THEY GROW CHERRIES IN MICHIGAN. IN GEORGIA/ THEY
   GROW PEACHES.
He studies from six until nine. He reads the newspaper from nine until ten.
   HE STUDIES FROM SIX UNTIL NINE. FROM NINE UNTIL TEN/
   HE READS THE NEWSPAPER.

1. John started his trip on Tuesday. He was in Chicago on Wednesday.
2. Ted saw an accident. He ran for the police immediately.
3. Mr. Martinez does not like American food. He will get accustomed to it eventually.
4. Bill has one class in the morning. He has three classes in the afternoon.
5. Mary had a headache yesterday. She feels better today.
6. The library has a reading room on the first floor. It has a large reference room on the second floor.
7. We find salt water in the Great Salt Lake. We find fresh water in other lakes.
8. It is 6:30 on my watch. It is 6:40 on Jim's watch.
9. The cold weather lasts four months in Michigan. It lasts three months in Kentucky.
10. The census is taken in June. The results are published in August.
11. Hockey is a favorite sport in Canada. Baseball is a favorite sport in the United States.
12. School begins at 9:00. Classes are over at 3:00, and the children go home.

EXERCISE 2.2. (To produce sentences related by time and place expressions with greater freedom.) Listen to the sentence. It will have a reference to time or place. Repeat the sentence and add another sentence introduced by a time or place expression. For example:

He eats breakfast early in the morning.
   HE EATS BREAKFAST EARLY IN THE MORNING. LATER/ HE
   GOES TO SCHOOL.
We see a table on the right.
   WE SEE A TABLE ON THE RIGHT. ON THE LEFT/ WE SEE A
   CHAIR.
John eats lunch at 12:00.
   JOHN EATS LUNCH AT 12:00. AT 1:00/ HE GOES TO THE OFFICE.

1. Robert has a pronunciation class in the morning.
2. We watched television in the lounge.
3. He eats breakfast at 8:00.
4. Birds go south in the fall.
5. There is a lecture by the speaker first.
6. We went to Detroit last week.
7. Jim is going to take a plane to Caracas tomorrow.
8. People go to church on Sunday.
9. Fred likes to swim and fish in the morning.
10. The winter is extremely cold in Michigan.
11. It rained very hard yesterday.
12. We lived at the dormitory this semester.
13. I am studying English at this university.

EXERCISE 2.3. (To use the pattern with THERE after initial expressions of time or place.) Listen to the two statements. Repeat the first statement, and change the second statement to the pattern with THERE after an expression of time or place. For example:

> The pronunciation class is in the morning. The grammar class is in the afternoon.
> THE PRONUNCIATION CLASS IS IN THE MORNING. IN THE AFTERNOON/ THERE IS THE GRAMMAR CLASS.
> The Smiths bought a new house. A small garden is behind the house.
> THE SMITHS BOUGHT A NEW HOUSE. BEHIND THE HOUSE/ THERE IS A SMALL GARDEN.
> China is situated here on the map. Siberia lies to the north.
> CHINA IS SITUATED HERE ON THE MAP. TO THE NORTH/ THERE LIES SIBERIA.

1. Canada is to the north of the United States. Mexico is to the south.
2. Cuba is a large island south of Florida. The Bahamas lie to the east.
3. The church is in the background. A statue is in the foreground.
4. The program comes first. The refreshments come afterwards.
5. The paper is in this drawer. Pencils are in that drawer.
6. A large painting hangs above the table. A smaller one hangs by the window.
7. Lake Michigan lies to the west of Michigan. Lake Huron lies to the east.
8. The women sat on the left. The men sat on the right.
9. The holiday comes first. The examinations come later.
10. An elm tree grows on the lawn. An apple tree grows in the garden.
11. There is a book in this desk. Pen and paper are on that desk.
12. The Atlantic Ocean is east of the United States. The Pacific is to the west.

3.   Key example: Business administration requires economics. It requires mathematics. It includes production, marketing, and accounting. IN OTHER WORDS/ it is a complex subject.

Observe the use of IN OTHER WORDS.

Joe is usually late to class. He is often absent. He doesn't study much. He failed in three courses last year.
IN OTHER WORDS/ he is a very bad student.

COMMENT

Use IN OTHER WORDS to introduce a statement which repeats or restates briefly information which has preceded and which is similar in at least one way.

ILLUSTRATIVE EXAMPLES

Bob enjoys swimming and playing tennis. He likes to watch football. In summer, he goes to a baseball game every Saturday.
IN OTHER WORDS/ he likes sports.
New York is famous for its tall buildings. It has a great library and many museums. It is the theatrical center of the United States. Its population includes people from every country in the world.
IN OTHER WORDS/ it is a fascinating city.

Many other expressions are used similarly to IN OTHER WORDS. You should learn to recognize these expressions, but elementary and intermediate students do not need to practice using them all.* Observe the following example:

The three branches of the U. S. Government have considerable control over each other. The President appoints the nine members of the Supreme Court for life and may veto legislation that has been passed by Congress. Congress may, in turn, override the President's veto. The Supreme Court may declare laws that have been passed by Congress and signed by the President to be unconstitutional.

IN OTHER WORDS/   we may say that equal distribution of power
IN SUMMARY/   constitutes an important part of govern-
IN A WORD/   ment in this country.
IN BRIEF/
BRIEFLY/
IN GENERAL/
TO SUMMARIZE/

PRACTICE

EXERCISE 3.1. (To use IN OTHER WORDS to relate sentences.) Listen to the statements. Repeat them, and produce a summarizing statement introduced by IN OTHER WORDS. For example:

I like fishing and golf. My wife likes tennis.
I LIKE FISHING AND GOLF. MY WIFE LIKES TENNIS. IN OTHER WORDS/ WE LIKE SPORTS.

---

*Advanced students who wish to practice these words should remember that they are slightly different in style and meaning.

Canada is larger than the United States. It is larger than Brazil or Argentina.

CANADA IS LARGER THAN THE UNITED STATES. IT IS LARGER THAN BRAZIL OR ARGENTINA. IN OTHER WORDS/ IT IS THE LARGEST COUNTRY IN THE WESTERN HEMISPHERE.

1. Tom reads a book a week. He subscribes to several newspapers and magazines.
2. Mary is having a difficult time with her pronunciation. Her sentence patterns are confused.
3. Tomás does all of his work. He never misses classes and he studies hard.
4. The play has started. The theater is several blocks away.
5. France has an area of 213,000 square miles. Spain has 195,000 square miles.
6. The weather is warm. The birds are singing. The trees are blooming.
7. The tickets are bought. Our baggage is packed.
8. John has a temperature of 100. His pulse is rapid and he has a cough.
9. We lost our tickets. Our baggage was stolen and we ran out of money.
10. The Red Cross gave us money. It provided us with food and shelter.
11. War kills and cripples. It destroys and creates misery.
12. He composes music. He plays the piano and violin.

KEY EXAMPLES OF LESSON XXIX

1. I haven't talked to my adviser yet. THEREFORE/ my plans are still indefinite.
2. I will finish this course first. THEN/ I'm going to study business administration.
3. Business administration requires economics. It requires mathematics. It includes production, marketing, and accounting. IN OTHER WORDS/ it is a complex subject.

Lesson XXX

EXERCISE 1. (To review answers to negative questions.) Answer the following negative questions with a negative or an affirmative short answer. For example:

Wasn't George Washington born in the nineteenth century?
NO, HE WASN'T.
Isn't her hat unusual?
YES, IT IS.
Can't you take the examination tomorrow?
NO, I CAN'T.

1. Didn't you take English last semester?
2. Couldn't he find the right room?
3. Don't you own a car?
4. Isn't Miss Francisco registered yet?
4. Didn't they go to the program last night?
6. Isn't your cold any better?
7. Doesn't she look pretty in her native costume?
8. Couldn't she have paid her tuition yesterday?
9. Won't you take a plane back to your country?
10. Wasn't he embarrassed?
11. Shouldn't you ask the teacher first?
12. Hadn't they eaten their breakfast?

EXERCISE 2. (To review attached questions.) Repeat the following statements and add an attached question. Add a negative question if the statement is affirmative, and an affirmative question if the statement is negative. For example:

He isn't sick.
HE ISN'T SICK, IS HE?
They answered all of the questions.
THEY ANSWERED ALL OF THE QUESTIONS, DIDN'T THEY?
They could have taken a later bus.
THEY COULD HAVE TAKEN A LATER BUS, COULDN'T THEY?

1. He is very young.
2. She has her bachelor's degree.
3. He won't return.
4. It's too late to write a letter now.
5. You haven't seen my pencil.

---

*TO THE TEACHER: Each teacher may plan a review lesson suited to the needs of his particular class by making a selection of exercises from the ones included in this lesson. Exercises from previous lessons may also be reviewed.

6. He never goes to his office in the morning.
7. They are going to see the play this afternoon.
8. We could have telephoned.
9. They can't see the building from here.
10. His foot looks bad.
11. I didn't get a letter.
12. We always wait for them.

EXERCISE 3. (To review attached questions.) Convert the following questions into statements with attached questions. Produce two forms of the attached question. For example:

Is John sick?
    JOHN IS SICK, ISN'T HE?
    JOHN ISN'T SICK, IS HE?
Have they answered your letter?
    THEY HAVE ANSWERED YOUR LETTER, HAVEN'T THEY?
    THEY HAVEN'T ANSWERED YOUR LETTER, HAVE THEY?
Has he offered to buy the book?
    HE HAS OFFERED TO BUY THE BOOK, HASN'T HE?
    HE HASN'T OFFERED TO BUY THE BOOK, HAS HE?

1. Is he a student?
2. Have you seen Tom?
3. Is she taking a course in biology?
4. Does he work for the government?
5. Can you come to the party?
6. Should I have opened the door?
7. Is she going to the program?
8. Did John promise to come?
9. Will you buy a subscription?
10. Are we going to take a plane?
11. Are they the same?
12. Did you find the correct answer?

EXERCISE 4. (To review short answers to questions with COULD HAVE, SHOULD HAVE BEEN, WILL, etc.) Produce a negative or affirmative short answer to the following questions. For example:

Should I have written a letter?
    YES, YOU SHOULD HAVE.
Won't you have another piece of pie?
    YES, I WILL.
Could you have lost the pencil on the way to school?
    NO, I COULDN'T HAVE.

1. Have you ever been to California?
2. Should I have gone to the picnic?
3. Could he have taken the book with him?
4. Will you be fifty years old this year?
5. Could you pay me for this picture tomorrow?
6. Might he have made a reservation with the travel bureau?

7. Would he have gone if I had asked him?
8. Would you have bought his typewriter from him?
9. Should we take our soccer ball to the picnic?
10. Could he have been talking to Professor Jones?
11. Should you have been taking notes?
12. Has he been studying in the library?

EXERCISE 5. (To review Class 3 words (GOOD, WHITE, etc.) in position after Class 1 words.) Substitute the following words. Include the Class 3 word after the Class 1 word. For example:

They washed the clothes white.
> table   THEY WASHED THE TABLE WHITE.
> painted   THEY PAINTED THE TABLE WHITE.
> blue   THEY PAINTED THE TABLE BLUE.

1. car	14. program	27. tough
2. house	15. interesting	28. wonderful
3. brown	16. found	29. play
4. wanted	17. delightful	30. painting
5. clean	18. movie	31. superb
6. kept	19. funny	32. judged
7. boy	20. thought	33. natural
8. happy	21. good	34. preferred
9. interested	22. food	35. color
10. class	23. delicious	36. red
11. busy	24. considered	37. car
12. lively	25. undigestable	38. painted
13. made	26. steak	

EXERCISE 6. (To review Class 1 words followed by -ING forms.) Listen to the statements. Combine the information so that a Class 1 word is followed by an -ING form. For example:

We saw John. He was walking to school.
> WE SAW JOHN WALKING TO SCHOOL.

They met Mary. She was hurrying to the concert.
> THEY MET MARY HURRYING TO THE CONCERT.

I found my watch. It was lying in the street.
> I FOUND MY WATCH LYING IN THE STREET.

1. They found us. We were preparing a program.
2. I can see Tom. He is riding a bicycle.
3. You couldn't have seen us. We were walking in the dark.
4. John heard me. I was talking with Fred.
5. I enjoyed seeing Fred. He was washing his car.
6. He remembers the car. It was going very slowly.
7. Jim had to pay the man. The man was standing by the gate.
8. We watched the camera man. He was taking a picture of the president.
9. We picked some berries. They were growing in the woods.
10. I discovered the owl. It was sitting on a branch.
11. We noticed Professor Ward. He was eating dinner with some friends.
12. He might have seen me. I was waiting for the bus.

EXERCISE 7. (To review -SELF forms as object.) Listen to the statements with the subject as receiver of the action. Produce corresponding statements with -SELF forms in which the same person is receiver and performer. For example:

The baby was fed yesterday.
THE BABY FED ITSELF YESTERDAY.
John was cured.
JOHN CURED HIMSELF.
The students are corrected in their pronunciation.
THE STUDENTS CORRECT THEMSELVES IN THEIR PRONUNCIATION.

1. The baby was fed some cereal.
2. John was hurt with a knife.
3. Mary was punished for telling a lie.
4. Fred was found in the hospital.
5. The patient was washed with hot water.
6. They were heard on the phonograph record.
7. The hunter was shot accidentally.
8. She was treated to a soda.
9. We were warmed by the fire.
10. He is considered a good student.
11. The country is protected with a good army.
12. Jane isn't understood.

EXERCISE 8. (To review -SELF forms as intensifier of the subject.) Substitute the following words and make the necessary changes in correlation. For example:

We talked to John ourselves.
    saw   WE SAW JOHN OURSELVES.
    him   WE SAW HIM OURSELVES.
    I   I SAW HIM MYSELF.
    the book   I SAW THE BOOK MYSELF.

1. it	11. them	21. the money
2. her	12. brought	22. I
3. they	13. the pencils	23. him
4. talked to	14. I	24. them
5. him	15. the apples	25. heard
6. he	16. we	26. her
7. me	17. you	27. she
8. her	18. found	28. me
9. us	19. it	29. saw
10. warned	20. she	30. us

EXERCISE 9. (To review the -ING expression as subject.) Listen to the statements. Use the information to make a generalizing statement with the -ING expression as subject. For example:

John has the bad habit of wasting time.
WASTING TIME IS A BAD HABIT.

Mary disturbs the teacher by talking in class.
TALKING IN CLASS DISTURBS THE TEACHER.
We work hard when we study.
STUDYING IS HARD WORK.

1. Mary has fun writing letters.
2. Jim has difficulty in pronouncing English.
3. They find it tiresome to study in the evening.
4. I help my pronunciation by listening to the radio.
5. John saves money by taking a bus to work.
6. I find fishing enjoyable.
7. It can be very expensive to go sightseeing.
8. John finds it a nuisance to eat alone.
9. It is dangerous to drive fast.
10. Our goal is to find the correct answer.
11. Fred thinks it is good exercise to play tennis.
12. Jane thinks it is a good hobby to write plays.

EXERCISE 10. (To review WHERE TO PLAY, HOW TO GO, etc.) Substitute the following words. For example:

I taught John how to play football.
   showed   I SHOWED JOHN HOW TO PLAY FOOTBALL.
   him   I SHOWED HIM HOW TO PLAY FOOTBALL.
   where   I SHOWED HIM WHERE TO PLAY FOOTBALL.
   tennis   I SHOWED HIM WHERE TO PLAY TENNIS.
   practice   I SHOWED HIM WHERE TO PRACTICE TENNIS.

1. golf
2. swimming
3. go
4. when
5. canoeing
6. told
7. where
8. how
9. enjoy
10. baseball
11. the program
12. prepare
13. why
14. Mary
15. when
16. leave
17. book
18. where
19. for whom
20. buy
21. where
22. find
23. how
24. the elevator
25. where
26. the typewriter
27. use
28. why

EXERCISE 11. (To review WISH with situations in present time.)
Listen to the situation in present time. Produce a response with WISH
+ a statement pattern. Use the -ED form of the Class 2 word in the
statement. For example:

John is sick.
   I WISH HE WAS WELL.
They made a lot of noise.
   I WISH THEY MADE LESS NOISE.
Jane works slowly.
   I WISH JANE WORKED FASTER.

1. Mary is tall.
2. They are sick.
3. The weather is bad.
4. He writes small on the blackboard.
5. She talkes quietly in the classroom.
6. You walk fast.
7. They are going to the movie.
8. He is coming today.
9. I am a student.
10. The book is very long.
11. The movie lasts one hour.
12. I read slowly.
13. I talk with an accent.
14. You stay up too late.
15. I get a letter every week.
16. He gets to class late.

EXERCISE 12. (To review WISH with situations in past time.) Listen to the situations in past time. Produce a response with WISH + a statement pattern. Use HAD + the -ED/-EN form of the Class 2 word in the statement. For example:

> John didn't eat much yesterday.
>   I WISH HE HAD EATEN MORE.
> I studied one hour each day last semester.
>   I WISH I HAD STUDIED TWO HOURS EACH DAY.
> They nominated Jack for president.
>   I WISH THEY HAD NOMINATED PETER.

1. I didn't see the program last Friday.
2. The newspaperman wrote an article about war.
3. We bought the less expensive rug.
4. All the students went to a movie this afternoon.
5. She sang a selection from an opera.
6. He was careless and lost his money.
7. We could have gone to the concert or the play.
8. I took a ship to Europe.
9. My friend sent me a post card.
10. I couldn't take professor Rolo's picture yesterday.
11. We waited for Fred in the corridor.
12. He sold his car to a stranger.

EXERCISE 13. (To review MUST, SHOULD, etc., + HAVE + the -ED/-EN form.) Listen to the situations in past time and the words which follow them. Produce comments which explain or elaborate the situation. Use MUST, MIGHT, COULD, SHOULD + HAVE + the -ED/-EN form. For example:

> I worked until ten o'clock yesterday.   could
>   I COULD HAVE WORKED UNTIL TWELVE.
> When I saw Mary, she was crying.   must
>   SHE MUST HAVE GOTTEN SOME BAD NEWS.
> John waited until yesterday to register.   should
>   HE SHOULD HAVE REGISTERED A WEEK AGO.
> He didn't come to the musical program last night.   might
>   HE MIGHT HAVE BEEN SICK.

1. I saw Mr. Rigs hurrying to the office.   must
2. John felt sick after dinner.   might
3. He walked in the rain and got wet.   should

4. She didn't know what to do with the book she found.   could
5. The teacher didn't give us a quiz today.   must
6. I wonder how they found out about my car accident.   might
7. Fred was supposed to meet me at the snack bar, but didn't.   could
8. Mary spent three months in Europe last year.   must
9. I looked for a pencil but couldn't find one.   could
10. He paid his bill on the third of this month.   should
11. We didn't see Jane arrive this afternoon.   might
12. John felt hungry all afternoon.   should

EXERCISE 14. (To review MUST, SHOULD, etc., + HAVE BEEN + the -ING form.) Listen to the situations in past time and the words which follow. Produce comments which explain or elaborate upon the situations. Use MUST, MIGHT, SHOULD, COULD + HAVE BEEN + the -ING form. For example:

I didn't see John at the program last night.   might
   HE MIGHT HAVE BEEN STUDYING.
Fred says that he didn't hear the telephone ring last night.   could
   HE COULD HAVE BEEN SLEEPING.
He was at the movie yesterday afternoon.   should
   HE SHOULD HAVE BEEN ATTENDING CLASS.
Paul's clothes are all wet.   must
   HE MUST HAVE BEEN WALKING IN THE RAIN.

1. I wonder what John was doing in the language laboratory.   might
2. Paul spent the day talking to his friends.   should
3. They weren't in their room when I knocked.   could
4. We saw John kicking a football on the lawn.   must
5. Mary got arrested for speeding yesterday.   should
6. The worker's face was covered with sweat.   must
7. I saw Fred lying on the couch.   might
8. I wonder why he didn't come to the program yesterday.   could
9. Jim talked over the telephone for two hours last night.   might
10. Mary was busy in the kitchen.   could
11. We missed the bus because we didn't see it arrive.   should
12. There was a foot of snow on the ground this morning.   must

EXERCISE 15. (To review Class 2 words not followed by TO.) Listen to the statements and combine them. Use a Class 2 word + a Class 1 word + a simple form of a Class 2 word or TO + a Class 2 word. Do not use TO after MAKE, LET, HAVE, HEAR, WATCH, SEE, OBSERVE, etc. For example:

I heard Fred. He talked about politics.
   I HEARD FRED TALK ABOUT POLITICS.
I selected John. He went.
   I SELECTED JOHN TO GO.
Mary bought a hat. We saw her.
   WE SAW MARY BUY A HAT.

1. They asked me. I took the book.
2. The teacher let him. He spoke to the class.
3. The teacher encouraged him. He spoke to the class.
4. I had the book brought. John brought it.
5. I helped John. He finished his work.
6. We saw the lightning. It struck a tree.
7. We observed the sky. It turned very dark.
8. We put on our lights. The policeman made us.
9. We put on our lights. The policeman told us.
10. I felt the toaster. It got hot.
11. He telephoned me. I sent his books.
12. I had a tooth pulled. Dr. Todd pulled it.

EXERCISE 16. (To review Class 2 words followed by an -ING form.)
Listen to the statements. Repeat the statements and after the Class 2
word add an -ING form or TO + a Class 2 word. For example:

    I enjoyed the program.
        I ENJOYED WATCHING THE PROGRAM.
    I forgot John.
        I FORGOT TO WRITE TO JOHN.
    Fred continued to town.
        FRED CONTINUED WALKING TO TOWN.

1. Jim enjoys football.
2. I wanted the book.
3. Mary finished the book.
4. They considered a trip.
5. He began the story.
6. They forgot the potatoes.
7. He got through first.
8. John insists on a pipe.
9. I expected Jim.
10. I remember Jim.
11. I recall Jim.
12. He likes cars.
13. She learned a song.
14. She avoided him.

EXERCISE 17. (To review Class 2 words with the -ING form, with TO
and without TO.) Substitute the following Class 2 words. For example:

    I wanted him to buy a car.
       had   I HAD HIM BUY A CAR.
       remembered I REMEMBERED HIM BUYING A CAR.
       asked   I ASKED HIM TO BUY A CAR.

1. watched
2. told
3. noticed
4. advised
5. encouraged
6. insisted on
7. sent
8. helped
9. expected
10. observed
11. persuaded
12. saw
13. wrote
14. found
15. got
16. begged
17. made
18. let
19. permitted
20. recalled

EXERCISE 18. (To review CAN, COULD, etc., in statements with IF.)
Listen to the situations. Expand the statements given with IF + a state-
ment with a Class 2 word in the simple or -ED form. After COULD,
WOULD, MIGHT, EXPECTED TO, PLANNED TO, etc., use the -ED form.
After CAN, MIGHT, WILL, EXPECT TO, PLAN TO, etc., use the simple
form. For example:

John is probably going to Detroit tomorrow. He is not going to New
York. I want to go to Detroit. I want to go to New York.
    I will go with John.
        I WILL GO WITH JOHN IF HE GOES TO DETROIT.
    I would go with him.
        I WOULD GO WITH HIM IF HE WENT TO NEW YORK.
    I can go with him.
        I CAN GO WITH HIM IF HE GOES TO DETROIT.
    I could go with him.
        I COULD GO WITH HIM IF HE WENT TO NEW YORK.
    I might go with him.
        I MIGHT GO WITH HIM IF HE GOES TO DETROIT.
    I might go with him.
        I MIGHT GO WITH HIM IF HE WENT TO NEW YORK.
    I expect to go with him.
        I EXPECT TO GO WITH HIM IF HE GOES TO DETROIT.
    I expected to go with him.
        I EXPECTED TO GO WITH HIM IF HE WENT TO NEW YORK.

A.   John is probably going to New York next week. He is not going to
Detroit. I want to go to Detroit. I don't want to go to New York.
   1. I won't go with John if he goes to New York.
   2. I would go with John.
   3. I could go with John.
   4. I can't go with John.
   5. I don't plan to go with John.
   6. I might go with John.

B.   Mary is probably going to the concert. She is not going to the play.
I want to go to either the concert or the play.
   1. I can go with Mary if she goes to the concert.
   2. I could go with Mary.
   3. I would go with Mary.
   4. Mary won't go with me.
   5. Mary wouldn't go with me.
   6. I might go with Mary.
   7. I will go with Mary.

EXERCISE 19. (To review WOULD HAVE, MIGHT HAVE, COULD HAVE
in statements connected with IF.) Listen to the improbable situations
with COULD, MIGHT, WOULD and IF + the -ED form. Convert the
statements into past-time situations with COULD HAVE, etc. Use HAD
+ the -ED/-EN form after IF. For example:

I would write if I knew his address.
I WOULD HAVE WRITTEN IF I HAD KNOWN HIS ADDRESS.
I might go to Detroit with John if he went by train.
I MIGHT HAVE GONE TO DETROIT WITH JOHN IF HE HAD GONE
BY TRAIN.
The director could see you if you waited.
THE DIRECTOR COULD HAVE SEEN YOU IF YOU HAD WAITED.

1. I could go with you if you went early.
2. John would take Mary if she wanted to go.
3. They could come if the program was short.
4. He might buy a raincoat if he needed it.
5. I would go with John if he drove his car.
6. The secretary could take your name if you were leaving.
7. I might buy it if it was for sale.
8. You could buy it if he gave you the money.
9. He would wait for you if you hurried.
10. I might study if I found my book.
11. We could call him if we knew his telephone number.
12. I would take a swim if I had a swim suit.

EXERCISE 20. (To review the connecting words IF, UNLESS, WHEN-
EVER, ALTHOUGH, BECAUSE, WHETHER OR NOT.) Listen to the
statement and the connecting word which follows. Repeat the statement
and use the connecting word to add another statement. For example:

He writes poetry.   although
HE WRITES POETRY ALTHOUGH HE NEVER WENT TO COLLEGE.
He writes poetry.   whenever
HE WRITES POETRY WHENEVER HE FEELS INSPIRED.
We will go on a picnic this afternoon.   whether or not
WE WILL GO ON A PICNIC THIS AFTERNOON WHETHER OR
NOT IT RAINS.
They won't go to the picnic.   unless
THEY WON'T GO TO THE PICNIC UNLESS SOMEONE TAKES
THEM.

1. The children get excited.   whenever
2. There is no school today.   because
3. He can't go to Canada.   if
4. She knows her lessons.   although
5. The program will go on.   whether or not
6. John never hurries.   unless
7. The desert cactus blooms.   whenever
8. The desert cactus never blooms.   unless
9. I have a difficult time with my pronunciation.   although
10. He must see a doctor.   whether or not
11. I like this city.   although
12. I feel happy.   whenever

EXERCISE 21. (To review the use of BECAUSE OF. . . and BECAUSE. . .)
Answer the following questions. Use the Class 1 words which follow
the question in your answer. Student A uses the word after BECAUSE
OF; student B uses the word in a statement after BECAUSE. For example:

Why is he going to the doctor?   cold
    Stud. A: HE IS GOING TO THE DOCTOR BECAUSE OF HIS COLD.
    Stud. B: HE IS GOING TO THE DOCTOR BECAUSE HE HAS A COLD.
Why is the teacher angry?   John
    Stud. A: THE TEACHER IS ANGRY BECAUSE OF JOHN.
    Stud. B: THE TEACHER IS ANGRY BECAUSE JOHN WAS TALKING
        IN CLASS.

1. Why couldn't Paul come to class today?   toothache
2. Why did he win the election?   personality
3. Why did he win the election?   hard work
4. Why was John late this morning?   watch
5. Why are you carrying an umbrella?   rain
6. Why can't Fred walk?   knee
7. Why is Tom popular?   good nature
8. Why have you stopped writing your letter?   pencil
9. Why can't you study tonight?   radio
10. Why doesn't your father visit the United States?   expense
11. Why can't he sleep at night?   noise
12. Why don't you write home oftener?   time

EXERCISE 22. (To review SO. . . THAT, SUCH . . . THAT.) Listen to
the statements. Compare them with SO . . . THAT and SUCH . . . THAT.
Use a Class 3 or Class 4 word with SO . . . THAT; use a Class 1 word
with SUCH . . . THAT. For example:

His talk was interesting. We listened for an hour.
    HIS TALK WAS SO INTERESTING THAT WE LISTENED FOR AN
      HOUR.
    HE GAVE SUCH AN INTERESTING TALK THAT WE LISTENED
      FOR AN HOUR.
The problem was easy. Everybody got the answer.
    THE PROBLEM WAS SO EASY THAT EVERYBODY GOT THE
      ANSWER.
    IT WAS SUCH AN EASY PROBLEM THAT EVERYBODY GOT THE
      ANSWER.

1. He is tall. He can't go through the door.
2. Her pronunciation is good. People think she is a native speaker.
3. He talks slowly. The new students can understand him.
4. Her dress was beautiful. All of the girls wanted one like it.
5. The doctor worked hard. He had a heart attack.
6. John's letters are long. It takes fifteen minutes to read them.
7. The clown was funny. We all laughed.
8. The building was huge. We couldn't believe it.
9. The little girl is bright. She talks like an adult.
10. The child is energetic. She runs and jumps all day.
11. The picture is blurred. We can't see it clearly.
12. The professor talks rapidly. We can't take notes.

EXERCISE 23. (To review ALSO, THEREFORE, HOWEVER.) Listen to the statements. Relate them with the expressions THEREFORE, ALSO, HOWEVER. For example:

> He is sick. He can't come.
> HE IS SICK. THEREFORE, HE CAN'T COME.
> He has a cold. He has a cough.
> HE HAS A COLD. ALSO, HE HAS A COUGH.
> He is in bed. He can get up tomorrow.
> HE IS IN BED. HOWEVER, HE CAN GET UP TOMORROW.

1. We like Mr. Blue as a teacher. We like Miss Meyner better.
2. Tom has a good vocabulary. He pronounces well.
3. I don't have a driver's license. I don't drive.
4. We haven't seen the new building. We don't know what it looks like.
5. I can't come today. I'll come tomorrow.
6. She bought her books today. She bought some pencils.
7. The carpenters worked hard. They didn't finish.
8. They are studying hard. They are learning English rapidly.
9. She knows how to play the piano. She can dance.
10. We like potatoes. We like rice.
11. I bought a boat last week. I haven't used it yet.
12. Bill left town. He won't be able to keep his appointment.

Lesson XXXI

SUMMARY OF QUESTION PATTERNS*

Observe these question patterns**

I		IS	music		one of the fine arts?	Yes, it is.
		IS	Mr. Smith	teaching	music to graduate students?	Yes, he is.
		HAS	he	taught	music history recently?	Yes, he has.
		CAN	he	teach	music history with recordings?	Yes, he can.
		DOES	he	teach	music because he likes it?	Yes, he does.
II	WHAT WHICH ART	IS	Mr. Smith	teaching?		Music.
		IS	he	teaching?		Music.
	WHO	IS	he	teaching	music to?	Graduate students.
	WHERE	HAS	he	taught	music history?	At the university.
	WHEN	HAS	he	taught	music history?	Recently.
	HOW	CAN	he	teach	music history?	With recordings.
	WHY	DOES	he	teach	music?	Because he likes it.
III			WHAT WHO	is is teaching	one of the fine arts? music to graduate students?	Music. Mr. Smith.
			WHICH TEACHER	has taught	music history recently?	Mr. Smith.

COMMENTS

(1) Use question patterns of Type I when you want an answer like YES, NO, CERTAINLY, CERTAINLY NOT, etc.

(2) Use question patterns of Type II when you know the performer and you want additional information in answer to WHAT, WHO, WHERE, WHEN, etc.

(3) Notice that a form of BE, or a form of HAVE, or CAN, MAY, SHOULD, etc., or a form of DO precedes the subject in all question patterns of Types I and II. This word order is the most important question signal in English.

(4) Use question patterns of Type III, putting WHAT, WHO, etc., in subject position, when you do not know the performer and you want the answer to identify the performer.

---

*Lessons XXXI to XXXIV are summary lessons. Their purpose is a) to give a more systematic presentation of some of the important sentence patterns of English; b) to give additional practice with these patterns.

**This lesson concerns only questions with falling intonation, so all exercises should be practiced with falling intonation. Questions with rising intonation are also used in English in certain social situations, or with certain special meanings.

ILLUSTRATIVE EXAMPLES OF QUESTION TYPE I

Observe the following questions without DO.

IS	there	a school of music in this university?	Yes, there is.
WERE	you	in Mr. Smith's music class last year?	Yes, I was.
ARE	you	taking a course from him now?	Yes, I am.
ARE	you	going to study music education next year?	Probably.
WERE	you	advised to take music theory?	Certainly.
MIGHT	you	play in the orchestra next year?	Yes, I might.
WILL	you	be studying harder next year?	Yes, I will.
COULD	you	have studied harder last year?	Yes, I could have.
SHOULD	you	have been studying harder this year?	Yes, I should have.
HAVE	you	studied the violin for very long?	Yes, I have.
HAVE	you	been practicing a lot recently?	I certainly have.
HAD	you	taken violin lessons before you came here?	Yes, I had.
HAVE	you	a good violin?	Yes, I have.

NOTE: Questions with HAVE plus the -ED/-EN form of the Class 2 word are not made with DO. Questions with HAVE, meaning "possess," without DO are uncommon in conversation but quite frequent in writing. However, questions with HAD, like "HAD you a good violin last year?" are very uncommon even in writing.

Observe the following questions with DO.

DO	you	go to the movies every Saturday night?	Yes, I do.
DID	you	see the show at the Liberty last week?	Yes, I did.
DOES	your	little brother like to go to cowboy movies?	Yes, he does.
DO	you	have a good violin?	Yes, I do.
DID	you	have a good violin when you were in high school?	No, I didn't.
DO	you	have to practice very much?	I certainly do.
DOES	your	teacher have him practice difficult exercises?	Of course.

NOTE: In conversation, questions with HAVE meaning "possess," are usually made with DO. Questions with HAVE TO and HAVE HIM PRACTICE, etc., are always made with DO in conversation and writing. Remember to use the simple form of the Class 2 word in questions with DO.

Observe the negative questions and their answers.

ISN'T	Rome the capital of Italy?	YES, IT IS.
ISN'T	Barcelona the capital of Spain?	NO, IT ISN'T.
DON'T	they grow oranges in California?	YES, THEY DO.
DON'T	they grow coffee in California?	NO, THEY DON'T.

NOTE: The speaker who asks a negative question with a falling intonation expects an affirmative answer, but he does not always receive one. The answers are the same as for affirmative questions in the same situation.

Observe the attached questions and their answers.

Rome is the capital of Italy,	ISN'T IT?	YES, IT IS.
Barcelona is the capital of Spain,	ISN'T IT?	NO, IT ISN'T.
They grow oranges in California,	DON'T THEY?	YES, THEY DO.
They grow coffee in California,	DON'T THEY?	NO, THEY DON'T.

NOTE: Use a negative attached question after an affirmative statement. Use an affirmative attached question after a negative statement. The speaker who asks an attached question with a falling intonation expects an answer to agree with his statement, but he does not always receive one. Answer attached questions according to the situation.

ILLUSTRATIVE EXAMPLES OF QUESTION TYPE II

Observe the various question words used in Type II and the kinds of answers they receive.

WHERE	IS	the violin concert going to be?	In the auditorium.
WHEN	IS	it going to be?	On Wednesday.
WHAT TIME	WILL	it begin?	At eight o'clock.
HOW LONG	WILL	it last?	For about two hours.
HOW FAR	IS	the auditorium from here?	About three miles.
HOW	CAN	we get there?	By car.
WHY	DON'T	we take a taxi?	Because it's expensive.
WHOSE CAR	SHOULD	we go in?	Mine.
WHOSE	DID	we go in last time?	Yours.
WHO(M)	SHOULD	we go with?	Mary and Betty.
WHAT KIND OF MUSIC	WILL	the violinist play?	Modern American music.
WHAT KIND	DO	you like?	Classical music.
WHICH COMPOSER	DO	you like best?	Bach.
WHICH	DOES	Mary prefer?	Beethoven.
HOW MUCH	WILL	the concert cost?	Two dollars.
HOW MANY PEOPLE	WILL	there probably be there?	About 1000.
HOW MANY	DOES	the auditorium hold?	Almost 2000.
WHAT	DO	you want to do after the concert?	Get something to eat.

ILLUSTRATIVE EXAMPLES OF TYPE III

Observe the question words used in Type III and the kinds of answers they receive.

WHAT	is an interesting course to take?	Music history.
WHO	teaches it?	Mr. Smith.
HOW MANY STUDENTS	take it?	All the music students.

HOW MANY	are taking it now?	About fifteen.
WHOSE BOOK	is used?	Mr. Smith's.
WHOSE	is the best?	His.
WHICH		
COMPOSERS	are studied?	All the great composers.
WHICH	is the most interesting?	Classical music.
WHAT KIND		
OF MUSIC	is the most difficult?	Modern music.

PRACTICE *

EXERCISE 1. (To practice questions of Type I with question word order.)
Convert the following statements into questions having a YES or NO
answer. Use question word order to signal the question. For example:

John is a good student.
    IS JOHN A GOOD STUDENT?
The man in the brown coat is his father.
    IS THE MAN IN THE BROWN COAT HIS FATHER?
He has attended many recitals.
    HAS HE ATTENDED MANY RECITALS?

1. Mr. Flynn is the founder of the company.
2. Ted may go on the trip.
3. The trip to Niagara Falls can be taken in June.
4. The light bulb has burned out.
5. The concert is being given in the auditorium.
6. We can take the test tomorrow.
7. She should take a taxi to the airport.
8. The books on our reading list are expensive.
9. The students are going on a picnic.
10. There's a student waiting in the classroom.
11. Our students will be taught to play baseball.
12. Jane is still reading her magazine.
13. She is going to study later.
14. They would go if they could get a ride.

EXERCISE 2. (To use Question Type I with the forms of DO.) Convert
the following statements into questions having a YES or NO answer. Use
the forms of the word DO and produce the necessary changes in the Class
2 word. For example:

We eat at six.
    DO WE EAT AT SIX?
The boys played football at the picnic.
    DID THE BOYS PLAY FOOTBALL AT THE PICNIC?
The man in the street hears the song.
    DOES THE MAN IN THE STREET HEAR THE SONG?

---

*The exercises in this lesson can be practiced in three ways:.
    1) the questions may be practiced without answers.
    2) the teacher can answer the questions which the students form.
    3) another student can answer the questions.

1. Americans read many magazines.
2. The professor spoke of cultural contacts.
3. Our physics teacher explained it.
4. The students who heard it agree.
5. Registration takes place on Monday.
6. John's father has a new car.
7. He drove his car to Chicago.
8. We have to go to Detroit.
9. They always go to the cafeteria for lunch.
10. Jane wanted to go to the movies.
11. The car which he is buying runs well.
12. He found the pen which belongs to Bill.
13. The students plan to take a plane if the weather is good.
14. They had a good plane trip last year.

EXERCISE 3. (To practice Question Type I.) Listen to the statement. Repeat the statement and convert it into a YES or NO question containing the form YOU or YOUR. For example:

I went to the movie last night.
    I WENT TO THE MOVIE LAST NIGHT. DID YOU GO TO THE
    MOVIE LAST NIGHT?
John likes skating.
    JOHN LIKES SKATING. DO YOU LIKE SKATING?
Tom is a good swimmer.
    TOM IS A GOOD SWIMMER. ARE YOU A GOOD SWIMMER?

1. We always drink coffee for breakfast.
2. John is a candidate for class president.
3. Fred can do his assignment in one hour.
4. He could see the building.
5. I think that democracy is the best form of government.
6. The Ford family has a lot of money.
7. She has taken two courses in the English Department.
8. In our country, we eat a lot of bread.
9. Bill has been asked to speak at the dinner.
10. Mary will go to the play with us.
11. They know that the ticket costs one dollar.
12. He was taken to see the director.
13. Jane asked for an extension of her visa.
14. Mrs. Brown had a headache last night.

EXERCISE 4. (To produce questions of Type I from suggested phrases.) Listen to the phrase given. It contains a Class 1 word and one or more Class 2 words. Expand the phrase to form a question by supplying more words and the signals for a question. For example:

Mary walks
    DOES MARY WALK TO SCHOOL IN THE MORNING?
made progress
    DID JOHN MAKE PROGRESS IN ENGLISH?
boy is
    IS THE BOY YOUR BROTHER?

1. Fred was writing	9. Jane listens
2. he heard	10. he was seen
3. took an examination	11. he has seen
4. John had	12. she can eat
5. likes winter sports	13. you traveled
6. is talking to Fred	14. get seasick
7. has been reading	15. they are going to
8. attended a concert	16. we had

EXERCISE 5. (To produce attached questions.) Convert the following statements into questions by repeating the statement and adding to it a form of BE, DO, or CAN, etc., plus a negative and the appropriate substitute word. If the statement contains a negative, then omit the negative in the attached portion. For example:

> He is a professor.
> HE IS A PROFESSOR, ISN'T HE?
> He isn't a lawyer.
> HE ISN'T A LAWYER, IS HE?
> Mary taught English in Cuba.
> MARY TAUGHT ENGLISH IN CUBA, DIDN'T SHE?
> They can sing folk songs.
> THEY CAN SING FOLK SONGS, CAN'T THEY?

1. He likes to discuss politics.
2. John and Mary are classmates.
3. They never go to a movie.
4. Alice bought a sewing machine.
5. It didn't cost much.
6. Professor James can play the piano.
7. May has a new dress.
8. Jane doesn't like writing compositions.
9. They should buy a season's ticket to the concert.
10. You will go to the dance.
11. The picture of Tom is a good one.
12. The semester will soon be over.
13. They don't like the new opera.
14. They have eaten dinner already.

EXERCISE 6. (To use Question Type II, and to practice discrimination in the use of question words.) Listen to the question of Type I. Without changing the wording, convert it into a Type II question, using the question words: WHO, WHEN, WHERE, HOW, WHY, WHAT. Use all the question words which fit the situation, omitting those which do not. For example:

Is Miss Jones teaching?
> WHAT IS SHE TEACHING?
> WHERE IS SHE TEACHING?
> WHEN IS SHE TEACHING?
> WHY IS SHE TEACHING?
> HOW IS SHE TEACHING?
> WHO IS SHE TEACHING?

Does the program begin at eight in the auditorium?
    WHY DOES THE PROGRAM BEGIN AT EIGHT IN THE AUDITORIUM?
    HOW DOES THE PROGRAM BEGIN AT EIGHT IN THE AUDITORIUM?

Is Mr. Smith working now?
    WHY IS HE WORKING NOW?
    WHERE IS HE WORKING NOW?
    HOW IS HE WORKING NOW?

1. Can he teach well?
2. Did you buy a ticket?
3. Will you travel by car?
4. May Ted go to the movie?
5. Does he write well?
6. Is the concert beginning now?
7. Did you see?
8. Is your friend coming?
9. Is Guatemala small or large?
10. Is the director here?
11. Can I ask at the desk now?
12. Can you sing immediately?

EXERCISE 7. (To practice Question Type II.) Listen to the following statements. One item will be selected from the statement. Convert the statement into a question asking for this item of information. Use the question words WHO, WHEN, WHAT, etc. For example:

He can teach physics.   physics
    WHAT CAN HE TEACH?
John and Mary heard an opera Saturday.   heard an opera
    WHAT DID JOHN AND MARY DO SATURDAY?
He knows Jim Santos.   Jim Santos
    WHO DOES HE KNOW?
Tom played the folk song at the program.   at the program
    WHERE DID TOM PLAY THE FOLK SONG?

1. Mary is going to Milwaukee tomorrow.   tomorrow
2. Professor Tomkin has taken a trip to Italy.   to Italy
3. He will spend a week in Rome.   a week
4. Fred listened to the radio last night.   the radio
5. A concert will be given next month.   next month
6. Mr. Mendes is here to study English.   to study English
7. Professor Dakin liked the symphony very much.   very much
8. Mr. Flores has studied music in Peru.   music
9. Jane goes to the recitals because she likes music.   because she likes music
10. She can play the piano and the violin.   the piano and the violin
11. They met Mr. Bell at the concert.   at the concert
12. The opera lasted four hours.   four hours
13. The singer dedicated a song to Mary.   to Mary
14. We waited in the auditorium for Paul.   for Paul
15. Mrs. Jimson found the program exciting.   exciting

EXERCISE 8. (To use Question Type III by forming questions in which the performer is not identified in the question.) Listen to the statements. Substitute WHO, WHAT, or WHICH in the position of the subject; substitute WHAT or WHICH + a Class 1 word in some statements. For example:

Mr. Smith is a good teacher.
     WHO IS A GOOD TEACHER?
The blue bird built a nest in the tree.
     WHICH BIRD BUILT A NEST IN THE TREE?
An insect bit him.
     WHAT BIT HIM?

1. I heard the opera last Saturday.
2. The first act was the most interesting.
3. The soprano forgot her part.
4. The opera has long been a classic.
5. The tenor in the leading role was outstanding.
6. This book is not for sale.
7. This kind of candy is too sweet.
8. His is the best.
9. The book cost five dollars.
10. John answered the telephone.
11. The cup fell off the table.
12. The red-haired boy broke the window.

EXERCISE 9. (To use Question Types II and III.) Listen to the following statements containing several items of information. Using the question words given, form questions which will ask for information contained in the statement. For example:

I went to South America by plane.
     Where: WHERE DID YOU GO BY PLANE?
       Who: WHO WENT TO SOUTH AMERICA BY PLANE?
       How: HOW DID YOU GO TO SOUTH AMERICA?
Tom is studying architecture at the University.
       Who: WHO IS STUDYING ARCHITECTURE AT THE UNIVERSITY?
     What: WHAT IS TOM STUDYING AT THE UNIVERSITY?
     Where: WHERE IS TOM STUDYING ARCHITECTURE?
Fred taught history in Detroit last year.
     When: WHEN DID FRED TEACH HISTORY IN DETROIT?
     Where: WHERE DID FRED TEACH HISTORY LAST YEAR?
       Who: WHO TAUGHT HISTORY IN DETROIT LAST YEAR?

1. He studied algebra yesterday.
     When
     Who
     What
2. He is Ted Reily.
     Who
     Who
3. We liked the concert very much.
     How
     Who
     What
4. He went to Detroit to see the opera.
     Why
     Who
     Where

5. Jack gave Bill a book.
   What
   Who
   Who
6. The pianist will arrive today by plane.
   Who
   How
   When
7. Fred bought Jim a radio today.
   Who
   Who
   When
   What
8. Ted works because he needs the money.
   Why
   Who
9. The concert last night was superb.
   What
   When
   How
10. Mary took a music appreciation course at the university.
    What
    Where
    Who
11. Jazz was popular in America in the thirties.
    When
    What
    Where
12. His lecture yesterday was about government.
    Whose
    When
    What

EXERCISE 10. (To review Question Types I, II, and III.) Convert the following statements into questions. The first question should have a YES or NO response and the second an information response. Use question word order or the forms of DO in the first question. Use the question words, WHAT, WHEN, WHERE, WHY, HOW, WHO, in the second. For example:

   This book is a good one.
      IS THIS BOOK A GOOD ONE?
      WHICH BOOK IS A GOOD ONE?
   John received good grades.
      DID JOHN RECEIVE GOOD GRADES?
      WHY DID JOHN RECEIVE GOOD GRADES?
   Mary is willing to go.
      IS MARY WILLING TO GO?
      WHEN IS MARY WILLING TO GO?

1. Time Magazine is a popular magazine.
2. They heard the National Anthem played.
3. Her father is a lawyer.
4. They told him to practice every day.
5. The book on the desk cost five dollars.
6. He traveled in Europe because he was wealthy.
7. It is three blocks from his house to the campus.
8. This kind of flower grows on sandy soil.
9. You can find the pattern on page eight.
10. He forgot his hat when he left the building.
11. It will take you one hour to get to Toledo.
12. This book is John's.

EXERCISE 11. (To practice free use of questions in a conversational situation.) Listen to the situation. Then ask all types of questions which may help to solve the problem. For example:

He invented a machine. I've forgotten what it does.
Questions: DOES IT FLY? DOES IT WASH DISHES? IS IT BIG OR SMALL? CAN IT PEEL POTATOES? HOW DOES IT WORK? WHO CAN USE IT?
    I had a dream last night. I saw something horrible. It was chasing me, so I ran.
Questions: WHERE DID YOU RUN? DID IT CATCH YOU? WHY DID IT CHASE YOU? WAS IT AN ANIMAL OR A HUMAN BEING? WHAT COLOR WAS IT? COULDN'T YOU CALL FOR HELP?

1. John went to the drugstore to buy something, but I can't remember what.
2. An important piece of news was broadcast over the radio.
3. I saw him doing something but I've forgotten what he was doing.
4. I went to a movie last night but I can't remember the story.
5. Mr. Johnson wrote a book but I don't know the title.
6. Jack went on a trip. I've forgotten exactly where he went.
7. They had a bad accident yesterday.
8. I have just subscribed to a magazine but I can't remember which one.
9. I saw something strange on State Street.
10. Marilyn is looking for something. She needs it immediately but she doesn't know the name of it.
11. Dick won a prize for something he did.
12. Her husband has an important job, but I'm not sure of his title.

Lesson XXXII

SUMMARY OF SUBJECT AND SUBJECT MODIFICATION

1. The Position of the Subject

Observe the words and patterns in subject position.

ART	requires ability and hard work.
MR. JOHNSON	is an artist.
HE	paints pictures.
THIS	is a difficult art.
THERE	are many beautiful pictures in his home.
IT	is a pleasure to look at them.
PAINTING	has always interested Mr. Johnson.
TO PAINT	is hard work.
WHAT TO PAINT	is never a problem.
WHAT PLEASES MR. JOHNSON MOST	is to paint well.
WHAT HE WANTS MOST	is to paint a great picture.

COMMENT

Use something in subject position in every English statement.* You have learned the following types of words and patterns which you can use in this position:

  a) Class 1 words (ART, MR. JOHNSON, etc.)
  b) Class 1 substitutes (HE, THIS, etc.)
  c) THERE, IT (See Lesson XIV, if necessary.)
  d) The -ING form of Class 2 words or TO + the simple form of Class 2 words (PAINTING, TO PAINT, etc. See Lesson XXVIII if necessary.)
  e) Expressions like WHAT TO PAINT. (You learned to use these expressions in object position in Lesson XXI.)
  f) Included sentences (WHAT PLEASES MR. JOHNSON MOST, WHAT HE WANTS MOST, etc. See Note at the end of Lesson XVII, if necessary.)

THE OLD MAN AND THE SEA   is about an old fisherman.
"TO BE OR NOT TO BE" is my favorite line from Shakespeare.

NOTE: You can use titles and quotations in subject position.

Should we go downtown in the morning or in the afternoon?
IN THE MORNING would be the best time.

---

*Observe the contrast between a statement, with a subject, like YOU PAINT WELL and a request, without a subject, like PAINT WELL. Complete questions like WHY DID YOU COME? contain a subject, but certain short questions like WHY? do not. Some answers to questions do not contain a subject. In works of literature, you will observe various other sentence patterns without a subject.

Should we meet at my house or at your house?
   AT MY HOUSE would be better.
Should we go quickly or slowly?
   QUICKLY would be preferable.

NOTE: You can use expressions of time, place, and manner in subject
         position in answers to questions.

What do YOU call that?   YOU call it a can opener.
What does ONE call that?   ONE calls it a can opener.
Where can YOU study here?   YOU can study in the library.
Where can ONE study here?   ONE can study in the library.

NOTE: Use YOU or ONE in subject position when you wish to refer to
         "people in general," not to any specific person. ONE is more
         formal than YOU.

Observe the use of Class 1 substitutes in sequence sentences.

Some STUDENTS were in the lounge.
         SEVERAL were watching television.
         A FEW were trying to study.
            ONE was writing a letter.
         ANOTHER was watching him.
            THREE were standing by the window.

George got to go to California last winter.
   THIS was just what he had wanted.
However, it rained every day he was there.
   THAT was unfortunate.

Observe the use of two or more subjects.

ART AND LITERATURE are important parts of a country's culture.
MR. JOHNSON, MR. EDWARDS, AND MR. BROWN are artists.
DRAWING AND PAINTING have always interested them.
A MUSEUM OR AN ART GALLERY is an interesting place to visit.
WHAT PLEASES MR. JOHNSON MOST AND WHAT HE ALWAYS TRIED
   TO DO is to paint well.

Observe the expansions of the Class 2 subjects.

PAINTING is a difficult art.
PAINTING PORTRAITS is a difficult art.
PAINTING PORTRAITS WELL is a difficult art.
TO PAINT is hard work.
TO PAINT WITH WATER COLORS is the easiest.
TO PAINT AN IMPORTANT PORTRAIT WITH WATER COLORS would
   be a mistake.

PRACTICE

EXERCISE 1.1. (To practice various types of subject.) Substitute the item given in the subject position of the statement. Make a change in the Class 2 word if necessary. For example:

The Metropolitan Museum of Art is world-famous.
1. Some painters and sculptors
   SOME PAINTERS AND SCULPTORS ARE WORLD-FAMOUS.
2. Diego Rivera
   DIEGO RIVERA IS WORLD-FAMOUS.
3. He
   HE IS WORLD-FAMOUS.
4. His painting
   HIS PAINTING IS WORLD-FAMOUS.
5. His murals
   HIS MURALS ARE WORLD-FAMOUS.
6. What he has painted
   WHAT HE HAS PAINTED IS WORLD-FAMOUS.

A. My friend's painting was shown at the art gallery.
   1. A Persian rug
   2. Others from Europe
   3. Picasso's work
   4. It
   5. What he had painted
   6. Pictures and statues
B. Dali's work created a sensation.
   1. He
   2. His work
   3. How he did it
   4. Hanging such unusual paintings in important museums
   5. His article, "What to Paint,"
   6. Whatever he said
C. To produce the pyramids of Egypt was a great achievement.
   1. The Cathedral of Notre Dame
   2. The artist's next painting
   3. Last night's program
   4. Learning to speak English
   5. The first airplane flight
   6. To climb Mt. Everest
D. The President honored our leading artist.
   1. The City of Detroit
   2. What he produced last year
   3. We
   4. Creating a new technique
   5. To paint such great pictures
   6. Whatever work he attempted

E. Mary and Fred have done good work.
  1. He and she
  2. Others
  3. Dr. Gonzales and he
  4. Those who took the intensive course in English
  5. These taking the summer course
  6. Everyone

EXERCISE 1.2. (To practice word groups in subject position.) Listen
to the statements. Convert the word group with -ING in subject position
to one with a word group prefaced by HOW, WHAT, WHEN, WHERE and
completed with   . . .IS A PROBLEM.   For example:

Painting requires great skill.
        WHAT TO PAINT IS A PROBLEM.
Buying a car is an expensive venture.
        WHAT CAR TO BUY IS A PROBLEM.
Getting a high score pleases Mary.
        HOW TO GET A HIGH SCORE IS A PROBLEM.
Swimming when the weather is hot is refreshing.
        WHERE TO SWIM WHEN THE WEATHER IS HOT IS A PROBLEM.

  1. Visiting art museums is a pleasant hobby.
  2. Sculpturing is a difficult art.
  3. Driving a car when you are sleepy is dangerous.
  4. Wood carving appeals to me.
  5. Working with Professor Smith made George a good painter.
  6. Doing good work is Bob's ambition.
  7. Eating alone irritates Mr. Swenson.
  8. Drinking tea in the afternoon is a custom in England.
  9. Getting rich in a short time is the ambition of many people.
 10. Asking for help when you are in trouble is a wise thing.
 11. Speaking loudly and clearly is a good habit.
 12. Writing letters makes Miss Darby happy.

EXERCISE 1.3. (To practice IT and THERE in subject position.) Convert
the following statements into statements having THERE or IT in subject
position. Use THERE when the statement contains a Class 1 word in subject position. Use IT when an -ING form or TO + a Class 2 word is the
subject. For example:

    Working hard is necessary.
        IT IS NECESSARY TO WORK HARD.
    A storm is coming from the West.
        THERE IS A STORM COMING FROM THE WEST.
    To paint with water colors requires skill.
        IT REQUIRES SKILL TO PAINT WITH WATER COLORS.
    A picture of the group will be taken tomorrow.
        THERE WILL BE A PICTURE OF THE GROUP TAKEN TOMORROW.

1. Working together is a good practice.
2. A painting by Grant Wood is on display at the Art Gallery.
3. To get a taxi in rainy weather is a problem.
4. Studying in the evening is difficult for me.
5. Five students are preparing a program.
6. Taking part in the program was requested of the students.
7. To protect the poor is a responsibility of the government.
8. A house on Main Street was on fire.
9. A girl in a blue coat was studying here.
10. When to return to Panama is hard to determine.
11. To hold a picnic on Sunday was suggested by the chairman.
12. An examination will be given on Tuesday morning.
13. A lecture on Whistler was presented by Professor Wallen.
14. Watching a football game is exciting.
15. Registration is at eight o'clock in the morning.

EXERCISE 1.4. (To produce included sentences in subject position.)
Listen to the statements. Add an appropriate comment by using an included sentence consisting of HOW, WHY, WHERE, WHEN, or WHAT + Class 1 + Class 2 in the position of subject. For example:

It is important that you study.
    I AGREE. BUT WHAT YOU STUDY IS ALSO IMPORTANT.
It is important that you travel.
    I AGREE. BUT WHERE YOU TRAVEL IS ALSO IMPORTANT.
It is important that you practice pronunciation.
    I AGREE. BUT HOW YOU PRACTICE PRONUNCIATION IS ALSO IMPORTANT.

1. It is important that you eat.
2. It is important that you work.
3. It is important that you go.
4. It is important that you co-operate.
5. It is important that you sing.
6. It is important that you drive.
7. It is important that you read.
8. It is important that you smile.
9. It is important that you paint.
10. It is important that you fly.
11. It is important that you listen.
12. It is important that you watch.

2. Subject Modification

Observe the modifiers of the Class 1 subject head.

MODIFIER		SUBJECT HEAD	MODIFIER	
Many	LARGE	cities		have art museums.
These	ART	museums		display the works of famous painters.
	BEGINNING	artists		sometimes have their pictures displayed too.
A	RECOGNIZED	painter		often receives large prices for his pictures.
		Artists	EVERYWHERE	like to display their pictures.
The		pictures	IN MUSEUMS	must be chosen very carefully.
The		men	CHOOSING THE PICTURES	have to work very carefully.
The		decision	TO CHOOSE A PICTURE	is often difficult.
The		men	WHO CHOOSE THE PICTURES	have a great responsibility.
The		pictures	WHICH THEY CHOOSE	are often very expensive.
The	FAMOUS ART	museums	WHERE GREAT PICTURES ARE DISPLAYED	attract hundreds of visitors every day.

COMMENTS

(1) Use most single word modifiers (LARGE, ART, BEGINNING, RECOGNIZED, etc.) before the subject head. However, use expressions of time and place (EVERYWHERE, etc.) after the subject head which they modify.

(2) Use word group and included sentence modifiers (IN MUSEUMS, CHOOSING THE PICTURES, WHO CHOOSE THE PICTURES, etc.) after the subject head.

(3) You can use several modifiers with one subject (THE <u>FAMOUS</u> <u>ART</u> MUSEUMS <u>WHERE GREAT PICTURES ARE DISPLAYED</u>, etc.).

ILLUSTRATIVE EXAMPLES

The ART instructor AT OUR SCHOOL works hard.
The YOUNG ART instructor TEACHING PAINTING works hard.
The VERY ENTHUSIASTIC
YOUNG ART instructor ASSIGNED TO TEACH PAINTING
works hard.

The WELL KNOWN ART instructor WHO TEACHES PAINTING HERE
works hard.

The YOUNG PAINTING instructor THAT I TOLD YOU ABOUT works
hard.

The YOUNG DRAWING
AND PAINTING instructor AT OUR SCHOOL WHO(M) I TOLD
YOU ABOUT works hard.

PRACTICE

EXERCISE 2.1. (To practice single word modification of a Class 1 word
in subject position.) Listen to the two statements. Combine them so that
the Class 1 word in subject position of the first statement is modified by
an additional word or words. For example:

The student is ambitious. He is learning English.
THE AMBITIOUS STUDENT IS LEARNING ENGLISH.
The north wind is bitter. It will bring snow.
THE BITTER NORTH WIND WILL BRING SNOW.
The man is weary and old. He cannot work.
THE WEARY OLD MAN CANNOT WORK.

1. The girl is dancing. She is wearing a Mexican costume.
2. Mary is busy. She always has her work done.
3. Our radio is broken. It was taken to the repair shop.
4. The book is missing. It belongs to Fred.
5. The sweater is washable. It will not fade or shrink.
6. The weather is cold and rainy. It is depressing.
7. The young child is very bright. He learns quickly.
8. The skiing season is past. It was very good.
9. Sally's flower is yellow. It smells nice.
10. The time has been well spent. It will profit our English.
11. The snow was pure white. It sparkled like diamonds.
12. The Boston Symphony Orchestra is excellent. It will play here next
    week.

EXERCISE 2.2. (To produce a Class 1 word as a modifier of another
Class 1 word in subject position.) Listen to the statements. Convert the
Class 1 word occurring in the word group into a single word modifier of
the Class 1 word in subject position. For example:

The book on Whitman has been lost.
THE WHITMAN BOOK HAS BEEN LOST.
The house on Main Street is a meeting place for artists.
THE MAIN STREET HOUSE IS A MEETING PLACE FOR ARTISTS.
The elevator in the Taylor Building is dangerous.
THE TAYLOR BUILDING ELEVATOR IS DANGEROUS.
The large painting by Norman Rockwell is owned by Mr. Loty.
THE LARGE NORMAN ROCKWELL PAINTING IS OWNED BY
MR. LOTY.

1. The Vice-President of the Association gave a talk.
2. His report on the book was well done.
3. The arts of weaving are practiced by the Hopi Indians.
4. This beautiful sculpture by Michelangelo is priceless.
5. Our time in class is well spent.
6. The attendance in summer set a new record.
7. Interest in jazz music has increased recently.
8. The window on the east faces the campus.
9. The new teacher in school read a story by Mark Twain.
10. Art in school has improved through better teaching.
11. The recent mural by Rivera has many admirers.
12. The policy of "English Only" is a tradition in the Institute.

EXERCISE 2.3. (To practice modification of a Class 1 word in subject position with -ING, or -ED/-EN, or TO + the simple form of the Class 2 word, word groups.) Listen to the statements. Combine them to form a single statement in which the Class 1 word in subject position is modified by a word group introduced by the -ING, or -ED/-EN form, or TO + the simple form of a Class 2 word. For example:

The boy is writing a letter. He has a headache.
THE BOY WRITING A LETTER HAS A HEADACHE.
The painting is being shown at the art gallery. It is by Thomas Eakins.
THE PAINTING BEING SHOWN AT THE ART GALLERY IS BY
THOMAS EAKINS.
The student was taken to the hospital. He has the flu.
THE STUDENT TAKEN TO THE HOSPITAL HAS THE FLU.
The drive is to help needy students. It begins today.
THE DRIVE TO HELP NEEDY STUDENTS BEGINS TODAY.

1. The girl is talking to Jim. She is Mary's roommate.
2. The movie was shown at the dormitory. It was about Glacier Park.
3. His aim is to get an "A" this semester. He may succeed.
4. The girl was singing the new song. She had a contralto voice.
5. The book is lying on the desk. It is by Willa Cather.
6. The group picture was taken yesterday. It pleased everybody.
7. The game was played at St. Louis. It decided the World Championship.
8. Their objective is to support art. It is a worthy cause.
9. The painting was produced in 1920. It was a masterpiece.
10. The tree is growing in the yard. It is an apple tree.
11. The young woman was sitting by the window. She was thinking of her children.
12. The exhibition was held in the school auditorium. It was well attended.
13. Our purpose is to learn to speak English fluently. It is being accomplished.
14. The secretary is typing a report. She is in a hurry.
15. The painting was displayed at the festival. It was returned last week.

EXERCISE 2.4. (To practice included sentence modification of a Class 1 word in subject position.) Listen to the two statements. Combine them so that the Class 1 word in the subject position of the first statement is modified by an included sentence. Introduce the included sentences with THAT, WHICH, WHO, WHOM, WHOSE, WHEN, WHERE. For example:

> The examinations are hard. They are taken in June.
> THE EXAMINATIONS WHICH ARE TAKEN IN JUNE ARE HARD.
> The boy is in the hospital. He broke his leg.
> THE BOY WHO BROKE HIS LEG IS IN THE HOSPITAL.
> The boy is in the hospital. His leg is broken.
> THE BOY WHOSE LEG IS BROKEN IS IN THE HOSPITAL.
> The young man is here. He likes Mary.
> THE YOUNG MAN WHO LIKES MARY IS HERE.
> The young man is here. Mary likes him.
> THE YOUNG MAN WHO(M) MARY LIKES IS HERE.

1. A student drew the picture. He is in art school.
2. Art civilizes man. It is the result of discipline.
3. Last summer was the best time to buy a car. Things were cheap.
4. The dog belongs to John. It ran away yesterday.
5. The boy threw a stone. He ran after Tom.
6. The boy threw a stone. Tom ran after him.
7. An old woman bought this home. Her son goes to school.
8. The University had its hundredth anniversary. The governor praised it.
9. The cat had no home. Tommy found him yesterday.
10. The place is on Washington Street. We will meet there tonight.
11. The boy can ride a bicycle. He likes his father.
12. The boy can ride a bicycle. His father likes him.
13. My neighbor takes good pictures. He owns an expensive camera.
14. The store is on State Street. I buy my shoes there.
15. The bald man teaches English. The President praised him.

SUMMARY EXERCISE (To practice various structures in subject position.) A word or group of words is given. Use it as the subject of a statement, freely composing the remainder of the statement. For example:

> The time when we meet
> THE TIME WHEN WE MEET HAS NOT BEEN DECIDED.
> The picture on the east wall
> THE PICTURE ON THE EAST WALL IS BY PABLO PICASSO.
> We
> WE TOOK A TRIP TO NEW YORK.
> Listening to music
> LISTENING TO MUSIC IS A FAVORITE PASTIME OF MANY PEOPLE.
> What Mr. Hanson likes
> WHAT MR. HANSON LIKES IS TO GO TO A MOVIE ON SUNDAY.

1. Where to go for a vacation
2. Tom and Harry
3. The book about contemporary painters
4. The dress which you bought
5. The First National Bank of New York

6. The big fire engine belonging to the city
7. To select a sport coat
8. Working for a degree in the United States
9. The modern apartment building at 112 Lexington
10. The factory where John works
11. The pen and pencil set which I got for my birthday
12. Talking about politics often
13. The friends whom he brought to the party
14. The person whom I talked to
15. The person who talked to me

Lesson XXXIII

SUMMARY OF CLASS 2 EXPRESSIONS AND CLASS 2 MODIFICATION

1.   Class 2 Expressions

Observe the Class 2 expressions.

Betty				WRITES	poetry.
Her friends				ADMIRE	it.
She				WROTE	poetry last year.
She				WROTE	a poem yesterday.
Her friends				ADMIRED	it.
She		IS		GOING TO WRITE	some poetry tomorrow.
She		WAS		GOING TO WRITE	some last week, but she didn't.
She		IS		WRITING	now.
She		WAS		WRITING	when I was here.
She		HAS		WRITTEN	many poems recently.
She		HAD		WRITTEN	many before I knew her.
She		HAS	BEEN	WRITING	poetry for several years.
She		HAD	BEEN	WRITING	it before she finished high school.
She	WILL			WRITE	some poetry tomorrow.
She	CAN			WRITE	poetry easily.
She	MIGHT	BE		WRITING	some now.
She	COULD	HAVE		WRITTEN	some last week.
She	WOULD	HAVE		WRITTEN	some if she had had time.
She	MUST	HAVE	BEEN	WRITING	when you called her up yesterday
Her poetry		IS		WRITTEN	on the typewriter.
It		WAS		WRITTEN	by hand before she got her typewriter.
It			IS BEING	WRITTEN	on the typewriter now.
It			WAS BEING	WRITTEN	by hand then.
This poem		HAS	BEEN	WRITTEN	by hand.
It	HAD		BEEN	WRITTEN	before she got her typewriter.
Poetry	SHOULD		BE	WRITTEN	carefully.
This poem	MUST	HAVE	BEEN	WRITTEN	when she was younger.

305

Betty					HAS TO STUDY	a lot.
She					WANTS TO WRITE	great poetry.
She					ENJOYS WRITING	poetry.
She	MIGHT	HAVE	BEEN		TRYING TO WRITE	a new poem when you called her up.
She	MUST	HAVE			DISLIKED BEING INTERRUPTED	while she was writing.

SUMMARY COMMENTS

(1) To indicate an action in progress at the time spoken about, use BE + an -ING form (IS WRIT<u>ING</u>, HAS <u>BEEN</u> WRIT<u>ING</u>, MIGHT <u>BE</u> WRIT<u>ING</u>, etc.).

(2) To indicate an action completed at the time spoken about, use HAVE + an -ED/-EN form (HAS WRITTEN, HAS BEEN WRITING, etc.). Also use HAVE + an -ED/-EN form to indicate an action begun at a past time and continued until the time spoken about.

(3) To indicate that the subject is the receiver of the action, not the performer, use BE directly before an -ED/-EN form (IS WRIT<u>TEN</u>, IS <u>BEING WRITTEN</u>, HAS <u>BEEN WRITTEN</u>, SHOULD <u>BE WRITTEN</u>, etc.).

(4) To indicate past time, use -ED forms (ADMIR<u>ED</u>, <u>WROTE</u>, <u>WAS</u> WRITING, <u>HAD</u> WRITTEN, etc.).

(5) To indicate an action qualified by the first Class 2 word, use a second Class 2 word (WANTS TO WRITE, ENJOYS WRITING, etc.).

ILLUSTRATIVE EXAMPLES

Observe the negative forms.

Betty DOESN'T write stories.
She NEVER tried to write one.
She ISN'T interested in writing them.
She HASN'T ever tried to write one.
She ISN'T going to try.
She CAN'T write essays very well either.
She tries NOT to write her poetry carelessly.
She DOESN'T try NOT to make her poetry difficult to understand.

Observe the special uses of DO.

DOES Betty write poetry? Yes, she DOES.
Betty DOESN'T write stories, but John DOES.

He DOESN'T write poetry, but he writes stories.*
He DOES it very well.
I am sure that he DOES.

Observe the Class 1 word between two Class 2 words.

Betty WANTS HER FRIENDS TO READ her poetry.
She LIKES THEM TO ADMIRE it.
She LETS THEM READ every poem she writes.
She HAS THE SCHOOL PAPER PUBLISH some of her poems.

Observe the correlation of the Class 2 expressions in the statements
before and after the connecting words.

Betty WILL GO to the bookstore IF you GO with her.
She WOULD GO IF John WENT with her.
She WOULD HAVE GONE yesterday IF someone HAD GONE with her.
She CAN'T BUY the books she wants UNLESS you LEND her some money.
She COULDN'T BUY any book UNLESS someone LENT her some money.
She COULD HAVE BOUGHT this book yesterday IF someone HAD lent
    her some money.

PRACTICE

EXERCISE 1.1. (To practice various Class 2 expressions.) Substitute
the following Class 2 expressions in the statements. For example:

    We study American literature.
1. have studied
    WE HAVE STUDIED AMERICAN LITERATURE.
2. will be studying
    WE WILL BE STUDYING AMERICAN LITERATURE.
3. are going to study
    WE ARE GOING TO STUDY AMERICAN LITERATURE.
4. have been studying
    WE HAVE BEEN STUDYING AMERICAN LITERATURE.
5. studied
    WE STUDIED AMERICAN LITERATURE.

A. American literature is taken by most students.
        1. was taken
        2. will be taken
        3. had been taken
        4. will have been taken
        5. can be taken
        6. should have been taken

---

*You will also hear "He DOESN'T write poetry, but he DOES write stories."
DO + the simple form of a Class 2 word is used for emphasis.

B. The students have found Mark Twain amusing.
 1. find
 2. are going to find
 3. have been finding
 4. were finding
 5. had found
 6. will find
C. John expects to read that novel.
 1. has expected
 2. has been expecting
 3. expected
 4. was expecting
 5. doesn't expect
 6. will be expecting
D. The play will be written by one of the students.
 1. can be written
 2. has been written
 3. was written
 4. has to be written
 5. is to be written
 6. was being written
E. Mary enjoys the work of Henry James.
 1. enjoyed
 2. is enjoying
 3. is going to enjoy
 4. has enjoyed
 5. should enjoy
 6. has been enjoying
F. His work is well written.
 1. has been. . .written
 2. is going to be. . .written
 3. was. . .written
 4. could have been. . .written
 5. can be. . .written
 6. is being. . .written
G. Melville wrote Moby Dick in 1851.
 1. was writing
 2. could have written
 3. must have been writing
 4. could have been writing
 5. had been writing
 6. had written

EXERCISE 1.2. (To produce statements expressing future time.) Convert the statements to express a situation in future time. Use BE + GOING TO. For example:

 He spent a lot of money on clothes.
  HE IS GOING TO SPEND A LOT OF MONEY ON CLOTHES.
 They can attend the university next year.
  THEY ARE GOING TO ATTEND THE UNIVERSITY NEXT YEAR.
 I might go to the movie if you do.
  I AM GOING TO GO TO THE MOVIE IF YOU DO.

1. She should visit her uncle.
2. He found where the house is located.
3. We can speak English fluently.
4. My wife would want a new hat.
5. They might come back tomorrow.
6. The people understand the instructions.
7. They could speak to the director if he was here.
8. The students leave the dormitory.
9. The dog barks when I walk by.
10. We must be careful in crossing the street.
11. I may take a train to St. Louis.
12. Dave telephones regularly in the morning.

EXERCISE 1.3. (To use the forms HAVE and HAD + an -ED/-EN form.)
Convert the following statements which indicate present or simple past
time situations into statements with HAVE and HAD + the -ED/ -EN form
of the Class 2 word. With HAVE use the word group FOR TWO MONTHS;
with HAD use the included sentence BEFORE HE CAME HERE. For
example:

I study English at the University of Michigan.
    I HAVE STUDIED ENGLISH AT THE UNIVERSITY OF MICHIGAN FOR
      TWO MONTHS.
    I HAD STUDIED ENGLISH AT THE UNIVERSITY OF MICHIGAN BE-
      FORE I CAME HERE.
John works in the cafeteria.
    JOHN HAS WORKED IN THE CAFETERIA FOR TWO MONTHS.
    JOHN HAD WORKED IN THE CAFETERIA BEFORE HE CAME HERE.
We took algebra.
    WE HAVE TAKEN ALGEBRA FOR TWO MONTHS.
    WE HAD TAKEN ALGEBRA BEFORE WE CAME HERE.

1. He teaches chemistry.	7. You knew the professor.
2. Mary worked at the library.	8. Jim speaks English clearly.
3. Tom sells insurance.	9. My watch loses time.
4. Jane sings in the chorus.	10. They let him use the car.
5. I drink coffee.	11. She wrote each day.
6. We travel by ship.	12. He does his work efficiently.

EXERCISE 1.4. (To use a form of BE + an -ING form to express action
in progress.) Listen to the statements which express present, past, or
future time. Convert them so that the action expressed is continuous.
Use a form of BE + an -ING form. For example:

John enjoys Mark Twain.
    JOHN IS ENJOYING MARK TWAIN.
He studied Walt Whitman.
    HE WAS STUDYING WALT WHITMAN.
He is going to study Henry James.
    HE IS GOING TO BE STUDYING HENRY JAMES.
He had read Uncle Tom's Cabin.
    HE HAD BEEN READING UNCLE TOM'S CABIN.

1. They have studied English poetry.
2. They enjoyed Benjamin Franklin's <u>Autobiography.</u>
3. She memorizes Emily Dickinson's poetry.
4. Faulkner will write more novels.
5. He has produced many good works.
6. You should write a composition on Melville.
7. Fred wrote an essay on Tom Paine.
8. We haven't studied English literature.
9. James Fenimore Cooper had written novels about Indians.
10. Mary takes two literature courses.
11. She took a course in French literature last summer.
12. We should have done our assignment this morning.
13. We didn't go to the lecture.
14. The students eat at twelve.
15. He has not read the book.

EXERCISE 1.5. (To practice statements in which the subject is the receiver of the action.) Listen to the statements. Convert them so that the subject receives the action. Do this by putting the object in subject position and using the -ED/-EN form of the Class 2 word, preceded by a form of BE. For example:

All freshmen read the book.
    THE BOOK IS READ.
Hemingway wrote the book.
    THE BOOK WAS WRITTEN.
The students are filling out the questionnaire.
    THE QUESTIONNAIRE IS BEING FILLED OUT.
Many readers will find this poem interesting.
    THIS POEM WILL BE FOUND INTERESTING.

1. Joseph Conrad wrote sea stories.
2. The librarian has requested me to return this book.
3. Shakespeare entertained us.
4. The teacher told them about realism.
5. The students are going to discuss the work of Sinclair Lewis.
6. The professor has given a lecture on Eugene O'Neill.
7. Professor Stack has published books on drama.
8. Students know the value of literature.
9. Miss Palermo does not teach pronunciation.
10. Rosalis is writing two essays on liberty.
11. Readers can see the relationship between culture and literature.
12. The work of Poe will amuse Tom.
13. Washington Irving has written humorous speeches.
14. The students could have presented a play.

EXERCISE 1.6. (To produce statements having two Class 2 words.)
Listen to the two statements. Combine them to form one statement with two Class 2 words. For example:

She watched him. He bought a hat.
SHE WATCHED HIM BUY A HAT.
He waited until the next day. Then he bought the car.
HE WAITED UNTIL THE NEXT DAY TO BUY THE CAR.
They will give a program. They want to.
THEY WANT TO GIVE A PROGRAM.

1. Fred listens to the opera. He likes it.
2. John taught his son. His son plays folk songs.
3. Mary will go. She wishes to.
4. He is buying a ticket. He will watch the game.
5. Our team is getting ready. It will play a team from Puerto Rico.
6. He tries hard. He will find a solution.
7. Tom is going to build a boat. His friends will help him.
8. He never smoked. He started recently.
9. I pay a high rent. I don't like to.
10. She makes her own dresses. She enjoys it.
11. We can hear him. He sings many songs.
12. We heard the speaker. He gave a wonderful lecture.

EXERCISE 1.7. (To practice correlation of Class 2 words in included sentences beginning with IF and UNLESS.) Listen to the partial statement. It contains a Class 2 word preceded by CAN, COULD, HAVE, WOULD, etc. Complete the statement by adding the included sentence, IF YOU ASK HIM TO, with proper correlation of the Class 2 word and substitute word to the previous structure. Substitute UNLESS for IF if the partial statement is negative. For example:

I can come.
I CAN COME IF YOU ASK ME TO.
Mary won't come.
MARY WON'T COME UNLESS YOU ASK HER TO.
She could recite a poem.
SHE COULD RECITE A POEM IF YOU ASKED HER TO.
They would have bought a ticket.
THEY WOULD HAVE BOUGHT A TICKET IF YOU HAD ASKED
THEM TO.

1. My friend will go.
2. The teacher would tell a story.
3. Miss Sanchez would sing.
4. The president would have spoken.
5. Jim might read the book.
6. The director will not give a speech.
7. Mr. Martin will teach the lesson over again.
8. He would have taught the lesson over again.
9. He can't come to the program.
10. Mr. Junger would have driven to Chicago.
11. Could he go?
12. Would she have written the story?

2.

Class 2 Modification

Observe the Class 2 modifications.

Poetry	is OFTEN difficult.			
Betty	OFTEN writes	poetry.		
She		wrote	a poem	YESTERDAY.
She		wrote	it	IN THE MORNING.
She		wrote	it	IN HER ROOM.
She	USUALLY writes		her poetry	THERE.
She		wrote	the poem	CAREFULLY.
She		wrote	it	ON HER TYPEWRITER.
She		wrote	it	IN HER ROOM YESTERDAY.
She		wrote	it	ON HER IN THE TYPEWRITER MORNING.
She	USUALLY writes		her poetry	IN HER ROOM ON HER TYPE- IN THE WRITER MORNING.
She	ALWAYS writes		it	BY HAND IN IN THE THE LIBRARY AFTERNOON.
She	OFTEN writes		poetry	BEFORE SHE GOES TO CLASS.
She	likes to write		it	WHERE SHE CAN BE ALONE.
She	wants to write			AS THE GREAT POETS DO.

IN THE AFTER-NOON/	She wrote one poem	IN THE MORNING.
	she wrote another.	
IN THE LIBRARY/	She wrote one poem	IN HER ROOM.
	she wrote another.	

COMMENTS

(1) Use single words (OFTEN, YESTERDAY, THERE, CAREFULLY, etc.), word groups (IN THE MORNING, IN HER ROOM, ON HER TYPEWRITER, etc.), and included sentences (BEFORE SHE GOES TO CLASS, etc.) to modify sentences or their Class 2 expressions.

(2) Use words of frequency (OFTEN, etc.) after BE and before other Class 2 words.*

(3) Use expressions of place (IN HER ROOM, THERE, etc.), manner (CAREFULLY ON HER TYPEWRITER, etc.), and time (YESTER-DAY, IN THE MORNING, etc.) after the object.**

(4) Use expressions of time after expressions of place and manner.

(5) You may use expressions of time and place before the subject in sequence sentences.

*You will also hear words of frequency at the end of the sentence: "Betty writes poetry OFTEN."

**You will also hear words of manner ending in -LY and certain other words, like NOW, SOON, ALSO, etc., after BE and before other Class 2 words: "Betty CARE-FULLY wrote the poem."

PRACTICE

EXERCISE 2.1. (To practice modification of Class 2 words with expressions of frequency, time, place, and manner). Substitute the word or group of words indicating manner, time, or place in the proper position in the given statement. For example:

We often study English very hard in the library in the morning.

every day   WE OFTEN STUDY ENGLISH VERY HARD IN THE LIBRARY EVERY DAY.

very diligently   WE OFTEN STUDY ENGLISH VERY DILIGENTLY IN THE LIBRARY EVERY DAY.

generally   WE GENERALLY STUDY ENGLISH VERY DILIGENTLY IN THE LIBRARY EVERY DAY.

1. usually
2. at home
3. in the evening
4. sometimes
5. when the weather is bad
6. very little
7. frequently
8. at my apartment
9. always
10. very much
11. during weekends
12. never
13. at the dormitory
14. quietly
15. often
16. in our rooms
17. seldom
18. before dinner
19. in summer
20. out-of-doors

EXERCISE 2.2. (To practice the various positions of expressions of time, place, and manner.) Listen to the statement and the expression of time, place, or manner said after it. Produce a statement introduced by a sequence expression and substituting the given expression of time, place, or manner in its proper place. Use the last time or place expression of the statement as a clue for the sequence expression. For example:

She often studies German in the morning.   Rarely
IN THE AFTERNOON, SHE RARELY STUDIES GERMAN.
John writes letters in the office in the afternoon.   At home
IN THE EVENING, JOHN WRITES LETTERS AT HOME.
Fred is often a student at the university in the summer.   Seldom
IN THE WINTER, FRED IS SELDOM A STUDENT AT THE UNIVERSITY.
The grass is usually green in the springtime.   After a rainfall
IN THE SUMMER, THE GRASS IS USUALLY GREEN AFTER A RAINFALL.

1. We usually eat lunch in the cafeteria on Friday.   Rarely
2. Tom celebrated his birthday proudly last year.   Very quietly
3. He will work on his book this week.   If he has time
4. He is going to work in the garden today.   In the basement
5. He usually studies French with a student from Korea in the evening.
   By himself

6. She seldom eats lunch alone at the dormitory.   Usually
7. He is seldom late for his classes in the morning.   On time
8. She takes the train to Detroit faithfully every day.   To Chicago
9. We frequently meet him going to the Chemistry Building at nine
    o'clock.   Very rarely
10. They went out during the intermission.   In
11. The Smiths generally have a picnic with their children by the
    river.   With their friends
12. He always wears a hat in winter.   When it rains.

EXERCISE 2.3. (To use various Class 2 expressions in correlation with
expressions of time.) Listen to the Class 2 expressions and the time
expressions. Use them in a statement freely, composing a context
which is suitable to their meaning. Use the words expressing time at
the end of the statement. For example:

    is taking. . . today
        HE IS TAKING AN EXAMINATION TODAY.
    have been walking. . . every day
        THE STUDENTS HAVE BEEN WALKING IN THE RAIN EVERY DAY.
    is going to. . . tomorrow
        MARY IS GOING TO EAT DINNER WITH ME TOMORROW.

1. had to buy. . . yesterday
2. has been listening. . . every day
3. will have completed. . . next month
4. will be announced. . . today
5. earns. . . a week
6. was earning. . . a week last year
7. must have been attended. . . during the summer
8. wants to study. . . in the morning
9. would like to write. . . next year
10. can be heard. . . in the springtime
11. respect. . . when they are polite
12. will learn. . . in time
13. have had. . . during November
14. might be willing to visit. . . in the future

Lesson XXXIV

SUMMARY OF OBJECT STRUCTURES

Observe the words in object position.

Mr. Smith teaches.

He	teaches			HIS STUDENTS.
He	teaches			GRAMMAR.
He	appointed			TOM.
He	likes			HIS STUDENTS.
He	teaches	HIS STUDENTS	GRAMMAR.	
He	appointed		TOM	SECRETARY.
He	likes		HIS STUDENTS	INTELLIGENT.
He	likes		HIS STUDENTS	CONSIDERED INTELLIGENT.

COMMENTS

(1) Use no object, one object, or two objects after Class 2 words. (However, you cannot use objects with certain Class 2 words. See Illustrative Examples.)

(2) Use a second object before the primary object to indicate the person or thing for whom the action is performed. (HE TEACHES HIS STUDENTS GRAMMAR, etc.)

(3) After certain Class 2 words like APPOINT, ELECT, NAME, CALL, etc., use a second object after the primary object to indicate a name or designation given to the primary object. (HE APPOINTED TOM SECRETARY, etc. See Lesson XXVII, if necessary.)

(4) Use describing words after the object to indicate its condition or quality as a receiver of the action. In this pattern, the describing words modify the object and the Class 2 word as a unit. (HE LIKES HIS STUDENTS INTELLIGENT, etc. See Lesson XXVII, if necessary.)

ILLUSTRATIVE EXAMPLES

John understands CHEMISTRY.
He   understands IT.
He   understands HOW TO DO EXPERIMENTS.
He   understands WHAT CAUSES REACTIONS.
He   understands HOW ORGANIC COMPOUNDS ARE FORMED.
He   understands (THAT) CARBON IS THE BASIC ELEMENT OF ORGANIC COMPOUNDS.

NOTE: Use Class 1 words or substitutes (CHEMISTRY, IT, etc.), word groups (HOW TO DO EXPERIMENTS, etc.), or included sentences (WHAT CAUSES REACTIONS, etc.) in object position.

315

The teacher told	THE CHILDREN	A STORY.
She	told THE LITTLE CHILDREN	AN AMUSING STORY.
She	told THE DELIGHTED CHILDREN	A STORY ABOUT A PRINCESS.
She	told THE CHILDREN SITTING AROUND HER	A STORY THEY LIKE VERY MUCH.

NOTE: Modify Class 1 objects like Class 1 subjects.

Observe the contrast between these patterns of modification.

George	painted the	WHITE	house.	
He	painted the		house	GREEN.
He	painted the	WHITE	house	GREEN.

We	washed our	DIRTY	clothes.	
We	washed our		clothes	CLEAN.
We	washed our	DIRTY	clothes	CLEAN.

The barber	cut	Betty's	LONG	hair.	
He	cut	her		hair	SHORT.
He	cut	her	LONG	hair	SHORT.

Observe what comes after the Class 2 words.

Juan	came	FROM MEXICO.
He	arrived	IN ANN ARBOR.
He	went	TO A HOTEL.
He	looked	AT MANY APARTMENTS,
He	listened	TO THE LANDLORDS.
He	smiled	AT THEM.
He	thought	ABOUT THE APARTMENTS.
He	insisted	ON A GOOD APARTMENT.

NOTE: Do not use a Class 1 object after certain Class 2 words like COME, ARRIVE, GO, LOOK, etc. Use word groups with FROM, IN, TO, AT, etc., to indicate a receiver. (See Vocabulary Lessons, if necessary.)

Mary said	"HELLO"	TO HER FRIENDS.
She introduced	JANE	TO ALICE AND BETTY.
She spoke	ENGLISH	TO THEM.
She described	THE COURSE	TO THEM.
She explained	THE CLASSES	TO THEM.
She answered	A QUESTION	FOR BETTY.
She changed	A DOLLAR BILL	FOR HER.

NOTE: After certain Class 2 words like SAY, INTRODUCE, SPEAK, ANSWER, etc., do not use a second Class 1 object before the primary object to indicate the person or thing for whom the action is performed. Use word groups with TO or FOR after the primary object. (See Lesson VIII, if necessary.)

PRACTICE

EXERCISE 1. (To practice the order of Class 1 words in object position.) Substitute the following word or words in the statement. Make the necessary changes in other forms for correlation. For example:

We gave her a watch for her birthday.
him   WE GAVE HIM A WATCH FOR HIS BIRTHDAY.
his sister   WE GAVE HIS SISTER A WATCH FOR HER BIRTHDAY.
diamond pin   WE GAVE HIS SISTER A DIAMOND PIN FOR HER
    BIRTHDAY.

1. a beautiful present
2. them
3. ourselves
4. our neighbor
5. what he wanted
6. her
7. our mother
8. six red roses
9. Miss Salinas
10. the girl who works here
11. a book
12. Tom, the janitor,
13. some fishing equipment
14. the boy
15. a dog
16. her
17. the boy who is sick
18. Bob
19. a dog like mine
20. a pair of shoes

EXERCISE 2. (To practice the positions of various kinds of objects, and to contrast object structures with word groups containing TO and FOR.) Listen to the word or words and the statements which follow. Include the word or words in the proper position in the statements. For example:

Him. I gave a book.
    I GAVE HIM A BOOK.
 or I GAVE A BOOK TO HIM.

Her. I said "Hello."
    I SAID HELLO TO HER.

The man. I asked his name.
    I ASKED THE MAN HIS NAME.

Chairman of the committee. They chose Fred.
    THEY CHOSE FRED CHAIRMAN OF THE COMMITTEE.

1. Them. He is going to give some advice.
2. The man who is here. He will give some money.
3. The school children. She explained the problem.
4. Her. They expect to get it.
5. Me. He will have a check today.
6. Her. He says "Good morning" every day.
7. Him. They bought his book.
8. Himself. John bought a tie yesterday.
9. Tom. They appointed the chairman.

10. Captain of the team. They selected Fred last night.
11. Us. He promised a book from the store.
12. Them. He paid the money he owed.
13. Him. He drew a picture of John on the wall.
14. Us. The dentist will talk about our teeth today.
15. The girl. The mother sent for the bread.
16. The professor. They asked some very difficult questions.
17. His employees. The president of the company always speaks
      cheerfully.
18. Secretary. They chose him by unanimous vote.
19. Jim. They tried to nominate the president.
20. His son. He is thinking of buying a car.

EXERCISE 3. (To contrast the object followed by a designation or name,
or by a describing word, with the object preceded by a second object.)
Listen to the statements. Convert them into statements having two objects,
or statements having an object followed by a describing word. Use the
word THEY as the subject of each statement. For example:

George was named boss.
    THEY NAMED GEORGE BOSS.
George was given the job.
    THEY GAVE GEORGE THE JOB.
The students are considered intelligent.
    THEY CONSIDER THE STUDENTS INTELLIGENT.
The students were bought a sandwich.
    THEY BOUGHT THE STUDENTS A SANDWICH.
Professor Dart was considered interesting.
    THEY CONSIDERED PROFESSOR DART INTERESTING.
Professor Dart was given a compliment.
    THEY GAVE PROFESSOR DART A COMPLIMENT.

1. Mr. Lanza was appointed chairman.
2. Mr. Lanza was given the position of chairman.
3. The baby was named Sue.
4. The baby was given the name Sue.
5. John Smith was appointed manager of the team.
6. John Smith was offered the job of manager.
7. The young lawyer was presented the office of judge.
8. The young lawyer was made judge.
9. Their baby was given a bath.
10. Their baby was called Richard.
11. Richard was promised a book.
12. Richard was called Dick.
14. Her hair was given a washing.
15. Fred was found discouraged.
16. Fred was given a pair of shoes.
17. The white house was painted yellow.
18. The white house was built a new roof.

19. They were selected Board of Directors.
20. John was voted most popular.
21. John was voted more money.
22. Her blue coat was given a cleaning.
23. Her blue coat was dyed black.

EXERCISE 4. (To correlate meaning with arrangement of items in object position.) Listen to the two statements. The subject and the Class 2 expression are the same in both. Combine them to form one statement with the same meaning as the two separate statements. There may be more than one way to express the statement. For example:

He bought a book. He bought it for Jane.
    HE BOUGHT JANE A BOOK.
    HE BOUGHT A BOOK FOR JANE.

He paid the man. He paid for the coat.
    HE PAID THE MAN FOR THE COAT.

He gave a dollar for a picture. He gave it to me.
    HE GAVE ME A DOLLAR FOR A PICTURE.

1. She sang the song. She sang "Home on the Range."
2. He promised a book. He promised it to Jane.
3. He promised to buy a book. He promised Jane.
4. He promised to buy a book. He promised a book to Jane.
5. He paid for the book. He paid John.
6. He paid the man. He paid for John.
7. He paid for the book. He paid for John.
8. She bought a car. She bought it herself.
9. She bought a car. She bought it for herself.
10. Mary wrote her mother. Mary wrote a long letter.
11. She wrote a letter today. She wrote it for her mother.
12. Mary wrote her mother. Mary wrote a long letter.
13. She paid the money. She paid him.
14. She paid him the money. She paid for it.
15. He received a hat. He received it soiled.
16. He made the boat. He made it big and heavy.
17. They saw him reading to himself. They saw the book.
18. We saw a note to his friend. We saw him writing it.
19. We are going to elect a president. We are going to elect Bob.
20. She wants a car. She wants him to get it.
21. She wants her car. She wants him to get it.

EXERCISE 4. (To practice various patterns after the Class 2 expression.) Listen to the two statements. Combine them to form a statement which will include the information of both statements and with the same meaning as the two statements. For example:

He is talking to my friend. My friend is a student.
    HE IS TALKING TO MY FRIEND WHO IS A STUDENT.

He saw her. She got the book.
HE SAW HER GET THE BOOK.

They watched Fred during the concert. They watched him reading the program.
THEY WATCHED FRED READING THE PROGRAM DURING THE CONCERT.

1. He knows it. It is not the truth.
2. We seldom see a movie. We seldom go because we have no time.
3. We waited while she shopped. We waited in the car.
4. They talked during the concert. They talked to me about music.
5. The doctor knows about the patient. The doctor knows about his illness.
6. They know about Fred Kana. They know he is going into the army.
7. They walked while the concert played. They walked in the park.
8. We are taking John. We will buy a suit for John.
9. John knows the doctor. The doctor cured Fred last year.
10. The doctor cured Fred last year. They know it.
11. They see the professor. The professor is working in his garden.
12. The car turned over on the hill. They saw the place.
13. The car turned over on the hill. They saw it.
14. They waited for the man. They waited in the apartment all day.
15. The man is sick. Jim knows about him.
16. The man is sick. Jim sees it.
17. The doctor treated the patient. They watched the patient.
18. The nurse whispered to the doctor. John heard the nurse.
19. The student was sick yesterday. We didn't realize it.
20. The baker burned his finger while baking bread. John saw how.
21. Mr. Dorik parks his car every day. They know where.
22. They plan to buy him the car. The car belongs to Jerry.

Lesson XXXV

STYLE

It is possible to recognize many styles in a language. For example, we may notice in English the styles that are used in various situations. One style is appropriate for conversations. Another style is appropriate to letters. A third style is found in scientific and business reports; a fourth in newspaper reports; a fifth in short stories; a sixth in poetry, etc.

These stylistic differences can be described. They are characterized by various combinations of patterns and vocabulary. The speaker or the writer must know what he wants to say and he must organize it. In saying it or in writing it, he adopts patterns and vocabulary that are customary in the style that he is using.

Conversations are characterized by greetings and a large proportion of questions and short answers. Words like "you," "I," and "he" are very frequent. Letters have salutations, introductory remarks, and complimentary closes. Scientific and business reports, whether they are oral or written, have many sentences with the word order which we often call "normal." The subject and its modifiers come first in these sentences. The Class 2 word comes next. The objects and expressions of place, manner, or time come last. Newspaper reports regularly begin with a relatively complex sentence. The purpose of this sentence is to give information concerning "who," "what," "where," and "when." In short stories you will find that authors often change the "normal" pattern to achieve artistic effect. The style of poetry permits even more extreme variation from the normal pattern. The result is that it is sometimes hard to understand a poem.

Following is a sample treatment of somewhat similar material communicated in the patterns of the styles we have just considered.

1. Conversational style:

"Good morning, Alfred."

"Good morning, Bob. I haven't seen you around lately. What have you been doing?"

"Oh, I've been working pretty hard lately. I'm trying to finish my report on the photosynthetic process for the next issue of the Journal."

"Say, that's interesting. What's new?"

"Well, it seems that plant organisms not only form a kind of reservoir of light energy but also convert it into chemical energy. Nature has covered the Earth with living plants which capture and store sunlight. They do this by converting it into an immobile form."

"I don't quite understand this."

"I don't have time to explain it now, Alfred, but I'll send you a copy of the report as soon as it's finished."

"Thanks a lot. So long, Bob."

"Goodby, Al."

2. Letter style:

Dear Alfred:

Sorry to have delayed so long in answering your most welcome letter. My only excuse is work. As a matter of fact, I've been working on a study of the photosynthetic process. I believe that the crux of the matter lies in the conversion of light energy into chemical energy. Green plants are a reservoir in which the sun's rays are stored and converted into another force. How considerate of Nature to provide such an abundance! And how dependent we human beings are upon it!

Enough of my work! What about you? I'm sorry to hear that little Al has been sick but I'm sure he's better now.

Your new project sounds most interesting. Keep me informed on the latest developments.

My best wishes to the family. Say hello to all our mutual friends for me.

Sincerely yours,

Bob

3. Scientific and business report style (oral or written):

Nature set herself the task of capturing the light flooding toward the Earth, and of storing this, the most elusive of all forces, by converting it into an immobile form. To achieve this, she has covered the Earth's surface with organisms which while living take up the sunlight and use its force to add continuously to a sum of chemical difference. These organisms are the plants. The plant world constitutes a reservoir in which the solar rays are fixed and ingeniously laid down for later use, a providential economic measure to which the very existence of the human race is inescapably bound. The plants take in a force, the light, and bring forth another force, the chemical difference.

Robert von Mayer's report, 1845

4. Newspaper report style:

Nature stores solar rays and converts them into an immobile form through the work of plants, prominent physicist Robert von Mayer reports from Germany. Living plants absorb the sunlight and utilize its force to add continuously to a sum of chemical energy. Plant life is the reservoir in which the sun's rays are stored for later use. Without such a reservoir human life could not continue.

5. Short story style:

The miracle happened again. It was the same old miracle which had been repeated countless times since life first appeared on earth, yet was new and fresh each time. Now under the observant eye of the scientist it had happened again. Now, for the first time in all the eons through which the miracle had repeated itself, a trained observer watched and understood. The photosynthetic process had been discovered. The questing mind of man had at last found out how nature utilized plant organisms as a reservoir of energy; how the solar rays were taken into living plants and converted into chemical energy; how oxygen, that element so essential to human existence, was produced. The miracle was finally appreciated, but not diminished.

6. Poetic Style

Across vast airless spaces streams the light,
Across the hollow dark until the earth
Comes reeling, spinning, twisting through the mirth—
Less rigid patterns of untrammeled night.
The planet rolls, alive and green, beneath
The life-outpouring light, the living flood
Of light—this light that is the very blood
In which the parasitic planets seethe.
The green things growing on this light-fed world
Raise hungry lips to drink the rays thus hurled
From parent sun. They gasp, inhale, and then
A miracle takes place. Within their green
Interiors is born a force unseen
Which holds and keeps the sun's rays here for men.

PRACTICE

EXERCISE 1. (To use English freely in conversational style.)

Simulate the meeting of two English-speaking friends in a downtown hotel lobby in St. Louis, Missouri. Include acceptable greetings, a short conversation, and acceptable leave-taking.

EXERCISE 2. (To use English freely in a speech style.)

Suppose that you have been asked to give a short talk to a mixed group about the people in your home town and about their activities and interests.

EXERCISE 3. (To use English freely in a letter style.)

Write a letter to a scientific or business associate whose interests are similar to yours.

EXERCISE 4. (To use English freely in a written report style.)

Write a summary report on some research that you have done or on the conditions in one school that you have attended.